Exploring Mathematics through Literature

Articles and Lessons for Prekindergarten through Grade 8

Edited by
Diane Thiessen
University of Northern Iowa
Cedar Falls, Iowa

NATIONAL COUNCIL OF
TEACHERS OF MATHEMATICS

Copyright © 2004
THE NATIONAL COUNCIL OF TEACHERS OF MATHEMATICS, INC.
1906 Association Drive, Reston, VA 20191-1502
(703) 620-9840; (800) 235-7566; www.nctm.org

Third printing 2006

Library of Congress Cataloging-in-Publication Data

Exploring mathematics through literature : articles and lessons for
prekindergarten through grade 8 / edited by Diane Thiessen.
     p. cm.
Includes bibliographical references.
  ISBN 0-87353-553-7
  1. Mathematics—Study and teaching (Primary) 2. Mathematics—Study
and teaching (Elementary) I. Thiessen, Diane.
  QA135.6.E86 2004
  372.7—dc22

                                   2003025744

The National Council of Teachers of Mathematics is a public voice of mathematics
education, providing vision, leadership, and professional development to support teachers in ensuring mathematics learning of the highest quality for all students.

Printed in the United States of America

Table of Contents

Preface

IN THE last two decades children's books in mathematics have continued to grow in popularity as more and more teachers have discovered the potential of their use in the classroom. Interest has grown not only in the books themselves but in more effective ways to use them. This collection of articles and lessons based on children's books in mathematics has been designed to help teachers of prekindergarten through eighth grade use children's literature to teach mathematics. The articles, previously published by the National Council of Teachers of Mathematics, describe how a lesson was used in a classroom. Each is followed by newly added teacher notes written by the authors.

Selection of the Articles

The articles for this collection were selected from previous issues of *Teaching Children Mathematics*, *Mathematics Teaching in the Middle School*, and *Arithmetic Teacher*. All articles were classified by using the content standards from *Principles and Standards for School Mathematics* (Reston, Va.: National Council of Teachers of Mathematics, 2000). Most of the articles involve communication, problem solving, representation, and reasoning, and some of them involve connections. Because the process standards were reflected if not explicitly discussed in many articles, their potential use as a classification scheme did not appear to make sense. Consequently, Number and Operations, Algebra, Measurement, Geometry, and Probability and Statistics became the bases of five sections of the book. The availability of appropriate articles in specific content areas or grade levels is reflected in each section's length. As anticipated, Number and Operations was the largest category, and Algebra, the smallest. Some articles fell into a miscellaneous category, in that they were related to a theme rather than a specific content standard or were simply more general in nature.

More than seventy articles were reviewed, and many high-quality ones had to be eliminated, largely for lack of space. Within each category, articles were selected to maximize representation across grade levels Pre-K–2, 3–5, and 6–8. Some articles were not selected because they were primarily descriptions of books rather than sample lessons. Some articles contained more general rather than specific mathematics content and were eliminated on that basis. Others focused on descriptions of specific books, such as ones written in Spanish or ones about geometry, and thus were considered too restrictive for inclusion in the present volume. The final collection brings under one cover articles deemed to have strong potential for teaching mathematical content through literature-based lessons that are both meaningful and enjoyable to students.

The Format of the Lessons

After the articles were selected, the authors were invited to submit lessons and recording sheets that reflected or extended the lesson described in their article. The type of lessons to include was their choice. Because many articles contained lessons that resulted in many different student strategies or were based on constructivist learning principles, recording sheets rather than worksheets were suggested. Additionally, when area teachers were consulted to determine their sentiments on the feasibility of activity or worksheets, they responded that they preferred recording sheets. They noted that worksheets can be overly restrictive, whereas a recording sheet can be just a blank page, since even the inclusion of blank lines on which to write can interfere with children's drawing or writing. Because of the explicit content to be investigated, some recording sheets are more structured; for example, those in Austin and Thompson's "Exploring Algebraic Patterns" have simply been reformatted from the original article.

As the teacher notes were compiled, the need for a common format to make the book more teacher-friendly and attractive became evident. The submitted teacher notes were rewritten using the format below and then resent to the authors for their feedback.

Grade range: The grid in the opening pages states the grade ranges that the individual authors or coauthors identified for their specific lesson.

Mathematical topic(s): Each article and lesson was originally classified as addressing one of five content areas; this list provides a more specific list of subtopics included in the lesson.

Children's book: Book(s) featured in the lesson

Materials: A listing of any materials needed to implement the lesson

Discussion of the mathematics: Two different approaches are used. One approach quotes specific sections from *Principles and Standards for School Mathematics* (Reston, Va.: National Council of Teachers of Mathematics, 2000). A second approach highlights explicit aspects of the mathematics, describes common misunderstandings, or includes suggestions on appropriate language.

Teacher notes and questions to ask students: These notes describe how to implement or extend the task discussed in the article.

References: The references include a citation of the original article and all resources mentioned in the teacher notes.

Recording sheets: Blackline masters were designed for most but not all lessons.

The lessons are designed as a resource to help you more successfully implement the use of children's books in your mathematics classroom. The hope is that you will find this resource valuable and will enjoy sharing the stories and teaching mathematics through children's books.

Introduction

As USING children's books to teach mathematics has become more and more popular, interest has grown not only in the books themselves but also in how to more effectively use them. The focus of this book of readings is to provide classroom examples of how to use children's literature to effectively teach mathematics. The collected articles describe how the different authors have used specific books to help their students learn mathematics. In all these articles and the related lessons, the focus is on learning mathematics.

What Are Some Ways That Children's Books Can Enhance Mathematics Learning?

Only a few of the many excellent children's books that can be used to teach mathematics are featured in this book. The purpose of this section is to highlight different qualities inherent in the books themselves that affect how the books can be used in teaching mathematics. The categories are designed to foster insights into the different ways that books can be used and to give guidance on how to more effectively select and use books. The categories are not exhaustive, nor are they disjoint. Some examples are highlighted in each category.

A context or story line is used to launch or develop mathematical concepts. Some children's books clearly represent a mathematical concept through their prose, illustrations, logical development, and context. These books provide excellent opportunities to launch a concept through a problem-solving situation. Often these books can be appreciated at many different grade levels. One of the issues for classroom teachers is to determine whether a particular book will be used to simply introduce or to thoroughly investigate the concept.

Pinczes's *A Remainder of One* (see the article and lesson by Patricia S. Moyer) is an excellent book to launch an investigation of division and remainders. The story line draws the reader into the dilemmas of Soldier Joe as he works though a social solution of not being left behind and a series of division problems. Students of various ages and backgrounds can enjoy this story and explore different division and remainder patterns.

In many situations the context clearly and cleverly represents one mathematical idea to be explored. For example, each semester prior to reading *Anno's Mysterious Multiplying Jar* to a class composed of elementary majors who are mathematics minors, a question is posed to them about the meaning of 5!. Their response is limited to a computational procedure as they note that the value of 5! is 120. When pressed for a context or an application of factorial, occasionally someone makes a vague reference to "something dealing with probability." After the book *Anno's Mysterious Multiplying Jar* is read to the class, the class discussion centers on the meaning of factorial as well as a better understanding of the magnitude of 10!. For the college students the book has provided an opportunity to revisit the concept of factorial. For children in the elementary grades, this same book can serve as an introduction to the power of multiplication and an introduction to factorial through the story line and the representations.

Introducing a concept in a context can be motivating to students. In some instances it may help students connect the mathematics with the real world. In other situations the context or story line may simply intrigue or entertain them. Both Myllar in *How Big Is a Foot?* and Matthews in *Gator Pie* use a humorous story line. As the story is read to them, preschool and primary-grade children giggle about the situations and readily solve the dilemma involving nonstandard units before the adults do in *How Big Is a Foot?* Both children and adults are entertained by Mathews's *Gator Pie*, in which the illustrations and prose depict the antics of Alice and Alex as they relate various fraction concepts.

Illustrations clearly represent mathematical concepts. Good illustrations are as essential as good text, and having illustrations that clearly represent mathematical concepts is essential in children's books in mathematics. The illustrations should not distract or confuse but should enhance the presentation. In the section above, *Anno's Magic Multiplying Jar* was noted for its story line, but the coupling of Anno's simple yet elegant prose with the beautiful illustrations clearly conveys the concept. The magnitude of 10! and the power of multiplication are clearly represented through the story line and by selected pages of red dots.

In *How Much Is a Million?* Schwartz introduces and describes excellent situations to depict millions, billions, and trillions. These number concepts are complemented by Kellogg's illustrations that clearly capture relative size through examples using height, volume, and time (measurement models) and stars (a set model).

Quality illustrations are motivating to the reader. All the books cited above as having illustrations that clearly represent mathematical concepts could also be discussed again in this section. Similarly, all the books discussed in this section could have been included in the previous section. Not all books whose illustrations clearly represent mathematical concepts have motivating illustrations. The purpose of this section is to highlight various types of high-quality illustrations that are motivating in different ways.

The photographic essays of Hoban, such as *Circles, Triangles, and Squares*; *Shapes, Shapes, Shapes*; and *Spirals, Curves, Fanshapes and Lines*, are beautifully done. Hoban's photographs, whether in black and white or color, capture our world with respect to both aesthetics and function. These photographs can prompt discussions connecting mathematics with the real world or simply foster an appreciation of viewing our world through the lens of mathematics. In *Eating Fractions*, McMillan also uses photographs to illuminate connections of mathematical ideas with our everyday lives.

High-quality artwork enhances many children's books. In *How Many Bears?* Edens presents an interesting set of related story problems, but the intricate illustrations by Marjett Schille dominate the book and will motivate readers to revisit the book. A number of books are based on a folktale about doubling, but Demi's illustrations in *One Grain of Rice: A Mathematical Folktale* make this version stand out. Similarly, Kim Howard's luminous watercolors in Friedman's *A Cloak for a Dreamer*, a carefully crafted story of a tailor and his three sons, add appeal to this book that introduces tessellations.

The humor reflected in illustrations can also be motivating. Clement's *Counting on Frank* is a favorite of children and adults for its clever and zany situations and illustrations. As readers revisit the book, they often discover new aspects of each double-page spread. In Burns's *Spaghetti and Meatballs for All!*, a story about perimeter and area, Tilley's illustrations depict the humor and increasing chaos in the lives of Mr. and Mrs. Comfort.

Books are a source of problems or a basis for generating problems. Clement's *Counting on Frank* and Scieszka's *Math Curse* provide intriguing problems to solve as well as a motivation for students to write their own "Counting on Frank" or "Math Curse" problems. Each double-page spread presents another real-life situation involving mathematics for the reader to contemplate. The situations and the illustrations have a zany humor that appeals to readers of many ages. Depending on their grade level, students will choose different concepts for their problems. But no matter what grade level, students will enjoy the challenge of writing their own problems that capture the unique style of each author. Class members may decide to organize their problems into a class collection that will be the basis of their own "Counting on Frank" or "Math Curse" book.

Some books may be related to mathematics, but they do not pose an explicit mathematics problem. Crews's *Ten Black Dots* does not pose the question "How many black dots in all?" but Weinberg (see the article and lesson by Susan Weinberg) found this counting book a natural way of launching a problem that she wanted her second graders to explore.

Style and format of book can motivate writing problems or designing your own book. As noted above, Clement's *Counting on Frank* and Scieszka's *Math Curse* could motivate the class to create their own book. In addition to examining the style and types of problems to be written, class discussion also needs to involve how to format and organize individual work so that it can become part of the class collection.

Books like Ash's *Incredible Comparisons* (see the article and lesson by Vicki L. Oleson) can also be used to generate problems or to design a class book. The structure and examples from this book can be used to help students develop number and measurement sense with respect to our world as well as provide a model for creating their own "Incredible Comparisons."

Brown's *The Important Book* is not about mathematics, but the book's format lends itself to investigating mathematics. For example, Bertheau (see the article and lesson by Myrna Bertheau) used *The Important Book* as a basis for her students to analyze the attributes of shape; the book itself focuses on attributes of nonmathematical ideas, such as snow, rain, and daisies.

Styles such as poetry and well-written prose are other aspects to be considered. Rhyming verse is found in many children's books; Brown's *The Important Book* and Pinczes's *A Reminder of One* can serve as models. Rather than create poetry, Ted Rand selected the poem *Arithmetic* by Carl Sandburg as the text for his illustrations. In "Mathematics and Poetry: Problem Solving in Context," Curcio, Zarnowski, and Vigliarolo use Silverstein's poem "Overdues" to pose a problem; they also list other examples of poetry that can be used to relate mathematics.

Why Use Children's Books in the Mathematics Classroom?

Using children's books in the mathematics classroom has become very popular in the last fifteen years. This effect can readily be seen at mathematics conferences by the popularity and the number of sessions on children's books as well as the number of customers at booths that sell children's books. In our professional journals, both "Links to Literature" and feature articles describe the use of children's books in mathematics classrooms. Publishers have produced teacher resources on how to use books in the mathematics classroom as well as an abundance of new children's books.

Teachers have found that high-quality, well-designed children's books in mathematics can become effective teaching tools. Some primary-grade teachers (Trafton 1999) report that initially they used teacher resources that described specific lessons using children's books to teach mathematics. As they acquired more expertise using children's books, they soon devised their own lessons with new books that they selected. Additionally, they continued to build their repertoire of exemplary lessons through reading journals, attending conferences, and conversing with other educators.

One of the concerns that have been raised with respect to children's books in mathematics is a direct result of the popularity of children's books in mathematics. Many new books have been written to cover parts of the curriculum, and consequently a large number of books are published that are mediocre at best. Some books closely resemble traditional textbooks but are being marketed as children's books. More than likely, the books rather than the curriculum are being promoted. When selecting books for your classroom, look beyond the illustrations and authors to determine the mathematical task for which you plan to use the book. Is the mathematics worthwhile? Is it accurate? Is the book appealing? Is it well illustrated?

Another concern involves maintaining the integrity of the book. The selected book should be treated as a whole and regarded as children's literature. When only parts of books are used in isolation and particular sections are overanalyzed, the story line can be lost. When using books in their classroom, most educators recommend first reading the entire book to the class. On rereading the selection, the teacher or the students then pose problems to make sense out of various aspects of the book. Hung (1999) found that the best tactic was to pursue contexts that made sense to students. Students may choose to reread the book individually, or teachers may read or lead a whole-class discussion of the book as a closing activity.

My hope is that the articles and accompanying lessons in the chapters that follow will furnish some additional ways for both you and your students to learn mathematics as well as to enjoy children's literature.

REFERENCES: CHILDREN'S BOOKS

Anno, Masaichiro, and Mitsumasa Anno. *Anno's Mysterious Multiplying Jar*. Illustrated by Mitsumasa Anno. New York: Philomel Books, 1983.

Ash, Russell. *Incredible Comparisons*. New York: Dorling Kindersley, 1996.

Brown, Margaret Wise. *The Important Book*. Illustrated by Leonard Weisgard. New York: HarperCollins Publishers, 1990.

Burns, Marilyn. *Spaghetti and Meatballs for All! A Mathematical Story*. Illustrated by Debbie Tilley. New York: Scholastic Press, 1997.

Clement, Rod. *Counting on Frank*. Milwaukee, Wis.: Gareth Stevens Children's Books, 1991.

Crews, Donald. *Ten Black Dots*. New York: Scholastic, 1968.

Demi. *One Grain of Rice: A Mathematical Folktale*. New York: Scholastic, 1997.

Edens, Cooper. *How Many Bears?* Illustrated by Marjett Schille. New York: Atheneum, 1994.

Friedman, Aileen. *A Cloak for a Dreamer*. Illustrated by Kim Howard. A Marilyn Burns Brainy Day Book. New York: Scholastic, 1994.

Hoban, Tana. *Circles, Triangles, and Squares*. New York: Macmillan Books for Young Readers, 1974.

_____. *Shapes, Shapes, Shapes*. New York: Greenwillow Books, 1986.

_____. *Spirals, Curves, Fanshapes and Lines*. New York: Greenwillow Books, 1992.

McMillan, Bruce. *Eating Fractions*. New York: Scholastic, 1991.

Mathews, Louise. *Gator Pie*. Illustrated by Jeni Bassett. Denver, Colo.: Sundance, 1995.

Myllar, Rolf. *How Big Is a Foot?* New York: Dell Publishing, 1991.

Pinczes, Elinor J. *A Reminder of One*. Illustrated by Bonnie Mackain. New York: Houghton Mifflin Co., 1995.

Sandburg, Carl. *Arithmetic*. Illustrated by Ted Rand. San Diego: Harcourt, Brace Jovanovich, 1993.

Schwartz, David M. *How Much Is a Million?* Illustrated by Steven Kellogg. New York: Lothrop, Lee & Shepherd Books, 1985.

Scieszka, Jon. *Math Curse*. Illustrated by Lane Smith. New York: Viking, 1995.

Silverstein, Shel. *A Light in the Attic*. New York: HarperCollins Publishers, 1981.

RESOURCES

Austin, Patricia. "Math Books as Literature: Which Ones Measure Up?" *New Advocate* 11, no. 2 (1998): 119–33.

Halpern, Pamela A. "Communicating the Mathematics in Children's Trade Books Using Mathematical Annotations." In *Communication in Mathematics*, edited by Portia C. Elliott, pp. 54–59. Reston, Va.: National Council of Teachers of Mathematics, 1996.

Hong, Haekyung. "Using Storybooks to Help Young Children Make Sense of Mathematics." In *Mathematics in the Early Years*, edited by Juanita V. Copley, pp. 162–68. Reston, Va.: National Council of Teachers of Mathematics, 1999.

_____. "Children Learning Mathematics through Literature." *Journal of Educational Research* 33, no. 1 (1995): 399–424.

_____. "Effects of Mathematics Learning through Children's Literature on Mathematical Achievement and Dispositional Outcomes." *Early Childhood Research Quarterly* 11 (1996): 477–94.

Jennings, Clara M., James E. Jennings, Joyce Richey, and Lisbeth D. Krass. "Increasing Interest and Achievement in Mathematics Learning through Children's Literature." *Early Childhood Research Quarterly* 7, no. 2 (1992): 263–76.

Thiessen, Diane, Margaret Matthias, and Jacquelin Smith. *The Wonderful World of Mathematics: A Critically Annotated List of Children's Books in Mathematics*. Reston, Va.: National Council of Teachers of Mathematics, 1998.

Trafton, Paul R., and Diane Thiessen. *Learning through Problems: Number Sense and Computational Strategies*. Portsmouth, N.H.: Heinemann, 1999.

Whitin, David J., and Sandra Wilde. *Read Any Good Math Lately? Children's Books for Mathematical Learning, K–6*. Portsmouth, N.H.: Heinemann, 1992.

Young, Terrell. "Master Class: Children's Literature and Mathematics—an Unhealthy Alliance?" *Journal of Children's Literature* 25, no. 1 (1999): 70–71.

Content Strands and Grade Levels for Articles

	Number and Operations	Algebra	Geometry	Measurement	Data Analysis and Probability
1 Mathematics Is Something Good!	1–3				
2 Going beyond Ten Black Dots	1–3				
3 Exploring Estimation through Children's Literature	3–5				
4 Mathematics and Poetry: Problem Solving in Context	3–5				
5 Amanda Bean and the Gator Girls: Writing and Solving Multiplication Stories	3–5				
6 *A Remainder of One:* Exploring Partitive Division	3–5				
7 Critical Thinking during the December Holidays	4–6				
8 Popping Up Number Sense	K–6				
9 Connecting Literature, Language, and Fractions	1–5				
10 Literature and Algebraic Reasoning		1–5			

Continued on page xiv

Content Strands and Grade Levels for Articles—Continued from page xiii

Content Strands and Grade Levels for Articles—Continued

	Number and Operations	Algebra	Geometry	Measurement	Data Analysis and Probability
22 *Incredible Comparisons:* Experiences with Data Collection	5–8			5–8	
23 Scrumptious Activities in the *Stew*	1–4			1–4	1–4
24 Investigating Probability and Patterns with *The Thirteen Days of Halloween*	3–5				3–5
25 *Socrates and the Three Little Pigs:* Connecting Patterns, Counting Trees, and Probability					7–8
26 From *The Giver* to *The Twenty-One Balloons:* Explorations with Probability					6–8
27 *Dumpling Soup:* Exploring Kitchens, Cultures, and Mathematics	1–3			1–3	
28 Telling Tales: Creating Graphs using Multicultural Literature		2–5		2–5	2–5
29 Feisty Females: Using Children's Literature with Strong Female Characters				4–6	4–6
30 On the Road with Cholo, Vato, and Pano	4–7			4–7	4–7

Content Strand:
Number and Operation

1

Mathematics Is Something Good!

Diane Cradick Oppedal

IT WAS the second week of a new school year, and my second-grade students were working together in pairs. They talked quietly as they arranged and counted interlocking cubes, buttons, plastic disks, counting bears, color tiles, and base-ten units, to name a few. Two students had asked where to find the rubber bands to wrap around their bundles of sticks.

I had just finished reading *Moira's Birthday* by Robert Munsch (1987). In the story, Moira orders 200 cakes and 200 pizzas for her birthday party because she has invited all of the kindergarten, all of the first grade, all of the second grade, all of the third grade, all of the fourth grade, all of the fifth grade, all of the sixth grade—the entire school—to her birthday party! The problem that I had posed to the second graders was "How can you show 200

From *Moira's Birthday,* ©1987 Annick Press; used with permission

things in different ways?" The busy scene just described was the second graders' response to my question.

As I watched and wandered around the room, I observed the ways students approached the problem. I listened to their conversations and asked questions. One group was setting out bear counters. "Would you count what you have for me, please?" I asked. They replied, "5, 10, 15, 20, 30, 40, . . ." as they miscounted their groups of five bear counters. In another group, Mindy and her partner were busy counting out Popsicle sticks and bundling them into piles of fives. When I inquired how many bundles they had made, they counted their bundles and gave the total. To my next question, "How many bundles of five will you need to make 200?" they responded, "Well, we're not done yet." Before most students were finished working, we stopped to get ready for lunch.

On the following day I asked the second graders to report to the class the different ways in which they had shown 200 things. All groups were able to tell how they did it. One group proudly showed how they had used the base-ten stamps (ones, rods, and flats) to show three different ways to represent 200 things.

After all the groups had had an opportunity to share, I considered posing a new problem for them to solve—a rate problem. Because of my concern about the difficulty of a rate problem for second graders, I pondered whether it would be an appropriate task but decided to go ahead and give it a try. "If it took 200 children 10 minutes to eat 200 cakes, how long would it take them to eat 100 cakes? 20 cakes?" I asked the student pairs first to talk with their partners to come up a plan for solving the problem, then to solve it, and finally to write down in their journals how they did it so that they could share that information with the rest of the class.

One pair of students chose the rubber base-ten stamps and an ink pad but could not agree on which stamp to use, so one person used the rod stamp and the other used the cube stamp. Later Mindy explained, "We both agreed, but we just did it different ways." When Cody showed his picture of two rubber-stamp cubes, he said, "This is 100 and this is 100." Jessica interjected with "I don't know how much that is, but it's not 100. I started counting once, and I know it is more than 100."

Again, I listened, observed, and asked a few questions. Students were able to explain what they were doing verbally but needed encouragement to put these same thoughts in writing.

- Jamie wrote in her journal that if it took 10 minutes for 200 kids to eat 200 cakes, it would take 5 minutes for them to eat 100 cakes because "half of 200 is 100 and half of 10 is 5." (See fig. 1.1.) As her partner reasoned, "You have to take away the half of 10 to get 5." Jamie went on to explain that "20 cakes would be 1 minute because half of 5 minutes is 2 and 3, half of 4 minutes is 2 minutes, and half of 2 minutes is 1 minute." I noted that Jamie was close to understanding that half of 5 is between 2 and 3.

- Todor *knew* it would take 1 minute to eat 20 cakes. "I don't know how it's right," he said, "but I know 1 + 1 + 1 + 1 + 1 = 5 and 20 + 20 + 20 + 20 + 20 = 100." It was exciting to hear Todor's thinking, as he was just beginning to read and write English.

- Two groups decided that it would take 1 minute to eat the 20 cakes because they "knew it would be smaller than 5 minutes" and 1 minute sounded "about right." Two other groups figured the time to eat 20 cakes would be 7 minutes. They argued that "there is less cake to eat" and that since 7 minutes is close to 10 minutes, it would be less than 10 minutes. "At times, guessing is okay," I noted, "but then you need to go on and figure out a way to solve the problem."

- One student pair filled their journal page with a drawing of a big star. To my inquiry about how they planned to use the star, they replied, "We're going to put our 100 cakes inside." I continued by asking, "Do you have a plan for doing that?" They responded, "Oh yes!" and proceeded to draw cakes in the center of their star. I had anticipated their drawing 20 cakes on each point of the star, but that was not the direction they took.

- Mindy wrote in her journal that "200 [cakes] – 100 [cakes] = 100 [cakes]" and that "10 [minutes] – 5 [minutes] = 5 [minutes]." (See fig. 1.2.) "If you take away 100 cakes that

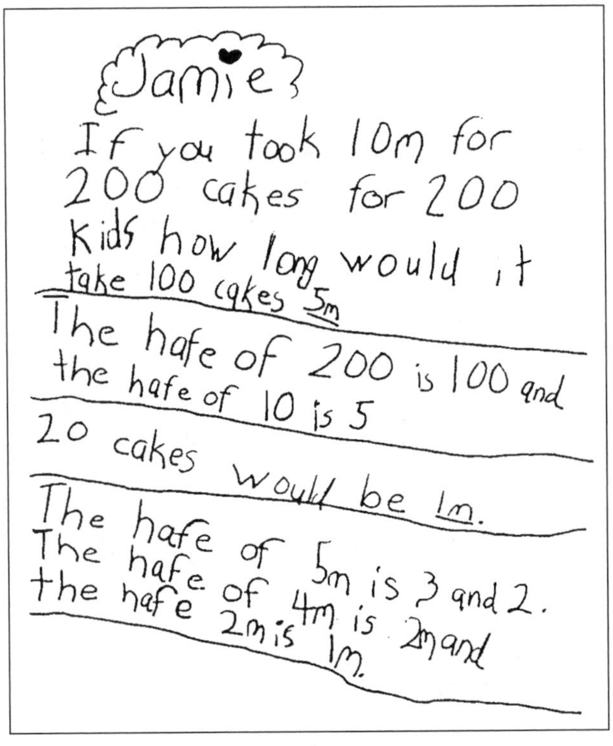

Fig. 1.1. Jamie's reasoning about the rate problem

Fig. 1.2. Mindy's journal entry for the rate problem

EXPLORING MATHEMATICS THROUGH LITERATURE

would be just like taking away 5 minutes," she explained. To solve the question about 20 cakes, she had drawn 5 circles and labeled them 1 through 5. She had crossed out the two circles on each end and had written "middle" under the third circle. "It will take 3 minutes to eat 20 cakes because 3 minutes is in the middle of 5 minutes," she explained. Mindy's strategy was limited; it only worked for the first part of the problem.

Although not all the children found a correct solution to both problems, all of them tackled the rate problems with enthusiasm and developed various strategies to explore and to make sense of the problem. The question of whether I should pose a rate problem for second graders had been answered. I plan to continue to pose such problems, although at the beginning of the school year, I probably will not make them as challenging as this one. At the end of this three-day mathematics-literature lesson, I was delighted with the children's thinking and their abilities to work in groups. I planned on using *Something Good*, another book by Munsch (1990), later in the year. I wondered if I would learn as much about my students' mathematical reasoning as I had with *Moira's Birthday*.

In January I shared Munsch's *Something Good* with the class. In this tale, Tyya goes grocery shopping with her brother, sister, and father. As Tyya pushes the cart up one aisle and down another, she contemplates buying good food. Her definition of "good food" differs from that of her father, so she makes some choices of her own, and the results are wild and crazy!

The second graders could envision the 100 boxes of ice cream and the 300 candy bars that Tyya loaded into her shopping cart. Since the beginning of school, my students had had many experiences with bundling objects and counting large sets by fives, tens, and twenties. They were gaining an understanding of place value, but I wanted to reassess their counting skills and use Munsch's book as a springboard to new questions. I wanted to begin our discussion with a question about an important part of problem solving, that of knowing and explaining how a solution is correct. Additionally, I wanted to introduce some new number problems.

To introduce the new tasks, I told the students that I knew they could easily show what 300 candy bars looked like by counting out 300 cubes or tiles. But could they show the quantity in such a way that

we could easily know that the counting was accurate and the total correct? Earlier I had observed that some students, when selecting and counting objects, did not have a strategy for placing objects, which made counting difficult.

- One student suggested laying out sets of five or ten objects in a row and then building additional rows directly underneath, so that one could see if each row was complete.

- Another student suggested stacking sets of five or ten and visually comparing the height of each stack to see if they were identical. Susan explained that she would use tiles to fill in a solid area. She would check her work by counting how many tiles were in one row and how many complete rows had been built.

As students began to devise strategies that would make counting more accurate, I posed the following problem: How could they estimate the number of cubes or tiles it would take to cover the surface of an eight-and-one-half-by-eleven-inch sheet of paper? After estimating, the children were to determine the actual number of tiles and record their findings. Cooperative groups were formed with two students in each group. Students wrote one sentence each about their estimation in their mathematics journals and then shared resources to begin work on solving the problem.

As they worked, I commented about the visual ease I had in seeing the exact number of tiles in each row. Some students were using their hands to "even up" the sides of their rows as they laid out their tiles. Mat and his partner were using connecting cubes and had created some middle rows that were a cube longer than the beginning rows. When I asked Mat if his rows looked even, he said, "Yes," as he moved his hand along one side, causing the rows with extra cubes to hang over the other side. I asked him to count the cubes in the first row and in a longer row to see if they were the same number. He found his discrepancy and removed the extra cubes. I noted this occasion as another example of Mat's difficulty with visual acuity.

David and his partner had chosen centimeter cubes and were slowly covering the surface of their paper. When I asked them if they thought they would have to cover the whole sheet to get their answer, David said they would not. But neither partner was able to explain how they could solve the problem without covering all the surface area, so they continued laying out each row.

We had just completed work with another measurement problem in which Pinocchio's nose became twice as long, or doubled, each time he told a lie. Students had determined how long his nose was after five lies and then after twenty lies. I thought that some transfer of the doubling strategy (adding a number to itself) might occur and that for the present problem, these students would cover half a page with tiles and double their count. Although Jamie volunteered just that solution, David and his partner continued slowly covering the entire sheet.

As students began to come up with their solutions, I asked each pair how many tiles they had placed in each row and how many rows they had made. I had previously asked these questions as I observed the small groups at work, so most students could answer my question. I had shared with each group that knowing the number of rows and the number of tiles in each row was important information because we could use the calculator to multiply those numbers to check their answer. Students exhibited many looks of surprise when they saw confirmation of their answer on the calculator.

When I questioned Jamie and her partner about the accuracy of their answer, she said, "I know it's right because I used the multiplication chart." Note: Jamie was the student who had correctly calculated by hand the seven-digit length of Pinocchio's nose by the twentieth lie and had declined the use of the calculator!

Our next task was estimating the number of tiles or squares that would cover one flat surface of a piece of Styrofoam. This surface was smaller than the surface of the typewriter-sized sheet of paper with which we had worked the previous day. The Styrofoam represented a floor that needed to be tiled. James estimated that 50 tiles would cover the surface. When he and his partner checked their estimate, they found that the task actually took 24 tiles. Although his estimate was not as close as it could have been, James learned an important aspect about estimation—that "estaments do not have to be perfekt." (See fig. 1.3) Another student, Jordan, initially estimated 500 tiles to cover the piece. As he worked, he realized that his estimate was too high, so he readjusted his thinking. (See fig. 1.4)

Swapomthi and her partner chose centimeter cubes for their work, but they had difficulty completing the task because of the size of the cubes compared with the large area. In Swapomthi's written eval-

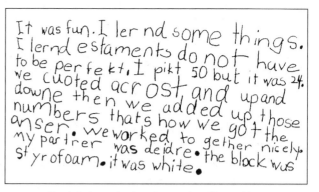

Fig. 1.3. James's thoughts on the tiling problem

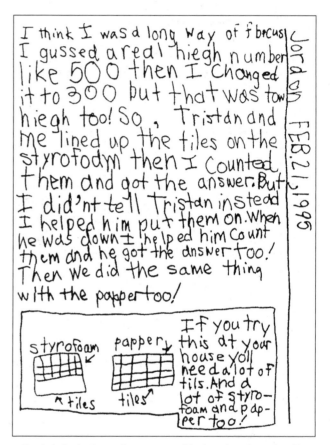

Fig. 1.4. Jordan's readjustments to his thoughts about the tiling problem.

uation, I was happy to read that the next time she would choose "something else to wrok with." (See fig. 1.5) It was also gratifying to read Swapomthi's statement "What I am not going to chace is couperating."

As I reflected on the children's work, I would also do something different next time. I would suggest to students who were working with colored counters that they devise a method so that they could see each unique set of ten at a glance. I would ask them how they could use color to separate visually each set of ten. Grouping by tens would reinforce place-value concepts as well as make the totals easier to count.

EXPLORING MATHEMATICS THROUGH LITERATURE

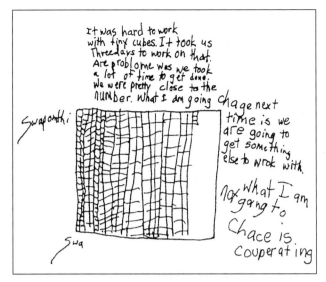

It was hard to work with tiny cubes. It took us Three days to work on that. Are problome was we took a lot of time to get done. We were pretty close to the number. What I am going chage next time is we are going to get something else to wrok with.

Now What I am gang to Chace is couperating

Fig. 1.5. Swapomthi's evaluation of her group's work on the tiling problem.

The students' last tasks was to calculate the difference between their estimations and actual counts. Most calculations involved subtracting three-digit numbers using regrouping, which was a challenge for most students and occupied most of the work period. As the mathematics period ended, I knew that my students had grown in number sense and had built on their understanding of estimation and place value. I also hoped that they were more aware of the importance of accuracy in their work and better able to explain strategies for knowing why their work was accurate. I planned to present many similar situations with a variety of materials so that my students would continue to develop number sense and increase their understanding of place value.

BIBLIOGRAPHY

Armstrong, Barbara E. "Implementing the *Professional Standards for Teaching Mathematics:* Teaching Patterns, Relationships, and Multiplication as Worthwhile Mathematical Tasks." *Teaching Children Mathematics* 1 (April 1995): 446–50.

Campbell, Patricia F. "Research into Practice: Place Value and Addition and Subtraction." *Arithmetic Teacher* 41 (January 1994): 272–74.

Harte, Sandra W., and Matthew J. Glover. "Estimating Is Mathematical Thinking." *Arithmetic Teacher* 41 (October 1993): 75–77.

Munsch, Rober. *Moira's Birthday.* Illustrated by Michael Martchenko. Toronto: Annick Press, 1987.

———. *Something Good.* Illustrated by Michael Martchenko. Toronto: Annick Press, 1990.

Sowder, Judith, and Bonnie Schappelle. "Research into Practice: Number Sense-Making." *Arithmetic Teacher* 41 (February 1994): 342–45.

Thornton, Carol A., Graham A. Jones, and Judy L. Neal. "The 100s Chart: A Stepping Stone to Mental Mathematics." *Teaching Children Mathematics* 1 (April 1995): 480–83.

"Mathematics Is Something Good!"

by Diane Cradick Oppedal

Grade range:	1–3
Mathematical topics:	Counting strategies, grouping, place value, estimation, introductory area and perimeter concepts
Children's books:	*Moira's Birthday*, written by Robert Munsch and illustrated by Michael Martchenko (1987)
	Something Good, written by Robert Munsch and illustrated by Michael Martchenko (1990)
Materials:	"Moira's Birthday" recording sheets 1 and 2; "Something Good" recording sheets 1 and 2; color tiles and other objects for counting, for example, unit cubes, counters, dominoes, or such junk-box items as soda-pop lids, shells, empty spools, or buttons

Discussion of the mathematics: Counting tasks lead naturally to grouping and to place-value concepts as children develop more efficient strategies to determine the number of objects in a set. Most children will begin counting large numbers of objects by ones, then progress to counting by twos, fives, or tens. Estimating the number of objects contained in a set before counting enhances number sense. Covering the paper's surface with tiles leads to an array representation (an area model). By carefully lining up the tiles in each row, students can see that each row contains the same number of objects. The rate problems involving three variables (kids, minutes, cakes) are accessible to children when they have the opportunity to represent the situation and use number sense and their reasoning skills.

Teacher notes and questions to ask students: Children need many informal opportunities to group and count a variety of objects before attempting the more formal problem-solving activities that require recording and sharing their problem-solving strategies with peers. Choose numbers that are appropriate to the ages of the children and that permit all students, regardless of abilities, to be successful with, yet challenged by, the task. An assortment of classroom objects for sorting and counting could include unit cubes, color tiles, counters, dominoes, and such junk-box items as soda-pop lids, shells, empty spools, and buttons. Pose questions that require counting and that encourage children to develop more efficient strategies involving grouping and counting by multiples. Some examples include the following:

- Can you count or write your numbers to 100? To 120? To 150?

- How many groups or bundles (e.g., 2, 5, 10) do you think you have?

- How many groups of 5 do you have?

Requiring students to record two or more solutions to a problem will stimulate their thinking and provide extension opportunities for students needing extra challenge. Once a problem is posed, the teacher is free to observe students' work and ask questions that move students' thinking forward in their work. Such questions as the following pose such challenges:

- What is a different way to count and show your number?

- Can you use a more efficient way to show your number?

- How can you be sure your number is accurate?

Students' recording of their thinking is an important part of problem solving. Students should be encouraged to record their work using pictures, words, numbers, or a combination of these tools. All students need to learn strategies for checking the accuracy of their work, whether in counting or recording. Finally, students' sharing of their problem-solving strategies with peers helps the teacher assess students' understanding, serves as a teaching resource for classmates, and may challenge peers to investigate new problem-solving strategies.

Recording sheets 1 and 2 were used after reading and discussing *Moria's Birthday*. The other recording sheets were designed for *Something Good*. Often the last questions I pose as we finish an activity are these:

- What did you learn?

- What would you like to learn next?

REFERENCES

Munsch, Robert. *Moira's Birthday*. Illustrated by Michael Martchenko. Toronto: Annick Press, 1987.

_____. *Something Good*. Illustrated by Michael Martchenko. Toronto: Annick Press, 1990.

Oppedal, Diane Cradick. "Links to Literature: Mathematics Is Something Good!" *Teaching Children Mathematics* 2 (September 1995): 36–40.

Moira's Birthday

Name_____

Date _____

Moira ordered 200 cakes for her birthday.

Choose a counting item from the room, and show how you would count out 200 things accurately. Record your solution using words, pictures, or numbers to show how you did it.

Name_____

Date _____

If 200 children needed 10 minutes to eat 200 cakes, how much time would they need to eat 100 cakes?

Show your work using pictures, words, or numbers. Be ready to explain your solution to the class.

Extension: How long would it take them to eat 20 cakes?

Something Good

Name_____

Date _____

How many color tiles would it take to cover the surface of a sheet of paper?

Write down your estimate.   Estimate _____

Cover the surface of the paper to find out how many tiles were needed.

Record your answer, and explain how you solved the problem.

Actual number _____

Extension activities: Can you get the answer to this problem without covering the whole sheet of paper? Explain your thinking.

Find a different item to cover your paper. Will you need more or fewer of this item? Why? What is your estimate? How many did you need?

Something Good   Recording Sheet 2

Name_____

Date _____

How many tiles would you need to go around the outside edge of this paper?

Write down your estimate.   Estimate _____

Use your tiles to find the exact number you would need.

Actual number _____

What is the difference between your estimate and the actual number?

2

Going beyond Ten Black Dots

Susan Weinberg

I FEAL beg, beg, beg, beg. I feel gronup bekoes meath is gronup stof." This comment was one second grader's reaction to studying mathematics through problem solving. (We have preserved the actual spelling used by these students throughout the article.—Ed.)

Children eagerly respond to the challenge when given the opportunity to solve difficult problems. One joy of posing problems to be solved mathematically is the discovery that students are also surprisingly capable of solving complex problems. Students come to school with informal mathematical knowledge and a bank of problem-solving strategies to apply to unusual problem situations. When given the opportunity, students rapidly develop positive, confident attitudes about their mathematical ability.

Students use strategies to solve problems appropriate to their mathematical ability in ways that never cease to amaze me. I was astounded by the second graders' responses to a problem that was posed after reading Donald Crews's *Ten Black Dots* (1968). In this book the numbers from 1 through

10 are introduced through rhyming text about simple, everyday objects with black dots incorporated into each drawing (see fig. 2.1 for an illustration).

The students thoroughly enjoyed this book and were delighted when we discussed the possibility of writing individual *Ten Black Dots* books. They recognized that their first task was to solve the problem of how many "dots" would be needed to create their individual books if each number of dots from 1 to 10 appeared only one time. This task proved to be easy for second graders, and they quickly solved the problem by determining that each student would need fifty-five dots. Figure 2.2 includes a cross section of students' work and a short description.

Posing the Big Problem

After solving the problem of the sum of the numbers from 1 through 10, the second graders wrote their rough drafts in ten-page, teacher-made student books. As my parent volunteer began typing each student's verses into a separate booklet, I knew I needed to buy dots for the illustrations. This situation triggered a thought that I might pose the problem of how many black dots I would need to buy for the class. I mentioned this possibility to Paul Trafton, a coleader in the Primary Mathematics Project at the University of Northern Iowa, in which I was a participant. He surprised me by asking if he and some undergraduate students could visit to observe the children at work. I consented and contemplated the scenario as it might unfold. I could imagine all my students counting out 1100 manipulatives, going to the neighboring classes and begging and borrowing manipulatives while I scurried around the classroom. In spite of my confidence in the children's abilities, I began to question the audacity of posing such a problem for children early in second grade.

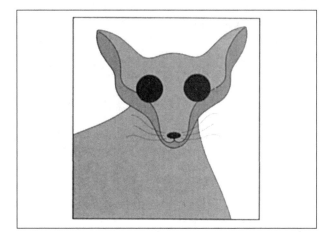

Fig. 2.1. A page from *Ten Black Dots*. Copyright 1968 by Donald Crews. Greenwillow Books. Used by permission of HarperCollins Publishers.

After listing the numerals vertically, Kevin added pairs of consecutive numbers. Then he added the resulting sums. His drawings clearly indicate his thinking as he mentally added different pairs of numbers.

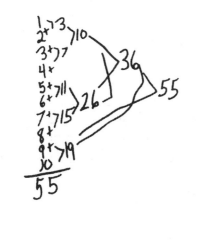

Lisa, who was not yet ready to use pencil-and-paper computation systematically, drew kitty-cat counters to represent all the black dots and then counted them for an answer of 55.

Erica began with the largest numbers. First she added 10 + 9 for an answer of 19. She then added 19 to 8 for an answer of 27 and continued 27 + 7 = 34, 34 + 6 = 40, and so on, to arrive at a final answer of 55.

$$10+9=19 \quad 19+8=27 \quad 27+7=34$$
$$34+6=40+5=45 \quad 45+4=49 \quad 49+3=52$$
$$52+2=54 \quad 54+1=55$$

Kayla found combinations of 10 and then added the tens together. She added 1 + 9 first and checked off those rows. Then she added 2 + 8 and checked off those rows. As "tens are easy," she added the numbers mentally. This pattern is parallel to a method credited to Carl Friedrich Gauss for adding a sequence of numbers.

Valerie vertically listed the numerals from 1 to 10. She added 1 and 2, recording the sum 3 to the side. After adding 3 and 4 and recording the sum 7, she then added 3 + 7 to obtain 10. She continued by adding 10 and 5, then adding that result to the next number 6, and so on. Her running total was recorded to the right of each new consecutive number, that is, 10 + 5 = 15, 15 + 6 = 21, and so on. Valerie used "counting on" to obtain each new sum.

Fig. 2.2. Various strategies attempted by students

The next morning my visitors arrived. I posed the problem, emphasizing that twenty students in the classroom each needed fifty-five dots to complete their booklets. I repeated this statement slowly three or four times so that my students could visualize the problem. When I was sure they understood it, I encouraged them by letting them work in pairs.

The students began working on this problem at 10:25 a.m. At 11:10 a.m. I invited pairs of students to share strategies with other classmates who were finished. A few pairs were still at work; however, I wanted the visiting undergraduate students to observe the power of the shared learning that occurs when pairs have a chance to share their problem-solving strategies with the rest of the class. The student work and quotes described in the next sections illustrate their mathematical power.

Kayla's and Danny's Thought Processes

Kayla and Danny wrote the numeral 55 twenty times on their paper, but they mentally considered 55 as 50 and 5 more. They proceeded by adding the 50s in pairs to make 100 (fig. 2.3). Kayla explained, "50 and 50 equals 100, and another 50 and 50 is 200, etcetera." They continued this pattern to 1000. Next, they added the twenty 5s together for an answer of 100. To obtain the final answer of 1100, they added 1000 and 100.

When Trafton asked Kayla if this problem was easy, medium, or hard, Kayla responded, "This was sort of easy problem because I can count by 50s and I can count by 5s, so this was easy." When Kayla was asked how solving this problem made her feel, she responded, "Good."

Jamie's Brandon's, and Hillary's Reasoning

The following written explanation was offered by Jamie, Brandon, and Hillary.

> I told Jamie to put 1 finger up each time I added 55 on the clacalaters and we got the anser 4240.

As Hillary explained her group's solution to the class, she concluded by stating, "We think our answer is wrong." One of their classmates, Danny, empathized, "You have a good strategy, but when you push so many numbers into the calculator, mistakes are easily made." Hillary admitted, "It was hard pushing the buttons and keeping up all the time. We kept messing up." The students were complimented on their reasoning and encouraged to try their strategy again to obtain the correct answer.

Erica's and Clint's Examples

Erica and Clint began by drawing twenty desks and writing the numeral 50 on each desk. They decided a calculator would be helpful for adding all of the 50s. When a 50 was entered into the calculator, a "D" was written above the desk, meaning it was "done." Erica wrote an explanation under their drawing: "We put a 50 on ech desk and counted then on the calculator. Then we counted evrybodys desk by 5." When their work was shared with the class, Erica noted that she was sure her answer was wrong. When Erica was asked what she thought went wrong, she commented, "I added some 50s without marking them off on the desks."

Adam's and Andrew's Calculation

Adam and Andrew solved the problem rapidly by using a calculator. To describe their reasoning, they wrote, "We used the caelcualatrs. We gat are anser by deying a teims, and we gat the anesr 1100. $20 \times 55 = 1100$."

Because Adam and Andrew got the answer so quickly, I asked them to solve this problem using another strategy. I suggested that they compare the answers and see if they were the same. They quickly began working and put together twenty trains of interlocking cubes. Each train had 5 cubes. When sharing their work, Adam explained, "One of these five-sticks really counted as 55. So we went 55, 110 [then Adam started picking up 2 five-sticks at a time and continued counting by 110 to 1100], 220, 330, 440, 550, 660, 770, 880, 990, and 1100."

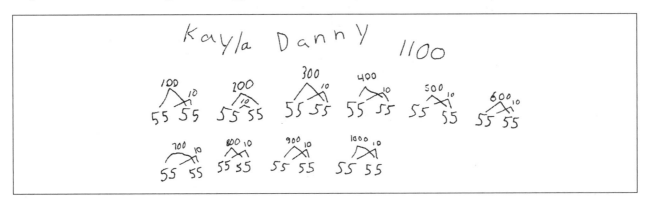

Fig. 2.3. These students decomposed each 55 into 50 + 5.

EXPLORING MATHEMATICS THROUGH LITERATURE

When Trafton inquired why they called a five-stick "55," Adam explained, "Because everybody in our class needed 55 dots." When asked whether this problem was easy or hard, Adam replied, "Easy problem because I'm pretty smart at math. Some problems Mrs. Weinberg gives us are easy and some are hard. This was an easy one." When students were asked whether they liked to think in mathematics class, Adam responded, "Yeah, because it is fun."

In Closing

This activity is another example of using children's literature as a vehicle for encouraging students to think, to develop mathematical strategies, and to increase their number sense. Basic computation skills begin to make sense through such problem-solving tasks.

As we have observed, students are capable of solving complex problems at an early stage of development. Adam was counting by 110s while B.J. was connecting links. A little later, B.J. realized that this method was not efficient for solving the problem. He appeared to be keenly interested in discovering how others solved the problem, since he observed other students working and eagerly listened during peer sharing. Valerie's interest in the problem was also sustained. She continued working on this problem throughout the day as well as through the noon recess, at her own choosing. After much confusion with her scribbled array of 5s, she chose a different and more efficient strategy.

The strength of students who work, learn, and share with others was evident in the results of their work. The advantages, both socially and academically, exist for all students. Nick, a very capable student, summed up his thoughts about working with others: "I feel happy it is fun. It is fun becus you can see how smart you are and lern stof from other kids."

We, as teachers, need to challenge students and then step back and encourage them to work through problems at their own rates. Students will not only gain a deeper understanding of mathematics but also develop a positive attitude toward mathematics and confidence in their ability to solve problems.

REFERENCE

Crews, Donald. *Ten Black Dots*. New York: Scholastic Books, 1968.

Teaching Notes for

"Going beyond Ten Black Dots"

by Susan Weinberg

Grade range:	1–3
Mathematical topic:	Strategies for solving computational problems
Children's book:	*Ten Black Dots*, by Donald Crews
Materials:	"Ten Black Dots" recording sheets 1 and 2

Discussion of the mathematics: By being posed questions to which they do not have a known procedure, students will be building new mathematical knowledge through problem solving. To solve such problems, students use their problem-solving strategies with such concepts as the commutative and associative properties, place value, doubles, "making tens," and the like. Another focus is the Communication Standard, in that students are asked to communicate their mathematical thinking coherently and clearly to peers, teachers, and others as well as to analyze and evaluate the mathematical thinking and strategies of others.

Teacher notes: After reading the book to the class, we discuss the features of the book, such as the rhyming verses and the big black dots. Various students comment on the different ways that Crews uses the dots in his artwork, and they often comment on their favorite black-dot picture. They also observe that Crews offers two examples of each number. To launch the problem, I pose the possibility of each student's making his or her own black-dot book, but using only one example of each number from 1 to 10. I ask, "How many 'dots' would you need to make your own *Ten Black Dots* book?"

After I am sure that the students understand the problem, I hand out the recording sheets. While they work, I make observations about their work and plan what should be shared in their seminar, or group-sharing, time. Below is a sample of a full-page grid used for recording students' strategies; each student's name is written on the grid. As I walk around, observing and visiting with different students, I jot down the strategies they are using to solve the problem, or anything of significance that I would like to remember or would like to have the students share. This type of recording sheet aids in conducting seminar time in which the students are sharing their strategies and work. For example, if four students used the same strategy, I may request that one student explain it and then ask the other three students whether they have additional comments.

Brian	Sara	Tasha	Kiah
Sarah P.	Kalin	Logan	Davian

REFERENCES

Crews, Donald. *Ten Black Dots*. New York: Scholastic, 1968.

Weinberg, Susan. "Links to Literature: Going beyond Ten Black Dots." *Teaching Children Mathematics* 2 (March 1996): 432–35.

Ten Black Dots

Name_____

Date _____

How many "dots" would you need to make your own *Ten Black Dots* book?

Please explain your answer using word, numbers, or pictures.

Ten Black Dots

Name_____

Date _____

How many dots would I need to buy if everyone in the class made a *Ten Black Dots* book?

Please explain your answer using words, numbers, or pictures.

3

Exploring Estimation
through Children's Literature

David J. Whitin

ESTIMATION is a crucial mathematical strategy that can be woven throughout the entire mathematics curriculum. The strategy can certainly foster the development of many of the goals advocated by the NCTM's curriculum and evaluation standards (1989). Since approximately 80 percent of real-world applications of mathematics involve estimation or mental computation, the goal of becoming an "informed electorate" requires us to use and analyze various estimation strategies.

Knowing when to use estimation in certain situations helps learners become more flexible problem solvers, another important goal of the curriculum standards. A focus on the use of estimation also gives learners a more balanced perspective about the nature of mathematics; they grow in their confidence about themselves as mathematicians when they see mathematics as a way of thinking, not a way of behaving according to certain algorithmic rules.

Children's literature can be an important vehicle for exploring ideas about estimation. Books supply a natural context for discussing mathematical ideas, including such strategies as estimation (Whitin and Wilde 1992). Through stories learners come to see that estimation is not a separate strategy that is studied and used in isolation but one that is put to good use by people in their daily living. Children's literature can help to highlight this purposeful and functional use of estimation. The following three classroom scenarios help to demonstrate the potential that children's literature holds for investigating this important mathematical strategy.

A First-Grade Scenario

Teacher Margaret Tuten created such an exploration when she shared the book *Many Is How Many?* by Illa Podendorf (1970) with her first-grade students. The book contrasts various comparison words, such as *a lot* and *a few*, *big* and *small*, and *long* and *short*. It concludes with a section entitled "What is many?" These comparison words are used to estimate the size of objects; their meaning is not absolute but rather dependent on each particular situation.

After reading the story to her students, Tuten asked them to list what they considered to be a few versus many pieces of candy. Some of their responses are included in table 3.1.

TABLE 3.1

First-Grade Students' Understanding of Few and Many

Few	Many
3	100
4	50
8	51
2	1000
5	100

They reached a general agreement that five pieces of candy would be considered *few*. However, when Tuten asked them if they would view five spoonfuls of yucky-tasting medicine as few, the students clamored "no" in unison. They felt that five spoonfuls of medicine would be considered as *many*. Tuten's question helped the students see that such estimating words as *few* and *many* are dependent on the context in which they appear. This same point was underscored when the students discussed temperature: 60° F seemed cool in the summer but warm in the winter. These kinds of discussions lie at the heart of what it means to "communicate mathematically" (NCTM 1989, p. 6), an important goal of the curriculum standards. Communication does not involve learning a list of mathematical terms in isolation; rather, communication involves an active negotiation among learners as they debate, revise, and clarify mathematical ideas. The student's tentative interpretations and explanations for the quantitative terms of *few* and *many* demonstrated to them that mathematics was not a system to accept and follow but rather a system to question and challenge.

Tuten posed a question about the mall because she knew that all her students had been there and had ridden the elevator. "If all the students in our class and the other first-grade class got into that elevator, would *a few* or *many* people be in the elevator?" The students felt the elevator would be quite crowded and agreed that *many* riders would be in the elevator. However, when Tuten asked them if that same group of children walked into the theater at the mall, would they consider the theater crowded with too many people, her first graders just laughed and said there would be plenty of room in the theater. In this situation they concluded that the group would be only *a few* in number.

"But how can you call this same group of students *many* on one occasion and *few* a little later on?" Tuten asked. Some students were not sure, but others thought that the amount of space made the difference in whether this group could be called *few* or *many*. Tuten then asked the students if they could think of other examples in which the same number of people seemed like *a few* in one place and *a lot* in another. They noted that their class seemed like *a lot* of people when they had to crowd into the bathroom area during the tornado drills. However, Monica recalled another time when their class seemed much smaller: "On the playground at second recess, there's not anybody out there except our little ol' class."

The students were beginning to realize that the mathematical language of *few* and *many* was used to estimate the size of a group. They were also discovering that this language could be used and interpreted in different ways depending on the context of the specific situation. One student realized that estimates permitted a numerical range and wished that her mom would allow her to have a "few" cookies rather than just "two," so that she could eat perhaps three or four. The language of estimation allowed for some freedom of interpretation that had some very definite benefits for those who liked cookies!

Second-Grade Scenario

One of the best children's books to incorporate the strategy of estimation is *Counting on Frank* by Rod Clement (1991). In this story a young boy, accompanied by his dog named Frank, presents the reader with a series of interesting facts and comparisons. Bespectacled and looking quite serious, a young boy, accompanied by his dog named Frank, performs most of their calculations around the house: they draw a long line across a wall, over a lamp, and across dad's body to show that the average ball-point pen draws a line twenty-three hundred yards long before the ink runs out; they calculate that twenty-four Franks could fit into the boy's bedroom; they estimate that it would take eleven hours and forty-five minutes to fill the entire bathroom with water with both faucets running; and because the young boy dislikes peas, he estimates that if he had accidentally knocked fifteen peas off his plate every night for the last eight years, the peas would now be level with the tabletop!

The illustrations humorously depict these wonderfully bizarre calculations. This book is important because it is one of only a few that address the strategy of estimation and it also demonstrates to the reader what it means to think mathematically. This young boy views the world with a pair of mathematical "lenses." He sees situations from a mathematical perspective and poses questions for himself to solve that involve various mathematical concepts, such as length, time, volume, and capacity.

Second-grade teacher Terri Bingham read this story to her students and invited them to write and illustrate their own calculations. Their work was later bound into a class book titled *Counting on Frank, Part 2*. Sean created an estimate that involved volume: "I think that it would take twenty thousand pieces of soap to fill my dad's garage. Only when my dad's car and tools are out. Also when my brother isn't using soap while he is taking a bath" (fig. 3.1). Sean's dad had in fact built a large shed next to their house and had recently stored four packs of soap. Sean used these two familiar events in his story.

Although Sean's actual figure of 20,000 was "just a guess," he did incorporate the concept of volume into a situation that made sense to him. In this way Sean was looking at his world from a mathematical perspective. This kind of thinking is advocated

I think that it would take twinty thousand pieces of soap to fill my dad's garage. Only when my dad's car and tools are out. Olso when my brother isn't using soap while he is taking a bath.

Figure 3.1. Sean's estimate

I don't like going to bed. I have to change my under wear. It would take 3 books to fill up my dad's under wear.

Figure 3.2. Adam's estimate

by the curriculum standards (NCTM 1989). It is a call for learners "to be active participants in creating knowledge" (p. 15) and to have regular opportunities "to read, write, and discuss ideas in which the use of the language of mathematics becomes natural" (p. 6). This story-writing by these second graders also underscores the notion that "everybody is a mathematician" and that "doing mathematics is a common human activity" (p. 6). It encourages learners "to value the mathematical enterprise, to develop mathematical habits of mind" (p. 5). One such habit is using the strategy of estimation across a variety of mathematical concepts. Sean and his classmates are learning that they can look at their world from a mathematical point of view. This more global realization underpins the mathematical literacy espoused by the curriculum standards.

Adam wrote an estimation story that also involved volume: "I don't like going to bed. I have to change my underwear. It would take 3 books to fill up my Dad's underwear" (fig. 3.2). Just as the young boy in the story disliked eating peas, so Adam shared a personal dislike of his own. In fact, he even went home and tested out his estimate and found that his dad's underwear held "3 1/2 books, and the 1/2 was a small book." Another student, Sam, also used volume and tried to describe exactly what a volume measurement was when he wrote, "My room is pretty big so I predict it would take 31 beds to fill, top to bottom and side to side in my room." Through writing, Sam had to clarify for himself what this particular kind of measurement entailed.

Anna was intrigued by that part of the story that discussed the length of a line from a ball-point pen.

She wrote her own estimation story using the concept of length: "If I were to take a big piece of chalk and go up and down the chalkboard ten times there would be no more chalk left" (fig. 3.3). Anna's mother is a teacher, and Anna was used to making designs on the chalkboard in her mother's classroom after school. She figured that "when I color in on my Mom's chalkboard I use up about a half of a piece," so she thought her estimate of ten times was fairly close. Here again Anna took a situation that was familiar to her and viewed it from a mathematical perspective. Carl used the concept of length to express his estimate about his savings account: "I calculate that if I take all my savings out of the jar and spread it out it would take 15 feet to do it." He said afterward that "I have a lot of money in my jar, but I don't know how much fifteen feet is." Nevertheless he created a unique comparison using the concepts of money and length that he could test out at a later date.

Jennifer incorporated the concept of time in her estimate: "If I were to watch one hundred movies it

Figure 3.3. Anna's estimate

Fifth-Grade Scenario

Teacher Kathryn McColskey shared several pieces of literature with her fifth- and sixth-grade students. At first she shared Shel Silverstein's poem "How Many, How Much" (1981), which highlights the contextual constraints that shape an estimate. In this poem the author poses some questions that must be answered conditionally. For instance, the number of slices in a loaf of bread depends on how thin you slice it; or the number of slams in an old screen door depends on how loud you shut it. Estimates are required in these situations because the value varies, that is, it depends on who is doing the slicing or who is doing the slamming. After reading the poem aloud several times, McColskey then invited her students to write their own personal variations. Some of the problems they posed appear in table 3.2. The answers to these questions will vary from person to person; their responses could only be estimates because they are influenced by so many different factors. Whether one is trying to determine the amount of water, the number of freckles, or the duration of dressing time, the answers will vary to reflect the natural diversity of individuals' lifestyles, habits, and interests. The students' personal examples serve to highlight the idea that estimates are always context dependent.

McColskey also shared with her students the books by Tom Parker titled *Rules of Thumb* (1983) and *Rules of Thumb #2* (1987). According to the author, rules of thumb are homemade recipes that fall somewhere between a mathematical formula and a shot in the dark. They have been honed, revised, and refined through hours of personal experience and enable people to make things work out most of the time. The author solicited these rules of thumb from people in all walks of life and includes such example as these: One acre will park 100 cars; you need one-half ton of hay per cow per month for feed, or six tons per cow per year; about four pounds of fresh herbs are needed to make one pound of dry herbs; about forty gallons of maple sap are required to make one gallon of maple syrup; no sizable apiary should be placed within two miles of another.

These examples underscore the diverse contexts in which people devise and apply their own personal estimates, or "rules of thumb." After sharing some of these examples with her students, McColsky asked them to record rules of thumb that they used in their own lives. Some of their responses, which were illustrated and bound into a class book, included these entries:

would take four months. My Dad would go crazy because he could not watch his favorite show" (fig. 3.4). Jennifer later explained her reasoning: "Well, I could probably only watch one or two a day 'cause we only have two TV's and Dad watches one and my Mom and sister watch the other. But when they cook supper I can go watch TV. That means in four months you could only see 100 movies." Jennifer used a personal interest and a common family situation to devise an estimate that was meaningful to her.

Figure 3.4. Jennifer's estimate

EXPLORING MATHEMATICS THROUGH LITERATURE

TABLE 3.2

Fifth Graders' Contexts For Estimation

How much water in a bathtub?	Depends on who is in it (fig. 3.5)
How many freckles on a freckle face?	It depends on whose face it is
How much hair spray do you use?	It depends on how many times your boy friend comes over
How long does it take to take a test?	It depends on how long you study (fig. 3.6)
How much time does it take to get dressed?	Depends on what you wear
How much hair does your teacher have?	Depends on how annoying you are
How long does it take your pimples to go away?	Depends on if you use OXY 5

- If you spend more than ten minutes on homework you have too much.

- Never go outside in 100° F weather.

- Always bring at least $600.00 on vacations.

- If you have more than two pimples use Stridex.

- Never wear make-up until you are thirteen years old.

- You should never have homework higher than one inch.

The last rule of thumb requires one to stack up the homework books and measure their height. If the stack measures more than one inch, the homework

Figure 3.5. Context-dependent estimate involving capacity

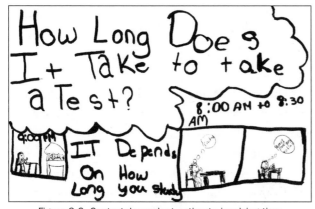

Figure 3.6. Context-dependent estimate involving time

assignment is too "lengthy" and time-consuming. The child who suggested $600.00 for vacations actually went on a vacation with his family and helped them make decisions on how to spend their fixed amount of money wisely. By sharing their rules of thumb, the students were coming to recognize the important role that estimation plays in their daily lives.

Conclusion

Children's literature can be an important avenue for exploring the strategy of estimation. Through books, children can read, write, and discuss the language of mathematics because it is naturally embedded in familiar situations. Stories also show how certain contextual factors influence the kind of estimates that we make; books demonstrate the use of estimation across various mathematical concepts, such as volume, length, time, and area. And, most important, children's literature powerfully demonstrates that mathematics is a way of thinking. For these reasons children's literature deserves a prominent role in the mathematics curriculum for all learners.

REFERENCES

Clement, Rod. *Counting on Frank.* Milwaukee, Wis.: Gareth Stevens Children's Book, 1991.

National Council of Teachers of Mathematics (NCTM). *Curriculum and Evaluation Standards for School Mathematics.* Reston, Va.: NCTM, 1989.

Parker, Tom. *Rules of Thumb.* Boston: Houghton Mifflin Co., 1983.

———. *Rules of Thumb #2.* Boston: Houghton Mifflin Co., 1987.

Podenforf, Illa. *Many Is How Many?* Chicago: Children's Press. 1970.

Silverstein, Shel. "How Many, How Much." In *A Light in the Attic.* New York: Harper & Row, 1981.

Whitin, David, and Sandra Wilde. *Read Any Good Math Lately? Children's Books for Matheamtical Learning K–6.* Portsmouth, N.H.: Heinemann Books, 1992.

"Exploring Estimation through Children's Literature"

by David J. Whitin

Grade range:	3–5
Mathematical topic:	Estimation
Children's books:	*Many Is How Many?* written by Illa Podendorf (1970)
	"How Many, How Much," in *A Light in the Attic*, by Shel Silverstein (1981)
	Counting on Frank, written by Rod Clement (1991)
	Rules of Thumb, written by Tom Parker (1983)
	Rules of Thumb #2, written by Tom Parker (1987)
Materials:	"Estimation" recording sheet

Discussion of the mathematics: Estimation is encountered in such different contexts as computational estimation, estimation of measures, and estimates of number. Estimating a measure, such as meters or square inches, requires developing a referent for that measure. Estimating number requires developing benchmarks, such as 10, 25, 100, or 1000.

Teacher notes: Estimation is a strategy that we use all the time but often take for granted. For students to recognize the prevalence of estimation in their lives, ask them to list the times they estimate. They might ask their parents to contribute ideas to the list. Next to each instance of estimating, have them record *why* they estimated instead of determining an exact answer. This second column can highlight the reasons for, and benefits of, estimating. For instance, some possible responses are included in the chart.

Make a classroom chart of these instances of estimating and the reasons that an estimate rather than an exact answer was appropriate. Invite the children to categorize each column. Some students

Estimate	Why I Estimated
I looked in my wallet to see if I had enough money to buy this toy.	I just looked at the ten- and five-dollar bills to get an estimate. This saved me some time.
My grandma is coming to visit. She wants to know the temperature in April.	I couldn't give her an exact answer because the temperature varies.
My little brother wanted to know how much money I had saved for my bike.	I told him about $50 because that's easier for him to understand.
My mother wanted to know if she had enough gas in the car to do all her errands.	She can't measure the gas in her car, so she had to estimate.

may find newspaper articles that involve estimation. The contexts for estimating might include cooking, money, weather, time, and so on. Such a list underscores the pervasive presence of estimation in our lives. The reasons for estimating might include saving time, making a situation easier to understand, and having no alternative (sometimes an estimate is the only choice, as in estimating the amount of gasoline in the car or the temperature in April). Children might add other examples to the list as the year progresses. An excellent article that describes these reasons, and others, in more detail is Usiskin's "Reasons for Estimating."

REFERENCES

Clements, Rod. *Counting on Frank.* Milwaukee: Gareth Stevens Children's Books, 1991.

Parker Tom. *Rules of Thumb.* Boston: Houghton Mifflin Co., 1983.

———. *Rules of Thumb #2.* Boston: Houghton Mifflin Co., 1987.

Podendorf, Illa. *Many Is How Many?* Chicago: Children's Press, 1970.

Silverstein, Shel. "How Many, How Much." In *A Light in the Attic.* New York: Harper & Row, 1981.

Usiskin, Zalman. "Reasons for Estimating." In *Estimation and Mental Computation,* 1986 Yearbook of the National Council of Teachers of Mathematics (NCTM), edited by Harold L. Schoen, pp. 1–15. Reston, Va.: NCTM, 1986.

Whitin, David J. "Exploring Estimation through Children's Literature." *Arithmetic Teacher* 41 (April 1994): 436–41.

Name_____

Date _____

At home: Share what you have learned about estimation with others, and interview them.

Ask them to describe when they use estimation and why an estimate rather than an exact answer is appropriate.

Record whom you interviewed, what they estimated, and why they estimated.

4

Mathematics and Poetry: Problem Solving in Context

Frances R. Curcio, Myra Zarnowski, and Susan Vigliarolo

ALTHOUGH many elementary school teachers routinely share poetry with their students to foster an appreciation of language and literature, poetry can also promote the learning of mathematics. Many poems—through rhythm, rhyme, story, and interesting word choices—evoke situations that engage children and can serve as a basis for mathematical problem solving.

Some ideas and activities designed to integrate poetry into the third-grade mathematics curriculum are presented in this article. The discussion demonstrates how a humorous poem sparked a great deal of lively talk about mathematics and involved third graders in estimating, devising and comparing problem-solving strategies, creating their own mathematical poems, and posing original problems based on their poems. Other poems have similar potential for strengthening students' interest and involvement in mathematics. Suggestions for selecting poetry to complement the mathematics curriculum are included, along with an annotated list of poems, call a "poemography," which is arranged by mathematics content.

Although these activities were implemented in a third-grade class, many of the ideas could be adapted for younger as well as older children on the basis of their interests and abilities. This approach begins with using poetry to generate ideas about mathematics. After sharing problem-solving strategies, children create their own poems using mathematical ideas. Children return to the mathematics as they share their original poems and pose and solve problems related to their friends' writing.

From Poetry to Mathematics

To begin, the classroom teacher read "Smart," "The Googies Are Coming," "Band-Aids," and "Overdues" by Shel Silverstein (1974, 1981). The poems were already familiar to many of the children, since they had been made available during sustained silent-reading time. Before making connections with mathematics, the teacher read the poems aloud to the children, enjoying the language, the sounds, and the thoughts expressed in the poems. She then posed the following question: What do these poems have in common?" The children responded enthusiastically, noting that all the poems had numbers in them, all rhymed, and all were written by the same author.

To pursue the mathematics objectives for the class of estimating and solving problems with large numbers, the teacher decided to focus on Silverstein's poem "Overdues" (see fig. 4.1). Since the poem deals with a potentially large, but unspecified, amount of money owed as a library fine for an outlandishly overdue book, it set the stage for problem solving in a meaningful yet humorous context.

The authors gratefully acknowledge Emily Rykert, a Queens College graduate intern at Public School 146Q, for her assistance during the 1993–94 academic year. Her position was a component of the Cognitively Guided Instruction Primary Preservice Teacher Education Project funded by the National Science Foundation through the University of Wisconsin—Madison to Queens College—CUNY.

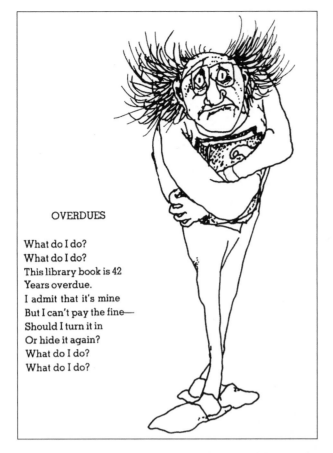

OVERDUES

What do I do?
What do I do?
This library book is 42
Years overdue.
I admit that it's mine
But I can't pay the fine—
Should I turn it in
Or hide it again?
What do I do?
What do I do?

Fig. 4.1. "Overdues" from *A Light in the Attic* by Shel Silverstein.
Copyright ©1981 by Evil Eye Music, Inc. Reprinted by permission
of HarperCollins Publishers.

After several children volunteered to read "Overdues" aloud, the class read the poem together. Since the poem ends with a question, the teacher asked the class, "Well, what should he do?" Suggestions included keeping the book or returning it, which prompted the opportunity for discussing the responsibilities related to borrowing library books. The children described what they would do. Jackie responded, "Pay the fine and be broke." When the teacher inquired why she would be broke, Jackie said "Because I'd have to pay *a lot* of money for forty-two years." This reason led naturally to key aspects of the lesson: *estimating* the fine for the overdue book, *formulating and solving* a problem related to the situation, *comparing* estimates and computed amounts, and *extending* the problem.

Estimating

The teacher probed, "How much does an overdue book cost for one day at your library?" Eric said that his library charges $0.10 a day. Although other children had suggested various amounts, the class decided to use Eric's rate. The teacher then asked the children, "How much money do you think the character in the poem owes for the overdue book?"

As the children offered estimates of $4.20, $50, $1000, $1001, $600, and $400, the teacher recorded them on chart paper, which remained visible during the next phase of the activity.

Formulating and Solving

Vinnie phrased the problem as follows: "How much does he have to pay for the library book that costs $0.10 a day for 42 years?" The children agreed with his phrasing and set to work, using a variety of strategies to solve the problem. Calculators expedited the computation.

Eric began by finding out the number of days in one year and multiplying by 42 years to find the total number of days the book was overdue. He entered 365×42 into the calculator and noted that the book was 15,330 days overdue. Then he multiplied 15,330 days by $0.10 a day and found that the character in the poem owed the library $1,533.

Jackie decided to estimate 30 days in a month, multiply by the number of months in a year, and multiply by the number of years to get the number of days that the book was overdue. Her calculation yielded about 15,120 days. When she multiplied 15,120 days by $0.10 a day, she found that the character owed about $1,512.

Shazim began with 7 days in a week. He multiplied by $0.10 a day and found that the rate for each week was $0.70. He estimated that a month has 4 weeks and multiplied 4 by $0.70 to get the amount owed in one month, $2.80. He then multiplied $2.80 a month by 12 months in a year, or $33.60. Multiplying $33.60 a year by 42 years yielded $1,411.20.

Stephanie started with 12 months in a year and multiplied by 42 years to determine the number of months the book was overdue. Then using Jackie's estimate of 30 days in a month, she found the monthly overdue rate to be $3. She multiplied 504 months by $3 a month and found that the character owed $1,512.

Comparing

As the children shared their strategies, they realized that different strategies yielded different solutions. They questioned each other to make sure that the different strategies made sense. For example, Chris asked Shazim why he did not use 52 weeks in a year. Shazim said that he estimated that each month had about 4 weeks and he based his calculation on this estimate. Using his calculator,

EXPLORING MATHEMATICS THROUGH LITERATURE

Child	Strategy	Solution
Eric	365 days × 42 years = 15 330 days 15 330 days × $0.10 a day	= $ 1533
Jackie	30 days in a month × 12 months in a year × 42 years = 15 120 days 15 120 days × $0.10 a day	= 1512
Shazim	7 days in a week × $0.10 a day × 4 weeks in a month × 12 months in a year = $33.60 year $33.60 a year × 42 years	= $1411.20
Stephanie	12 months in a year × 42 years × 30 days in a month = 15 120 days 15 120 days × $0.10 a day	= $1512
Chris	7 days in a week × $0.10 a day × 52 weeks in a year = $36.40 a year $36.40 a year × 42 years	= $1528.80

Fig. 4.2. Problem-solving strategies used by third graders to compute the amount of an overdue fine at $0.10 a day for forty-two years

Chris found that $0.70 a week times 52 weeks a year yields $36.40 a year. The total amount owed after 42 years would be $1,528.80, much closer to the amounts calculated by Eric, Jackie, and Stephanie. See figure 4.2.

When the children compared their original estimates with the actual calculations, everyone agreed that the estimate of $1,001 was the closest. By revising their initial estimates, the children had the opportunity to evaluate and refine their thinking beyond mere guessing.

Extending

Once the problem was solved and strategies were shared, children were prepared to talk about ways to change the problem. They were asked to consider a situation in which a librarian gives the character in the poem a choice. He could either pay $0.10 a day for 42 years, that is, pay about $1,533, or he could pay the amount arrived at by doubling $0.01 for 30 days. The children were asked to estimate the cost of doubling $0.01 each day for 30 days and to recommend an option for the character in the poem. Additionally, they were asked to explain their reasoning.

Before computing, the children gave the following estimates: $0.40; $10; $30; $20; $1,000; $16; $100. After making the problem simpler by comparing $0.10 a day for 5 days, that is, $0.50, with

doubling $0.01 for 5 days, that is $0.16, Jackie suggested the 30-day option. Most of the children in the class were convinced by her example. Rafael thought that the 42-year option was better because it would be easier to compute.

The children worked in pairs to double, $0.01 for 30 days. Jackie and Chris constructed a table, systematically listing the 30 days and the doubled amount from the preceding day (see fig. 4.3). When they got to the tenth day, Jackie remarked, "Oh, no! It's better to pay $1,512." On the tenth day, doubling $0.01 yielded $5.12, whereas paying $0.10 a day yielded only $1.00. Chris used a calculator to check Jackie's doubles. They agreed that on the thirtieth

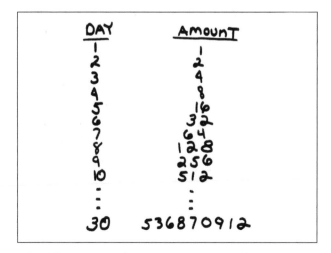

Fig. 4.3. An excerpt of Jackie and Chris's table of doubles

day, the character would owe over $5 million! They decided to advise the character in the poem to pay $0.10 a day for 42 years. The children were excited by, and amazed at, the power of doubling.

From Mathematics to Poetry

After reading Silverstein's humorous poems and solving mathematics problems related to "Overdues," the children were ready to create their own mathematical poems. Eric and Dina decided to write poems about money (see fig. 4.4).

. . . and Back Again

Once the children wrote their own poems using mathematics and poetic language, they challenged each other to pose and solve the problems embedded in their writing. After reading Eric's poem, Allison said that Eric did not have any money left because he probably bought something for $22. She indicated that after Eric's mom and dad gave him a total of $11, he put it with the $11 that he had already, yielding $22. She made up the following word problem: "If Eric wants to buy a doll for $24, how much more money does he need?" She answered her own question—$2.

When challenged to think of something else Eric might be interested in buying, Allison posed another problem: "If Eric wants to buy a Nintendo game for $100, how much more money does he need?" Using paper and pencil, she proceeded to solve her own problem: $100 – $22 = $78.

Selecting Poetry to Complement the Mathematics Curriculum

When poetry is combined with mathematics instruction, emotion and feeling are evoked. Poetry sparks wonder, surprise, and insight. It appeals to children's sense of humor and their delight in language. At the same time, poetry helps children find depth and personal meaning within the subject matter.

When selecting poems to share with children, it is best to start with poetry the children enjoy most. National studies of children's poetry preferences (Fisher and Natarella 1982; Terry 1974) have found that the poems children like most have rhyme and rhythm, tell a story, and deal with everyday experiences. Fortunately, many of these well-liked poems also afford a context for discussing mathematics. The poems listed in the poemography are excellent starting points for primary school investigations.

> Mother gave me ten dollars
> My father game me one
> I had eleven dollars
> But now I have none.
>
> *by Eric*
>
> "Funny Money" *by Dina*
>
> Soon my picture
> Will be on the
> MONEY!
> My friend thinks that's funny
> What's funny
> About it?
> They will have a
> New bill
> It will
> Be $101
> That's the one with
> My picture on it
> Then let's see them laugh.

Fig. 4.4. Examples of poems written by third graders

Teachers interested in helping children write poetry about mathematics topics or other curriculum areas will find Donald Graves's book *Exploring Poetry* (1992) to be a practical source of ideas. In the section specifically devoted to mathematics and poetry, Graves remarks that "numbers are always more than numbers" (p. 163), meaning that within the study of mathematics are intriguing stories of people, events, and ideas. Graves demonstrates how to access these stories through writing and sharing poetry. Graves's ideas appear right on target, and their potential is just being realized.

As the connections between mathematics and literature continue to be explored, more of the artificial boundaries that exist between them will be removed. In the process, both subjects will be better understood.

Poemography

Combinations

"Bleezer's Ice Cream" by Jack Prelutsky (1984, p. 49)

"Eighteen Flavors" by Shel Silverstein (1974, p. 116)

"The Ice Cream Fountain Mountain" by Eve Merriam (1989, pp. 20–21)

The twenty-eight, eighteen, and thirty-one ice-cream flavors, respectively, that are illustrated in these poems offer a rich context for posing combination problems related to making double- and triple-scoop ice-cream cones with different flavors.

EXPLORING MATHEMATICS THROUGH LITERATURE

Fractions

"The Will" by Ian Serraillier (in Rosen [1985, pp. 232–33])

The attempt to partition an inheritance of seventeen horses among three sons explores divisibility and fractions as three sons try to fulfill the terms of a will in which the eldest son gets one-half, the middle son gets one-third, and the youngest son gets one-ninth of the seventeen horses.

Money

"Smart" by Shel Silverstein (1974, p. 35)

As a "smart" child exchanges money by ignoring the value of coins and thinking that the more coins he receives, the more money he has, problems related to the value of the coins and the amount of money lost through the exchanges can be posed, discussed, and solved.

Ratio and Proportion

"One Inch Tall" by Shel Silverstein (1974, p. 55)

A discussion of ratio and proportion can be initiated as a character who is one inch tall encounters some challenging situations.

Word Problems: Join, Separate, and Compare

"Baloney Belly Billy" by Jack Prelutsky (1984, p. 134)

As the character charges different amounts of money to eat nonedible items, "join," "separate," and "compare" problems can be formulated and solved.

"Band-Aids" by Shel Silverstein (1974, p. 140)

"Join," "separate," and "compare" problems can be formulated and solved as the character describes the number of Band-Aids located on different body parts.

"The Googies Are Coming" by Shel Silverstein (1974, p. 50)

The different amounts of money offered by the Googies for children with certain characteristics can be the basis for formulating "join," "separate," and "compare" problems.

"How Much Is a Gross?" by John Ciardi (1985, p. 28)

Kangaroos in tennis shoes provide a context for computing the number of items in a gross.

"Hungry Mungry" by Shel Silverstein (1974, p. 160–61)

"Join," "separate," and "compare" problems can be formulated and solved on the basis of the different portions of food and nonedible items consumed by the hungry character.

BIBLIOGRAPHY

Ciardi, John. *Doodle Soup.* Boston, Mass.: Houghton Mifflin Co., 1985.

Fisher, Carol J., and Margaret A. Natarella. "Young Children's Preferences in Poetry: A National Survey of First, Second and Third Graders." *Research in the Teaching of English* 16 (December 1982): 339–54.

Graves, Donald H. *Explore Poetry.* Portsmouth, N.H.: Heinemann Educational Books, 1992.

Merriam, Eve. *A Poem for a Pickle.* New York: Morrow Junior Books, 1989.

Prelutsky, Jack. *The New Kid on the Block.* New York: Greenwillow Books, 1984.

Silverstein, Shel. *A Light in the Attic.* New York: HarperCollins Publishers, 1981.

———. *Where the Sidewalk Ends.* New York: HarperCollins Publishers, 1974.

Rosen, Michael, ed. *The Kingfisher Book of Children's Poetry.* New York: Kingfisher Books, 1985.

Terry, Ann. *Children's Poetry Preferences: A National Survey of Upper Elementary Grades.* 1974. Reprint, Urbana, Ill.: National Council of Teachers of English, 1984.

Wilner, Isabel, ed. *The Poetry Troupe.* New York: Charles Scribner's Sons, 1977.

Teaching Notes for

"Mathematics and Poetry: Problem Solving in Context"

by Frances R. Curcio, Myra Zarnowski, and Susan Vigliarolo

Grade range:	3–5
Mathematical topics:	Estimation, whole-number multiplication
Children's poem:	"Overdues," in *A Light in the Attic*, by Shel Silverstein (1981)
Materials:	The poem with illustration; "Overdues" recording sheets; and one calculator for each pair of students

Discussion of the mathematics: Prior to grade 3, children have had extensive experience developing additive reasoning by posing and solving problems involving joining, separating, and comparing quantities. By developing multiplicative reasoning in grades 3–5, children extend their understanding of number relationships, (*a*) becoming familiar with situations that illustrate multiplication as repeated addition and multiplication as area as well as notions of sharing and partitioning, (*b*) examining patterns involving multiples, (*c*) applying the operations of multiplication and division to appropriate situations, and (*d*) building an understanding of the underlying structure of the base-ten number system (NCTM 2000, pp. 143–46), while establishing a foundation for future study of proportional reasoning in the middle grades. This activity supports the development of multiplicative reasoning by setting the stage for children to discuss and experience the repeated-addition interpretation of multiplication (i.e., 42 years × approximately 365 days per year × the daily fine of an overdue library book) as they formulate a mathematical problem based on the situation described in the poem "Overdues." Built into the activity is the opportunity for children to strengthen their computational-estimation strategies as they reflect on, and discuss the reasonableness of, the estimates and the answers (NCTM 2000, p. 144) to the problems they formulate.

Teacher notes and questions for students: Working in pairs, students read and discuss the poem, examine the illustration, and formulate word and number problems. The possibility exists that different pairs of students may create different problems. Encourage children to formulate problems that are of interest to them and that challenge their thinking.

Although the library's fines for late books never exceed the cost of the book and dues are not paid for the days the library is closed, children may formulate word problems and number problems that go beyond the cost of a typical children's library book and that include payments for every day of the year for 42 years. Once children have a chance to estimate the answer to their problems, they can calculate their answers and compare their actual answers with their estimates.

Different pairs of students can share their word or number problems and compare their answers. The class can compile and display a collection of problems composed by the students.

Following a class discussion of problems and solutions, an extension could include instruction about various forms of poetry and children could be asked to write their own mathematical poems. Other possibilities include using poems listed in the poemography in the article or using the children's book

34

The Rajah's Rice (see Curcio and Zarnowski [1996] for a more detailed description of how to use the book) for continuing work related to developing multiplicative reasoning.

In addition to the questions formulated in the article, other questions might include these:

- How did your answer compare with your estimate?

- How did you solve your problem?

- How did the problem posed by you and your partner compare with the problem posed by another team?

REFERENCES

Barry, David. *The Rajah's Rice: A Mathematical Folktale from India.* Illustrated by Donna Perrone. New York: W. H. Freeman & Co., 1994.

Curcio, Frances R., and Myra Zarnowski. "Revisiting the Powers of Two." *Teaching Children Mathematics* 2 (January 1996): 300–304.

Curcio, Frances R., Myra Zarnowski, and Susan Vigliarolo. "Links to Literature: Mathematics and Poetry: Problem Solving in Context." *Teaching Children Mathematics* 1 (February 1995): 370–74.

National Council of Teachers of Mathematics (NCTM). *Principles and Standards for School Mathematics.* Reston, Va.: NCTM, 2000.

Silverstein, Shel. *A Light in the Attic.* New York: HarperCollins Publishers, 1981.

Name_____

Date _____

Work with a partner as you read and discuss the poem.

1. Read the poem, look at the illustration, and tell what you think.

2. If this poem was written as a math problem using words or numbers, what would the problem be?

3. What is an estimate for the answer to your problem?

4. How would you solve this problem?

5. Solve the problem, and show your work.

5

Amanda Bean and the Gator Girls: Writing and Solving Multiplication Stories

Maryann S. Wickett

HAVING children create and solve their own story problems is a valuable activity. It encourages the child to think carefully about and apply a concept to create and solve a problem. In addition, teachers can gain valuable insights into the child's thinking and level of understanding, enabling them to guide students' thinking more effectively. Several curriculum units written for third grade, such as *Math by All Means: Multiplication, Grade 3* (Burns 1991) and *Investigations in Number, Data, and Space* (TERC 1995), suggest using this strategy.

Amanda Bean's Amazing Dream

This year, as part of our third-grade multiplication unit based on previously mentioned resources, I decided to add a twist to the unit by using literature to provide a context for writing multiplication stories. I selected two books, one to be used midway through the unit and the other, at the end, to offer additional experience in writing multiplication stories. The first book was *Amanda Bean's Amazing Dream* (Neuschwander 1998).

Amanda Bean is a third grader who loves to count. She does not see any need to learn her multiplication facts, until one night when she has a wild dream about sheep riding bicycles and grandmas knitting sweaters. The sheep and the grandmas help convince Amanda that multiplication is a very useful tool for finding out "how many" in a hurry!

As I shared this story with the children, we paused and talked about how multiplication was shown in the book's illustrations. "Look carefully at the loaves of bread in the store window," I said,

pointing to the illustration at the bottom of the first page. "Is there anything about the picture of the bread that reminds you of multiplication?"

"It has two pans with two breads on each pan," answered Chris.

"That's like two groups of two," added Ryan.

"The cookies are like a multiplication problem, too. There are three rows of three on each tray, then there are two trays," observed Nicholas.

"How many cookies in all?" I asked. After a few moments, the students started to raise their hands.

"I think there are nine on each tray because I counted '3,' '6,' '9' and then I would have to add '9' two times to figure out how many altogether," explained Genean. I paused to give her a chance to figure out the total. "I think it would be eighteen." Several students nodded their agreement.

I was interested in Genean's approach. We were about halfway through our unit on multiplication. I was listening to find out whether she would use multiplication as a tool to help her solve this problem. She used skip counting to figure out the number of cookies on one tray, but when she had to think about combining the two trays to find the total number of cookies, she fell back on addition instead of using multiplication. I continued reading the story, giving the students various opportunities to figure out the total number of objects in the illustrations and watching for the types of strategies that they used.

When we finished the book, I asked the students the following question: "As we read the story, we sometimes stopped and I gave you a multiplication story based on an illustration. You had to solve these problems. When I gave you these problems, what sorts of information did I tell you?" My goal was to help the children realize that when writing multiplication stories, they needed to include complete information, as well as a question that could be solved using multiplication.

"You told us some information that was in the picture," said Chase.

"You said some numbers, usually," added Katherine.

"You asked us a question," said Austin.

I listed the children's ideas on the chalkboard. "You are going to have the chance to write some multiplication stories, too," I continued. "When you do, you must be sure to include all the necessary information and ask a question about the information that can be solved using multiplication. Then turn your paper over and solve your problem on the back." I circulated through the classroom to observe as the children worked, redirecting them when necessary to ensure that stories included all the necessary information and a question that could be solved using multiplication.

Some students based their multiplication stories on illustrations from *Amanda Bean*. Others thought up stories that were unrelated to the book. Both types of stories offered insights into how the students were thinking about multiplication and whether they had begun to see multiplication as a useful tool to solve problems. Chris and Hunter wrote a story based on an illustration in *Amanda Bean* in which eight sheep with red-and-white-striped helmets are riding bicycles. The boys noticed that all the helmets had the same number of stripes and used this information in their problem: "There were 8 sheep riding bikes. Each sheep had a helmet. There were 7 stripes on the helmets. How many stripes altogether?"

Hunter's paper (see fig. 5.1) demonstrates several ways of approaching the problem. He used tally marks, skip counting, repeated addition, multiplication, and an illustration. He also successfully calculated the correct answer.

I was pleased with Hunter's work and confident that he was developing a firm understanding of multiplication. I asked him to write a second, more challenging, problem. He studied the book for awhile and came up with this problem: "Which has more, a building with 6 windows with 20 panes in each window or a building with 8 windows with 10 panes in each?" (A special section for parents and teachers in the back of *Amanda Bean's Amazing Dream*

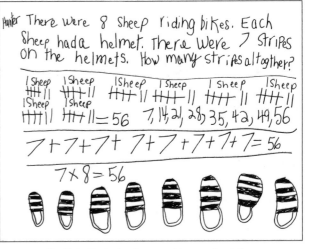

Fig. 5.1. Hunter's sheep problem and solution

offers suggestions for many problems, including one similar to this.)

Chris, who was initially working with Hunter, came up with a different solution to their sheep problem. He found that the helmet had 47 stripes altogether rather than 56, as Hunter had found. When I looked at his work, I saw that he had actually solved a slightly different problem. His illustration showed 7 sheep with 7 stripes on each helmet. The answer to the problem that he had illustrated should have been 49. I also noticed that he had added 7 eight times and had written the multiplication problem 7×8. I showed Chris the illustration in the book and asked whether he noticed anything different about the number of sheep in his illustration and the one in the book. He grinned, took his paper back to his seat, revised it, and came up with the correct solution.

All the students were able to write multiplication stories, some of which were more complex than others. I think that the reason for their success is that *Amanda Bean* is enjoyable and uses concrete examples to show students exactly what is needed to write multiplication stories correctly. The errors that students made were in counting or figuring out the products, which indicated that they needed many more ongoing, concrete experiences to practice finding products.

Get Well, Gators!

Toward the end of the unit, I shared the second book that I had selected, *Get Well, Gators!* (Calmenson and Cole 1998), as the context for an additional experience in writing multiplication stores. In this story, the Gator Girls, Amy and Allie, decide to help raise money for repairs to the local playground. I read chapter 9, "Get Your Instant Story Here!" The girls' plan was to raise money by telling stories. For a fee, the girls would ask their customers to tell three facts about themselves. In return, the girls would create a story based on the facts given.

After reading the chapter, I explained to the students that they were to think up three facts about themselves, then write and solve a multiplication story using those three facts. This task proved to be difficult for the students. After a few moments of watching the students struggle with this assignment, I asked for their attention.

"I notice that some of you seem to be having difficulty. Would someone be willing to share with us what is causing the trouble?" I asked the class.

"I can think of things about me, like my favorite color, but that doesn't work when I have to write a multiplication story," said Sarah.

"I have two brothers and one mother and one father and me," said Matt, "but I can't think of a multiplication question about that."

"You could write a multiplication story about us," suggested Matt's twin, Chris. "You could say there are two twins, they each have two eyes, and their eyes are brown. How many eyes? That would be multiplication."

"Oh, I get it. I could write that I have cats, then to make it multiplication, I could figure out how many feet or whiskers or stripes or something," said Shelby.

The difficulty for students seemed to be in thinking of facts about themselves that could be used in the context of multiplication. I gave the students the option of not using facts about themselves. Also, three facts seemed to be too many for the task, so I changed the number to two facts. Taking a few minutes to talk about the problem seemed to help. The students quickly got back to work.

This assignment again gave me insights into the students' levels of understanding. Most students did well. Allison's work is typical of what many students accomplished (see fig. 5.2).

A few students made mistakes that indicated that they still needed to develop their understanding of multiplication. Ariana's initial work (fig. 5.3a) shows that she still had not grasped the important idea that multiplication is about combining groups of equal size. Both the written part of her problem and her solution show this lack of understanding. To help Ariana, I gave her counters and asked her to use them to answer such questions as "How many is five groups of three?" I focused her attention on the idea

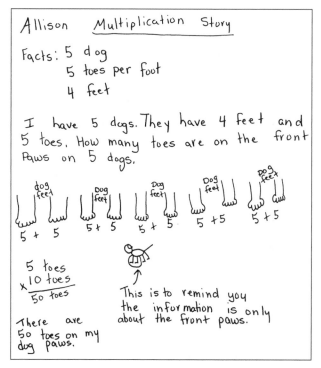

Fig. 5.2. Allison's problem using facts about her dogs

of equal groups. Then I showed her how to write a multiplication problem to represent the counters. For example, five groups of three counters would be written 5 × 3. I explained that she could think of the × sign as meaning "groups of." After several such experiences spread over two or three days, I asked Ariana to write another multiplication story. Figure 5.3b shows her effort and gives evidence of her emerging understanding.

Cody had great fun with this assignment and wrote the following problem:

> We have 5 cats at our house. Each of them has six whiskers on each cheek, 1 tail, and 4 paws. How many feet, tails, and whiskers altogether?

He listed his facts, wrote his multiplication story, and went to great lengths to show how he solved his problem. Cody wrote a fairly complex problem, however, and never quite arrived at an answer. In one part of his solution, he found the total number of whiskers to be 60, yet when he skip counted in another part, he counted only one cheek per cat and found 30 whiskers rather than 60. Despite Cody's errors, he understands that multiplication involves combining equal groups. He shows this grasp through his illustrations and his use of repeated addition and skip counting. I appreciated his enthusiasm and his willingness to create and solve a complicated problem.

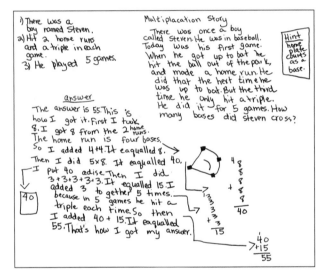

(a) Ariana's problem using facts about herself

Ariana

Multiplication Story

My mom has 6 Childern. She wants to buy us 2 pairs of shoes per child. How many shoes in all?

6 × 4 = 24

(b) Ariana's second problem, showing greater understanding

Fig. 5.3. Ariana's work, showing increased understanding after several days

1) There was a boy named Steven.
2) Hit 2 home runs and a triple in each game.
3) He played 5 games.

Multiplacation Story
There was once a boy called Steven. He was in baseball. Today was his first game. When he got up to bat he hit the ball out of the park, and made a home run. He did that the next time he was up to bat. But the third time he only hit a triple. He did it for 5 games. How many bases did steven cross?

Hint home plate counts as a base.

answer
The answer is 55. This is how I got it. First I took 8. I got 8 from the 2 home runs. The home run is four bases. So I added 4+4. It eaqualled 8. Then I did 5×8. It eaqualled 40. I put 40 adise. Then I did 3+3+3+3+3. It equalled 15. I added 3 to gether 5 times, because in 5 games he hit a triple each time. So then I added 40+15. It eaqualled 55. That's how I got my answer.

40

Fig. 5.4. Kyle's baseball problem and solution

Like Cody, Kyle approached this task with enthusiasm and loved the challenge of this open-ended assignment. Kyle organized his thinking well enough to come up with a correct solution for his multiplication story (see fig. 5.4).

Conclusion

The students enjoyed both books. *Get Well, Gators!* is an easy-to-read book that third graders find amusing and entertaining. Many students chose to read the book on their own after I read chapter 9 in class. *Amanda Bean's Amazing Dream* is a picture book that the students have revisited after our lesson. In fact, they continue to find new multiplication stories to solve in the illustrations. Students

I went to the woods and I saw 9 aliens. They each had 4 eyes. How many eyes are there in all?

By Genean

Once there was a six-legged dragon. It was with five other dragons. How many legs on all the dragons?

By Meline

There were three spiders. The three spiders had 6 eyes and 8 legs. How many eyes and legs in all?

By Breanna

Fig. 5.5. The published multiplication stories

also continue to write and edit their own stories, publishing them in the computer lab after I do the final editing. When the stories are competed, they are photocopied and placed in books so that each student has a book of problems to solve (see fig. 5.5). The students enjoyed both pieces of literature and have fun creating and solving multiplication stories. These activities give me insight into their thinking and help them correct misconceptions when necessary or pose additional challenges to those students who are ready for them.

REFERENCES

Burns, Marilyn. *Math by All Means: Multiplication, Grade 3.* New York: Cuisenaire Co. of America, 1991.

Calmenson, Stephanie, and Joanna Cole. *Get Well, Gators!* New York: Morrow Junior Books, 1998.

Neuschwander, Cindy. *Amanda Bean's Amazing Dream—a Mathematical Story.* New York: Scholastic, 1998.

TERC. *Investigations in Number, Data, and Space.* Palo Alto, Calif.: Dale Seymour Publications, 1995.

"Amanda Bean and the Gator Girls: Writing and Solving Multiplication Stories"

by Maryann S. Wickett

Grade range:	3–5
Mathematical topic:	Solving and writing multiplication story problems
Children's books:	*Amanda Bean's Amazing Dream*, story by Cindy Neuschwander, illustrated by Liza Woodruff, math activities by Marilyn Burns (1998)
	Get Well, Gators! written by Stephanie Calmenson and Joanna Cole and illustrated by Lynn Munsinger (1998)
Materials:	One "Amanda Bean's Amazing Dream" recording sheet for each student or pair of students

Discussion of the mathematics: One of the first of four types of multiplication story problems that students encounter is that of problems involving groups. For this type of problem, students need to recognize that the situation involves a certain number of equal-sized groups and asks for how many. The lesson based on *Amanda Bean's Amazing Dream* involves recognizing multiplication situations, being able to discuss what is known, solving the problem, and discussing solution strategies. Writing story situations extends students' understanding because to do so, they need to know what factors comprise a multiplication situation and how to write appropriate questions.

Teacher notes and questions to ask students: Share the book *Amanda Bean's Amazing Dream*, stopping at appropriate intervals to discuss and solve the multiplication problems presented in the story. Have the students share the strategies they are using.

After finishing the book, pose the question below to the students. Students' responses should include complete information about the problem to be solved, as well as a question that could be solved using multiplication. Students should form a generalization regarding the common structure: number of groups, equal-sized groups, and an appropriate question.

- When I read the problems from the story, what sorts of information did you need about each problem?

Using the information gathered in the discussion, have students work independently or in pairs to write multiplication stories based on the book or other situations familiar to them. The students should include a solution on the back of the paper. Students can edit their multiplication stories for publication or for other students to solve.

After additional experiences with multiplication, repeat the foregoing activity using the book *Get Well, Gators!* Note in the article that initially students had difficulties using three facts about themselves to write multiplication problems. Brainstorming a variety of common situations before writing their problems is helpful for them. The hope is that some students will write situations that involve other types of multiplication, such as comparison or combination.

Another challenge would be to have students write problems that involve more than one operation or involve three factors.

REFERENCES

Calmenson, Stephanie, and Joanna Cole. *Get Well, Gators!* Illustrated by Lynn Munsinger. New York: Morrow Junior Books, 1998.

Neuschwander, Cindy. *Amanda Bean's Amazing Dream*, illustrated by Liza Woodruff, math activities by Marilyn Burns. New York: Scholastic, 1998.

Wickett, Maryann. "Links to Literature: Amanda Bean and the Gator Girls: Writing and Solving Multiplication Stories." *Teaching Children Mathematics* 6 (January 2000): 282–85, 303.

Amanda Bean's Amazing Dream Recording Sheet

Name_____

Date _____

Facts used to write my multiplication story:

My multiplication problem:

Solve your problem on the back of this sheet.

6

A Remainder of One: Exploring Partitive Division

Patricia Seray Moyer

CHILDREN'S literature can be a springboard for conversations about mathematical concepts. Austin (1998) suggests that good children's literature with a mathematical theme provides a context for both exploring and extending mathematics problems embedded in stories. In the context of discussing a story, children connect their everyday experiences with mathematics and have opportunities to make conjectures about quantities, equalities, or other mathematical ideas; negotiate their understanding of mathematical concepts; and verbalize their thinking. Children's books that prompt mathematical conversations also lead to rich, dynamic communication in the mathematics classroom and develop the use of mathematical symbols in the context of communicating. The National Council of Teachers of Mathematics (1989) emphasizes the importance of communication in helping children both construct mathematical knowledge and link their informal notions with the abstract symbols used to express mathematical ideas.

This article relates how the book *A Remainder of One* (Pinczes 1995) was used in a fourth-grade classroom to teach the concept of *partitive division*. In partitive division, the student separates a group of objects into a given number of equivalent groups and finds the number in each group.

About the Book

A Remainder of One is written in a lyrical style that makes reading the story melodic, and the colorful bugs illustrated by Bonnie MacKain are a visual delight for students. The book tells the story of Soldier Joe, a lovable bug who always seems to find himself labeled as the "remainder of one" by the other insects in the bug squadron.

In this story, Joe is a member of the twenty-fifth squadron, a group of twenty-five bugs that is marching in a parade before the queen. When the bugs divide themselves into two lines, Joe becomes the odd bug out. Because he is a determined little bug, Joe tries to find a way to divide the members of the bug squadron into even rows with no remainders so that he can participate in the parade. He divides the bug squadron into three rows for the next parade. When he is still the "remainder of one," Joe does not give up but instead divides the bug troop into four rows. Children quickly relate to Soldier Joe's feeling of wanting to belong and are motivated to work along with him to solve the problem. Joe eventually solves the problem by dividing the bug squadron into five rows, which evenly divides the twenty-five bugs in the squadron and eliminates the remainder of one.

Exploring Division Concepts in the Text

The students were very receptive when I introduced *A Remainder of One* and told them that the star character was an insect. The illustrations, as well as the current popularity of animated movies that feature insects with human qualities, immediately captured the students' interest. I began the lesson by asking students what they knew about the word *remainder*. Shanequa said, "It's the last one there." Brittany explained, "A remainder is like when you are playing a game and you're the last one left." Then Laquisha said, "Like in division, a remainder of one." This discussion was the perfect lead-in to the book, which I read aloud to familiarize students with the story. I asked them to pay particular attention to the mathematics that they saw in the book. When I finished reading, the students commented that they saw "lots of division" in the story.

At this point, I told the students that we were going to read through the story again but that this time, we would model and record the division that we saw in the book. Each student was given a small plastic bag filled with twenty-five centimeter cubes to represent the bugs in the story. The students were delighted to have their own "bugs" to manipulate as the story was reread. Many of the students counted to be sure that they had exactly twenty-five bugs, and I allowed for exploration time, during which students stacked the cubes and made arrays.

Once students had become familiar with the bugs, I reread the story up to the point at which the bugs divided into two lines. I asked, "How might we model the bugs' dividing into two lines to find out how many bugs were in each line?" The students replied that we could group the cubes or make lines, as the bugs in the book had done. As they began making two lines, one student asked, "How long should the lines be?" I replied, "I guess we'll have to see how long it turns out to be when we make the two lines. Try to make them even." Shanequa remarked cleverly, "But we can't if there are twenty-five." As the students rearranged the bugs on their desks into two even lines, I heard a number of mathematical conversations throughout the room. "I've got one left over," someone said, "a remainder of one!"

After the children had the opportunity to divide their bugs into two even rows, we talked about the mathematics. I revisited the question asked earlier by a student, "How long should the lines be?" We talked as a class about how we might be sure that the same number of bugs was in each line. One student said that we could match the bugs in a one-to-one correspondence to be sure that the same number was in each line. Another student explained a strategy of "one for you and one for me," in which the bugs are placed in each line until they are all distributed. I modeled the one-for-you, one-for-me method for the students by starting with a group of twenty-five bugs on the back of my clipboard and partitioning the bugs into two lines until only one bug was left as the remainder. After this partitioning, we all agreed that each line had twelve bugs with a remainder of one. I wrote this number sentence on the chalkboard: $25 \div 2 = 12$ R 1.

I then continued reading the story up to the point at which the bug squadron divided into three lines. This time, I asked the students to model the bugs' dividing, to find the number of bugs in each line, and to write the resulting division sentence.

Dividing the bugs into three even rows with a remainder of one was easy for the children (see fig. 6.1), but it was not as easy for them to develop number sentences that captured the situation that they had modeled with bugs. When I asked students for their number sentences, they gave a variety of answers, including "eight divided by three," "twenty-five divided by eight," and "twenty-five divided by three."

Fig. 6.1. Fredneshia divides her "bugs" into three rows.

Many students can solve mathematical exercises but have difficulty expressing their work using mathematical symbols when solving word problems (Witherspoon 1999). They also struggle when they are not sure what the problems require or how to translate them into symbolic equations. Developing the language of mathematics, including both the words that students use to communicate orally and the written symbol system, is essential for mathematical understanding yet lags behind the performance of mathematics. I helped students make these connections by showing them what each of the numbers in the division number sentence represented. The first number was the total number of bugs in the bug squadron, and the second number was the number of rows that we made with our bugs. The students then realized that the number that followed the equals sign told us how many bugs were in each of the lines after we had divided them. They agreed that "twenty-five divided by three" was the number sentence that represented dividing the bugs into three rows, and I wrote that sentence on the chalkboard ($25 \div 3 = 8$ R 1).

I continued to reread the story in this manner, allowing the students to rearrange their centimeter-cube bugs to find the number of bugs in each row and to write the resulting mathematical sentences. When we agreed on a number sentence represented in the story, I wrote it on the chalkboard: $25 \div 4 = 6$ R 1 and $25 \div 5 = 5$. When the bugs divided evenly into five rows, I asked students about the remainder. They replied that it was "none," or "zero."

To wrap up our lesson on the first day, I asked students what might happen if the pattern of dividing from the book had continued. The students said that the bugs would have divided into six rows, then seven. Before we manipulated the bugs, I asked students to predict whether they thought that a remainder might result when we divided by six, and if so, would the remainder be one? Most of the students thought that a remainder would occur, but they were not sure whether it would be a remainder of one. We investigated this problem by making six rows of bugs and found that, once again, we had a remainder of one. I wrote this division sentence on the chalkboard with the others: $25 \div 6 = 4$ R 1. Students noticed that "the six and the four just changed places." These connections are important for students to make as they build an understanding of the underlying patterns in mathematics. We finished that day by reviewing some of the patterns that we had noticed in our division and by speculating whether other numbers might result in a remainder of one as often as had the number of bugs in our story.

Extending the Lesson—Using Concrete and Pictorial Representations

On the second day, I took the lesson one step further. I had two goals for the second part of this lesson. I wanted students to transfer the problem-solving skills that they had used in the first part of the lesson to a new, yet similar, problem situation. I also wanted to demonstrate a method for creating a pictorial model of the mathematics. Instead of using the number of bugs from the story, each student was given a different number. I began the lesson by telling the students that they would each work with their own bug squadron that day. Each student received a bag containing from twenty-six to fifty centimeter cubes and a number card that showed how many cubes were in the bag.

The students were excited about continuing our activities from the previous day. When the bags were distributed, they started counting and checking their bugs. "I've got thirty." "I've got thirty-one." "I have an even number." "I've got thirty-four." "I have forty-

two." I told the students that they would each be dividing their own bug squadrons, so their answers and number sentences would be different from those of everyone else in the class. The students also received sheets of twelve-by-eighteen-inch drawing paper that were divided into six equal sections, to be used as storyboards for their bug squadrons.

We continued the lesson by reviewing the things that we had learned about division the day before. We talked about how we had used partitioning to divide the bugs into rows during the previous day's lesson and how we might divide the new bugs during the lesson that day. The students remarked that they had received more than twenty-five bugs in their bags that day and so might not be able to do all the division in their heads as they had done the day before.

Then I posed a two-part question: How many bugs will be in each line if your bug squadron divides into two lines for the parade, and will you have a remainder? I asked the students to write the number sentences that represented their individual bug squadrons divided into two lines. The children used the centimeter-cube bugs to make two even rows to find their answers (see fig. 6.2).

Fig. 6.2. Chaquetta lines up the forty-one bugs in two even rows of twenty with a remainder of one.

As I walked around the room, I asked students to tell me what they were doing and to state the number sentences that represented their bug squadrons divided into two lines. Some students reported only parts of their number sentences: "I have forty-two divided by two," "thirty-seven divided by two," "forty divided by two . . . twenty." Other students stated the entire number sentence. When I asked Jennifer about her number sentence, she replied, "Twenty-eight divided by two is fourteen." Kayla said, "Thirty divided by two is fifteen." I asked the students to put these number sentences and any illustrations that would help others understand the division of their bug squadrons on the storyboard. Some students found that they had remainders, whereas others did not. Before she divided the bugs into two rows, Shanequa said, "I have an even number, so I'm not going to have a remainder." As I walked around the room, the students shared their number sentences with me and showed me what they were writing on their storyboards.

After the students finished dividing their bug squadrons into two lines and writing their corresponding number sentences, I asked the students how I might model what "divided by three" means. One student said, "Make three lines." The students quickly began grouping their centimeter cubes and making three lines of bugs. Some students gave others mathematical suggestions or directions: "Make sure you divide them up." "Make three lines." "Make them even." They also questioned one another: "Three lines of what—six?" Some students verbalized their thinking to others: "Thirty-three divided by three equals eleven." After students divided the bugs into three lines, they wrote number sentences to show what they had found. Some students also drew on their storyboards illustrations showing a pictorial representation of the mathematics. A few of the students shared their division sentences and drawings with the rest of the class.

Next, I told the students that the last division problem we were going to do would create four rows, and we were going to illustrate our last number sentence in a way that would make the bugs on our storyboards look like the ones in the book. Students need to see models of mathematical symbols as their mathematical language develops, and they need to see examples of how to create pictorial models. This activity gave students an example of using information from a problem-solving situation, manipulating concrete objects to model the situation, illustrating the solution route in the form of a picture, and writing the mathematical symbols.

I demonstrated my method of partitioning my bugs into four equal rows. Then I counted aloud the number of bugs in each row. To create the pictorial model, I showed the students how to make the bugs by using their fingers and stamp pads to make fingerprints on the storyboards. I modeled this technique on a sheet of paper taped to the chalkboard. To make my fingerprints look more like the

bugs in the story, I used a marker to add antennae, legs, eyes, and a mouth.

Students quickly began dividing their individual bug squadrons into four groups so that they would know how many fingerprint bugs to place in each row on their storyboards. Once again, the mathematical talk in the classroom began. I heard several conversations in which students helped one another make sense of the mathematics. I overheard one child explain to another, "There's eight in your row, so you put down thirty-three divided by four equals eight." The students used the bottom half of their storyboards for their final number sentences and fingerprint illustrations (see fig. 6.3).

Fig. 6.3. Jennifer adds legs and antennae to her bug illustrations.

At the end of class, the students shared their work. Students found patterns in the numbers that divided evenly. They noticed that sometimes no remainder occurred and that sometimes the remainder was more than one. Some of the students found that their numbers created an array. Students' illustrations, their use of spoken language, and their written number sentences gave the teacher insights into the depth of their understanding of division in the context of this problem situation. Their manipulation of the centimeter cubes and their drawings and number sentences helped us interpret students' developing understanding of what it means to divide. The book presented a problem-solving context for communicating, understanding, and exploring division concepts. Experiences such as these further students' development of number sense and pattern recognition, foundational skills for the higher-level mathematics that they will encounter later in their educational careers.

EXPLORING MATHEMATICS THROUGH LITERATURE

Conclusion

Children need many and varied experiences with mathematical concepts and symbols to develop fluency with them. It is important for teachers to promote conceptual understanding of what it means to divide before teaching the procedures for division. These experiences with division situations should include developing pictorial models and using both the spoken vocabulary and the written symbol systems of the language of mathematics. Opportunities to manipulate objects, illustrate mathematical thinking, and use the language of mathematics in oral and written form should be integral parts of the daily activities in an elementary mathematics classroom.

This activity dealt with partitive division, in which a group is separated into a given number of equivalent groups and the students find the number of items in each group. Other examples of problem-solving contexts may also be used for *measurement division*, in which the number of items in each group is known and the number of groups must be determined. Developing an understanding of both partitive and measurement division in a variety of contexts gives students a foundation for transferring this skill to dividing fractions, decimals, integers, and algebraic expressions.

It is equally important for students to develop the ability to translate the information embedded in a problem context into an equation to solve the problem. Students see many number sentences on worksheets throughout their school years. Yet the ability to extract the information needed to create number sentences from real-world situations promotes students' problem-solving skills, which is an important developmental step in students' mathematical learning. Yet the ability to translate information in a problem context into a symbolic representation models the work that real mathematicians do. Experiencing many opportunities to read and interpret mathematics in a variety of contexts also enables students to become successful problem solvers. Children's books in which mathematics naturally emerges as a part of the story supply one meaningful context for modeling and exploring real problems.

REFERENCES

Austin, Patricia. "Math Books as Literature: Which Ones Measure Up?" *New Advocate* 11 (spring 1998): 119–33.

National Council of Teachers of Mathematics (NCTM). *Curriculum and Evaluation Standards for School Mathematics.* Reston, Va.: NCTM, 1989.

Pinczes, Elinor J. *A Remainder of One.* New York: Houghton Mifflin Co., 1995.

Witherspoon, Mary Lou. "And the Answer Is . . . Symbolic Literacy." *Teaching Children Mathematics* 5 (March 1999): 396–99.

Teaching Notes for

"A Remainder of One: Exploring Partitive Division"

by Patricia Seray Moyer

Grade range:	3–5
Mathematical topics:	Exploring division and remainders, number sense
Children's book:	*A Remainder of One*, written by Elinor J. Pinczes and illustrated by Bonnie Mackain (1995)
Materials:	*"A Remainder of One"* recording sheets 1–3, a bag of twenty-five centimeter cubes, beans, or other counters (any manipulative that is easy to count and sort) for each student

Discussion of the mathematics: The purpose of this activity is to support the development of number sense and encourage students to use different forms of representation to express numerical relationships through an exploration of the concept of partitive division. The book's repetitive story line reflects partitive division, in that the number of objects and the number of rows is known. Part of number sense is breaking apart numbers. What happens as the size of the divisor changes? Under what conditions will the remainder be 0, 1, or 2?

Teacher notes: The investigation can be completed in two or more class sessions. During the first class session, the teacher and students should read the book *A Remainder of One* together. During the first and subsequent class sessions, the teacher and students can explore the mathematics concepts introduced in the book.

Before the Activity

- Introduce the book to students by sharing the title and the name of the author. Ask students to tell what they know about the word remainder. This information can be recorded on large chart paper.

- Read the book aloud to students. Ask students to pay particular attention to any mathematics they identify in the story. Have students share their observations following the reading of the story.

During the Activity

- Distribute *"A Remainder of One"* recording sheet 1 and a bag of twenty-five centimeter cubes, beans, or other counters to each student. Reread the story, and have students use their counters to model the division that takes place as events unfold in the story.

- Use question prompts to support students' thinking: "How might we model the bugs' dividing into two lines to find out how many bugs were in each line?" "How long should the lines be?" "How do we know how many bugs will be in each line?"

- After the "bugs" are grouped, students can use a pictorial model to record their concrete model on the recording sheet.

- Assist students in writing number sentences that capture the mathematical processes. For example, when twenty-five bugs in the story divide themelves into two lines with one bug left over, students should draw this pictorial model and should write the corresponding number sentence $25 \div 2 \rightarrow 12 \text{ r } 1$.

Extending the Activity

1. Assign each student a different number between 26 and 50.

2. Students may use centimeter cubes, beans, other counters, or other mathematical representations to support their problem solving.

3. Students should divide their numbers by 2, 3, 4, and 5. For example, a student who is assigned the number 28 should write the following number sentences:

$$28 \div 2 = 14$$
$$28 \div 3 \rightarrow 9 \text{ remainder } 1$$
$$28 \div 4 = 7$$
$$28 \div 5 \rightarrow 5 \text{ remainder } 3.$$

4. Students write the appropriate number sentences on student recording sheet 2 and use a pictorial model to represent their division situation.

Follow-Up Activity

1. Encourage students' investigation of number patterns by working as a group to divide a variety of numbers by 2, 3, 4, or 5 (or other numbers as appropriate).

2. Students can then select their own "remainder number" to create personalized remainder stories. For example, if a student chooses to write a "Remainder of Two" story, she or he may write such number sentences such as these:

$$27 \div 5 \rightarrow 5 \text{ remainder } 2$$
$$30 \div 4 \rightarrow 7 \text{ remainder } 2$$
$$8 \div 3 \rightarrow 2 \text{ remainder } 2$$
$$14 \div 3 \rightarrow 4 \text{ remainder } 2.$$

3. Students can share their pictorial models, number sentences, and remainder stories with their peers.

REFERENCES

Moyer, Patricia Seray. "*A Remainder of One:* Exploring Partitive Division." *Teaching Children Mathematics* 6 (April 2000): 516–21.

Pinczes, Elinor J. *A Remainder of One.* Illustrated by Bonnie Mackain. New York: Houghton Mifflin Co., 1995.

Date _____

Record the mathematics that you identify in the story.

A Remainder of One by Elinor J. Pinczes

Mathematics by: _____

Mathematical sentence:	Mathematical sentence:
_____	_____
Pictorial model:	Pictorial model:

(Print two copies of this sheet for each group.)

Date _____

Divide your number by 2, 3, 4, and 5.

A Remainder of One by Elinor J. Pinczes

Mathematics by: _____

My number is _____.

Mathematical sentence:	Mathematical sentence:
_____	_____
Pictorial model:	Pictorial model:

(Print two copies of this sheet for each group.)

A Remainder of One

Date _____

Write four different number sentences that all have the same number as the remainder.

A Remainder of _____ by _____

Mathematical sentence:	Mathematical sentence:
_____	_____
Pictorial model:	Pictorial model:

(Print two copies of this sheet for each group.)

7

Critical Thinking during the December Holidays

Annette Raphel

IN A conscious effort to make mathematics more open-ended and relevant and to dispel the myth that the discipline is a series of easily solved and discrete experiences, the curriculum has been reshaped in the author's school to allow for some more lengthy investigations and projects. These lessons take more than one period, ask students to extend their thinking, and require them to relate several disciplines to mathematics. Many of the experiences start with sketchy ideas and without firm notions about answers on the part of the teachers. These experiences become the foundation for deep understanding and appreciation of the power of mathematics beyond computation.

One of the fourth-grade investigations is detailed here. This project was prompted by the seasonal excitement surrounding the winter holidays and astounded students and teachers with its richness.

In teaching series (sums of sequences of numbers), the subject of Hanukkah candles was discussed, and the students decided to figure out how many candles are needed for the eight nights of Hanukkah. On the first night, two are needed; on the second night, three are needed; and so on, until the eighth night. The numbers 2, 3, 4, 5, 6, 7, 8, and 9

were added to find out how many candles the candle makers have to put in the box. The students were led to observe that the sum of the first and last term of the series is 11. Amazingly, the sum of the second and next-to-last term of that series was the same. So, as a class, we made the discovery that we had four pairs of numbers that each had a sum of 11. Other series were also investigated. If the interval between the numbers in an arithmetic series was constant, the students could use this new information to made additional work much easier. In fact, the topic of series was tremendously empowering and enabled fourth graders to feel like real mathematicians. They used this strategy for efficient addition many times during the year.

A mathematical investigation of the song "The Twelve Days of Christmas" followed. The reader might remember that a lovesick gentleman had a great deal of gift ordering to do to impress the object of his affection. In fact, this very complex mathematics problem involves series and patterns galore and can be solved in many different ways. The gifts included—

- a partridge in a pear tree;
- two turtle doves;
- three french hens;
- four calling birds;
- five gold rings;
- six geese a-laying;
- seven swans a-swimming;
- eight maids a-milking;

The author would like to thank the two fourth-grade teachers, Carolyn Damp and Connie Dodes, at Milton Academy, in whose room she worked; and she would like to acknowledge the contribution of Mary Crist, former director, and the teachers at the Academy Hill Center for Gifted Children in Wilbraham, Massachusetts, who shared the idea for pricing the gifts at a conference of the Independent School Association of Massachusetts (ISAM).

- nine ladies dancing;

- ten lords a-leaping

- eleven pipers piping;

- twelve drummers drumming.

The reader might also remember that the present giving was cumulative. That is, on the fifth day, the lady received five of the gift for the fifth day as well as the same thing she had received on day 4 (which included the gifts for day 4 and day 3 and day 2 and day 1).

This gift-giving problem was separated into three parts. Here are the first two parts:

Imagine the plight of the poor lovesick gentleman who is arranging for gifts for the twelve days of Christmas. This task will take a fair amount of organization. I think it is only right that our mathematics classes help out. Basically, we have three jobs:

1. Figure out how many presents in total he will have to buy to send all the things mentioned in the song to his true love. See if you can find a system and patterns to help you. Record your work and be able to explain how you arrived at your answer. Many clever ways can be used to approach this problem.

2. Figure out how much of each item he actually has to order. For example, if he was calling the partridge-in-the-pear-tree company, he would be ordering twelve partridges in pear trees—one for each day of the twelve days! (Do you suppose that the company has a package deal and he can get a cheaper rate by ordering them as a set?)

The students worked in random groups of two, which were created by passing out playing cards; students had to find a partner with a matching card from a different suit.

The variety of ways in which the problem was attacked roughly matched the number of groups. Some students found out how many gifts arrived on the first day, then how many on the second, then on the third, and so on. They identified a pattern, and one very precocious student recognized the triangular numbers (one gift on day 1, three gifts on day 2, six gifts on day 3, and so on). With a calculator, they added the total number of each day's presents.

Another group noticed that twelve partridges in pear trees were sent (one for each of twelve days), twenty-two turtle doves (two on each of eleven

days), and so on. They added all these numbers. They discovered that six geese a-laying sent for seven days and seven swans a-swimming ordered for six days resulted in the same number of geese as swans. The excitement of this discovery was heightened when the pattern held fast. The number of gold rings (five each for eight days) was the same as the number of maids a-milking (eight for each of five days), and so on.

Still another group started with the last day and found that they had to add $1 + 2 + 3 + 4 + 5 + 6 + 7 + 8 + 9 + 10 + 11 + 12$ (a series!) to get seventy-eight total gifts for that day, and that on the next-to-last day, they had to add the same string of numbers except for the 12. That group used the strategy of working backward.

A different group produced a series that was quite interesting. They added 12 (drummers drumming) to 11 and then 11 again (for the pipers piping on days 11 and 12), then 10 appeared three times for the three days on which the lords a-leaping had to be ordered. Their list looked like this:

$$12 + 11 + 11$$
$$+ 10 + 10 + 10$$
$$+ 9 + 9 + 9 + 9$$
$$+ 8 + 8 + 8 + 8 + 8$$
$$+ 7 + 7 + 7 + 7 + 7 + 7$$
$$+ 6 + 6 + 6 + 6 + 6 + 6 + 6$$
$$+ 5 + 5 + 5 + 5 + 5 + 5 + 5 + 5$$
$$+ 4 + 4 + 4 + 4 + 4 + 4 + 4 + 4 + 4$$
$$+ 3 + 3 + 3 + 3 + 3 + 3 + 3 + 3 + 3 + 3$$
$$+ 2 + 2 + 2 + 2 + 2 + 2 + 2 + 2 + 2 + 2 + 2$$
$$+ 1 + 1 + 1 + 1 + 1 + 1 + 1 + 1 + 1 + 1 + 1 + 1$$

This group then linked all pairs of numbers summing to 10 (2 appeared on their list eleven times and 8 appeared on their list five times, so they made five pairs equaling 10s and continued bunching five of the extra 2s together to make another 10, etc.)

Every group, regardless of their method, arrived at the staggering and unexpected total of 364 gifts that had to be ordered. They also all figured out, some more elegantly than others, that the order form would look something like this:

12 partridges in pear trees

22 turtle doves

30 french hens

36 calling birds

40 gold rings

42 geese a-laying

42 swans a-swimming

40 maids a-milking

36 ladies dancing

30 lords a-leaping

22 pipers piping

12 drummers drumming

Look at the wonderful patterns, the diminishing intervals between numbers, and the symmetry of the numerical list! The students were fascinated and energized, and all were eager to share their methods of arriving at the answer; many shared the moment at which they stopped dealing with raw data and let the emerging pattern do the work for them.

The last part of the assignment was, in many ways, the most interesting. Our students had one full week to do this research, and they could work together or receive any support they wished.

3. Help figure out approximately, in 1990 dollars, what this chap needs to pay to send all these gifts. We'll work on this project as a whole class. We'll divide up the gifts, and each person will have only one to research. You may have to make some telephone calls and speak to some people. For example, how much would it cost to rent eleven musicians to be the pipers piping? For how many days would you need them? How much would you have to budget for pipers piping? The person investigating this gift might call the New England Conservatory, the Boston Symphony Orchestra, or a person who advertises musical entertainment for parties. Explain the project, get an estimate, and be prepared to report to the class next week. (You may find pipers piping as a small statue at the local mall and decide to send eleven of those instead of the real thing—it is your decision how and in what form the gift will be sent. One caution: drawings are not allowed.) Have a good time with this activity!

Take notes on your research, and attach all work to this sheet.

The data and the stories that came back a week later were wonderful. All the students were eager to share their experiences, and the explanations of the mathematics assignment to the outside world had met, with a few exceptions, with delight. Some stu-

dents chose to work together and help each other out. Some did the research by telephone; some did it in person. Parents, babysitters, older siblings, and community merchants were called on frequently.

Two classes were involved in this project, so we ended up with two sets of independently researched data. The students were interested in their own information but were also curious to compare their findings with those of others.

We collected the information by asking the fourth graders to fill out a chart. Headings on the chart were as follows:

Gift	Researcher	Source of price
Price for one	Number needed	Total

Although relating these anecdotes may not advance anyone's mathematical understandings, the author thinks that some are so irresistible, they deserve to be shared. Terrence called the Boston Recreation Department to find out how much it would cost to rent the swanboats for "swans a-swimming" and came back with awesome information about the New Kids on the Block and what the group's cost had been to rent the swanboats for a videotaping session. Danny's family called France to speak with his mother's former roommate and find out about how much "french hens" would cost. Danny had to translate francs into dollars as well as do the pricing research. Joe had such a good time researching his "ladies dancing" that he voluntarily researched a couple of other items. Justin couldn't find out about live "geese a-laying" but did go to a butcher shop and found out the price per pound for a goose and the average weight of the geese that were available. He had to deal with fractions and decimals! Beth used a tree catalog. Diana asked a high school teacher known for playing the bagpipes during special occasions how much it would cost to rent his services. Amelia figured in money to buy cages and food with her partridges to that they would feel comfortable and stay alive. Kiran had to tell the maid service she called about "maids a-milking" how many room her house had and how many times a month she was considering using the service, as well as assure the service that the house was in their regional district. Tatiana, researching "ladies dancing," asked questions of the ballerinas at the Boston Ballet while she was rehearsing for her part in the *Nutcracker*.

Almost as many entertaining stories were related as students involved. Some dealt with the interactions with adults while trying to get the information. Many dealt with the problems of interpretation that had to be solved. Would the lords a-leaping be rented, and if so, for how long? Would students have to figure out transportation costs? What is a partridge, anyway, and if you can't find one, what would be a good substitute? What would be a good source for the required data? And how much cooperation was needed from a friend or a parent? Because this was a group project and the class as a community was depending on these data, no student came unprepared, although some were more heavily invested in the elegant possibilities than others.

Finally, it was time to determine the grand totals, and quiet descended over the room as students focused on the data that were unfolding in front of them. Because two classes were involved, two sets of data could be compared when the students were finished. Table 7.1 and table 7.2 report the results.

One group also wanted to figure out the Massachusetts tax of 5 percent, which led to a rich, if somewhat off the main track, conversation about computing it.

Both classes saw the data at recess. A great deal of conversation ensued. Were the totals far apart? The consensus was that $5,000 was a lot of money, generally, but in relation to the two big amounts, the totals were fairly close. What factor accounted for the discrepancies? Was it interpretation or computation? What was the average of the two figures? (Although one group figured the average with a calculator, a large section of the class did it ingeniously by making a line with 162,357.83 on one side and 167,045.56 on the other. Then they performed inverse operations on both numbers until the numbers were the same, that is, if they added $1,000.00 to the smaller number, they subtracted it from the larger number. They started with big increments and worked their way downward. They also had to deal with reporting an average where the difference between the two numbers was odd.) Students came up with $164,706.14 as the average.

The tax and the average were not computations on a worksheet. They were not part of the lesson but rather were responses to students' questions about data that they had created and of which they were struggling to make sense.

Although the annual holiday music-assembly schedule permitted no time to share information about the problem with parents, we really needed

TABLE 7.1

Total Price for Gifts—First-Period Class

12 partridges (cockatiels)	$ 720.00
12 pear trees	360.00
22 turtle doves	660.00
30 french hens	269.91
36 calling birds	108,000.00
40 gold rings	33,460.00
42 geese a-laying	966.00
42 swans a-swimming	840.00
40 maids a-milking	3,620.00
40 cows for milking	2,000.00
36 ladies dancing	360.00
30 lords a-leaping	1,500.00
22 pipers piping	7,921.92
12 drummers drumming	1,680.00
Grand total	$162,357.83

TABLE 7.2

Total Price for Gifts—Second-Period Class

12 partridges	$ 186.00
12 pear trees	167.00
22 turtle doves	595.00
30 french hens	297.00
36 calling birds (parrots)	108,000.00
40 gold rings	2,200.00
42 geese a-laying	1,239.00
42 swans a-swimming	1,050.00
40 maids a-milking	2,000.00
40 cows for milking	36,000.00
36 ladies dancing	9,671.60
30 lords a-leaping	3,000.00
22 pipers piping	2,168.96
12 drummers drumming	480.00
Grand total	$167,054.56

an audience for our results. After all, great discoveries assume a larger importance only if they are shared, and we were determined to capture the vital energy and mathematical power of our experience and to display what we had learned. Using a half-sheet of posterboard each, the students illustrated their research and included the same important information we had collected on our class graph. These boards were hung proudly in the corridors leading to the gymnasium where the assembly would be held.

Our fourth grade was not the only group enchanted with the possibilities of "The Twelve Days of Christmas." Irene Trivias's marvelous picture book called *Emma's Christmas* (1988) tells of Emma, the object of a prince's affections, who receive the aforementioned presents. What happens at the end of this tale is simply a delight, and reading the story would make a wonderful finale to this project.

Lauren Resnick (1987) offers a list of nine valuable criteria for identifying higher-order thinking. The filters that Resnick had delineated are useful in measuring the capability of this project to promote the kind of thinking that should be valued in schools.

1. Higher-order thinking is nonalgorithmic. That is, the path of action is not fully specified in advance.
2. Higher-order thinking tends to be complex. The total path is not visible, mentally speaking, from any single vantage point.
3. Higher-order thinking often yields multiple solutions, each with costs and benefits, rather than unique solutions.
4. Higher-order thinking involves nuance and judgment.
5. Higher-order thinking involves the application of multiple criteria that sometimes conflict with one another.
6. Higher-order thinking often involves uncertainty. Not everything that bears on the task is known.
7. Higher-order thinking involves self-regulation of the thinking process. We do not recognize higher-order thinking in an individual when someone else calls the plays at every step.
8. Higher-order thinking involves imposing meaning, finding structure in apparent disorder.
9. Higher-order thinking is effortful. Considerable mental work is involved in the kinds of elaborations and judgments required.

The fourth graders who responded to this problem were given little direction in how to solve it. Parts of the problem had one correct answer, and parts were open to interpretation. How to define the problem, where to gather information, and how to deal with information that was not in the clean form that was asked for created true problem solving. The community of learners was creating information that was interesting—a product of their interpretations—and was not subject to the ultimate test of "Did we get it right?" Listening to the students talk about their initial ideas—why some ideas were rejected, where they went for help, and what kind of help they sought—made it clear that many of these students were as aware of their strategies as they were of the mathematical problem they were interpreting.

For some, this pursuit may not look enough like mathematics, or it may be too time-consuming, or students may not generally do well with long-range projects. These factors should all be considered before embarking on this project. But it this is the kind of thinking of which we want our students to be capable, we have to give them opportunities to practice. This is one experience in a long line of independent and open-ended opportunities. Students get better at making plans, identifying sources, dealing with inconsistencies, and making decisions—but only when we give them chances to try, to learn, and to grow.

REFERENCES

Resnick, Lauren B. *Education and Learning to Think.* Washington, D.C.: National Academy Press, 1987.

Trivias, Irene. *Emma's Christmas.* New York: Orchard Books, 1988.

Teaching Notes for

"Critical Thinking During the December Holidays"

by Annette Raphel

Grade range:	4–6
Mathematical topic:	Exploring patterns in sum of sequences by using mathematics in a project situation
Children's books:	*The Twelve Days of Christmas* (a number of versions are available); *Emma's Christmas*, by Irene Trivias
Materials:	"Twelve Days of Christmas Project Guidelines" handout

Discussion of the mathematics: As discussed in the article, many different patterns, such as symmetry and triangular numbers, can be found in determining the sum of the sequence. One aspect of the problem—finding the sum of the numbers from 1 through 12—can result in a discussion of triangular numbers. Different representations for each day's cumulative sum will lead to different strategies. The mathematics encountered in finding the costs of the gifts will vary; the topics to be discussed could include calculation of percents (sales tax), estimation, use of a price index, and the like.

Teacher notes: Guidelines for the three different aspects of the projects and how they were implemented are detailed in the article. Also included in the article are examples of students' strategies.

For some, this pursuit may not appear sufficiently mathematical, or it may be too time-consuming, or students may generally not do well with long-range projects. Here are some ways that teachers have modified this project to fit the needs of the children they are teaching:

1. Make the song more relevant by asking children to go through catalogues or circulars to choose gifts in which they might be interested. This tactic also eliminates the problem of asking children to do outside research in communities where little scaffolding is available for this kind of activity. One class chose twelve talking games, eleven walkie-talkies, ten pairs of roller blades, nine junior goal sets, and so on.

2. Pass out file cards listing the gifts to be researched, so that the items to be researched are randomly assigned. Separate some of the tasks (e.g., the cows from the maids-a-milking, the partridges from the pear trees, etc.) so that some groups need to collaborate to determine the amount of money that was spent on any given gift.

3. Provide data from newspapers or magazines that annually release information on the current cost of the "twelve days of Christmas"; one World Wide Web source is the PNC Bank Christmas Price Index. Note that such figures are generally given only for the last day rather than cumulatively. Students will enjoy comparing the results of their own research with those of others. If you choose to use externally gathered information instead of class research, investigating the data will still provide plenty of computational practice.

4. Take this project out of the realm of Christmas by using another book with the same mathematics, such as Seymour Chwast's *Twelve Circus Rings*, Elizabeth Lee O'Donnell's *The Twelve Days of Summer*, or Rebecca Dickenson's *The Thirteen*

Nights of Halloween. These books lend themselves to the same mathematical pattern seeking, although the pricing exercise will not work as well with any of these choices.

5. Encourage students to use the World Wide Web for their research. This approach, done either with the help of a school technology specialist or independently, has made a significant positive difference in the success of the research aspect of this project in the last five years. Below are the data collected by one class.

REFERENCES

Chwast, Seymour. *Twelve Circus Rings.* San Diego: Gulliver Books, Harcourt Brace Jovanovich, 1993.

Dickenson, Rebecca. *The Thirteen Nights of Halloween.* New York: Scholastic, 1996.

O'Donnell, Elizabeth Lee. *The Twelve Days of Summer.* Illustrated by Karen Ann Schmidt. New York: Morrow Junior Books, 1991.

Raphel, Annette. "Critical Thinking during the December Holidays." *Arithmetic Teacher* 41 (December 1993): 216–19.

Trivas, Irene. *Emma's Christmas.* New York: Orchard Books, 1988.

Present	Researcher	Source	Price for Each	No. Needed	Total Price
Partridge (price per pound of turkey, roughly doubled because partridges are more rare)	Alisha	Shaw's Supermarket	$2.80 per pound. 21 lb. average	12	$705.60
Pear tree—4 ft.	Elizabeth	Internet—Fla. company, followed by phone call	$25.00	12	$300.00
Turtle doves—Radko ornament	Grant	eBay final auction price	$178.00	22	$3,916.00
French hens	Alec	Yahoo.com	$5.00	30	$150.00
Calling birds	James K.	Yellow Pages pet shop, followed by phone call	$89.99	36	$1,239.64
Golden rings—sale priced for the holidays	Alli	*E. B. Horn Magazine* ad	$100.00	40	$4,000.00
Geese-a-laying	Gavin	Phone call to Dewar's store	$3.99 per pound, avg. 13 lbs. = $51.87	42	$2,178.54
Swans-a-swimming	Keller	Don Decker	$250.00	42	$10,500.00
Maids	Molly	Internet source—12daysofchristmas.com	$41.20	40	$1,648.00
Cows	Jasmine	Iwon.com (more open-minded than askjeeves.com)	$459.50	40	$18,398.00
Ladies dancing	Hillary	Magazine on fitness	$150.00	36	$5,400.00
Lords-a-leaping (performers)	Samara	Her dad	$300.00 per person	30	$9,000.00
Pipes (bagpipes)	Nikki	Scottish neighbor	$500.00	22	$11,000.00
Pipers (people to play the pipes)	Alex M.	Dad's orchestra	$50.00 per hour	22	$1,100.00
Drummers	Will T.	Mom's friend Taki	$225.00 per drummer	12	$2,700.00
Drums (African drums)	Andre	Internet	$350.00	12	$4,200.00

The Twelve Days of Christmas
Project Guidelines

Name_____

Date _____

Remember that the gift-giving was cumulative. That is, on the fifth day, the lady received five of the gift for the fifth day as well as the same thing she had received on day 4 (which included the gift for day 4 plus those for day 3 and day 2 and day 1).

Imagine that you are the lovesick gentleman who is arranging for gifts for the twelve days of Christmas. This task will require quite a lot of organization on our part. Basically we have three jobs:

1. Figure out how many presents in total the giver will have to buy to send all the things mentioned in the song to his true love. See if you can find a system and patterns to help you. Record your work, and be able to explain how you arrived at your answer. Many clever ways can be used to approach this problem.

2. Figure out how much of each item he actually has to order. For example, if he were calling the partridge-in-the-pear-tree company, he would be ordering twelve partridges in pear trees—one for each day of the twelve days! (Do you suppose the company has a package deal that will give him a cheaper rate by ordering them as a set?)

3. Help figure out what this chap must pay to send all these gifts. We will work on this investigation as a whole class. We will divide up the gifts so that each person will have just one to research. You may have to make some telephone calls and speak to some merchants and suppliers. For example, how much would you have to pay to rent eleven musicians to be the pipers piping? For how many days would you need them? How much would you have to budget for pipers piping? The person investigating this gift might call the city orchestra or a person who advertises musical entertainment for parties. Explain the project, get a ballpark figure, and be prepared to report back to class next week. (You may find pipers piping as a small statue at the local mall and decide to send eleven of those instead of the real thing—it is your decision how and in what form the gift will be sent. One caution: drawings are not allowed.)

Have a good time with this activity! Take notes on your research, and attach all work to this sheet.

Clearly organize your data, because we will be filling out a class chart with the headings listed below.

Present	Researcher	Source	Price for Each	No. Needed	Total Price

8

Popping Up Number Sense

Lindy Hopkins

Popcorn. This simple, inexpensive manipulative led to myriad unforeseen benefits—student excitement, whole-school participation, and even community involvement—as our project to count a million popped pieces unfolded.

Several teachers from Saltillo Elementary school, a K–5 school in rural Mississippi, had met David Schwartz, author of *How Much Is a Million?*, at a reading conference. Intrigued with his display of bags holding 10, 100, 1000, and 10,000 pieces of popped corn and equipped with autographed copies of his book, we planned a schoolwide project to help our students gain number sense by learning more about a million.

As we discussed working together to pop a million pieces of popcorn, we realized that neither our students nor we, their teachers, could picture a million very well. To display the popcorn, and on the basis of what we thought a million pieces might look like, we arranged for a huge, empty cotton wagon to be parked at the side of the school's parking lot to hold the popcorn. One teacher acted as spokesperson for our "million project" steering committee, obtaining approval for the location for the wagon from the school's principal, Ruth Stanford. She enthusiastically supported our plan, and when we presented it to colleagues at the weekly faculty meeting, the majority began to share ideas for making the project schoolwide and for incorporating many curricular areas.

Books about a Million . . . and Popcorn Too!

As the project was implemented, many teachers used Schwartz's *How Much Is a Million?* (1985) and *If You Made a Million* (1989) as sources for background information. Illustrated by Steven Kellogg, the books feature facts about one million with engaging prose and detailed, amusing pastel illustrations of people, animals, and objects. *How Much is a Million?* presents the huge number with such analogies as these: Counting aloud to a million, nonstop, would take about twenty-three days; a million youngsters standing on one another's shoulders would be "higher than the highest mountain." *If You Made a Million* features photographs and fanciful, information-rich drawings. Each book concludes with notes by the author that describe his procedures for calculating and estimating the facts presented in the books.

Teachers found that the books were effective for children in grades K–5. Each teacher who used the books highlighted and emphasized the information that would be most understandable to the children in a given classroom. Undoubtedly most of the fifth graders made more sense of Schwartz's analogies and descriptions than did the kindergartners, but each group grasped the idea that a million was a huge number and that it could be imagined in many different ways and applied to a variety of situations.

Since this "million project" involved popcorn, Tomie de Paola's *The Popcorn Book* (1978) proved to be another valuable resource. This book spins a tale of the many facts that two children discover as they prepare popcorn. Incorporating history, science, consumer information, and folktale, the book concludes that "the best thing about popcorn . . . is eating it!" De Paola's clear sketches, often showing present-day children as well as historical characters in a split-page format (fig. 8.1), present a great deal of information in a coherent, amusing way. *The Popcorn Book* describes popcorn as a food and a valuable commodity. Although not much popcorn is grown in the Saltillo area, the children could relate to its value as a crop because it was harvest time for many other agricultural products.

A Fifth-Grade Classroom Gets Popping

One fifth-grade inclusion classroom has two teachers and fourteen learning disabled students, four talented and gifted students, and ten regular education students. Although they work as a team, one teacher serves as a full-time special education teacher, and the other is the regular education teacher. Because these students have a wide range of abilities and interests, general themes like the millions project work well in this classroom. Students are able to work on their own levels; everyone is able to participate and experience success as all learn more about the broad topic or theme.

After reading *How Much Is a Million?*, teachers and students brainstormed about where they could find a million things. On the first day, students made inaccurate comments, such as "You can see a million cars at the mall." Near the end of the project,

the students had better number sense and shared such ideas as finding a million leaves in a forest or a million grains of sand at the beach.

Almost every day, the fifth graders popped corn. Students worked in self-selected, cooperative groups and counted out sets of 100 pieces of popcorn, combined ten sets to make thousands, then poured these larger sets into a large class bag. Finally, the students counted by thousands to get a daily total. Students not only used place-value skills as they worked but also developed a tremendous number sense as they saw sets of popped corn and thought about their relationships. Some students were content to count by ones and twos each day; others filled containers, established average numbers per container, and figured their totals using calculators. Still other students created and solved original problems, building from the author's notes in the Schwartz books.

Many facts about popcorn were learned as students read de Paolo's *The Popcorn Book*. The topic fit well with a unit on Native American culture scheduled to begin at harvest time. The students enjoyed the book so much that one teacher developed an author study on de Paolo. After reading, comparing, and contrasting several of de Paolo's books, the students wrote to him. He responded by sending them autographed bookmarks.

The millions project also incorporated many communication skills. In addition to the constant oral communication that took place as students devised approaches, carried out their plans, and shared their feelings about the project, written

Fig. 8.1. Illustration from *The Popcorn Book* by Tomie de Paolo (1978) © Holiday House. All rights reserved; used with permission.

POPPING UP NUMBER SENSE

communication was emphasized. Students made millions-project journals and wrote in them daily (fig. 8.2). Many students created word problems, illustrated them, solved and checked them, and shared their thinking with their peers and teachers. Some problems were simple, but others, like Jessica and Michelle's (fig. 8.3), were complex. The girls wondered aloud if the popcorn would cover the floor of a classroom or gymnasium; after they decided that it would, they extended their question to the community. They ascertained the approximate area covered by a single piece of popcorn by experimenting with many different pieces of popped corn, then based the rest of their problem on information obtained from city hall. Their work indicates that they know a good deal about estimation and number sense but that they need to learn more about the relationship of linear measures to area measures.

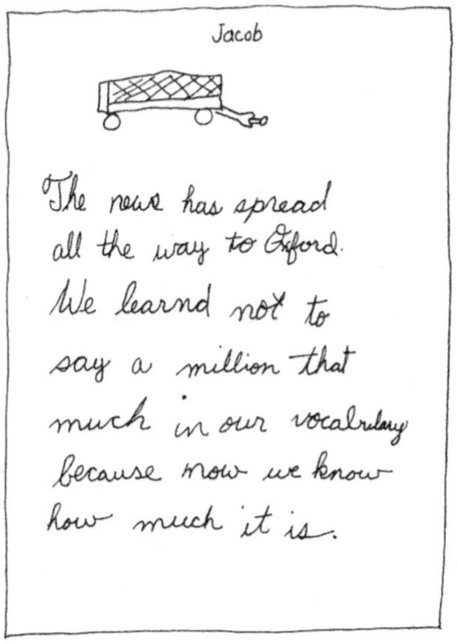

As all the participating classes accounted for daily totals of popcorn, they packaged it in plastic bags and put it in the cotton wagon. The numbers were reported to a member of the office staff, who posted the results near the office where the students could see them. As news of the project spread through the small southern community, people drove through the school's parking lot to see the popcorn mounting up, to comment on the progress, and, often, to shout encouragement to the students. At the end of the project, students found that a million pieces of popped corn, in bags, filled about one-third of the cotton wagon.

News of the learning project was featured in a regional newspaper and in the newsletter of the Mississippi Council of Teachers of Mathematics. Thus many citizens heard about this intriguing number-sense project and commented about their interest in it.

Fig. 8.2. Journal page from the millions project

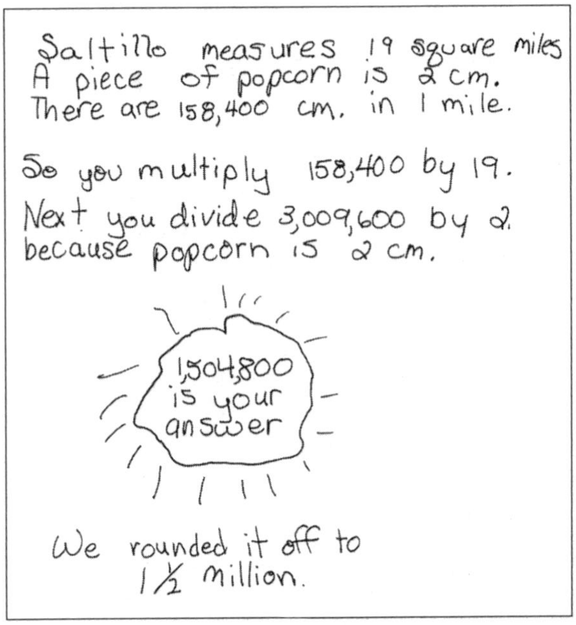

Fig. 8.3. Jessica and Michelle's estimate of the number of popcorn pieces needed to cover their city

Popping throughout the School

The million project's activities varied from teacher to teacher and grade level to grade level. In kindergarten, teachers drew pictures of what the cotton wagon might look like when filled with a million pieces of popcorn. The children compared the appearance of 10 kernels of unpopped and popped corn in small cups. Counting by 1's, over several days, the children contributed 1000 pieces of popcorn to the wagon.

First graders counted popped corn by 1's, 2's, 5's, and 10's; one class made a poster showing different configurations for 100—two 50's, four 25's, five 20's, and ten 10's. Children made sets of 10, then bagged 10's to make 100. The children were amused when popcorn overflowed from their popper, since a similar situation had been illustrated in de Paola's book. The children's interest in popcorn led to graphing favorite popcorn flavors and listing places where people eat popcorn. First-grade teachers noted one added benefit: the children enjoyed cleaning up any popcorn that spilled on the floor because it gave them more pieces to count!

After second-grade teachers read the books aloud, the children discussed them and made and displayed group compositions about the books. The children worked in groups and counted popped corn by 2's, 5's, and 10's. They packaged 100 kernels in sandwich bags, then counted the bags by 100's. Each day, they graphed the number of pieces they had counted. After counting it, the children put the corn in a bucket and, on the basis of the number of kernels they saw, estimated how many kernels would fill the entire bucket. Another popular estimating activity involved taking handfuls of popcorn, estimating the number of pieces, and then counting them. Children recorded their activities and results in their journals.

Parental involvement make it possible for the third graders to make and count over 20,000 kernels of corn. As they worked with popcorn as a concrete material to practice estimating and rounding to the nearest hundred and thousand.

A delightful diary idea "popped up" in the fourth-grade classrooms. Children created accounts of what they did using a pop-up-book format. They wrote about and illustrated data daily during the millions project. When they were not counting, they kept busy grouping numbers and finding average numbers for various containers of popped corn.

The talented and gifted class's letter to Orville Reddenbacher elicited a gracious response. Although Reddenbacher declined an invitation to visit, he sent information about popcorn—and samples! The class members brainstormed ideas for disposing of the "white wonder" once they counted, photographed, and discussed the million pieces of popcorn. Among their ideas were giving it to the principal, making a giant "snowman" of it, using it for packaging, and feeding it to animals. The class took the last piece of advice and gave the popcorn to a local farmer who was happy to feed it to his hogs.

Benefits of the Project

The project was memorable, enjoyable, and worthwhile. Since it involved most of the children and teachers at our school, it built a feeling of community. Each child could feel a part of the endeavor and become involved on his or her own level. Seeing the project to completion was rewarding: it took longer—about six weeks—then the two weeks originally expected; at times, we wanted to quit. But teachers and children encouraged each other and met our commitment to finish. Everyone was very proud to see one million pieces of popcorn!

Teachers and children alike developed tremendous number sense from working on the project. We can now picture numbers like 10, 100, 1000, and 1,000,000,000. We really understand what a huge number a million is! Although not every school and community has access to cotton wagons and to hogs to eat the leftover popcorn, we heartily recommend our project ideas to others—to modify, benefit from, and remember as a powerful, participatory learning experience.

REFERENCES

de Paola, Tomie. *The Popcorn Book.* New York: Holiday House, 1978.

Schwartz, David M. *How Much Is a Million?* Illustrated by Steven Kellogg. New York: Scholastic, 1985.

———. *If You Made a Million.* Illustrated by Steven Kellogg. New York: Scholastic, 1989.

Teaching Notes for

"Popping Up Number Sense"

by Lindy Hopkins

Grade range:	K–6
Mathematical topic:	Developing number sense by counting, estimating, and reasoning
Children's books:	*How Much Is A Million?* written by David M. Schwartz and illustrated by Steven Kellogg (1985n)
	If You Made A Million, written by David M. Schwartz and illustrated by Steven Kellogg (1989)
Materials:	Popcorn, containers

Discussion of the mathematics: By using popcorn to explore large quantities, students can develop number sense for quantities from one to one million. The calculation and estimation activities also help develop reasoning skills. Through writing and graphing, students improve their ability to communicate mathematical thinking and reasoning. Although primary-grade children may not be able to pursue some of the sophisticated investigations that fifth and sixth graders can, they still enjoy the illustrations of, and discussions about, millions, billions, and other very large numbers and can pursue investigations that are appropriate for their abilities.

Teacher notes: By working on a smaller scale, students could estimate the number of pieces of popcorn that would fill a given bucket or aquarium. After discussing different strategies, students could devise a plan to calculate the number of kernels without counting each one. An example of such a plan is counting one handful of popped corn and then counting the number of handfuls required to fill the container. For more advanced children, the teacher could bring up the concept of averaging or using standard measure. Does everyone have the same size hand in your class? The children may then choose to find the average hand's capacity or to use a standard measure, such as a one-cup measure, for the activity. The students would then record and share their solution to the capacity problem.

After students have determined the number of pieces in the smaller container, they could determine whether a million pieces of popcorn would fill the classroom. Would that quantity fill the gymnasium? A nearby swimming pool? After the students have discussed estimates, they need to devise and then test strategies for comparing the capacity of the original container with that of the larger "container."

Another activity would be for students to use the format found in the back of *How Much Is A Million?* to write their own mathematical facts. An example of such a fact is "It would take ____ days to say 'popcorn' one million times." Students will have to use reasoning and calculating skills to complete this activity. Much of the background research can be found in the text on the back pages of the book.

REFERENCES

Hopkins, Lindy. "Links to Literature: Popping Up Number Sense." *Teaching Children Mathematics* 2 (October 1995): 82–85.

Schwartz, David M. *G is for Googol: A Math Alphabet Book*. Illustrated by Marissa Moss. Berkeley, Calif.: Tricyle Press, 1998.

____. *How Much Is a Million?* Illustrated by Steven Kellogg. New York: Scholastic, 1985.

____. *If You Made a Million*. Illustrated by Steven Kellogg. New York: Scholastic, 1989.

Schwartz, David M., and David J. Whitin. *The Magic of a Million: Activity Book*. New York: Scholastic, 1998.

9

Connecting Literature, Language, and Fractions

Betty Conaway and Ruby Bostick Midkiff

BECAUSE of the symbolic nature of fractions and the procedural operations required to manipulate fractions mathematically, the concept of fractions is often difficult for students in early grades to master (Van de Walle 1990). Perhaps this difficulty results in part from the numerical contradictions presented by fractions. Furthermore, fractions are part of a mathematical language that is often foreign to students until they develop a personal understanding. "Children's literature presents a natural way to connect language and mathematics" (Midkiff and Cramer 1993, p. 303) and furnishes a foundation on which an understanding of concepts can be based. As students read, write, and discuss real-life situations requiring the use of fractions, they develop personal meanings for the abstract concepts.

Numerical Contradictions

Elementary school students have had many experiences with numbers. They know that as numbers increase in size, the amount represented by that number also increases. However, the amounts represented by fractional numbers do not always have the same relationships as those expressed in whole numbers. For example, as denominators increase numerically, the portion represented by that fraction actually decreases in size when the numerator remains constant.

Another complication is that a fractional number is read from top to bottom, but the top number cannot be fully understood unless the bottom number is visualized first. For example, 1/4 is read as "one-fourth," but the "one" has meaning only when the segment "fourth" is visualized as a section of a whole

or a part of a set. Reading this fraction as "one part of four" or "one of four equal parts" may be more meaningful for some students. Other children will benefit by referring to the numerator as the "counting number" and the denominator as "what is being counted" (Van de Walle 1990, p. 178). In other words, students must develop a concrete and personal understanding of fractions on the basis of a knowledge of both terms (Cruikshank and Sheffield 1992).

Developing Personal Understandings

Students cannot develop thorough understandings of the characteristics of fractions if they only listen to the teacher "tell" about the concepts. Children must discover the mathematical relationships themselves, creating this information from their own experiences visually, tactually, and auditorily. Furthermore, opportunities to develop an understanding of fractions through writing should be offered so that students can express the characteristics of fractions in terms that are meaningful to them.

For example, after students have experienced fractions through the use of patterning-block manipulatives and selections of children's literature, ask them to write personal definitions for such fractions as 1/2. When students have worked with the manipulatives (tactile), seen illustrations in books (visual), and talked about the relationships (auditory), their definitions will contain specific examples instead of simple repetitions of the definitions stated by the teacher. These experiences enable students to see that the quantity represented by 1/2 changes according to the context. As a result, one-half may be half of the class (twelve people), half of a pizza (four pieces), or two of four triangles.

One way to assist students in developing a schema for fractional concepts is to use children's literature. Almost all students in the early grades have developed a firm understanding of story grammar (Brown and Murphy 1975). They recognize that stories have a beginning, a middle, and an end, and they know that stories communicate information (Whaley 1981). This existing schema for the story can be used to introduce new concepts in other content areas, especially mathematics. This instructional strategy not only builds background information for mathematical concepts but also enhances children's ability to communicate mathematically, which is one of the standards in the NCTM's *Curriculum and Evaluation Standards for School Mathematics* (1989). Numerous children's books suitable for students in grades K–6 include specific mathematical concepts as part of the story. These stories can "help build bridges between the concrete and the abstract" (Slaughter 1993, p. 4). Books of this type also present opportunities for extension activities that focus on developing a thorough understanding of fractional concepts.

Fractions in Children's Literature

Students in grades K–3 will enjoy reading *Eating Fractions* by Bruce McMillian (1991). This book introduces the fractional concepts of whole, halves, thirds, and fourths using photographs of real children dividing and eating various foods. *Eating Fractions* is essentially a wordless picture book, since only the fraction words and numerals are included in the text. Two children are pictured eating two halves of a banana and two halves of an ear of corn. Thirds are demonstrated as the children divide a yeast roll into three pieces and a gelatin salad into three portions. Fourths are illustrated using a small pizza and a strawberry pie. Each food is first pictured as a whole and then pictured after it has been segmented into fractional parts.

This book offers many possibilities for discovery-learning activities. Simple recipes for the foods pictured in the book are given in an appendix at the end of the book. Each recipe uses fractions to measure the ingredients. Students can measure the ingredients and later divide the cooked foods. Older students can calculate new quantities for the ingredients if the recipes were to be doubled, tripled, or halved. Primary students enjoy working with foods that require no cooking and are "soft" or easy to divide, such as bananas, English muffins, or peanut butter sandwiches. Ask the children to use plastic knives to divide the bananas into halves, the English muffins into thirds, and the peanut butter sandwiches into fourths. Encourage them to compare the sizes of the portions and finally eat the foods.

An additional activity using raisins, small crackers, or bite-sized cookies can demonstrate the parts of a set. During this lesson, the teacher should ask students to work individually or in small groups to arrange the foods in sets of various sizes on paper plates. Then the teacher leads a discussion of the way to represent various fractional parts of each set. The following is an example:

> Show me a set of 5 cookies on your plate.
>
> What number represents 1/5 of the cookies?
>
> Divide your set to show 1/5 of the cookies.
>
> How do you know that 1/5 of the cookies are represented this way?
>
> Divide your set to show 3/5 of the cookies.
>
> How do you know that 3/5 of the cookies are represented this way?

The Doorbell Rang by Pat Hutchins (1986) can be used to extend the understanding of fractions. This book tells the story of Victoria and Sam as they prepare to share a dozen cookies. As the two children begin to divide the twelve cookies equally between themselves, the doorbell rings and two more children arrive, then two more children, and finally six more come to visit. After each group arrives, the children decide how to divide the cookies evenly among those present. Although this book does not directly discuss fractional concepts, the story provides a real-life problem-solving situation using fractional portions of 12. After the students have listened to the teacher read the book and have discussed ways to divide twelve items, ask the students to divide twelve paper cookies, twelve real cookies, or twelve pieces of popcorn. Extend this discussion by writing similar problems using a different number of children and cookies. For example, these two bags contain twelve cookies each. How many cookies do we have? (24) We have twelve students in our group. How many cookies will each student receive? (2) What fractional part of the cookies is that? (2/12) Then, depending on the grade level of the students, explore the concepts of simplifying or renaming.

Moria's Birthday by R. Munsch (1987) incorporates the concept of dividing a whole into portions while working with large numbers. Moria invites all the students who attend her school in "grade 1, grade 2, grade 3, grade 4, grade 5, grade 6, a-a-n-d-d kindergarten" to her birthday party. Then she orders 200 pizzas and 200 birthday cakes. The story explains the complications resulting from the delivery of the food and dividing the food among all the children. Although very young children enjoy hearing this story, the situation described is an opportunity to discuss with middle-grade students how many children 200 pizzas would feed if each one received one piece and each pizza was divided into eighths. Apply the same situation to the classroom. How many pizzas would be needed to feed all the students in this class? In the whole school? If each student ate two pieces, how many students would 200 pizzas serve?

Using the same procedures, lead students in a discussion of how to divide the cakes to serve all those attending the party. What fractional portion of each cake would each student receive? Other applications for older students include determining the total cost of the pizzas and the cakes, as well as the cost for each guest. Extend this activity by asking students to measure the number of servings in a quart or a two-liter container of punch and then to determine how many containers would be needed to serve all the students at Moria's party. Ask older students to calculate what fractional parts of a quart or a two-liter bottle each guest will receive.

Another book that includes fractions and food is *Tom Fox and the Apple Pie* by Clyde Watson (1972). Tom Fox is the youngest in a family of fourteen little foxes. With Ma and Pa Fox, they live at the end of Mulberry Lane. Tom buys an apple pie at the fair. As he walks home, he imagines the pie being divided into sixteen pieces to serve everyone in the family, and he concludes that each piece will be very small. Tom decides to wait until eight of his brothers and sisters are outside counting stars, divide the pie into eight pieces, and serve one piece to himself and one piece to each of the remaining seven family members. Again he concludes that these pieces will be too small to satisfy his appetite. Next he visualizes the pie cut into fourths, with one piece for Ma, one for Pa, one for Lou-Lou, his favorite sister, and one for himself. Tom finally concludes that he would much rather eat the whole pie himself, which he does. This book is one way to reinforce the concept that as the denominator decreases, the portion it represents becomes larger. Sample questions that lead the students to visualize this concept follow:

- What happens to the pieces of pie when they are changed from sixteenths to eighths? From eighths to fourths?
- What would happen if the pie were divided into halves?
- As the denominator decreases in these fractions—1/16, 1/8, 1/4, 1/2—what happens to the piece of pie?
- Match these fractions to pie-shaped pieces. Which piece would you rather have? Why?

Extension activities for this book include asking students to draw a pie on paper and divide it into sixteen sections using one colored marker. Next ask students to use a different color to divide the pie into eight sections and then to use another color to divide the pie into four sections. Ask the students how many sixteenths are in each eighth and in each fourth.

Practicing with fractional parts using patterning blocks or other manipulative counters also builds understanding. When patterning blocks are used, a hexagon can represent one whole. The trapezoid would then represent one-half; the parallelogram would represent one-third; and the triangles, one-sixth. Construct a variety of shapes to reinforce the concept that as the denominator of a fraction increases and the numerator stays the same, the portion the fraction represents becomes smaller. Ask students to cut one paper pie into four pieces, another into eight pieces, and another into sixteen pieces and to compare the sections. Ask students to reassemble the pie using different numbers of pieces of each size. Another way to use the same type of activity would be to use circular pieces of felt. Use one color of felt for the whole pie. Use different colors of felt for halves, fourths, eights, and sixteenths. Students will compare the various fractional parts by arranging the halves, fourths, eighths, and sixteenths on top of the whole.

The concept of one-half is presented in a variety of formats in *The Half-Birthday Party* by Charlotte Pomerantz (1984). Daniel's sister, Katie, who is six months old, has just learned to stand, and Daniel wants to have a half-birthday party to celebrate. He invites his friend Lily, Mr. Bangs, Grandma, Mom, and Dad. Each guest is to bring half of a gift and a whole story about the half present. Lily brings one earring, or half of a pair. Mr. Bangs and Grandma each bring half of a birthday cake. Daniel shows Katie the half-moon. The book has many possible extensions. Ask older students to determine their own half-birthdays. Ask younger students to select a half present for Katie and write a whole story explaining their choice.

Other Connections in Literature

Other books that are easily integrated into the study of fractions can be found through such resources as *How to Use Children's Literature to Teach Mathematics* (Welchman-Tischler 1992); *Books You Can Count On* (Griffiths and Clyne 1988); and *Read Any Good Math Lately? Children's Books for Mathematical Learning, K–6* (Whitin and Wilde 1992). *Book Cooks* (Bruno 1991) is a collection of recipes and extension activities based on thirty-five different books. This resource gives teachers a wide variety of activities for teaching fractions in the primary grades through classroom cooking.

Reviewing classroom collections from a mathematical point of view yields another source of books related to the study of fractions. A few of these might include the following:

- *Caps for Sale* (Slobodkina 1968) is an entertaining story for children in the primary grades that tells of a peddler who sells caps and whose caps are stolen by monkeys while he is resting. Use the illustrations of caps of five different colors as the basis for a discussion of fractions.

- *The Toothpaste Millionaire* (Merrill 1972) is embedded with mathematical content suitable for students in the middle grades. For example, the story includes one passage that reads, "You will need 2 1/4 yards of 36-inch-wide nylon, which is 97 cents a yard at Vince's, which will come to $2.18 1/4 plus sales tax" (p. 12).

- *A Rainbow Balloon* (Lenssen 1992) introduces such concepts as *rise* and *fall*, and *one* and *many* while following a colorful hot-air balloon. Ask primary students to draw a picture of the balloon in the story. Then ask students to draw a set of three balloons. Discuss how individual balloons in each set can be identified. Although this book is intended for younger audiences, it could also be used in the middle grades to integrate mathematics and science. Building and launching miniature hot-air balloons as a class project is one way to incorporate numerous mathematical concepts, including fractions, as well

as to develop an understanding of the science concepts presented in the book.

- *Wilbur's Space Machine* (Balian 1990) tells the story of a couple who builds a space machine to get away from pollution and noise. Illustrations of balloons furnish excellent examples of parts of sets to discuss and identify with primary students.

- *Earrings!* (Viorst 1990) tells the humorous story of a young girl who wants to have her ears pierced. Girls of all ages will enjoy reading this story, which could serve as the foundation for numerous problems involving fractions for several grade levels.

- *Seven Little Hippos* (Thaler and Smath 1991) uses a predictable pattern rhyme to tell the story of seven hippos who enjoy jumping on the bed. Each hippo falls off the bed one at a time until none are left. This story presents an opportunity to introduce primary children to the concept of the numerator as the "counting" part of the fraction and the denominator as the "number of things counted." After the students have listened to the story, give them a set of seven small plastic [counting] bears. As the story is read a second time, ask the children to arrange the set of seven into subsets that represent the hippos still on the bed and those that fell off the bed. Identify each of these fractions and discuss the changing relationship with the students.

- *Ten Little Rabbits* (Grossman and Long 1991) is a counting book for primary children. Read the story aloud to the children. As the book is read a second time, write the fraction representing the part of the set of rabbits counted on each page (1/10, 2/10, 3/10, and so on). Young children enjoy drawing pictures of rabbits to illustrate each fraction.

Conclusion

Effective and meaningful instruction in fractional computation requires students to have a thorough understanding of basic fractional concepts. The books described here are only a small sampling of children's literature that can assist in the formation of personal understandings of this topic. When students are actively engaged in activities that portray fractions as one-third of a yeast roll, one-half of a dozen cookies, one-eighth of a pizza, one-fourth of an apple pie, and one-half of a birthday gift, they form concrete connections between abstract number concepts and real-life experiences. When students work with fractions in a variety of formats, including literature, communication, and manipulatives, they are able to form personal definitions and thus to develop the understandings and readiness necessary to master more complex fractional concepts.

REFERENCES

Balian, Lorna. *Wilbur's Space Machine*. New York: Holiday House, 1990.

Brown, A. L., and M. D. Murphy. "Reconstruction of Arbitrary versus Logical Sequences by Preschool Children." *Journal of Experimental Psychology* 20 (1975): 307–26.

Bruno, Janet. *Book Cooks*. Cypress, Calif.: Creative Teaching Press, 1991.

Cruikshank, Douglas E., and Linda Jensen Sheffield. *Teaching and Learning Elementary and Middle School Mathematics*. 2nd ed. New York: Merrill Publishing Co., 1992.

Griffiths, Rachael, and Margaret Clyne. *Books You Can Count On*. Portsmouth, N.H.: Heinemann Educational Books, 1988.

Grossman, Virginia, and Sylvia Long. *Ten Little Rabbits*. San Francisco: Chronicle Books, 1991.

Hutchins, Pat. *The Doorbell Rang*. New York: Greenwillow Books, 1986.

Lenssen, Ann. *A Rainbow Balloon*. New York: Cobblehill Books, 1992.

McMillan, Bruce. *Eating Fractions*. New York: Scholastic, 1991.

Merrill, Jean. *The Toothpaste Millionaire*. Boston: Houghton Mifflin Co., 1972.

Midkiff, Ruby Bostick, and Mary McCart Cramer. "Stepping Stones to Mathematical Understanding." *Arithmetic Teacher* 40 (February 1993): 303–5.

Munsch, R. *Moria's Birthday*. Toronto: Annick Press, 1987.

National Council of Teachers of Mathematics (NCTM). *Curriculum and Evaluation Standards for School Mathematics*. Reston, Va.: NCTM, 1989.

Pomerantz, Charlotte. *The Half-Birthday Party*. New York: Clarion Books, 1984.

Slaughter, Judith Pollard. *Beyond Storybooks: Young Children and the Shared Book Experience*. Newark, Dela.: International Reading Association, 1993.

Slobodkina, Esphyr. *Caps for Sale: A Tale of a Peddler, Some Monkeys, and Their Monkey Business*. Reading, Mass.: Addison-Wesley Publishing Co., 1968.

Thaler, Mike, and Jerry Smath. *Seven Little Hippos*. New York: Simon & Schuster, 1991.

Van de Walle, John A. *Elementary School Mathematics: Teaching Developmentally*. New York: Longman, 1990.

Viorst, Judith. *Earrings!* New York: Atheneum Publishers. 1990.

Watson, Clyde. *Tom Fox and the Apple Pie*. New York: Thomas Y. Crowell Co., 1972.

Welchman-Tischler, Rosamond. *How to Use Children's Literature to Teach Mathematics*. Reston, Va.: National Council of Teachers of Mathematics, 1992.

Whaley, J. F. "Reader's Expectations for Story Structures." *Reading Research Quarterly* 17 (1981): 90–114.

Whitin, David J., and Sandra Wilde. *Read Any Good Math Lately? Children's Books for Mathematical Learning, K–6*. Portsmouth, N.H.: Heinemann Educational Books, 1992.

Teaching Notes for

"Connecting Literature, Language, and Fractions"

by Betty Conaway and Ruby Bostick Midkiff

Grade range:	1–5
Mathematical topic:	Fraction concepts including comparison and equivalence
Children's book:	*Eating Fractions*, by Bruce McMillan
Materials:	Construction paper of various colors cut into lengthwise strips about one inch wide and eleven inches long with a paper cutter

Discussion of the mathematics: Students need to explore many different representations of fractions. The task below focuses on a measurement model that involves folding strips of paper. Paper strips are especially appropriate for students because they are concrete region or area models but are also similar to a more abstract number-line model.

Teacher notes and questions for students: Read *Eating Fractions* to the class, showing the pictures as the book is read. After reading the book, explain that students will be using paper strips to construct fractions like those described in the book. Have the students work individually while sitting in groups of two or three. Distribute the paper strips so that each group has a sufficient number. Allow extra paper strips for "mistakes."

Note: These activities can be spread out over a period of time appropriate to students' abilities and background. Provide an envelope for each student to use for storing the fraction strips. Begin each fraction lesson for the next several days by taking out the fraction strips and comparing one with another as a group and as individuals, using the language described below.

One whole. Ask each student to select one strip of paper and to write "whole = 1" on the strip. Demonstrate how to do so by using a strip of paper that can be seen by everyone.

Halves. Have students choose another strip of paper in a different color. Ask the students to compare the lengths of the paper strips. They should note that the lengths are the same. Have students divide the second strip of paper into two equal pieces by folding (not cutting) the paper lengthwise into two pieces. Have students write 1/2 on each portion of the strip of paper. Ask, "How many halves are in the whole?" (Ans.: 2) Ask the students to place the strip of paper divided into halves next to the strip for one whole and to compare the two strips of paper.

Fourths. Have the student select a third strip of paper in a third color, and ask them how this strip could be folded to show fourths. Have one of the students demonstrate that folding the strip in half and then again in half will result in fourths. Have them write 1/4 on each section, then place the strip of paper next to the strip divided into halves. The following are appropriate questions to ask:

- How many fourths in one-half? (2)
- How many fourths are in one whole? (4)

Extensions to eighths and sixteenths: Continue this process, folding different colored strips of paper into eighths and sixteenths. Ask the same questions for each fraction, and have students write the fractional number on each section of the folded paper. As each strip is divided into a fraction, stack the strips of paper on top of one another for comparison.

Thirds. Ask the students how they could fold strips to represent thirds. Note: One method is to form a circle with the paper strip, overlapping the two ends until they are opposite as you hold the strip in the air, then crease the two opposites sides.

Extensions to sixths and twelfths. Have the students determine and then discuss their strategies to fold a strip of paper into sixths and another into twelfths. Ask the same questions.

- How many thirds in one whole? (3)
- How many sixths in one-third? (2)
- How many sixths in one whole? (6)

Then ask students to compare the "halves" strip and the "sixths" strip of paper.

- How many sixths in one-half? (3)
- How many thirds in one-half?

For the latter question, encourage an answer such as "more than one-third, but not two-thirds." Some students will explain that we can divide the third into sixths and then find the number of sixths in one-half. If your students are not ready for this discussion, continue to compare the fractional parts but encourage such explanations as that 5 fifths are in one whole, and so on.

Fifths and tenths. Continue this activity by folding strips of paper into fifths and tenths. Ask students to compare the sizes of each fractional part.

Grade range:	1–3
Mathematical topic:	Counting with fractions
Children's book:	*Seven Little Hippos*, written by Mike Thaler and illustrated by Jerry Smath
Materials:	For each student group, one "*Seven Little Hippos*" recording sheet, seven counting bears (or blocks or other counters), and a rectangular piece of paper labeled "bed"; for the overhead projector, a transparency marked "bed," seven counting blocks, and a transparency of the recording sheet

Discussion of the mathematics: In this counting task the students will need to recognize the set of counters as one whole and each individual counter as a fractional part of the whole. The lesson focuses on the concept of fractions as another way to represent numbers, where the numerator is the "counter" of the individual pieces and the concept of the denominator is the total number of pieces.

Teacher notes: Read *Seven Little Hippos* aloud to the students. As you read, ask the children how they can identify the individual hippos so that they can confirm that a different hippo falls off the bed each time. They should observe that each hippo's pajamas are different from the others'. For very young students, you may need to explain what a hippopotamus is and that *hippo* is a shortened form of the word. Note: A transparency marked "bed" and seven counting blocks for the overhead projector can be used by the teacher to demonstrate various aspects of the story or by the students to share their thinking.

Have the students work in groups of two or three, and distribute to each group a set of seven counters and a rectangular piece of paper labeled "bed." Have each group count the total number of blocks to verify that they have seven counters. Explain to the students that the seven counters form one whole group. Have each group arrange its whole set of counting blocks on the "bed." Ask the students to move the counters from "on the bed" to "off the bed." This step is important, especially with young students, to be certain that they understand the concept of "on the bed" and "off the bed." Also discuss with them that if only six counters are on the bed, that number is not the whole set.

Distribute the "Seven Little Hippos" recording sheets. Have a duplicate recording sheet for the overhead projector. In each group of students, appoint one student as the "writer," one student as the "mover," and for a three-student group, one student as the "checker" or "counter."

Begin with part 1 of the recording sheet. Ask each group to write the total number of counters (7). Then explain that 7/7 is read as "7-sevenths" and represents two things. First, the 7 on top explains the number of counting blocks on the bed and the 7 on the bottom explains the total number of counting blocks in the group. Ask the students how they would write the fraction to show that zero hippos were off the bed. The language used to introduce this concept to young children is important and should be consistent with many visual demonstrations.

Reread the book aloud. As each hippo falls, ask the students to (a) move a hippo "off the bed," (b) count the number of hippos on the bed, and (c) count the number of hippos off the bed. As you read the story have the students relate both the oral name and the symbol form for the fraction represented. As they fill in their recording sheets, groups of students can take turns recording their results on the transparency. Ask each group to check its answers with the overhead projector. Some students may understand this activity immediately and move ahead quickly until they finish the recording sheet. Other students may need more time to think about their answers. Pace the reading of the book aloud as needed.

REFERENCES

Conaway, Betty, and Ruby Bostick Midkiff. "Connecting Literature, Language, and Fractions." *Arithmetic Teacher* 41 (April 1994): 430–33.

McMillan, Bruce. *Eating Fractions.* New York: Scholastic, 1991.

Thaler, Mike. *Seven Little Hippos.* Illustrated by Jerry Smath. New York: Simon & Schuster, 1991.

Seven Little Hippos

Writer _____ Date _____

Mover _____

Counter _____

Part 1

Total number of hippos in the story _____

Total number of counters in one group _____

Write the fraction for the number of hippos "on the bed" and the fraction for the number "off the bed."

At the beginning of the story, all the hippos were on the bed.

Number of counters on the bed ⟶ ☐
Number of counters in one group ⟶ ☐

Number of counters off the bed ⟶ ☐
Number of counters in one group ⟶ ☐

(Continued on next page)

After one hippo falls off ....

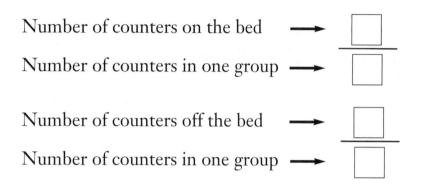

Number of counters on the bed ⟶ ☐

Number of counters in one group ⟶ ☐

Number of counters off the bed ⟶ ☐

Number of counters in one group ⟶ ☐

Part 2

Number of Hippos on the Bed	Number of Hippos That Fell off the Bed	Fraction of Hippos on the Bed	Fraction of Hippos off the Bed
7	0	$\frac{7}{7}$	$\frac{0}{7}$
6	1	$\frac{6}{7}$	$\frac{1}{7}$

Content Strand:
<u>Algebra</u>

10

Literature and Algebraic Reasoning

Cheryl A. Lubinski and Albert D. Otto

THE K–4 *Curriculum and Evaluation Standards for School Mathematics* (NCTM 1989) encourages teachers to broaden and develop their students' mathematical understandings by providing students with opportunities to explore and discuss patterns and relationships. A crucial aspect of this view is for students to realize that the role of the variable extends beyond that of an "unknown," particularly the role variables play in generalizing patterns and in describing change relationships among quantities (Philipp 1992; Usiskin 1988). The notion that young students can experience on an informal basis relationships describing change is now realized as important to the development of algebraic reasoning in early grades as recommended by reform documents.

With these thoughts in mind and using literature as our vehicle for developing algebraic reasoning, we taught in two classrooms to better determine how algebra can be informally introduced into the K–4 curriculum. In this article we share our experiences and discuss what we learned about the manner in which students describe and understand relationships involving change. In each case, the teacher to whom we refer is one of us. The primary focus of our instruction was to provide opportunities for students to facilitate the development of their algebraic reasoning so as to be better prepared to study formal algebra. We selected two books and two grade levels to assist us with our endeavors. *The Doorbell Rang* (Hutchins 1986) was used for a first-grade class, and *One Hundred Hungry Ants* (Pinczes 1993) was selected for a fourth-grade class.

The Doorbell Rang in First Grade

As the story unfolds in *The Doorbell Rang* (see fig. 10.1), two children are equally sharing twelve cookies that mom just baked, and then the doorbell rings. Two more children enter to share the cookies fairly, and then again the doorbell rings and two more children arrive who will also share the twelve cookies. As the story unfolds, it is apparent that as the number of children increases, the number of cookies each child receives decreases. The mathematical idea of change, as described in this situation, is an inverse relationship between two variables, that is, as one quantity increases, another quantity decreases, extending the role of variable beyond that of being an "unknown."

After reading the story, a two-column chart (see fig. 10.2) was carefully developed on the chalkboard as the students discussed what happened as more children arrived. We found it important in developing algebraic reasoning to have the students describe the situation and explain their answers *and* to realize that the number of cookies each child receives depends on the number of children. The students were quick to realize this fact.

Fig. 10.1. Two children sharing twelve cookies fairly. Illustration is from *The Doorbell Rang* by Pat Hutchins, © 1986 by Greenwillow Books. All rights reserved. Used with permission.

Number of Children	Number of Cookies
2	6
4	3
6	2
12	1
24	

Fig. 10.2. The students produced a chart to track cookies and children.

We asked the students to describe what they saw happening with the two columns of numbers. They responded that as the number of children got larger, the number of cookies each received got smaller, and they were able to describe their reasoning as to why this result was occurring. For example, John said, "Because there's more people, more people come and the cookies go down less because you have to share them evenly."

Although the situation in the book went from two children with six cookies each to twelve children with one cookie each, we added the additional number of 24 (referring to the number of children) to the chart to ascertain whether the students could extend their quantitative reasoning about change. The discussion proceeded as follows:

Teacher: We're going to pretend that twenty-four kids come in the door. What happens to the number of cookies? We've already decided it's going down because the more that come in, the numbers on the other side [of the chart] go down. If when there were twelve, they each got one, what happens when there's twenty-four children?

Anthony: They each get one-half.

Teacher: I'm going to write "one-half" up here [on the chart]. If you have twelve of these cookies [and 24 children], how many halves will you have?

Colton: Twenty-four.

Teacher: Emily, do you agree with that? [Emily agrees.] So, why do you think I picked the number 24? I went from 6 to 12 to 24. Why did I do that?

Brian: Maybe because it's 24 and then you took 12 away.

Teacher: I see what you're doing. I went from 6 to 12. Why did I go from 6 to 12?

Megan: Because you added on 6.

As illustrated, the first graders initially focused only on additive relationships by responding "you took 12 away" or "you added on 6." Since we wanted to focus on the multiplicative relationship between the numbers, we continued to probe the relationship of the numbers as follows:

Teacher: One of the things . . . that Brian said is that he added on. What did I do going from here to here [6 to 12] and then from here to here [12 to 24] besides adding on? Katie?

Katie: It's 6 and 6 is 12, 12 and 12 is 24.

Teacher: Okay, what else am I doing? John?

John: Pairing.

Teacher: Maria, what else am I doing?

Maria: You're doubling.

Teacher: I doubled it. That's another thing I did, too, besides pairing, John. Very good. What does it mean to double something?

Maria: If you double a number, it means that if you get that number twice, it goes to a higher number.

Teacher: So, I doubled here [referring to the number of people on the chart], and I doubled here. When I doubled the number of people, let's look at what happened to the number of cookies.

John: [I]f more people came, they have to split in half the cookies still.

This discussion on doubling proceeded reasonably easily, and many children continued to explain their answers using the phrase "splitting in half."

We found that using pictorial representations helped the students to focus on their reasoning rather than on what operation to use with the numbers. It was important to relate the children's explanations of doubling with a pictorial representation. At one point, the teacher drew on the chalkboard the situation of two children with the number of cookies each had (see fig. 10.3).

Fig. 10.3. Two children each with six cookies is illustrated.

Again, we asked the students to describe what happens to the number of cookies each child receives when the number of children doubles from two to four. The students could see from the chart that each child would then receive three cookies. However, the teacher probed for the reason by drawing the students' attention to the pictorial representation on the chalkboard, wherein two additional children had been added. She said that if "I doubled the amount of people, what happens to the [number of] cookies?" Aaron was able to show his reasoning of "splitting in half" by illustrating on the chalkboard how the two groups of six cookies could be split into four groups of three cookies by splitting a group of six into two groups of three.

Teacher: First of all, we have two people [referring to the picture on the chalkboard]; each has six cookies. Now, if two more people come, so that I doubled the number of people, what happens to the cookies? Aaron, what would you do?

Aaron: They each get three cookies.

Teacher: Show us how you would do that.

Aaron: [T]hese three here to there and these three. (See fig. 10.4.)

Teacher: When the number of people doubled, the number of cookies for this person . . . what had to happen, Maria?

Maria: They had to split it . . . in half.

In the case of how many cookies each child receives when there are forty-eight children, the students gave answers of "one-fourth" or "one-half of one-half."

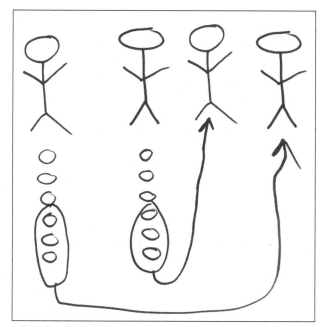

Fig. 10.4. Four children are pictured, having three cookies each.

Teacher: What would that new number be if I doubled that number? [24] Kramer?

Kramer: 48.

Teacher: I just doubled the number of people. What does that tell you about the number of cookies that each person's going to get?

Maria: I think you have to split it into sections. The cookies.

Teacher: Well, how were they split with twenty-four?

Maria: In half.

Teacher: Can you come and show me?

Maria represented the cookies' being split in half and then in half again for the forty-eight people (see fig. 10.5).

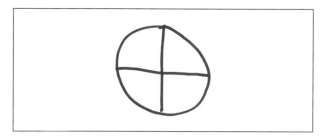

Fig. 10.5. The cookie is divided into fourths.

To provide a generalization focusing on the multiplicative relationship, the teacher then asked, "When the number of children doubles, what happens to the number of cookies each child receives?" Some students realized that as the number of children doubles, the groups of cookies will always be "split in half," the term they used. So the students realized that the number of cookies each child would receive would be only half the previous number. Thus in this way students were experiencing the mathematical concept of change as described by an inverse relationship between two quantities.

An extension of this lesson was to focus on what happens to the number of cookies each child receives if the number of children is tripled, as when the number of children is increased from 2 to 6.

Teacher: Look what I'm going to do to these numbers. We have doubled here and the number of cookies split in half. What happens if I go from two cookies to six cookies. It didn't double. What did I do?

Theodore: You added four more on.

Teacher: That's one thing that happened. What's another word [that describes what happened] besides adding?

John: You tripled . . . . You did it three times.

Teacher: Show me on the board. Start with two people. Now, what did I do with the number of people?

John: Tripled.

Teacher: How many people is he going to have if he triples the number? Anna?

Anna: Six . . . because 2 plus 2 plus 2 is 6.

Teacher: Now what happens to these cookies that these two people have if we triple the number of people? Emily, show us what's going to happen to the twelve we have.

Emily goes to the chalkboard, points to the cookies, and says, "Two will go here, and these two will go here, and then these two will go here, and these two will go here, and these two will go here, and these two will go here." The teacher asked John to use Emily's explanation and draw circles around groups of cookies to show what children get which cookies (see fig. 10.6).

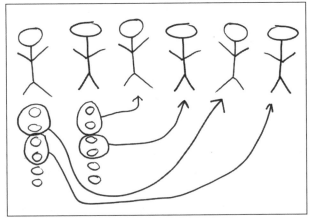

Fig. 10.6. Each child gets two cookies, as illustrated here.

The idea of change as described by an inverse relationship between the variables (the number of children and the number of cookies each child receives) was the primary focus of this lesson. As we worked, we found it important to encourage students to describe what is happening and to provide explanations for their responses. It appeared that a crucial part of these explanations was the pictorial representations. We found that if we proceeded too quickly to "make a chart," the focus seemed to shift to numerical calculating and away from reasoning. Thus, "Why?" was an important question to keep asking. Also it was important to ask "What does the 2 [the 4, the 6, or the 12] represent?" and "What does the 6 [the 3, the 2, or the 1] represent?" This questioning helped to keep the focus on the quantities involved and their relationships rather than

just on the numbers and the numerical relationships. The context of the situation was also important to developing the understanding that a change in one quantity caused a change in a second quantity. Further, if the context was not kept in focus, the emphasis of the students seemed to shift away from understanding the relationships of the changes to understanding just the properties of numbers and computation.

We suggest that during the school year, the idea of doubling and splitting in half or tripling and splitting in thirds be developed as early as first grade. Over time the students would become more flexible in their thinking, that is, they would not only be focusing on adding on or taking away, which is typical of the curriculum content in first grade. This flexibility in thought, we believe, is necessary to be able to reason algebraically and can be successfully developed at the primary level.

One Hundred Hungry Ants in Fourth Grade

The story of *One Hundred Hungry Ants* [Pinczes 1993] is about 100 ants going to a picnic in one long line. … Early in the story, the ants thought that they could all get to the picnic faster if they formed two lines instead of one, even faster if they formed four lines, and faster yet if they formed five lines. Ultimately they arrived at the picnic late after all the time spent reorganizing themselves in lines of ten. The mathematical idea of change found in this story is similar to that found in the story read to the first-grade class.

Working with fourth graders, we started in much the same way as we did in the first grade, making a chart on the chalkboard with the students quickly providing the numbers in the second column (see fig. 10.7).

Students were then asked to describe the relationships they saw. One student said that "as the number of rows get larger, the number of ants in a row gets smaller." In fact, most students realized that as the number of lines increased, the number of ants in each line decreased. Further, the students

Number of Lines	Number of Ants in Each Line
1	100
2	50
4	25
⋮	⋮

Fig. 10.7. Charting ants

EXPLORING MATHEMATICS THROUGH LITERATURE

recognized other relationships, such as when the numbers across from each other on the chart are multiplied, they always produce an answer of 100. When asked to fill in other possible numbers for the chart, the students added the following:

Number of Lines	Number of Ants in Each Line
⋮	⋮
20	5
25	4
50	2

The teacher asked, "What if I double the number of lines. What happens to the number of ants in each line?" One student responded, "Divided by 2." A discussion ensued that provided examples of where on the chart this relationship occurs.

At this point we developed the concern that the focus of the lesson had become one of computation. That is, the students knew that division is the inverse of multiplication and that multiplying the number of lines by 2 meant dividing the number of ants in each line by 2. The students were focusing on the multiplying and dividing aspects of the numbers in the chart rather than on the reasons for the changes in the numbers of ants and lines. The first graders had not done so, probably because of their limited experiences with multiplication and division facts. To bring the focus back on quantitative reasoning, we modified our teaching strategy by reinforcing the importance of having the students develop a strategy that would lend itself to a reasoning process about changes rather than focus on the computation. We believe that this strategy ensued because the fourth graders quickly recognized the number facts of the numbers being used.

To shift our focus back to our purpose of developing quantitative reasoning, we used pictorial representations. The teacher drew a line of points on the chalkboard and suggested that it represented the 100 ants. Then she asked, "If the number of lines is one, what happens to the number of ants in each line when we double the number of lines?" One student said, "It is divided into half and half the ants," meaning that 100 is divided or split in half and that 50 ants are in each half. When the teacher asked what happens when the number of lines doubled again, the students realized that each group of 50 ants is split into half and that the number of lines would be four and the number of ants in each line

would be half of 50, or 25. We illustrated this fact by using the pictorial representation of what was happening to the number of lines. Students were also able to explain what happened to the number of ants in a line if the number of lines of ants was five times as many. The teacher asked if it were possible to have eight lines, and the students explained why some numbers could not be used if we were talking about whole ants!

As an extension, we changed our context to cookies (because cookies can be split in half) in a line to be able to develop our chart further and to focus on reasoning about quantities.

Teacher: We're going from twenty rows to forty. We're doubling the number of rows. What happens to the number of cookies in a row? It used to be five; it's now going to be what?

Marcia: Two and a half.

Teacher: Two and a half. Why?

Sergio: There's two cookies and then 2 times 2 is 4 and that's only part of 5, and then you divide the other cookie in half.

We believe that students' focusing on the kind of changes that can take place between two quantities is important in developing their preparation for algebra.

Reflections

In high school algebra courses, the type of change relationship described in our two stories is referred to as *inverse variation* and described algebraically as $y = k/x$. Even though we did not use this algebraic representation, the primary-age students were still able to discuss and understand the concept, since we focused on quantities and their relationships and not just on the numbers and the numerical relationships. Although our emphasis was on change described by an inverse relationship, both situations are also examples of functions because a value for one quantity determines a value for the other quantity. While developing the charts, we focused on "the number of" to reinforce the concept that a variable represents a number and is not merely a label for children, cookies, ants, or lines. The use of a letter as a label seems to present students with difficulties when first studying algebra.

Since pictorial representations seemed to assist the students in developing an understanding of how a change in one quantity produced a change in a second, we prefer that students draw their own pictures because it is easy for teachers to misrepresent the reasoning of the student. Further, we believe that even young students can reason algebraically if given the opportunity. However, we also believe that unless these opportunities are provided, understanding formal algebra will continue to be a struggle for most students. We suggest that teachers' instructional decision making incorporate mathematics topics that encourage flexibility of thought about situations involving patterns and relationships among quantities. To do so successfully, the focus of instruction needs to be on reasoning, *not* on the manipulation of numbers. We found it helpful to be aware of recommendations in such reform documents as the *Curriculum and Evaluation Standards*, which provided the basis for our decision making about the type of reasoning opportunities that we could give primary-age students.

We believe that opportunities exist for primary-age students to experience algebraic reasoning with patterns and relationships and that these situations should be varied to include multiplicative reasoning and inverse variation. Children's literature was an effective vehicle for us to use to explore change and relationships and begin to develop algebraic reasoning.

REFERENCES

Hutchins, Pat. *The Doorbell Rang*. New York: Greenwillow Books, 1986.

National Council of Teachers of Mathematics (NCTM). *Curriculum and Evaluation Standards for School Mathematics*. Reston, Va.: NCTM, 1989.

Philipp, Randolph A. "The Many Uses of Algebraic Variables." *Mathematics Teacher* 85 (October 1992): 557–61.

Pinczes, Elinor J. *One Hundred Hungry Ants*. Boston: Houghton Mifflin Co., 1993.

Usiskin, Zalman. "Conceptions of School Algebra and Uses of Variables." In *The Ideas of Algebra, K–12*, 1988 Yearbook of the National Council of Teachers of Mathematics (NCTM), edited by Arthur F. Coxford, pp. 8–19. Reston, Va.: NCTM, 1988.

Teaching Notes for

"Literature and Algebraic Reasoning"

by Cheryl A. Lubinski and Albert D. Otto

Grade range:	1–5
Mathematical topic:	Patterns and tables leading to algebra
Children's books:	*The Doorbell Rang* by Pat Hutchins
	One Hundred Hungry Ants by Elinor Pinczes
Materials:	"Algebraic Reasoning" recording sheets 1 and 2

Discussion of the mathematics: The Algebra Standard for grades Pre-K–2 recommends that young students "analyze how both repeating and growing patterns are generated" (NCTM 2000, p. 90) and further that "[t]eachers in grades 1 and 2 should provide experiences for students to learn to use charts and tables for recording and organizing information in varying formats" (NCTM 2000, p. 92).

In grades 3–5 "[a]s students explore patterns and note relationships, they should be encouraged to represent their thinking" (NCTM 2000, p. 161), and further, teachers will need to assist students with how to symbolically represent their thinking. Also in these grades, "[s]tudents should have opportunities to study situations that display different patterns of change—change that occurs at a constant rate . . . and rates of change that increase or decrease" (NCTM 2000, p.163). The Algebra Standard presents examples for teachers so that they can provide "opportunities to engage students in thinking about how to articulate and express a generalization" (NCTM 2000, p. 160).

Teacher notes: In our article the children's books *The Doorbell Rang* and *One Hundred Hungry Ants* were the bases of tasks that focus on reasoning and the underpinnings of algebra. Teacher questions as well as the thinking of first and fourth graders are

also featured in the article. The problems posed below are designed as additional tasks that can be used to extend this type of thinking. The purposes of these tasks are to help students use charts and tables for recording and organizing information about various patterns of change, to learn to better articulate what changes occur and why, and to begin to express a generalization about a change situation.

To launch the task, discuss the problem with the class. Students could initially work the problem in pairs or individually. A whole-class discussion should highlight the strategies that students used as well as their generalizations; this forum would also be an opportunity to extend the solution to a graph and an equation, depending on students' backgrounds. Note: Some students may observe that their state requires a five-cent deposit and may decide to solve this related problem.

Soft-Drink-Can Task

For every soft-drink can that you return to the store, you receive 10¢. What happens if you return 1 can? If you return 2 cans? How much do you get for 4 cans? For 8 cans? Or any number (x) of cans? How can we represent this information using a chart?

Develop the table below with the students. Note: this task is appropriate for first and second graders.

Number of Soft-Drink Cans	Number of Cents
0	
1	
2	
3	
4	
5	
.	
.	
.	
x	$10x$

An important point for students to note is that as the number of soft-drink cans increases by 1, the number of cents increases by 10. In grades 3–5, this relationship could also be represented with a graph in which the horizontal axis represents the number of soft-drink cans and the vertical axis represents the number of cents. (Teacher note: This change situation is described as *direct variation* (proportional) because the graph is linear and goes through the origin.) On the graph, the number of cents received depends on the number of soft-drink cans collected. The graph is also *discrete;* that is, the situation is best represented as a set of points on a line. Numbers cannot occur between the points because we cannot reasonably talk about fractional parts of cans or cents in this situation.

Generalization. The number of soft-drink cans (x) is multiplied by the number of cents received for each can to get the total number of cents.

Equation. If y represents the total number of cents and x represents the number of soft-drink cans, then $y = 10x$.

Author note: The variables x and y are used to better connect with the typical axes labels; however, we most often use other letters to represent situations.

For example, the number of soft-drink cans can be represented by the letter n and the total number of cents can be represented by c. Thus the equation becomes $c = 10n$ and the axes are labeled n and c, respectively, instead of x and y.

Birthday-Money Task

My grandpa gave me $7.00 for my birthday. If I spend $0.75 on candy every day, how much money will I have left after 3 days? After 6 days? After 9 days? Also, for how many days can I expect to be able to buy candy? Note: this task is appropriate for grades 1 through 5.

As with the soft-drink-can task, the class can develop a chart with the labels, number of days buying candy (d), and number of dollars left (l). The number of dollars left depends on the number of days buying candy and therefore would be used to label the vertical axis of a graph. The situation would be represented by the equation $l = 7.00 - .75d$, where d represents the number of days one bought candy.

Teacher note: For better understanding, the term *number* should be used consistently in these change situations. That is, the "number of" (specific object) rather than *only* the object's name (e.g. soft-drink cans). Also, if the recording sheets are sent home, we recommend including both tasks on the recording sheets, no matter what the grade level, so that parents can see how the algebraic concepts are developed over grade levels.

REFERENCES

Hutchins, Pat. *The Doorbell Rang.* New York: Greenwillow Books, 1986.

Lubinski Cheryl A., and Albert D. Otto. "Literature and Algebraic Reasoning." *Teaching Children Mathematics* 3 (February 1997): 290–95.

National Council of Teachers of Mathematics (NCTM). *Principles and Standards for School Mathematics.* Reston, Va.: NCTM, 2000.

Pinczes, Elinor. *One Hundred Hungry Ants.* Boston: Houghton Mifflin Co., 1993.

Algebraic Reasoning

Name_____

Date _____

SOFT-DRINK-CAN TASK: (Appropriate for grades 1 and 2) For every soft-drink can that you return to the store, you receive 10¢. What happens if you return 1 can? If you return 2 cans? How much do you get for 4 cans? For 8 cans? Or any number (x) of cans? How can we represent this information using a chart?

Number of Soft-Drink Cans   **Number of Cents**

Generalization: (Appropriate for grades 3 through 5) Write a sentence that describes the relationship between the number of soft-drink cans and the number of cents.

Algebraic Reasoning

Recording Sheet 2

Name_____

Date _____

BIRTHDAY-MONEY TASK: (Appropriate for grades 1 and 2) My grandpa gave me $7.00 for my birthday. If I spend $0.75 on candy every day, how much money will I have left after 3 days? After 6 days? After 9 days? Also, for how many days can I expect to be able to buy candy?

Generalization: (Appropriate for grades 3 through 5) Write a sentence or an equation that describes the relationship between the number of days buying candy (*d*) and the number of dollars left (*l*).

11

Exploring Algebraic Patterns through Literature

Richard A. Austin and Denisse R. Thompson

ACTIVITIES that engage middle school students in investigating and extending patterns are essential in developing students' algebraic thinking. The *Curriculum and Evaluation Standards for School Mathematics* (NCTM 1989) for grades 5–8 and the position statement on "Algebra for Everyone" (NCTM 1994) describe the importance of using patterns and relationships to develop algebraic thinking. Hence, it seems reasonable that many activities describing, extending, and modifying patterns should be part of the middle school mathematics experience, both before and during formal algebra study.

This article presents an example of using literature to develop or expand algebraic thinking in an interesting environment that connects algebra to various situations. Many books classified as children's literature and used in K–5 classrooms contain mathematical content appropriate for use in a middle school class. The mathematics embedded in the story can be explored at an introductory level by elementary children; the more advanced mathematical abilities of middle school children can elicit a deeper and richer discussion of the mathematics. Because children's literature is a natural hook to interest and to motivate students of many ages, middle-grades teachers should also consider how this tool might effectively be used in the classroom.

We have found a number of children's books that can be used to introduce and encourage algebraic thinking. See the additional resources list following the references. Any one of these books could be used to explore rich mathe-matical patterns.

The particular lessons and activities discussed in this article relate to *Anno's Magic Seeds* (Anno 1995).

Summary of *Anno's Magic Seeds*

Jack is a young man who is given two magic seeds by a wise man and instructed to eat one and bury, or plant, the other. He will not be hungry for an entire year, and the planted seed will yield two more magic seeds the next year. Jack continues this process for several years until he decides to plant both seeds. When Jack plants two seeds, his yield is four seeds. He eats one seed and buries the others. This pattern of eating one and burying the other continues until he meets Alice. At this point, the process again changes and becomes more complex. Jack and Alice eventually marry, have a child, and begin selling seeds. Ultimately, a storm brings destruction, but a few seeds are preserved, and life with all its patterns begins again.

Development of the lessons

Anno asks questions within the story to encourage the reader to use mathematics to describe what is happening to both Jack and his seeds. The patterns developed in the story can be expressed in various ways. Although the ability to express the patterns using symbolic algebra is often beyond them, most middle school students are able to give verbal and written descriptions, as well as extensions, of the patterns.

We visited both a sixth-grade-mathematics class and a seventh-grade-prealgebra class to investigate *Anno's Magic Seeds*. We discovered that sixth- and seventh-grade students enjoyed listening to the story, which then became a motivational device for exploring the patterns presented. The activities described here required two sessions per class to complete and could easily have taken a third day to tie up loose ends and to investigate extensions. At the end of the first day with the seventh-grade class, one student said to another, "I thought today was going to be boring." She was surprised to find that the story was interesting and that exploring the mathematics was entertaining.

Students were given activity sheets (see the figs. 11.1–11.3) developed by the authors to guide their thinking and help them organize their data tables. For these students, this early experience with such a lesson required a level of structure to ensure that students were engaged in the mathematics that we were interested in discussing. Students were encouraged to use calculators. The activities to accompany *Anno's Magic Seeds* are designed to bridge the gap from simply extending patterns to the more formal use of variables to express the patterns symbolically.

When literature is connected to a mathematics lesson, one usually reads the entire story and then deals with the mathematics. However, we wanted students to extend a pattern beyond the time frame allotted in the story, so we designed the lessons so that a portion of the story was read, patterns were explored and discussed, and then the story was continued. Each time that the patterns changed—because of planting both seeds, meeting Alice, or having a baby—we stopped the story and explored the mathematics.

Activity sheet 1

The first activity sheet (see fig. 11.1) was designed so that students would begin to think about and describe patterns in a simple situation. Table 11.1 contains a completed table from activity sheet 1. Although the patterns in this table may seem repetitious, they can be described by *constant functions*, one of the function families studied in an algebra course.

When asked to describe the patterns seen in the table, such responses as the following were obtained:

He had two seeds produced, one eaten, and one buried, for six years. (Justin, grade 6)

2 seeds are produced every year. 1 seed was buried every year and 1 seed was eaten every year. (Kristy, grade 7)

2 is repeating, 1 is repeating, 1 is repeating. (Jamal, grade 7)

At both grade levels, students noticed that the patterns were the same each year. When asked to explain this result, students recognized that Jack did the same thing each year and so the patterns did not change.

When asked if Jack was correct in thinking that this pattern would continue forever, we got mixed opinions. Michelle, grade 6, said, "No, because he might not get a chance to let the rest grow." "No, if he stops planting one seed," replied Laurie, grade 6. "Yes, because if he doesn't change the pattern of his actions, then the results will continually stay the same until he decides to stop or change his pattern," said Kristy, grade 7. "Yes, because he will always do the exact amount he was directed to, which is 2 produced, 1 eaten, 1 buried," offered Heather, grade 7. Thus, this exploration gave students a concrete example of a constant function, and they recognized that the constant patterns would continue as long as Jack continued to do the same thing. The patterns would change only if Jack's actions changed.

Neither group of students had yet been exposed to variables. When asked to write a relationship between the number of seeds eaten, e, the number buried, b, and the number produced, p, students initially wondered what e, b, and p could represent. Such questions offered an opportunity to discuss the fact that variables could take on any values. The only constraint was the information in the given situation $e + b = p$. Thus, knowing values for e and b allows the values for p to be found.

We spent roughly one-third of the first class period on the beginning of the story and activity sheet 1.

Activity sheet 2

Before we continued the story, students were asked what might happen next and speculated that Jack might bury both seeds and eat something else for that year, which is exactly what happens. We continued reading the story from the time that Jack buried both seeds until he met Alice. Throughout the reading, students were asked to predict how Jack would use the seeds in a given year. Jack always ate one and buried the rest. Each buried seed produced twice that number of seeds the following year. Hence, by the time students received activity sheet 2 (see fig. 11.2), they had orally produced several of the values reconstructed in table 11.2.

Sixth and seventh graders differed in their ability to articulate their descriptions of the pattern, but almost all were able to operationalize the patterns by completing the table. In the first question, students were asked what they noticed about the number of

Anno's Magic Seeds

Activity sheet 1

Name_____

Read the story until Jack says, "This can just go on and on in the same way forever." Use the information in the story to complete the table below.

Year	0	1	2	3	4	5	6
Number of seeds produced	——						
Number of seeds eaten	1						
Number of seeds buried	1						

Use the results in the table to answer the following questions.

1. a. What do you notice about the number of seeds produced each year?

   b. Explain why you get this result.

2. Describe all the patterns you see in the table.

3. Jack thought, "This can just go on and on in the same way forever." Is he right? How do you know?

4. If the patterns in the table continued in the same way, what would the next four columns be?

Year	7	8	9	10
Number of seeds produced				
Number of seeds eaten				
Number of seeds buried				

5. a. Describe, in words, a relationship among the number of seeds eaten, the number of seeds buried, and the number of seeds produced.

   b. If p = number of seeds produced, e = number of seeds eaten, and b = number of seeds buried, describe the relationship from part (a) using p, e, and b.

Fig. 11.1. Activity sheet 1

TABLE 11.1

A Completed Table from Activity Sheet 1

Year	0	1	2	3	4	5	6
Number of seeds produced	——	2	2	2	2	2	2
Number of seeds eaten	1	1	1	1	1	1	1
Number of seeds buried	1	1	1	1	1	1	1

seeds produced in a year and to explain their thinking. Seventh graders were more likely to try to write the relationship with a number sentence and to articulate that the number buried in *this* year is used to find the number produced *next* year. Here are some sample responses.

They double each year. They are even because you double the number of seeds buried that year. (Laurie, grade 6)

2 × the buried number [because] he didn't bury one, he buried two. (Darrell, grade 6)

Two times the bottom number you get your answer because I multiplyed [sic] 2 times the bottom number. (Joshua, grade 6)

It's the number of seeds burried [sic] plus itself because that's what you get on the table with your calculation. (Heather, grade 7)

[T]here are twice as many as planted the year before. [B]ecause each year two seeds are grown for each seed planted and he eats one and burrys [sic] the other. (Joshua, grade 7)

The number of seeds buried × 2 = the number of seeds produced for the next year because each plant gets 2 seeds, so if 5 seeds are buried, then the next year there will be 10 seeds. (Kristy, grade 7)

When asked to complete the table for the next five years if the patterns continued in the same way, students used their calculators to complete the patterns efficiently. Students also began to engage in more cooperative group dialogue as they compared values.

Sixth graders had more difficulty than seventh graders in trying to determine whether it would have been possible for Jack to bury 2025 seeds. We had expected students to consider the types of numbers in the table and determine whether this figure would

have been reasonable. Instead, students used the current values in the extended table. In year 10, 1025 seeds would be buried. Hence, we obtained responses along the following lines:

No, because if he planted again, he would have 2050, so he would have to save some or something. (Joyce, grade 7)

No, because 1025 × 2 = 2050 – 1 = 2049, it still [doesn't] equal 2025. (Marjorie, grade 7)

A couple of seventh graders mirrored Katrina's response: "Yes, because each year he gets an even number of seeds, eats one, and buries an odd number of seeds." One sixth grader did not think Jack could bury that many seeds because his yard could not get any larger.

This situation could be interpreted in a variety of ways. If students used only the values given in the story, then planting the given number of seeds was not possible. If the problem was hypothetical, then it would be possible to bury 2025 seeds, assuming that 2026 were produced that year and Jack ate one. The focus of the activity was not to find one specific answer but rather to apply algebraic thinking to make a decision and then to give a reasonable justification for it.

After having completed the extended table, students had little difficulty in determining the number of seeds that would be produced if 2000 seeds were buried. However, an interesting extension developed in the seventh-grade class. Students wondered how long it would take to plant or bury 2000 seeds. We used this teachable moment to ask students to determine how long it would take to bury that many seeds if we could bury one seed every two seconds. We found that we could bury 2000 seeds in about 66 minutes. Then we extended this question to determine the number of seeds we could bury in a year if we buried 1 seed every 2 seconds and worked 4 hours per day for 5 days a week. Students became

Anno's Magic Seeds

Activity sheet 2

Name_____

Continue reading the story from the time that Jack decides to bury both seeds until he meets Alice. Use the information in the story to complete the table below. The year that Jack buries both seeds is labeled Year 0.

Year	0	1	2	3	4	5
Number of seeds produced	——	4				
Number of seeds eaten	0	1				
Number of seeds buried	2	3				

Use the results in the table to answer the following questions.

1. a. What do you notice about the number of seeds produced each year?
   b. Explain why you get this result.
2. Describe all the patterns you see in the table.
3. If the patterns in the table continued in the same way, what would the next five columns be?

Year	6	7	8	9	10
Number of seeds produced	——				
Number of seeds eaten					
Number of seeds buried					

4. Suppose that Jack lost track of the number of seeds. He told a friend that he thought he buried 2025 seeds. Is this value possible? Explain your answer.
5. a. To find the number of seeds produced in any year, what information from the table do you need to know?
   b. Suppose that in some year 2000 seeds were buried. How many seeds would be produced and how many seeds would be buried the next year?
6. a. Describe in words a relationship among the number of seeds eaten, the number of seeds buried, and the number of seeds produced.
   b. If p = the number of seeds produced, e = the number of seeds eaten, and b = the number of seeds buried, describe the relationship from part (a) using p, e, and b.
   c. Suppose that in some year 88 seeds are buried. How many seeds would be produced the next year?
   d. Suppose that in some year b seeds are buried. How many seeds would be produced the next year?
7. Use the results from your table to complete the graph you were given.

Challenge: Suppose that y represents the year. Find a rule that gives the number of seeds buried in year y.

Fig. 11.2. Activity sheet 2

TABLE 11.2

A Completed Table from Activity Sheet 2

Year	0	1	2	3	4	5
Number of seeds produced	——	4	6	10	18	34
Number of seeds eaten	0	1	1	1	1	1
Number of seeds buried	2	3	5	9	17	33

excited as they found the number of seeds buried in a week and then used the number of weeks in a year to determine the total number of seeds buried in a year. The result was quite large, and students had to write their answers in scientific notation, a topic that they had recently been studying. The extension to rates and scientific notation was an added bonus that we had not previously considered.

It was very instructive to have students graph the data in the table, placing the "year" on the horizontal axis and the "number of seeds buried" on the vertical axis marked off in increments of 10. Even though students were not prepared to express the relationship algebraically, they were able to graph the relationship. The number of seeds buried in year y can be represented by $2^y + 1$, with the understanding that year 0 represents the first year that two seeds were buried. Hence, middle school students were introduced to graphing exponential functions. We believe that it is very important that students have the opportunity to graph not only linear functions but a wide variety of functions. An added benefit of this graphing exercise was that students had to use different scales on the two axes.

We spent roughly two-thirds of the first class period on activity sheet 2 and began the second class period with the graph.

Activity sheet 3

Once Jack meets Alice, the patterns become more complex. Hence, activity sheet 3 was handed out to students so that they could complete the patterns as we read the third portion of the story (see fig. 11.3). Table 11.3 contains a completed table for activity sheet 3 through year 9.

Several interesting results occurred while completing this table. Although the number of seeds produced in one year continued to be twice the number of seeds buried the previous year, other relationships also had to be considered. Students had to recognize that the sum of the number of

seeds eaten, the number given away, the number stored, the number sold but not stored, and the number buried had to equal the number of seeds produced from those planted the previous year. When students attempted to determine the number of seeds buried each year, they had to use this relationship to justify their results.

Several students had initial difficulty with some of the language in the story that related to selling seeds. During year 7, Jack stored 16 seeds. In year 8, Jack sold 60 seeds, including the 16 stored the previous year. Some students initially thought that he sold 76, not understanding the meaning of the word *including*. Students had to argue their position with one another until the class was convinced about which result was more appropriate for the number sold.

In addition to using the story to complete the table for years 6–9, we asked students to complete the table for years 10 and 11. Many reasonable results are possible, subject to the following constraints: the number of seeds produced in year 10 must be 240; the number of seeds produced in year 11 must be twice the number buried in year 10; and the sum of the number eaten, given away, stored, sold but not stored, and buried must equal the number produced in that year. We found that some of the students were quite proficient in completing their tables while considering these constraints. Others determined the number produced in year 10 correctly and then completed the remainder of the table haphazardly without regard to the physical constraints of the problem. A third day on this lesson would have given us time to address these difficulties.

Assigning the students to write an ending to the story and then write two problems was quite revealing. Some of the students focused on Jack's dying or being killed, since the seventh-grade visit occurred on Halloween. Others wrote interesting twists to the story, as evident in the student samples in figures 11.4–11.5.

Anno's Magic Seeds

Name_____

Read the story from the time when Jack meets Alice until Jack says, "The wind is blowing awfully hard!" Use the information in the story to complete the table below for years 6, 7, 8, and 9. In the story, Jack meets Alice in year 6.

Year	6	7	8	9	10	11
Number of seeds produced	66					
Number of seeds eaten	2					
Number of seeds given away	_____					
Number of seeds stored	_____					
Number of seeds sold that have not been stored	_____					
Number of seeds buried	64					

1. Describe all the patterns that you see in the table.

2. If the patterns were to continue in the same way, predict the values in the table for years 10 and 11.

3. a. For years 8 and 9, describe in words a relationship among the number of seeds produced, the number of seeds eaten, the number of seeds stored, the number of seeds sold that had not been stored, and the number of seeds buried.
   b. How can you describe the relationship in part (a) using symbols?

4. From the table, there seems to be a maximum number of seeds that can be produced in any year. What are some reasons why such a maximum number exists?

5. Write an ending to the story. Then write two problems that other students could answer after reading your ending.

Read the rest of the story.

6. Jack is able to save 10 seeds. The family eats 3 and buries 7. Suppose that Jack will sell some of the seeds as soon as he produces at least 35 in one year. How long will it be before Jack sells some of the seeds?

7. Suppose that Jack and Alice have another child as soon as the storm is over. How much longer would it take before Jack produces at least 35 seeds in one year?

Fig. 11.3. Activity sheet 3

TABLE 11.3
A Completed Table from Activity Sheet 3

Year	6	7	8	9	10	11
Number of seeds produced	66	128	200	240		
Number of seeds eaten	2	2	2	3		
Number of seeds given away	____	10	____	____		
Number of seeds stored	____	16	34	51		
Number of seeds sold that have not been stored	____	____	44	66		
Number of seeds buried	64	100	120	120		

After students completed their story endings and presented some of them to the class, we read the ending of the story. Students then completed the final two questions on activity sheet 3 and had no difficulty following the patterns and determining the number of years before the condition was met.

Conclusion

Currently in our society, the mention of the word *algebra* causes many people to experience discomfort. Even middle school students who have not yet taken an algebra course often have negative

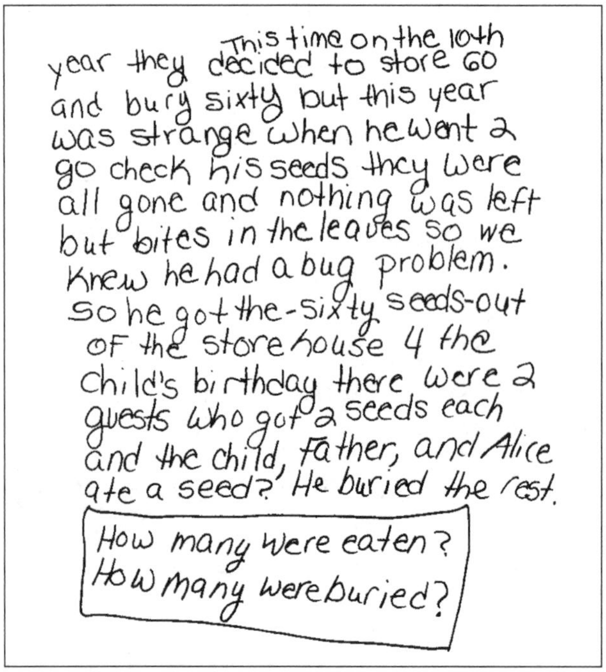

Fig. 11.4 Story written by Joyce, grade 7

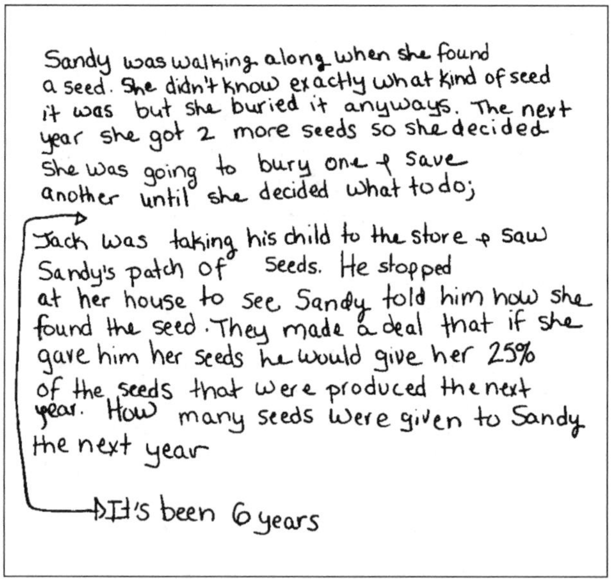

Fig. 11.5 Story written by Kristy, grade 7

views about algebra and do not believe they are capable of exploring algebraic relationships. Using literature as a vehicle to introduce patterns and then explore, describe, and extend those patterns creates algebraic experiences in an interesting and non-threatening manner. Students appeared to enjoy the lessons and were able to express a constant function, an exponential function, and a recursive function in their own words. Having students write about the mathematical patterns found in the story and extend those patterns helps develop algebraic thinking, since they will need to express these relationships symbolically in an algebra class. With the building of algebraic thinking from activities like those developed here, students will be better able to understand the more abstract symbolic approach to functions and patterns used to model real-world situations.

REFERENCES

Anno, Mitsumasa. *Anno's Magic Seeds*. New York: Philomel Books, 1995.

National Council of Teachers of Mathematics (NCTM). *Curriculum and Evaluation Standards for School Mathematics*. Reston, Va.: NCTM, 1989.

————. "Algebra for Everyone . . . More Than a Change in Enrollment Patterns." Reston, Va.: NCTM, 1994. Position statement.

ADDITIONAL RESOURCES

Anno, Masaichiro, and Mitsumasa Anno. *Anno's Mysterious Multiplying Jar*. New York: Philomel Books, 1983.

Interesting patterns of objects found in a jar are used to develop factorials.

Barry, David. *The Rajah's Rice: A Mathematical Folktale from India*. New York: W. H. Freeman & Co., 1994.

In this folktale a pattern is started by placing two grains of rice on the first square of a chessboard, four on the second square, and so on, doubling the number of grains of rice on each new square.

Birch, David. *The King's Chessboard*. New York: Puffin Pied Piper Books, 1988.

This retelling of the Indian folktale *The Rajah's Rice* begins with one grain of rice on the first square.

Clement, Rod. *Counting on Frank*. Milwaukee, Wisc.: Gareth Stevens Publishing, 1991.

Although the primary focus of this story is on counting, proportions and rates are used throughout in humorous ways.

Hong, Lily Toy. *Two of Everything*. Morton Grove, Ill.: Albert Whitman & Co., 1993.

This tale from China deals with a pot that doubles everything placed into it.

Pittman, Helena Clare. *A Grain of Rice*. New York: Bantam Skylark Books, 1986.

A humble servant requests one grain of rice on the first day, with the amount of rice to be doubled each day for 100 days. This version of the tale is set in China.

Teaching Notes for

"Exploring Algebraic Patterns through Literature"

by Richard A. Austin and Denisse R. Thompson

Grade range:	6–8
Mathematical topics:	Algebraic patterns, tables, and data collection
Children's book:	*Anno's Magic Seeds* by Mitsumasa Anno
Materials:	*"Anno's Magic Seeds"* recording sheets 1–3, graph paper, graphing calculators (optional)

Discussion of the mathematics: The Algebra Standard for grades 6–8 recommends that students "represent, analyze, and generalize a variety of patterns with tables, graphs, words, and when possible, symbolic rules" (NCTM 2000, p. 222). The activity sheets, teacher notes, and the article focus on collecting data, making tables, writing equations, and plotting graphs to pursue the questions posed.

"A major goal in the middle grades is to develop students' facility with using patterns and functions to represent, model, and analyze a variety of phenomena and relationships in mathematical problems or in the real world" (NCTM 2000, p. 227). The problems posed in *Anno's Magic Seeds* provide middle-grades students with an opportunity to pursue that goal as well as to pursue another NCTM recommendation, that of exploring nonlinear functions.

Teacher notes: The activity sheets discussed in the article have been reproduced and follow these notes. As detailed in the article, the activity sheets helped our students keep track of their data and also managed to keep their focus on the patterns that were well developed in the story. In particular, *"Anno's Magic Seeds"* recording sheet 3, through question 5, provides quite a nice, open-ended inquiry. Guidelines on suggested time frame, details of how we

launched the activity, and examples of students' thinking are included in the article.

Our recording sheets focused on collecting data and making tables to answer questions. The students moved to graphing the data from the tables. They also had an opportunity to generate equations from a real context.

In *"Anno's Magic Seeds"* recording sheet 1, students construct a constant function showing that two seeds were produced over a number of years.

In *"Anno's Magic Seeds"* recording sheet 2, students are asked to graph the number of seeds buried versus the number of years transpired, and they obtain an exponential graph. They could also graph the number of seeds produced versus the number of years transpired and obtain another exponential graph. Observe that this graph ($p = 2^y + 2$) is different from the graph of the number of seeds buried versus number of years, which is $b = 2^y + 1$. In both situations y is the number of years.

An additional graphing exercise might involve changing the story. Again, have Jack eat one seed and plant the rest. Each buried seed would then produce three seeds rather than two. This variation would allow the exploration of yet another relationship. Students might investigate the following question: How much faster (in years) would Jack produce 1000 seeds if 3 seeds were produced for each seed buried rather than 2 seeds for each seed buried? Students could find the answer from a table or from a graph, or both.

Some teachers might want to use this story as an entry into a writing assignment. For example, have students write a sequel to the story. After the storm Jack and his family started over with only the ten seeds Jack saved. What happened? Note: two examples of student writing are included in the article.

We would also like to recommend some children's books that involve doubling. In the list below, the last four books all revolve around a scenario in which an amount of rice doubles on each consecutive day. Each book has a different setting, but they also have a great deal in common.

Hong, Lily Toy. *Two of Everything*. Morton Grove, Ill.: Albert Whitman & Co., 1993.

> This story is a Chinese folktale about a couple who find a brass pot that doubles whatever is placed inside it.

Barry, David. *The Rajah's Rice: A Mathematical Folktale from India*. Illustrated by Donna Perrone. New York: W. H. Freeman & Co., 1994.

> A young girl is rewarded for healing sick elephants by receiving two grains of rice from the rajah on the first day, with the amount doubling each day until all the squares of his chessboard are covered.

Birch, David. *The King's Chessboard*. Illustrated by Devis Grebu. New York: Puffin Pied Piper Books, 1988.

> For a reward a wise man requests of the King one grain of rice for the first day, with the amount doubling each day for the number of days equal to the number of squares on the King's chessboard.

Demi. *One Grain of Rice: A Mathematical Folktale*. New York: Scholastic, 1997.

> A young girl uses her wits and helps feed starving people as she receives an amount of rice that doubles each day.

Pittman, Helena Clare. *A Grain of Rice*. New York: Bantam Skylark Books, 1986.

> A humble servant gets one grain of rice on the first day from the Emperor, with the amount to double each day for 100 days. (Several activities that can be completed using this book as a resource can be found in Thompson, Chappell, and Austin [1999].)

REFERENCES

Anno, Mitsumasa. *Anno's Magic Seeds*. New York: Philomel Books, 1995.

Austin, Richard A., and Denisse R. Thompson. "Exploring Algebraic Patterns through Literature." *Mathematics Teaching in the Middle School 2* (February 1997): 274–81.

National Council of Teachers of Mathematics (NCTM). *Principles and Standards for School Mathematics*. Reston, Va.: NCTM, 2000.

Thompson, Denisse R., Michaele F. Chappell, and Richard A. Austin. "Exploring Mathematics through Asian Folktales." In *Changing the Faces of Mathematics: Perspectives on Asian Americans and Pacific Islanders*, edited by Carol A. Edwards, pp. 1–11. Reston, Va.: National Council of Teachers of Mathematics, 1999.

Name _____ Date _____

Read the story until Jack says, "This can just go on and on in the same way forever." Use the information in the story to complete the table below.

Year	0	1	2	3	4	5	6
Number of seeds produced	——						
Number of seeds eaten	1						
Number of seeds buried	1						

Use the results in the table to answer the following questions on a separate sheet of paper.

1. a. What do you notice about the number of seeds produced each year?

   b. Explain why you get this result.

2. Describe all the patterns you see in the table.

3. Jack thought, "This can just go on and on in the same way forever." Is he right? How do you know?

4. If the patterns in the table continued in the same way, what would the next four columns be?

Year	7	8	9	10
Number of seeds produced				
Number of seeds eaten				
Number of seeds buried				

5. a. Describe, in words, a relationship among the number of seeds eaten, the number of seeds buried, and the number of seeds produced.

   b. If p = number of seeds produced, e = number of seeds eaten, and b = number of seeds buried, describe the relationship from part (a) using p, e, and b.

Anno's Magic Seeds
Recording Sheet 2

Name _____ Date _____

Continue reading the story from the time that Jack decides to bury both seeds until he meets Alice. Use the information in the story to complete the table below. The year that Jack buries both seeds is labeled Year 0.

Year	0	1	2	3	4	5
Number of seeds produced	——	4				
Number of seeds eaten	0	1				
Number of seeds buried	2	3				

Use the results in the table to answer the following questions on a separate sheet of paper.

1. a. What do you notice about the number of seeds produced each year?
   b. Explain why you get this result.
2. Describe all the patterns you see in the table.
3. If the patterns in the table continued in the same way, what would the next five columns be?

Year	6	7	8	9	10
Number of seeds produced	——				
Number of seeds eaten					
Number of seeds buried					

4. Suppose that Jack lost track of the number of seeds. He told a friend that he thought he buried 2025 seeds. Is this value possible? Explain your answer.
5. a. To find the number of seeds produced in any year, what information from the table do you need to know?
   b. Suppose that in some year 2000 seeds were buried. How many seeds would be produced, and how many seeds would be buried the next year?
6. a. Describe in words a relationship among the number of seeds eaten, the number of seeds buried, and the number of seeds produced.
   b. If p = the number of seeds produced, e = the number of seeds eaten, and b = the number of seeds buried, describe the relationship from part (a) using p, e, and b.
   c. Suppose that in some year 88 seeds are buried. How many seeds would be produced the next year?
   d. Suppose that in some year b seeds are buried. How many seeds would be produced the next year?
7. Use the results from your table to complete the graph you were given.

Challenge: Suppose that y represents the year. Find a rule that gives the number of seeds buried in year y.

Name _____ Date _____

Read the story from the time when Jack meets Alice until Jack says, "The wind is blowing awfully hard!" Use the information in the story to complete the table below for years 6, 7, 8, and 9. In the story, Jack meets Alice in year 6. Next, answer the questions below on a separate sheet of paper.

Year	6	7	8	9	10	11
Number of seeds produced	66					
Number of seeds eaten	2					
Number of seeds given away	____					
Number of seeds stored	____					
Number of seeds sold that have not been stored	____					
Number of seeds buried	64					

1. Describe all the patterns that you see in the table.

2. If the patterns were to continue in the same way, predict the values in the table for years 10 and 11.

3. a. For years 8 and 9, describe in words a relationship among the number of seeds produced, the number of seeds eaten, the number of seeds stored, the number of seeds sold that had not been stored, and the number of seeds buried.
   b. How can you describe the relationship in part (a) using symbols?

4. From the table, there seems to be a maximum number of seeds that can be produced in any year. What are some reasons why such a maximum number exists?

5. Write an ending to the story. Then write two problems that other students could answer after reading your ending.

Read the rest of the story.

6. Jack is able to save 10 seeds. The family eats 3 and buries 7. Suppose that Jack will sell some of the seeds as soon as he produces at least 35 in one year. How long will it be before Jack sells some of the seeds?

7. Suppose that Jack and Alice have another child as soon as the storm is over. How much longer would it take before Jack produces at least 35 seeds in one year?

Content Strand:
Geometry

12

The Most Important Thing Is . . .

Myrna Bertheau

The most important thing about a square is that it is a polygon with four sides and four corners. All four of its sides are equal. All four of its corners are equal. A square has four square corners. Square corners are 90 degrees and look like an L. All four sides are congruent and all four angles are congruent. I can have a square meal and get a square deal but I do not want to be a square. A square is used for a lot of things but the most important thing is that it is a polygon with four sides.

The foregoing paragraph was authored by third graders as part of a culminating activity from a project centered on Margaret Wise Brown's *The Important Book* ([1949] 1990)*. Various aspects of a project were incorporated throughout the third graders' study of geometry, which included using resources, conducting interviews, compiling lists, and writing paragraphs. Throughout their study children were involved in both written and oral discourse in individual as well as large- and small-group settings.

Observing a Relationship

Various discussions and tasks evolved from an observation that third graders made one morning as they examined a map of the United States that hung at the back of the classroom. They observed that an equilateral triangle could be formed by connecting the capitals of Iowa, Minnesota, and Wisconsin. To extend their thinking, the author used a chalkboard compass at the front chalkboard to draw a large circle and to divide it into six congruent parts. An equilateral triangle was formed by connecting every other point that was marked on the circle (fig. 12.1). Students enthusiastically discussed what would happen if different points on the circle were connected. Students were delighted to find shapes inside other shapes.

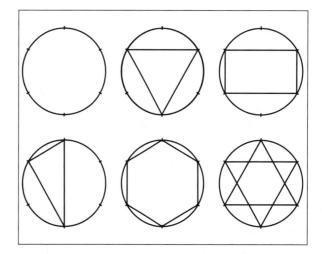

Figure 12.1. Students enjoyed finding shapes inside of shapes.

This exploration of polygons inscribed in a circle let to a general discussion about shapes. The class shifted to small-group work in which each of five groups were to select a shape that they would like to study further. Each group also listed different ways to collect more information about the chosen shape. Later each unit reporter shared the group's methods with the class. Some of their suggestions included visiting the media center, asking their parents, and consulting their mathematics books.

---

*The featured book in this [chapter] is not related to mathematics, but the theme and style of *The Important Book* is appropriate for helping to extend children's study of concepts. Each paragraph describes several attributes about a different concept with a focus on the most important attribute about that concept. Each double-page layout consistently starts and ends with the same refrain emphasizing "the important thing." The simple prose is complemented by Leonard Weisgard's dark illustrations that are composed with a minimum of detail.

Launching the Project

At this time *The Important Book* (Brown [1949] 1990) was selected to share with the children. The third graders were seated on the floor in a semicircle so that they could see the illustrations as the book was read to them. The children commented on the recurring pattern in the opening and closing sentences. A discussion evolved on what other descriptions could have been included for the different topics in the book. Some students found that they did not always agree on what they would list as being the most important thing.

Since the class had written books about topics that they were studying, they suggested that we write our own "important book" about shapes. The class discussed what pages *could* be included in the book. What concepts could be represented? What figures could be included in the illustrations? What ideas could be expressed in the poetry? From resulting answers, they decided to build a class list of all of the shapes that they remembered, which was then divided among the five groups.

Both inside and outside class the children collected information about the different shapes. They compiled their lists of attributes for each shape while working in small groups. As they worked, the children discussed which of these ideas they would note as being "the most important thing."

As the project continued, other concepts, such as line segment, angles, obtuse, acute, and congruent, were added to their list of topics for the book. Students observed that the number of topics they could learn about appeared to have no end. As the list grew, both individual students and pairs of students started researching other shapes to add to "the important book."

Exploring Geometric Concepts

Over the next three weeks various other tasks were designed to involve children in the continued exploration of shape. The tasks included both two- and three-dimensional shapes. As the shapes were analyzed, such concepts as sides, faces, angles, parallel lines, and perpendicular lines naturally evolved from the descriptions. The children found that one couldn't talk about a 90-degree angle unless everyone knew what that concept meant. These subjects were also added to the growing list.

One task involved handing out labeled geometric solids to the children. Each pair of children generated a list of three to four attributes that described the shape. Later the geometric solids were all placed so that the entire class could see the objects as the lists were read. The children's task was to determine which shape was being described. As this discussion unfolded, such terms as *flat, curved, corner, point, edge, surface, rectangular, circular,* and *square* were reinforced.

The relationship between two- and three-dimensional shapes was extended by placing different solids on the overhead projector. It was noted that a cube's projected image could be a square. Predictions were made of the projected images of different solids. As the predictions were checked out, the cylinder's projections presented some surprises, as rectangular and circular images were possible, whereas the sphere's image remained constant no matter how it was positioned. Throughout these discussions, the children were prompted when they used terms inappropriately. If a child used the term *square*, rather than *cube*, he or she realized that a cube's flat surfaces consisted of squares or that its projected image could be a square.

Composing Their Own Book

Writing involved different stages, which is reflected in Brittney's work shown in figure 12.2. Her initial paper involved both drawings and a list of attributes. This work was followed by a paragraph that was later rewritten in prose parallel to *The Important Book* (Brown [1949] 1990).

Brittney notes that *October* comes from the Latin word for *eight*. The children had been encouraged to determine the origin of different names by using resources from the library. The subsequent paragraph reflects the various facts that were found about the word *pentagon*.

> The most important thing about a pentagon is that it is a shape with 5 sides and 5 angles. An equilateral pentagon has 5 equal obtuse angles and no acute (angles) or square corners. You can make a 5 pointed star inside the pentagon and there will be a pentagon inside of the star. The largest office building in the world is the Pentagon. It has 5 stories and is in the shape of a pentagon. Not every pentagon has to have all of its sides the same. Pentagons are interesting but the most important thing about a pentagon is that it is a shape with 5 sides and 5 angles.

Children also interviewed family members and others to learn more about the names of different shapes. One result was the many uses of the word *square* in different contexts, as stated in the opening

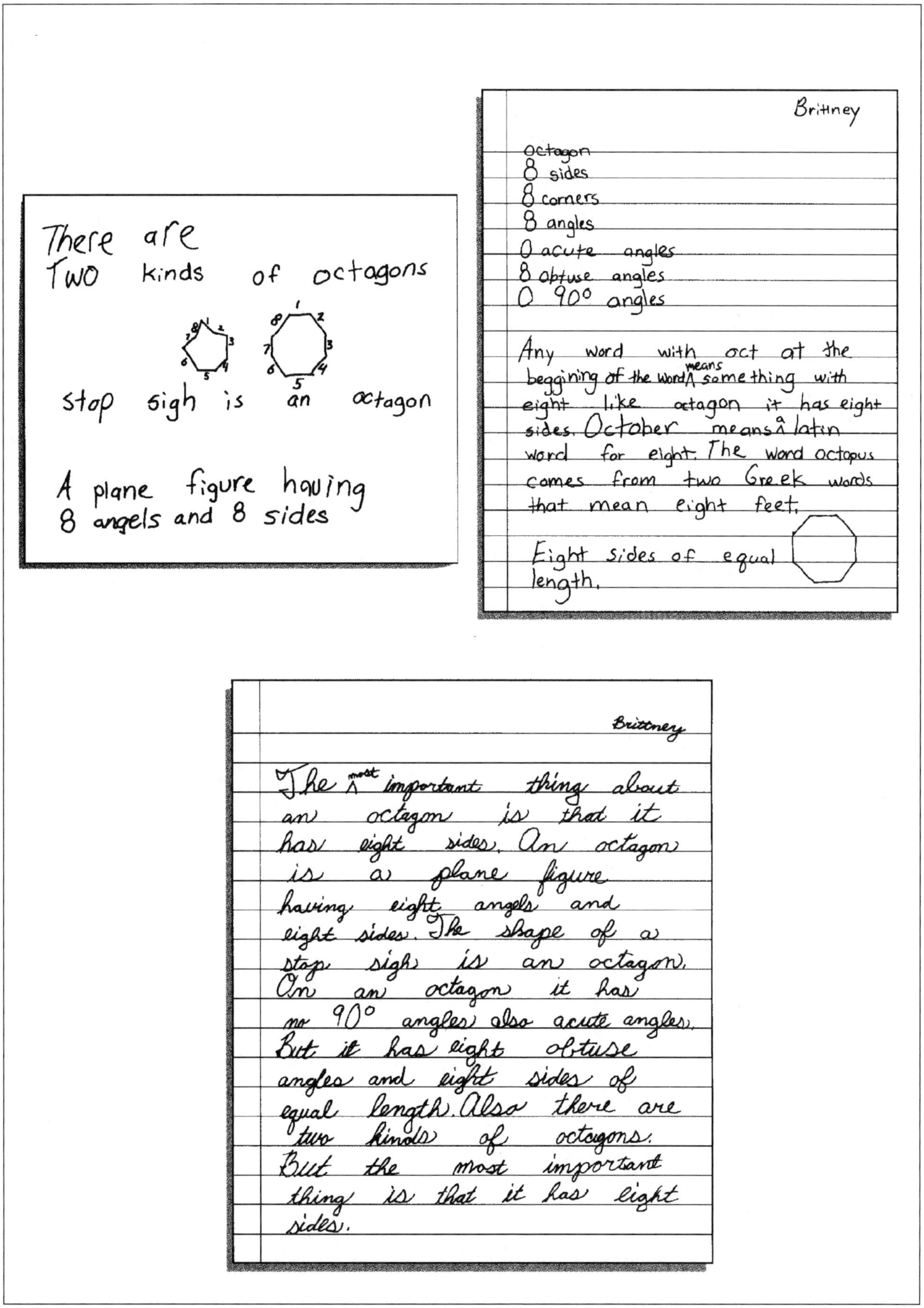

There are
TWO kinds of octagons

stop sigh is an octagon

A plane figure having
8 angels and 8 sides

Brittney

Octagon
8 sides
8 corners
8 angles
0 acute angles
8 obtuse angles
0 90° angles

Any word with oct at the
beggining of the word means some thing with
eight like octagon it has eight
sides. October means a latin
word for eight. The word octopus
comes from two Greek words
that mean eight feet.

Eight sides of equal
length.

Brittney

The most important thing about
an octagon is that it
has eight sides. An octagon
is a plane figure
having eight angels and
eight sides. The shape of a
stop sigh is an octagon.
On an octagon it has
no 90° angles also acute angles.
But it has eight obtuse
angles and eight sides of
equal length. Also there are
two kinds of octagons.
But the most important
thing is that it has eight
sides.

Figure 12.2. Brittney's work on octagons

paragraph, "I can have a square meal and get a square deal but I do not want to be a square." Another example involving the word *shape* is illustrated in the following excerpt:

> The important thing about a shape is that it is the outline or form of something. Things come in many different shapes. Shapes are made of line segments. We are sometimes told to shape up. If we don't shape up, we might have to ship out. And Mrs. Harken certainly wants us to shape up which means to be in good physical shape. But the important thing about a shape is that it is the outline or form of something.

The results of each group's work were shared by posting their written work and presenting their research. As can be seen from the foregoing examples, the project encompasses many goals—in mathematics and writing as well as other subjects. It is also a good opportunity to involve the family and to connect mathematics to our world. Although this article describes the children's work in geometry, the project can be modified for other concepts in mathematics as well as other subject areas.

REFERENCE

Brown, Margaret Wise. *The Important Book*. New York: Harper-Collins Children's Books, 1949; New York: Harper Collins Publishers, 1990.

Teaching Notes for

"The Most Important Thing Is . . ."

by Myrna Bertheau

Grade range:	2–5
Mathematical topic:	Analyzing and describing geometric concepts
Children's book:	*The Important Book*, written by Margaret Wise Brown and illustrated by Leonard Weisgard
Materials:	*"The Important Book"* recording sheets 1 and 2

Discussion of the mathematics: This task helps students move from the visualization level (level 0 of van Hiele's levels of geometric thought) to the analysis level (level 1). Traditionally geometry for elementary-grades children has been little more than shape identification with an emphasis on vocabulary. Students do need to know appropriate vocabulary, but a more important objective is that they have the opportunity to learn the attributes of geometric shapes and concepts by exploring and analyzing them. This task could readily be extended to include relationships among shapes or geometric concepts, for example, "a square is a rectangle with four equal sides." The task is also appropriate for analyzing three-dimensional shapes.

Teacher notes: Prior to the task involving *The Important Book*, I read and discuss with the class such children's books as *The Greedy Triangle* by Marilyn Burns. After reading the poem "Shapes," by Shel Silverstein, students write their own "shape" poems. Students are encouraged to find and share other literature selections that relate to geometry concepts. The children are also involved in using two or more shapes to construct new shapes, such as with tangrams or in exploring the 2-triangle and the 4-triangle problems from *Math by All Means: Geometry*.

Throughout the unit, the class works on constructing a geometry word wall and writing an individual notebook. Each student describes and illustrates each new geometry term and includes some additional information about the concept. For example for the term *acute angle*, the student would draw a diagram representing the concept and write a simple definition. She or he might also write a poem, a joke, or a cartoon about it.

Toward the end of the unit of study, I read *The Important Book*, by Margaret Wise Brown. Students are asked to think about the geometry word wall or their geometry notebook. Each student selects one of the geometry terms and lists all the information he or she knows about that term. Students share their recording sheets with their families and interview them for further information. Students also use the Internet to find additional information.

Students could use a recording sheet that lists their shape or term at the top and that provides space below for listing the individual they interviewed and recording that person's comments. An example of such a recording sheet is seen at the top of the next page.

Have students make presentations to the class sharing the information that they have found about their geometric term. Allow time for their classmates to ask questions or to share any additional information they may know concerning the term.

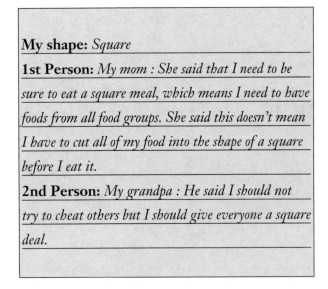

My shape: *Square*

1st Person: *My mom : She said that I need to be sure to eat a square meal, which means I need to have foods from all food groups. She said this doesn't mean I have to cut all of my food into the shape of a square before I eat it.*

2nd Person: *My grandpa : He said I should not try to cheat others but I should give everyone a square deal.*

After students have researched their geometric term, revisit the format of *The Important Book* and discuss with students how to write their own "important page" about their selected shape. Encourage students to be creative while still giving accurate geometric information about their term. The students' finished pages can be placed in a class book, which can be displayed at the local library or shared with other classes.

REFERENCES

Bertheau, Myrna. "Links to Literature: The Most Important Thing Is …" *Teaching Children Mathematics* 1 (October 1994): 112–15.

Brown, Margaret Wise. *The Important Book*. Illustrated by Leonard Weisgard. New York: HarperCollins Publishers, 1990.

Burns, Marilyn. *The Greedy Triangle*. Illustrated by Gordon Silveria. New York: Scholastic, 1994.

Rectanus, Cheryl. *Math by All Means: Geometry, Grades 3–4*. Sausalito, Calif.: Math Solutions Publications, 1994.

Silverstein, Shel. "Shapes." In *A Light in the Attic*, p. 77. New York: Harper Collins, 1981.

The Important Book

Name_____

Date _____

My Shape_____

Some facts about my selected shape:

At home: Share what you have learned about your selected shape with others outside school. Interview them. Record who you interviewed and what you learned from each person about your selected shape.

The Important Book

Name_____

Date _____

An important thing about a _____ is _____

_____.

_____

_____

_____

_____

_____

_____

_____

_____

But the most important thing about a _____ is _____

_____.

13

An Old Tale with a New Turn—and Flip and Slide

Pat Margerm

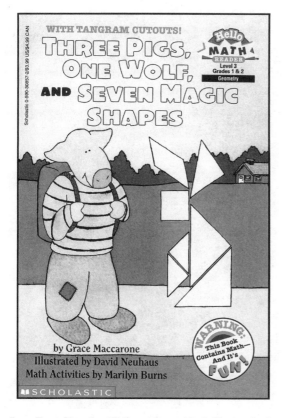

From *Three Pigs, One Wolf, and Seven Magic Shapes*, by Grace Maccarone. Reprinted courtesy of the publisher, Scholastic/Hello Math Readers. Used with permission.

IN *How to Use Children's Literature to Teach Mathematics*, Welchman-Tischler (1997, pp. 1–2) makes the following observation, "Some [children's books] are explicitly about mathematics, for example, counting books, books about shapes, and a variety of trade books that aim to teach specific mathematics concepts. Children can learn about mathematics directly from these books. . . . Other children's books involve mathematics in more subtle ways.

They might not be called 'math books' by teachers or students, yet they suggest rich possibilities for extended mathematical investigations. . . . [A]lmost all stand on their own as good books. . . ."

What Makes a Good Mathematics Book?

Limitations are often encountered when using picture books that are explicitly about mathematics. Sometimes they do not stand on their own as good stories that can be used to teach skills and concepts in language arts. At other times an obvious mathematical connection overshadows other opportunities for mathematical links or investigations. However, the mathematics picture book *Three Pigs, One Wolf, and Seven Magic Shapes* (Maccarone 1997) meets many criteria—it tells a good story *and* presents many opportunities to make both obvious and subtle mathematical links. It provides a context for introducing tangrams to children and suggests possibilities for additional mathematical connections.

The book is a variation of the traditional tale that tells the story of three little pigs from the village next to that of the original three little pigs. While seeking their fortune as a group, each pig meets an animal made from a set of tangrams and, in turn, is given a set of seven magic shapes to use to solve problems. Each pig then meets Big Brad Wolf, the twin brother of the Big Bad Wolf from the original story. Only the third pig survives because she has used her tangrams wisely, making a house to protect herself from danger. The story continues as this pig meets and decides to marry the third pig from the other village. They keep one sturdy house of bricks and decide to use the tangram pieces from the other house to build something else.

Introducing the Story

This book was introduced to the students in Pansy MacInnes's fourth-grade classroom at Our Lady of Lourdes Catholic School. To set the stage for comparing this book with the traditional version of the fairy tale, the children retold the story of the "Three Little Pigs" from memory.

The teacher then read the new version, *Three Pigs, One Wolf, and Seven Magic Shapes* (Maccarone 1997), telling her students that this story "had math in it" and that the seven magic shapes are called *tangrams*: "While I am reading this story, I'd like you to listen for the math in the story and for how it is different from the story of the three little pigs that you know." Since the basic plot was familiar to the children, the story was interrupted several times for them to model, identify, and extend the mathematics presented in the story.

Like the traditional tale, the book's story structure involves a pattern. In keeping with this idea, the names of the tangram pieces are repeated as a refrain: "Two large triangles, a medium triangle, two small triangles, a square, and a parallelogram." This refrain encourages children to repeat the names of the shapes to become familiar with the vocabulary, and, in fact, the refrain was repeated naturally by the students as the story was read.

The story begins by identifying these three pigs as living in the village next to that of the original three little pigs, which gives the children an opportunity to count by threes, skip count, or multiply. As they gave their answers, the teacher recorded them by coloring numbers on a hundred chart.

Teacher: How many pigs would there be altogether in both villages?
Students: Six.
Teacher: What if there were three pigs in another village? How many pigs would there be altogether?
Students: Nine.
Teacher: And another?
Students: Twelve. . . . Fifteen. . . . Eighteen. . . .
Teacher: What are we doing?

The students gave various responses: "Counting by threes . . . multiplying . . . adding. . . ." The story continued with the children's responding to similarities and differences; for example, two of the three pigs in the original tale were also eaten, and one pig in the new tale was female.

Using Mathematical Language

At the point in the story when the first little pig meets a duck made of seven magic shapes, a large version of this tangram animal, prepared ahead of time, was shown to the children. (See fig. 13.1.) The large picture made it possible for the children to see the animal, note the ways in which the pieces were used to make it, and match the names of the pieces to the shapes seen in the picture. When the first pig became lonely, the children were asked for possible solutions to his problem. They suggested that the pig could make an animal with tangram pieces.

The teacher continued the story, saying, "The first little pig decided to use his seven magic shapes to make a cat, and this is how he did it." At this point, the teacher used a giant set of tangrams to construct the cat from the story by moving the pieces on the chalkboard. Geometric translations were linked to the story by orally modeling the language of flips, slides, and turns as the pieces were manipulated to create the cat.

Teacher: The square was used to make the cat's head. It could look like this ■ or be rotated to look like this ◆ .

The children thought that this rotated square looked like a diamond. Some of the children who had previously thought of squares and diamonds as being two unrelated shapes were surprised to see that a diamond is actually a rotated square.

Teacher: What do you think he used for the ears?
Students: The small triangles.

The triangles were used in various positions to make them look like ears. The language of transformation geometry was used to describe the trials, for example, "Let's try flipping them."

Teacher: What do you think he used for the body?
Students: The large triangles.

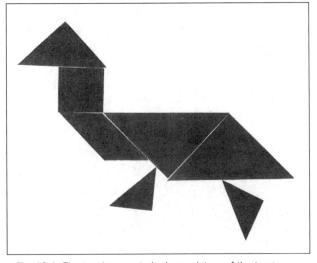

Fig. 13.1. The teacher created a large picture of the tangram duck for her presentation.

EXPLORING MATHEMATICS THROUGH LITERATURE

Various new shapes were created with the two large triangles and tested as possible bodies—a triangle, a square, and a parallelogram. Again, this activity modeled the use of mathematical language and some children found relationships among the pieces.

In *Integrating Children's Literature and Mathematics in the Classroom*, Schiro (1997) suggests that a book can be enhanced by altering its text to clarify or highlight mathematical ideas. The class decided that it would be useful to describe the pieces as being two *congruent* small triangles, a medium triangle, two *congruent* large triangles, a square, and a parallelogram. The word *congruent* was then added to the refrain.

The story continued. The third little pig meets the third pig from the original story, the two fall in love, and they get married. They have both a brick house and a tangram house and no longer need two dwellings. The teacher asked, "What should they do?" Children responded that the pigs should make something else with the shapes.

At this point, sets of precut tangrams were distributed to each group of children, and their first task was to separate the pieces into sets of tangrams. While collecting their sets of tangrams, the children could be heard using the language from the story to identify the shapes, for example, "I need another large triangle." When all groups had a complete set of tangrams, the children were instructed to try to make something that the pigs could use instead of the second house. (See fig. 13.2.)

Student Work

As the children were working, the teacher looked for and recorded on the chalkboard new shapes that resulted from combining two or more of the pieces, for example, a trapezoid made from

Fig. 13.2. The children were asked to make something that pigs could use instead of a second house.

the parallelogram and a small triangle. When the groups were finished experimenting with the pieces and were satisfied with what they had made, they glued them on pieces of paper. (See fig. 13.3.) Regardless of their level of mathematics or language ability, the children were able to participate by using the tangrams to create an object. For example, Yonas used the tangrams to make triangular corners for his baseball diamond and, with direction, was able to combine two triangles to complete its frame. (See fig. 13.4.) Brownson created a cat with his set of tangrams by reproducing the puzzles from the book. (See fig. 13.5.)

The children were asked to write an ending for the story on the basis of the shape they had created from the tangrams. (See fig. 13.6.) They were encouraged to incorporate mathematical language in their writing. To facilitate the children's use of language, the names of the shapes were listed on the chalkboard. The children's writing reflected a wide range of understanding of the ideas presented in the story and supplied important information for planning future lessons. For example, Jonathan attempted to describe the creation of his cat by using some

Fig. 13.3. The students glued their completed shapes onto paper.

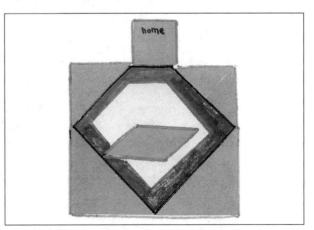

Fig. 13.4. Yonas made a baseball diamond where the pigs could play.

of the transformation geometry language modeled during the lesson. (See fig. 13.7.) Rachelle was one of several children who used much of the vocabulary from the lesson to label her creation. (See fig. 13.8.) Rachelle's labels demonstrate a familiarity with the term *congruent* and with the names of the geometric shapes. Her work reveals an understanding that new shapes can be formed by combining shapes, for example, "congruent triangles making a parallelogram."

One group of children made an exciting discovery while exchanging their papers and sharing their stories. When they passed their papers to someone opposite, they noticed that the upside-down, or rotated, view of their tangram puzzle resulted in a different object.

Fig. 13.5. Brownson reproduced the cat from the book.

Fig. 13.6. The children wrote an ending for the story on the basis of the shape that they created from the tangrams.

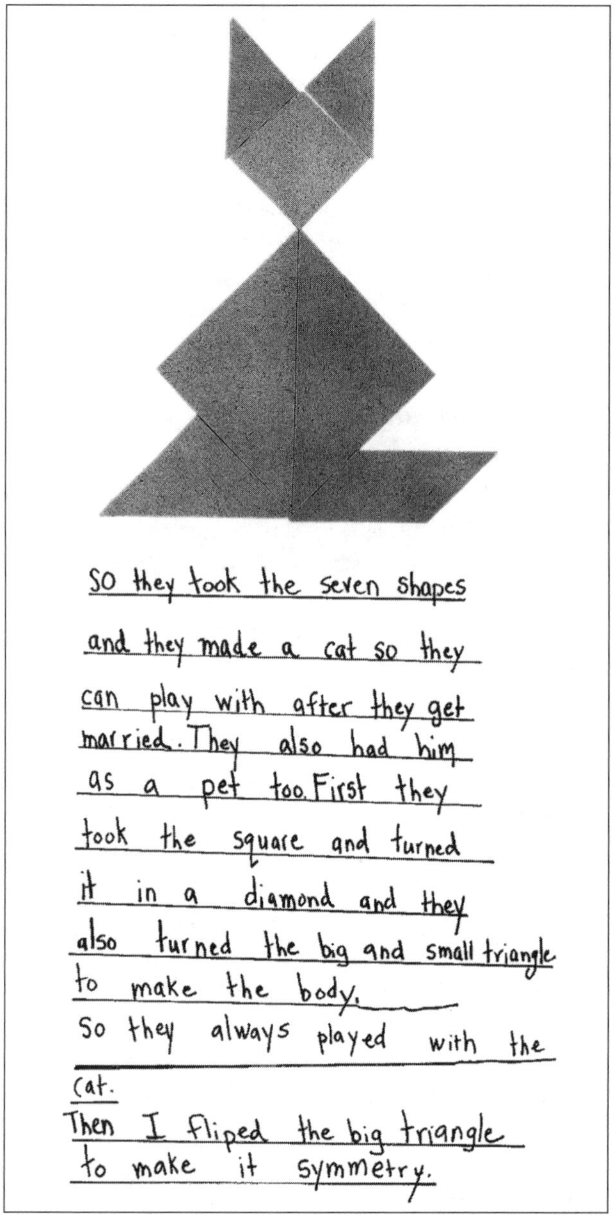

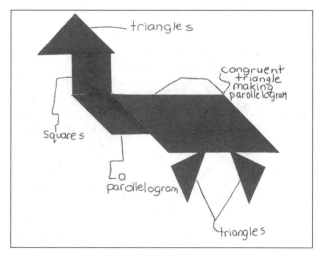

so they took the seven shapes and they made a cat so they can play with after they get married. They also had him as a pet too. First they took the square and turned it in a diamond and they also turned the big and small triangle to make the body. So they always played with the cat.
Then I fliped the big triangle to make it symmetry.

Fig. 13.7a. Jonathan attempted to use mathematical language in describing his cat.

triangles

congruent triangle making parollelogram

Squares

a parollelogram

triangles

Fig. 13.8. Rachelle showed her familiarity with the vocabulary of the shapes.

EXPLORING MATHEMATICS THROUGH LITERATURE

Conclusion

By working with *Three Pigs, One Wolf, and Seven Magic Shapes*, children were given opportunities to create tangram shapes and discuss and write about mathematical transformations. They were engaged in mathematics, and their enthusiasm was reflected in their work.

Extending the Lesson

In addition to the activities already mentioned, this book and lesson present a context for further mathematical explorations that may be less obvious than the ones described thus far. These additional mathematical links include patterns, measurement, and transformation geometry.

Patterns

Students can identify patterns, relationships, and divisibility rules with multiples of 3 on a hundred chart. They can describe the patterns that they see in the colored squares of the hundred chart, for example, diagonal. They can also organize the numbers (3, 6, 9, . . .) in columns to investigate the patterns in numbers in the times 3 table. Is the difference between the numbers always the same? Three multiples of 3 are found between 10 and 19 and between 20 and 29; four multiples of 3 occur in the numbers from 30 to 39. Why?

Measurement

Students can investigate variations in perimeter with pictures that have a constant area. Ask students to determine the area of their tangram shapes.

How did they solve this problem? Why is the area of all their different shapes the same? Will the perimeters be the same? Why? Can they estimate the perimeter of their shapes? Can they predict which shape will have the greatest perimeter? The least? Have them compare their predictions with the actual perimeters. What methods did they use to determine the perimeter of their shapes? To compare shapes? To estimate and predict?

Transformation geometry

Ask students to investigate similarities when performing translations with similar and congruent shapes. Have students give oral descriptions of how to create their tangram shape as another student tries to build it from the instructions, for example, "Take the medium triangle. Put it on the paper so that the right angle is pointing straight up. Next . . . ." These instructions could also be written on the back of the shapes and placed at an activity center.

REFERENCES

Maccarone, Grace. *Three Pigs, One Wolf, and Seven Magic Shapes*. New York: Scholastic, 1997.

Schiro, Michael. *Integrating Children's Literature and Mathematics in the Classroom—Children as Meaning Makers, Problem Solvers and Literary Critics*. New York: Teachers College Press, 1997.

Welchman-Tischler, Rosamond. *How to Use Children's Literature to Teach Mathematics*. Reston, Va.: National Council of Teachers of Mathematics, 1997.

"An Old Tale with a New Turn—and Flip and Slide"

by Pat Margerm

Grade range:	3–5
Mathematical topic:	Describing and building puzzles using two-dimensional shapes
Children's book:	*Three Pigs, One Wolf, and Seven Magic Shapes*, story by Grace Maccarone, illustrated by David Neuhaus, and mathematics activities by Marilyn Burns
Materials:	Tangram pieces and *"Three Pigs, One Wolf, and Seven Magic Shapes"* recording sheet

Discussion of the mathematics: Two-dimensional puzzles built from tangram pieces involve many geometric skills. When copying a puzzle, students need to recognize the congruent pieces and the orientation of each piece; for example, children may choose the appropriate-sized triangle but may set it aside because they do not realize that it needs to be turned or flipped. Some students may perceive that the different puzzles have different areas; but if the puzzles are made from the same seven shapes, the areas of the puzzles must be the same.

For a more sophisticated version of this task, just the outline of the puzzle could be given. Solving these puzzles involves comparing and estimating the length of edges, the size of angles formed by edges, and the relative size of areas.

Teacher notes: After initially reading through the book, explain that the class will revisit the book and build one or more of the shapes. Use a large picture for this presentation (see fig. 13.1 in the article), and talk though the placement of each tangram piece. Use the language of the refrain in the book as each piece is chosen. As the tangram piece is placed, model and use the language of geometric transformations—"slide," "flip," and "turn."

Before individually working with all seven pieces, students can work with two shapes to build another shape, for instance, use the two small triangles to build the tangram square, the parallelogram, and the medium-sized triangle. Students should discuss the idea that all these shapes are different but have the same area.

Continue such discussions when working with all seven pieces. For students who are not convinced that the areas are the same, reaffirm that although the areas do look different, students can convince themselves otherwise by remembering which pieces were used for each puzzle. Another teaching strategy is to use only the small triangles to cover each puzzle; students will understand that the areas are the same when they notice that they used the same number of small triangles to construct each one.

Children who are ready for a new challenge can try puzzles that show the outline of only one or two of the small pieces or that provide only the outline of the completed puzzle.

To engage students in writing their own ending to the story, revisit the book and ask them to decide what they would build and then to complete the sentence stem from the book. Explain that they need to use all seven shapes and that they are to describe mathematically how they constructed their shape. A list of shapes and the sentence stem could be written on the board, or the stem could be written across the top of a recording sheet.

Two additional children's books include *Grandfather Tang's Story*, a tale that uses tangram pieces to create different shapes, and *The Warlord's Puzzle*, a picture book that tells the story of the origin of tangrams.

REFERENCES

Maccarone, Grace. *Three Pigs, One Wolf, and Seven Magic Shapes*. Illustrated by David Neuhaus, math activities by Marilyn Burns. New York: Scholastic, 1997.

Margerm, Pat. "Links to Literature: An Old Tale with a New Turn—and Flip and Slide." *Teaching Children Mathematics* 6 (October 1999): 86–90.

Pilegard, Virginia Walton. *The Warlord's Puzzle*. Illustrated by Nicolas Debon. Gretna, La.: Pelican Publishing Co., 2000.

Tompert, Ann. *Grandfather Tang's Story*. Illustrated by Robert Andrew Parker. New York: Crown Publishers, 1990.

Three Pigs, One Wolf, and Seven Magic Shapes

Name_____

Date _____

They fell in love and were married, and they no longer needed two houses. The pig who built a house of shapes had an idea. She took her house apart and used the seven shapes to build _____.

Build and glue your shape on a separate sheet of paper. Use the space below to write a mathematical description of how you constructed your shape.

Description:

.

Small Triangle	Medium Triangle	Large Triangle	Square	Parallelogram

14

Pablo's Tree: Mathematics in a Different Light

Maryann Wickett

M^Y THIRD- and fourth-grade students began to look at mathematics in a different light after we read *Pablo's Tree* (Mora 1994). It is a story about a young Mexican boy named Pablo. Every year, in celebration of Pablo's birthday, his grandfather makes special decorations for the tree he planted the day Pablo was born.

As I shared the story with the class, Kevin wondered aloud about Pablo's age. I asked the students to put their thumbs up if they thought Pablo was older than they were or put their thumbs down if they thought he was younger. "I bet the book gives us enough clues to figure it out," giggled Christina, "she's always asking us to figure out stuff like that!" Christina was right. I often ask students to make predictions and check their predictions as we gather additional information to see if their thinking makes sense. As I continued to read, students listened carefully and discovered that Pablo was five years old.

We read about the different ways that Lito, Pablo's grandfather, had decorated the tree for each birthday. "If Lito decorated a tree for you on your next birthday, what would you like him to use?" I questioned the class.

"Candy!" yelled Hannah. "How about books!" suggested Tiffany. "Maybe paper birds," replied Juan. "Lito could use paper chains," said Oscar.

Mathematical Gifts

Since I wanted the students to apply their knowledge of previously studied geometric terms as we looked for the beauty of mathematics and mathematical "gifts," I held up a small origami box, explaining that the box was filled with imagination and something magical that was also mathematical. "I'm going to read you some clues. Your job is to use the clues to figure out my special magical mathematical gift to Pablo. My gift is a geometric shape."

"It's a triangle! That's my favorite," shared Jennifer.

"Maybe it could be a quadrilateral," thought Oscar aloud.

"Mrs. Wickett, I have been watching you and you have that look in your eye. I don't think it's a polygon at all!" grinned Andrew.

"Andrew is absolutely correct and very observant. Andrew has given you my second clue—my gift for Pablo is not a polygon."

"It's a polyhedron, like a cube," interrupted Fercie.

"It could be a hexagon," volunteered Maritza.

"I disagree, a hexagon is a polygon, and Mrs. Wickett said her gift was not a polygon, so it can't be a hexagon," explained Juliette, who had not only listened carefully but had a well-developed sense of the relationships of geometric figures.

"I need to give you another clue. My gift has no sides and no corners." Hands danced in the air. "Keep your ideas to yourself for just a moment. See if your idea still makes sense after I share my last clue. My last clue is that you can fold my geometric shape in half any place and it will be symmetrical. Using a whisper voice, tell me what you think my gift to Pablo is."

"A circle!" the class exclaimed in an almost whisper. "You've got it! My gift box to Pablo is filled with imagination and a circle. I am giving Pablo imagination to dream of exciting, clever things. I am giving Pablo a circle because I love geometry, and a circle is an important part of geometry. It is special because it is the shape of the sun and the moon—the sun, which will warm Pablo's body and spirit, and the moon, which will provide light and guidance when Pablo dreams his wonderful dreams. Circles because they are the shape of eyes through which Pablo can see the beauty of his dreams and the world around him. Circles because they can help him fly like the wind when he skates or drives his convertible when he grows up. A circle because it is the shape of zero, a lonely but most unique, interesting number."

"Oooouuuuuh! That's cool! I hadn't thought of that," replied Hannah quietly.

Making a Gift Box

With the students seated in a circle so that they could easily see what I was doing, I was ready to show them how to make an origami box. Making the box would provide a meaningful way to use the language of geometry. "I am going to show you how to fold your own gift box so that you can also give Pablo a mathematical gift. Before we start, I want you to take a moment to think quietly in your brain about something mathematical you could give Pablo. Let me know when you have an idea by putting your thumb up." The students thought quietly and slowly their thumbs began to go up. When most of the students had indicated that they had an idea for a gift, I began to show them how to fold an origami box.

"You will need a paper rectangle. How many lines of symmetry are there in a rectangle?" I asked. The class responded with "Two." "Fold your rectangle along both lines of symmetry," I instructed [for details consult "Links to Literature: Pablo's Tree: Mathematics in a Different Light," by Maryann Wickett, in the October 1996 issue of *Teaching Children Mathematics*, p. 97]. I wonder how many rectangles my paper has now?" I mused aloud. "Four," "eight," "ten," were some of the answers I heard.

"If you just look at one side of the paper, you have four," said Ellis.

"If you count both sides, then there are eight," pointed out Todd.

"I think there are ten. . . . Maybe more, I'm not sure yet," Juliette added, "There are at least four small ones on each side, so that's eight. Then there is the paper itself, which is a rectangle, which is two big ones if you count both sides, so that's ten. I think there are more, 'cause when you only fold it into half, that makes medium-sized rectangles. Could I figure it out tonight with my mom?"

"That's a great idea! You can report back to us tomorrow about what you and your mom discover," I replied.

I explained and demonstrated the subsequent steps in making the box, encouraging the children to name the figures that emerged. As we proceeded, we continued to discuss and predict the outcomes of subsequent steps. The students worked cooperatively to help each other as they retold the steps to their classmates. This opportunity was especially empowering for many students who had often struggled with number activities but who were able to use their spatial skills well and so became a resource to other students.

Filling the boxes with gifts and riddles

The next day, we admired our boxes then proceeded: "Before we made our boxes, I asked you to think of a gift to give Pablo. Remember, the box will be filled with imagination and something mathematical." I paused for a few moments. I find that if students are given a few moments to think quietly about something before being asked to share with others, they are more likely to come up with interesting, creative ideas. "Who would like to share an idea?" I continued. The students quickly raised their hands. "If you would like to, share your idea with your neighbors." I gave the students a few minutes to share. This process allowed all children to be involved and to become a resource for those unable to formulate their own ideas. "Would anyone like to share an idea they heard?"

"We could do one about triangles," suggested Jennifer.

"You could use any of the quadrilaterals up there," said Jessica, pointing to the polygon chart that was still on the wall from our unit on geometry.

"Mrs. Wickett, could I give Pablo a piano—because it plays music and music is mathematical?" asked Hannah.

"That sounds like a creative, interesting idea to me. I will be excited to read about your thinking. Remember to write clues about what is inside your box and to write a paragraph about why you chose the gift you did," I reminded the class. About half of the students were ready to work. Others took a few more moments to think before coming up with ideas but soon started to work intently and quietly.

I walked around the room glancing over students' shoulders and monitoring their work to ensure that their clues were clear and made sense. When the clues were vague or confusing, I asked questions to help guide the students. One common problem is that students often do not give enough clues to come up with a single answer. As I read their work, I encouraged them to try their clues on a neighbor, explaining that well-written clues will narrow the possible answers until the final clue leads to one answer only. When I saw that the clues did not lead to a single answer, I discussed this situation with the child, explaining what I thought could be the possible answers, thereby helping the child to add an additional clue to make the riddle successful.

As students finished, they posed their riddles. Oscar shared, "My gift can glide. It is a polygon. It has three corners." Joanna correctly guessed that Oscar's gift was a triangle. "Could it be anything but a triangle?" I asked the class. They agreed that it could be nothing else. Oscar then shared the reasons

he chose a triangle. As the other students finished their work, they joined us on the rug.

Sarah was next to share. Her explanation is shown in figure 14.1. "It is a number. It has two vertices. It has one right angle. $1 \times 2 + 3$ equals the answer."

"Is your gift the number 5?" asked Tiffany, tentatively.

"Yes, I chose the number 5 because Pablo is five years old and so he could hang it on his tree. So if anyone comes, they will know how old he is. I chose 5 because if he hangs it on the tree every year, he could think about how much older he is getting. I see the number 5 on birthday cakes and on the clock," explained Sarah.

"My gift makes shapes symmetrical so they have congruent parts. You can't see my gift, and it can be on many shapes," shared Juliette. The class looked a little puzzled by Juliette's clues.

"Can you give them one more clue?" I prompted.

Juliette thought very intently then grinned. "A rectangle has two and a square has four of them—I think," she said, grinning.

"Are you talking about symmetry?" asked Maritza.

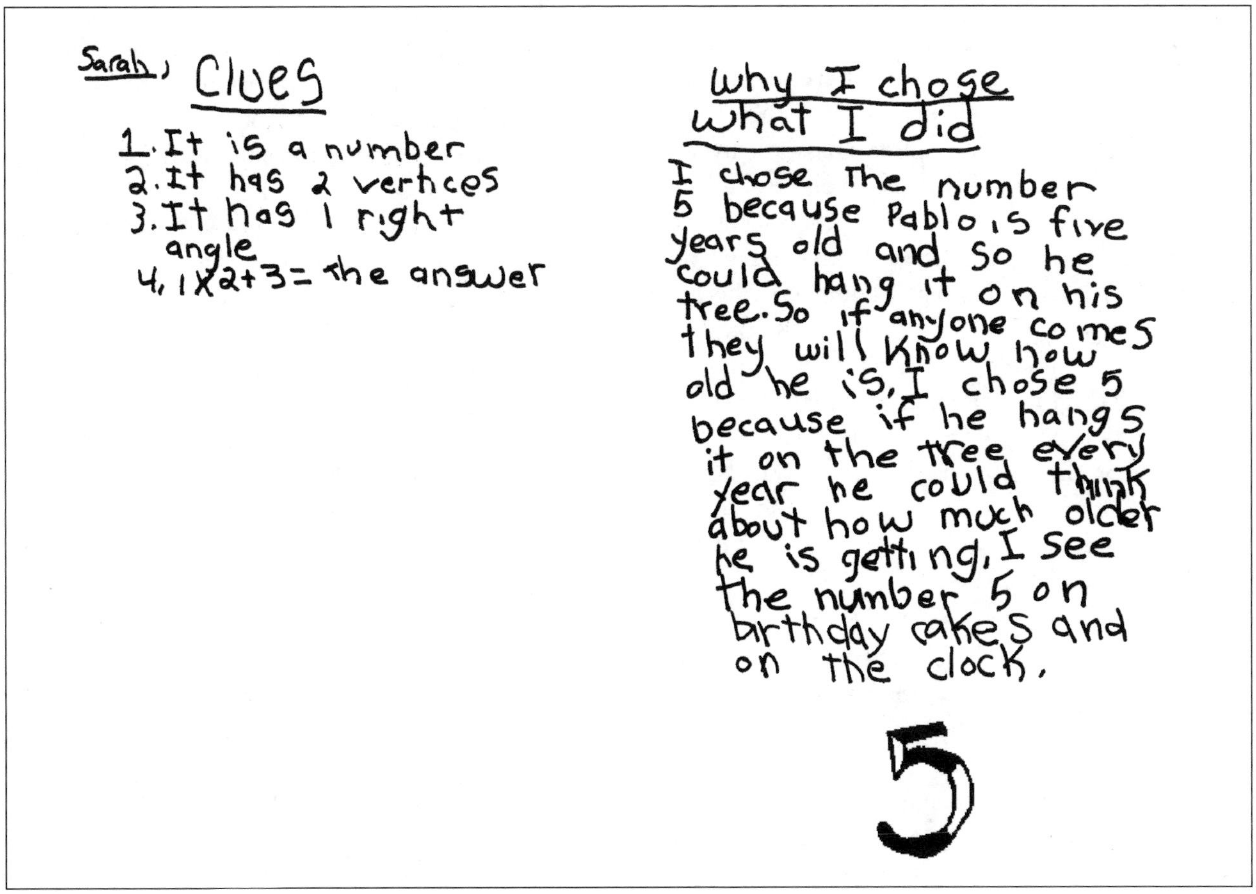

Fig. 14.1. Pablo's becomes the object of discussion.

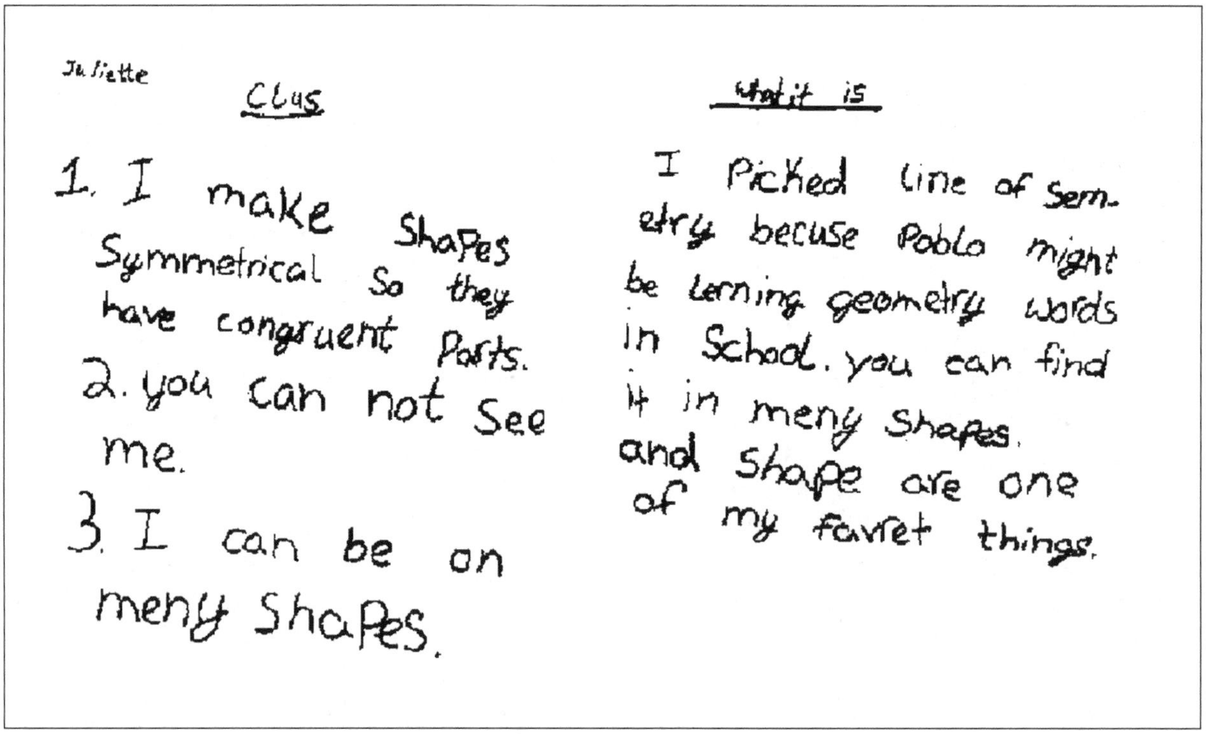

Juliette

Clus

1. I make Shapes Symmetrical So they have congruent Parts.
2. you can not See me.
3. I can be on meny Shapes.

What it is

I Picked line of Semetry becuse Pablo might be lerning geometry words in School. you can find it in meny Shapes. and Shape are one of my favret things.

Fig. 14.2. Clues and the answer are explained

"Uh huh! A line of symmetry. I picked line of symmetry because Pablo might be learning geometry words in school. You find it in many shapes, and shapes are one of my favorite things." (See the clues and explanations in fig. 14.2.)

The students continued to share. Samples of their work are shown in figure 14.3. Julie gave Pablo the gift of 2407 "because nobody has ever lived to be this age." Ellis gave the gift of circles and rectangles in the form of money. Juan chose a polygon for his gift … because "it looks like a part of a house." A decagon was what Arleigh chose because "I could see it at night. I could see it in constellations. Pablo would like it because it could go on the tree and it's bright." Arleigh envisioned his decagon as being a five-pointed star (see fig. 14.3).

When Shelly shared her clues with the class, we were not led to a single answer. She shared, "It's not a hexagon. It has four sides. Their sides don't match. It's shaped like a chalkboard."

"Shelly," began Shawn, "I think you gave a rectangle because that's the shape of the chalkboard. But you said the sides don't match, but the top and the bottom match, and the left and right side match each other."

"Oh," replied Shelly, quietly.

"Does someone have a suggestion for how Shelly could clarify what she means?" I asked the class.

"Well, maybe she needs to get rid of that one clue and just say it like Shawn did," suggested Yessika.

"Could I fix it, Mrs. Wickett?" Shelly asked.

"Certainly," I encouraged.

Shelly's problem is not uncommon. Gentle suggestions, along with the opportunity to revise immediately, help students to be more successful with this type of activity. The children's riddles provide an opportunity to assess misconceptions that students may have, and they pinpoint those fundamental geometric concepts for which additional experiences are needed to develop fully. For example, Chris described a rectangle in the following way, "Mine has four corners, four sides. It has eight vertex, six faces. It's a shap. It could be part of a rowbhote [robot] and it isant a line of sematry." His clues revealed to me that Chris needed additional experience with the concepts of rectangle, vertex, face, and line of symmetry. These boxes represent geometry and imagination to these students.

Conclusion

This lesson allowed my students to see mathematics in a different light. Making boxes was interesting and rewarding as we turned flat paper into three-dimensional boxes. As they worked with riddles, students practiced reasoning and communication skills, and I could informally assess their levels of thinking and understanding. This experience gave

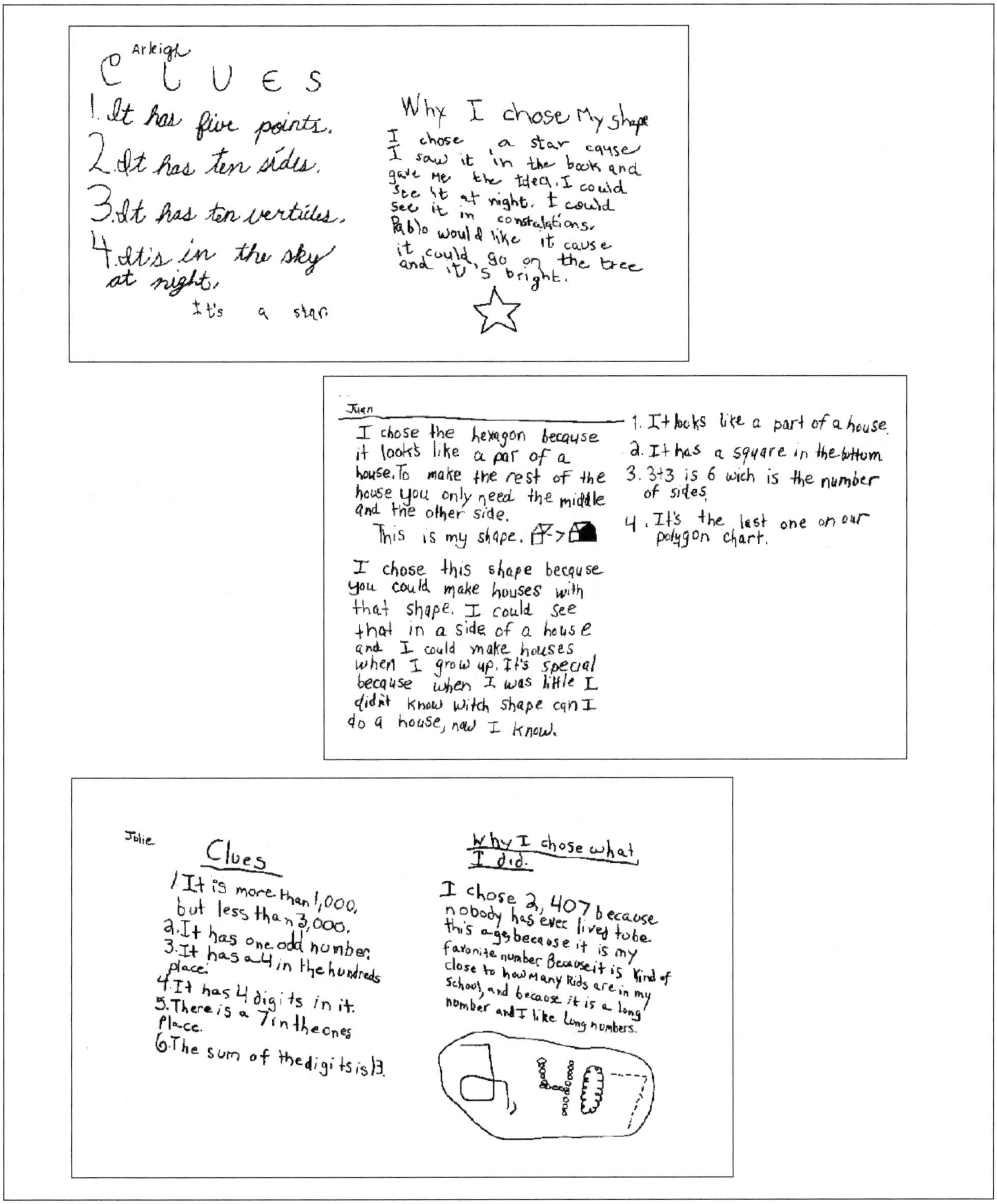

Arleigh

C L U E S

1. It has five points.
2. It has ten sides.
3. It has ten verticles.
4. It's in the sky at night.

It's a star.

Why I chose My shape

I chose a star cause I saw it in the book and gave me the idea. I could see it at night. I could see it in constalations. Pablo would like it cause it could go on the tree and it's bright.

Juan

I chose the hexagon because it looks like a par of a house. To make the rest of the house you only need the middle and the other side.

This is my shape.

1. It looks like a part of a house.
2. It has a square in the bottom.
3. 3+3 is 6 wich is the number of sides.
4. It's the last one on our polygon chart.

I chose this shape because you could make houses with that shape. I could see that in a side of a house and I could make houses when I grow up. It's special because when I was little I didn't know witch shape can I do a house, now I know.

Julie

Clues

1. It is more than 1,000, but less than 3,000.
2. It has one odd number.
3. It has a 4 in the hundreds place.
4. It has 4 digits in it.
5. There is a 7 in the ones place.
6. The sum of the digits is 13.

Why I chose what I did.

I chose 2,407 because nobody has ever lived to be this age because it is my favorite number. Because it is kind of close to how many kids are in my school, and because it is a long number and I like long numbers.

Fig. 14.3. Ingenuity is revealed in students' work.

students a meaningful context in which to apply mathematical language and to understand its usefulness in communicating clearly. By giving mathematical gifts and explaining why each gift was given, children could develop an appreciation of mathematics and its beauty and relate it to their own world.

REFERENCES

Mora, Pat. *Pablo's Tree.* Illustrated by Cecily Lang. New York: Macmillan Publishing Co., 1994.

Needham, Kate. *The Usborne Book of Origami.* Illustrated by Angie Sage. London: Usborne Publishing, 1992.

"Pablo's Tree: Mathematics in a Different Light"

by Maryann Wickett

Grade range:	3–6
Mathematical topics:	Identify and analyze attributes of two- and three-dimensional shapes, and develop vocabulary to describe the attributes
Children's book:	*Pablo's Tree*, written by Pat Mora and illustrated by Cecily Lang (1994)
Materials:	8 1/2 × 11 paper, prefolded origami box, *"Pablo's Tree"* recording sheet

Discussion of the mathematics: The topic explored could vary, but most of the mathematical topics illustrated in the article relate to attributes of two-dimensional shapes. Using and developing appropriate vocabulary is also inherent in this task, since students write clues as well as listen to clues written by their peers. The task also provides an excellent opportunity to develop awareness of the relevance of mathematics by building connections between geometry and the real world. Such connections can include the function of shape as well as the aesthetics of shape.

Teacher notes and questions to ask students: Begin by sharing the story with students. Discuss Pablo's age on the basis of clues given in the book. Discuss the various ways that Lito, Pablo's grandfather, decorated the tree.

- How old do you think Pablo is?

- What clues from the book helped you make your prediction?

- If Lito decorated a tree for you on your next birthday, how would you like him to decorate it?

Show the students the prefolded origami box. Explain that the box is a gift for Pablo. It contains imagination and something magical and mathematical. Read the following clues to the students:

- My gift is a geometric shape.

- My gift for Pablo is not a polygon.

- My gift has no sides or corners.

- I can fold my shape in half at any place, and it will be symmetrical.

As the clues are given, encourage students to share what they think the gift might be. After the students have figured out the gift, explain why it was chosen:

My gift to Pablo is filled with imagination and a circle. I am giving Pablo imagination to dream exciting, clever things. I am giving Pablo a circle because I love geometry, and a circle is an important part of geometry. It is special because it is the shape of the sun and the moon—the sun, which will warm Pablo's body and spirit and the moon, which will provide light and guidance when Pablo dreams his wonderful dreams. [A circle is special because it is] the shape of eyes through which Pablo can see the beauty of his dreams and the world around him. [I am giving Pablo a circle] because they can help him fly like the wind when he skates or drives his convertible when he grows up. [I am giving Pablo] a circle because it is the shape of zero, a lonely but most unique and interesting number.

To demonstrate how to fold an origami box, use the instructions from the article and appropriate mathematical language. The students need to be situated so they can easily see the demonstration, yet still have a surface on which to fold. Having the students seated on the floor works well. Note: As related in the article, this activity presents a good opportunity to discuss attributes of a rectangle, such as lines of symmetry.

Once students have folded their boxes, remind them that they are going to fill their boxes with imagination and a mathematical gift for Pablo. Give students a few moments to think about what they might give before asking them to share their initial ideas.

After students have decided on their mathematical gift, have them write clues about what is in their box. Monitor their work by asking questions and offering suggestions; one helpful approach may be for pairs of students to proof each other's work.

When students are ready to share their riddles, ask for volunteers to read their clues to the class. Allow the volunteers to call on classmates who think they have used the shared clues to solve the riddle. Have the class discuss the geometric concept and the clues; some students may suggest additional clues or attributes that could have been used.

REFERENCES

Mora, Pat. *Pablo's Tree*. Illustrated by Cecily Lang. New York: Macmillan Publishing Co., 1994.

Wickett, Maryann. "Links to Literature: Pablo's Tree: Mathematics in a Different Light." *Teaching Children Mathematics* 3 (October 1996): 96–100.

Pablo's Tree

Recording Sheet

Name _____

Date _____

I chose _____ .

Why I chose what I did:

_____ Clues _____
_____ Why the Clue Helps _____

15

Using Literature to Investigate Transformations

Jacqueline Harris

I AM ALWAYS looking for children's literature to make and enrich connections to the elementary school curriculum. In particular, books and stories that use mathematical problem solving not only engage children in the narrative but also give them opportunities to see how mathematics is used in everyday life. *A Cloak for the Dreamer* by Aileen Friedman (1994) investigates relationships among shapes and, at the same time, tells a wonderful story.

About the Story

This story is about a tailor and his three sons, who are asked to design and sew cloaks for an archduke as he embarks on an important journey. The older sons, Ivan and Alex, want to be tailors like their father and show their talent by creating fine cloaks for the archduke to wear. Each cloak is made with a carefully chosen repeating geometric pattern. Ivan creates a rectangular pattern resembling the bricks on the floor. Alex sews two different patterns, using squares and triangles, which combine the colors of the archduke's carriage and his coat of arms. The youngest son, Misha, who would rather travel the world than work as a tailor, willingly makes an attractive cloak to please his father, choosing colors that represent his love of nature. Unfortunately, the cloak is made of circles and is full of holes. The tailor realizes that Misha has other dreams, and with the help of his older sons, transforms the useless garment into a warm cloak as a gift for Misha to wear on his travels around the world.

This beautifully illustrated book captures the intricacies of family relationships as children grow up and make their way in the world. It is a story to which ten- and eleven-year-olds might well relate from a literature perspective and, at the same time, would serve as an interesting and solid introduction to the topic of transformations in geometry. Therefore, I chose to use this tale with a grade 5–6 class to introduce tessellations, tiling, and symmetry.

Predicting, Guessing, and Possibilities

I started the lesson by reading the story to the class up to the point at which the father and the two older sons decide to fix Misha's cloak. As I read, I posted diagrams of the patterns of the cloaks that the three sons had made (see fig. 15.1), asking the students to describe each pattern. The class quickly identified the familiar shapes—the rectangle patterns in Ivan's cloak, the square and triangle patterns in the two cloaks that Alex had made, and the circles in Misha's cloak.

I asked the students how the characters might fix the cloak of circles, and we brainstormed a list of responses. Their ideas included placing a piece of cloth behind the circles, sewing small pieces of cloth between the circles, and cutting the circles to make squares or hexagons. I then asked them if their suggestions were predictions or guesses. They agreed that they were guessing about possible solutions rather than predicting, because the book did not give any clues up to this point as to how the problem might be solved. Any one of the suggestions might have been correct. I finished reading the story, and we discovered that the tailor and his two older sons decided to cut the circles into hexagons. Our discussion then focused on the many ways in which the tailors might have created patterns. The students brainstormed many suggestions, such as using different colors; patterning colors in different ways; choosing different shapes, such as triangles; and mixing shapes, such as a square and a rectangle.

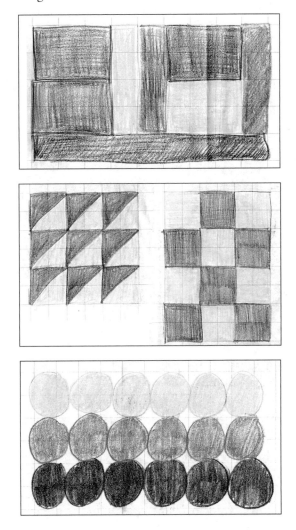

Fig. 15.1. The patterns made by the tailor's three sons

Tiling with Pattern-Block Shapes

The students then used pattern blocks to make their own cloak patterns. Using one shape only, they worked in small groups of two, three, or four students. As they worked, I circulated about the room, asking students whether they could fashion patterns without holes. They had little difficulty responding to my questions and building the patterns, but they quickly recognized that some shapes required more complex configurations than others. For example, the students quickly created patterns with pattern-block hexagons, trapezoids, squares, and triangles,

but they experienced more difficulty with the rhombi, particularly the thin beige rhombus.

Using Mathematical Language

Next, the students designed shapes with combinations of two and then three pattern-block shapes. Again, the students found that some shapes were easier to use, specifically, the hexagons, trapezoids, squares, and triangles. At the same time, they began to investigate the relationships among the shapes. Eugene shared his new knowledge, saying, "The trapezoid is half the hexagon." I suggested that his group look for other relationships, and they quickly discovered various fraction relationships among the shapes. As they experimented with circular patterns, Norali and Natalie found it challenging to tile with the rhombi (see fig. 15.2).

Fig. 15.2. Tiling with the rhombi presented difficulty.

As the students worked, we considered ways to describe patterns and I asked more questions: "Did you fill in the entire area?" "Are your patterns repeated?" "In which ways?" "How would you reproduce your pattern on paper?" "If you had just one piece of each shape, how would you move your pieces to draw your design?" After students had time to experiment with building patterns, we discussed these questions as a class. Through questioning and classroom discussion, the necessary mathematical language—slide, flip, turn, tessellation, tiling, and symmetry—was introduced. Our descriptions also included our own movements, as some students demonstrated slides, flips, and turns by moving their bodies and then the pattern-block shapes. Together we created and posted a chart to reference these mathematical terms (see fig. 15.3).

EXPLORING MATHEMATICS THROUGH LITERATURE

Fig. 15.3. A glossary of terms

Making Their Own Patterns

In small groups, students then created their own pattern designs, using as many shapes as they wished. When they were satisfied with their designs, they sketched and wrote about them. Their patterns varied from simple repetitions with two shapes and colors to more complex patterns. I was interested to hear them describe the many ways that they put the pattern blocks together. Many students worked from the inside out, whereas others attempted to make and then repeat a pattern. Adrian explained, "I made an outline of a shape and then filled in the middle, trying to make a pattern as I built." In addition, as they worked with the pattern blocks, students recognized relationships among the shapes. Some shapes could be described as fractions of other shapes, such as that each triangle was one-sixth of a hexagon. Some shapes could be tiled to create an enlargement of one of the pattern-block shapes. Daniel wrote, "My shapes are [a] trapezoid and triangles . . . . And it flips and the triangles can turn and it looks like a huge trapezoid."

Talking about their Work

As the students worked on building and recording their patterns, I continued to circulate around the room, asking them to tell me about their designs. With encouragement and reference to the chart when necessary, the students were able to articulate a description of their pattern, using the mathematical language we had developed. They all remem-bered that their patterns should not have holes and could identify at least one line of symmetry. Although they had had little experience with specific geometric concepts, the opportunities during this lesson to manipulate materials and to describe their patterns orally enabled them to use and become comfortable with the mathematical language. The charts were important visual clues as they worked, enabling them to recall and extend new information.

Talk is an important component of any lesson, and students should share ideas in large and small groups as well as in individual conferences with the teacher. In this lesson, the large-group discussion about the story gave students the opportunity to share ideas and led to the realization that their ideas are valid. In small groups, they had opportunities to construct a variety of tiling patterns, create their own designs, and describe them orally, using appropriate mathematical language, before putting their ideas in written format.

Writing about their Work

The students also characterized their patterns in writing. Some students described their work using concrete, real-life examples (e.g., sun, ribbon, trivet), some used mathematical language and named specific two-dimensional shapes (e.g., hexagon, parallelogram, triangle), and others used both concrete examples and mathematical language. For example, Michael used mathematical language. He recognized the relationships among the shapes and reported that his tiled pattern could be divided to create two equilateral triangles. Andrea also used mathematical language ("yellow hexagon, red trapezoid, blue parallelogram"), and she identified and sketched each shape, her symmetrical pattern, and her completed tiled pattern (fig. 15.4). Terra, by

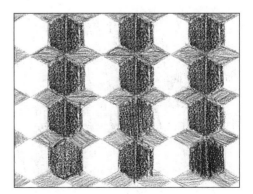

Fig. 15.4. Andrea's completed tiled pattern

contrast, described the development of her repeated-hexagon pattern using real-life examples as well as mathematical language: "In the middle is the shape of a sun. And then after I put the blue on, it looked like a hexagon. Then I put the green on, [and] it looked like a flower. And then I put blue in the spots that did not have anything, and it looked like a hexagon again." Many students used only real-life examples. Charles, for example, designed a symmetrical cowboy; Liliana wrote that her pattern "is a symbol of a ribbon . . . . Ribbons to me are very beautiful and also a symbol of winning." In fact, many students built their patterns around their personal knowledge while adding their new understanding of transformations.

A Successful Lesson: Kinesthetic, Visual, and Auditory Components

Kinesthetic, visual, and auditory components were embedded in this lesson. The use of manipu-lative materials, the various ongoing discussions, the visual cues and key words on the charts, and the opportunity to write about their work enabled these students to develop and express their learning about important geometric concepts in many ways.

A Cloak for the Dreamer allowed students their first opportunity to investigate transformations in the classroom and served as an excellent introduction to a complex idea. The students became familiar with some of the terminology of transformation geometry. As they continue their study of geometry, they will be able to revisit and refine their understandings of these geometric ideas.

REFERENCE

Friedman, Aileen. *A Cloak for the Dreamer*. New York: Scholastic Books, 1994.

"Using Literature to Investigate Transformations"

by Jacqueline Harris

Grade range:	4-6
Mathematical topics:	Tiling, tessellations, transformations, and symmetry
Children's book:	*A Cloak for the Dreamer*, written by Aileen Friedman and illustrated by Kim Howard
Materials:	Pattern blocks or other two-dimensional shapes

Discussion of the mathematics: The activities described in the article provide opportunities for students to create and describe transformations, in both oral and written format, while familiarizing themselves with the appropriate terminology. These explorations are an intuitive introduction to a more formal transformational geometry that students may study later, that is, "slides" lead to translations; "turns," to rotations; and "flips," to reflections.

Teacher's notes: The following activities are suggestions for extending students' understanding of the characteristics and properties of two-dimensional shapes.

1. One game involving communication and geometry is played in pairs. One student creates a shape using several pattern blocks, with the configuration hidden behind a barrier. The designer, using appropriate terminology, describes his or her work to a second student, whose job is to reproduce the design using only the verbal description. After students have worked through a design, they should discuss the appropriateness of the directions given and alternate giving the directions. Initially this game could be introduced to the whole class with a student or the teacher modeling the instructions.

Another option is to have students work in pairs or small groups until a satisfactory description is written. Other students can then build a design from the description and provide feedback to the designers.

Variations of this activity include (*a*) using different materials, such as paper shapes, tangrams, Power Polygons, and so on; (*b*) limiting the number of pieces used; or (*c*) allowing the second person to ask two or three questions or an unlimited number of questions for clarification.

2. In the end pages of *A Cloak for a Dreamer* is a section titled "About the Mathematics," which explains how angle size is related to tessellating shapes. This information can be the basis of a class investigation to determine which shapes tessellate and why.

3. To build awareness of transformations, tessellations, or symmetry in the world around us, the class could collect a variety of examples from school, home, or local public buildings and post them on a classroom bulletin board or in a class book. Students could photograph and describe their findings.

4. To become familiar with the similarities and differences among slides, flips, and turns, students can create simple two-dimensional designs by

repeating one shape (e.g., a square, a triangle, or a parallelogram). They can then try to duplicate the design by using only flips. Will this tactic work? Why or why not? Can the design be built using only slides or only turns? Or does it require a combination of transformations? Can the design be described in more than one way?

REFERENCES

Friedman, Aileen. *A Cloak for the Dreamer*. Illustrated by Kim Howard. New York: Scholastic, 1994.

Harris, Jacqueline. "Links to Literature: Using Literature to Investigate Transformations." *Teaching Children Mathematics* 4 (May 1998): 510–13.

16

Adventures with Sir Cumference: Standard Shapes and Nonstandard Units

Betty B. Long and Deborah A. Crocker

CINDY Neuschwander, author of *Sir Cumference and the First Round Table: A Math Adventure* (1997), commented on her work for this article:

> I wrote *Sir Cumference and the First Round Table* to help make abstract mathematical terms and ideas more concrete and more memorable. I would love to see students read or listen to the story and then try to re-create all the shapes in the book. This sort of activity should help students internalize and retain the terms and ideas that I have written about.

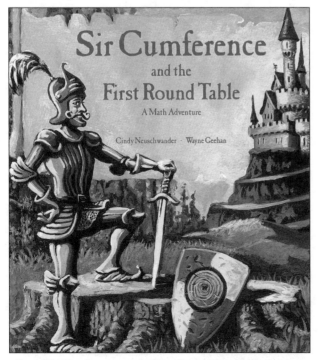

From *Sir Cumference and the First Round Table: A Math Adventure*, by Cindy Neuschwander, illustrated by Wayne Geehan. Text copyright © 1997 Cindy Neuschwander. Illustrations copyright © Wayne Geehan. Used with permission by Charlesbridge Publishing, Inc. All rights reserved.

Neuschwander's book highlights shape recognition and spatial visualization. It also serves as an excellent lead-in for several other topics, including area and perimeter.

Standard Shapes

We used *Sir Cumference and the First Round Table* with Krista Travis's fifth-grade class at Wittenburg Elementary School in Taylorsville, North Carolina. In the book, Sir Cumference, a knight in King Arthur's court; his wife, Lady Di of Ameter; and their son, Radius, are involved in the search for the perfect table to use when King Arthur meets with all the knights to discuss a possible invasion from a neighboring kingdom. They create tables of various shapes and discard them because problems arise with each shape.

We started our lesson with an activity that focused on both shape recognition and spatial visualization. We handed out paper rectangles that modeled the long rectangular table that Sir Cumference and the other knights used on the first day of their meetings. We then asked the fifth-grade students to use the rectangles to make the other geometric shapes mentioned in the book as we read the book aloud to them.

Teacher. Can you make a square out of your rectangle? You may fold and cut along the folds. You may not throw away any part of the rectangle.

Students. Yes! We can cut it in half and put one half above the other. (See fig. 16.1.)

We continued reading the book up to the point at which Lady Di suggests a diamond-shaped table. Some of the students turned their squares and claimed that they had produced diamond shapes.

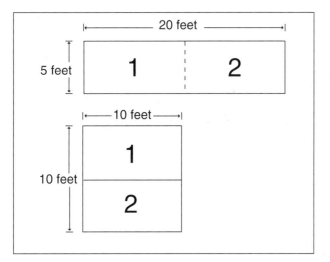

Fig. 16.1. The rectangular "table" is used to make other geometric shapes.

Because *diamond shape* is not a geometric term with a specific definition, we showed the students the illustration in the book and asked whether they could make a parallelogram that was not a square. We instructed the students to fold and cut along one diagonal of their squares. The students then put the two resulting triangles together to form the diamond-shaped table: a nonsquare parallelogram (see fig. 16.2). At this point, we discussed the concept of parallel lines and the properties of a parallelogram.

Teacher. What is a parallelogram?
Students. It has four sides, and the opposite ones are parallel.
Teacher. What does *parallel* mean?
John. They don't cross.
Katie. It's like railroad tracks.

As the story progresses, all the shapes suggested for the best possible table are ruled out because of their geometric attributes. Some have corners, for example, or not enough sides or sides that are too short or too long. After King Arthur

Fig. 16.2. Students put the triangles together to form the diamond-shaped table: a parallelogram.

complains, "The diamond point sticks into me like an enemy sword," Lady Di suggests an octagonal table. We asked the fifth graders to create an octagon from the diamond. When we saw that they were cutting out eight-sided figures but not regular octagons, we paused to talk about the difference between a regular octagon and the octagons that they were cutting.

One goal of the book is to provide a table that would give each person the same amount of room. This requirement leads to a regular octagon that has sides of equal length and angles of equal measure, rather than any arbitrary octagon. We used the book to guide the students in making a regular octagon. The text shows how to cut off irregular quadrilaterals from the corners of the parallelogram to form an octagon; parts of the quadrilaterals are then attached to the first octagon formed to make it a regular octagon (Neuschwander 1997, p. 17). We continued to read the story to the point at which Sir Cumference orders the carpenter to build an egg-shaped table. The students then cut an oval shape from the octagon.

We finished this portion of the lesson by reading the rest of the story. Ultimately, the best shape for the table is a circle. It has no corners, people can be spaced around it evenly because it has no sides, and everyone can see and hear everyone else. We asked the students to identify the *diameter, radius,* and *circumference* of a circle.

Teacher. What is the *diameter* of a circle?
Students. The distance across the circle.
Teacher. Across any place on the circle?
Students. It has to cross through the middle.
Teacher. What is the *radius* of a circle?
Carl. It's how far it is from the middle to the side.
Teacher. What is the distance around a circle?
Gail. Is it the perimeter?
Teacher. Yes, but it has another name. Does anyone know that name? Think about the names of the characters in the book.
Callie. It's circumference!

We suggested that the students might remember these terms by thinking about the Knights of the Round Table and the characters in the story: Sir Cumference, Lady Di of Ameter, and their son, Radius. Because the book helped the students remember the terminology during our discussion, it will probably also help them recall the terms later. Neuschwander hopes that teachers will use the

EXPLORING MATHEMATICS THROUGH LITERATURE

book to introduce and reinforce this vocabulary in their classrooms.

Nonstandard Units for Measuring Perimeter and Area

We used *Sir Cumference* as our lead-in for a second activity involving area and perimeter. At the end of the story, the characters discover that the suspected invaders from a neighboring kingdom, the Circumscribers, were attempting to measure the area of their kingdom, not plan for an attack. For our activity, we had the students work in groups of four. We gave each group a sheet of posterboard and markers, and we gave each student a set of pattern blocks. We asked the students to name all the shapes in their pattern blocks sets. Next, we discussed the meaning of *area* and *perimeter* with the students:

Teacher. Does anyone know what the words *area* and *perimeter* mean?

Jody. I think area is the space inside of something, like a square.

Teacher. You could measure it by covering up the shape?

Students. Yes!

Teacher. What about *perimeter*?

Sara. Is that how far around it is?

Teacher. Do you mean around the outside of a shape?

Sara. Yes, along the sides.

Teacher. That's right. You could measure perimeter by figuring out the distance around the edges.

We then suggested to the students which shapes from their pattern blocks sets to use as their units of measurement.

Principles and Standards for School Mathematics (NCTM 2000) supports the use of nonstandard units of measure as a means for making the transition to standard units of measure for grades 3–5:

> Students in grades 3–5 should be able to recognize the need to select units appropriate to the attribute being measured. Different kinds of units are needed for measuring area than for measuring length. At first they might use convenient nonstandard units such as lima beans to estimate area and then come to recognize the need for a standard unit such as a unit square (p. 172).

For their units of nonstandard measurement, we told the students to use one side of the green triangle in the pattern blocks set as the unit of measure for length and use the area of the green triangle as the unit of measure for area. We selected the green

triangle from the pattern blocks set because it has one of the smallest areas in the set; thus the students could use it to surround and cover the other shapes to find the perimeters and areas. This approach requires only addition or multiplication to compute the areas and perimeters of most of the other shapes.

The student groups drew diagrams on one side of the posterboard to illustrate how they found the perimeter of each of the shapes in their pattern blocks sets (see fig. 16.3). After sharing their methods (see fig. 16.4), the students worked in groups again to determine the area of each shape. They then drew diagrams on the reverse side of the posterboard to illustrate their methods for determining area (see fig. 16.5). The students found the areas of most of the shapes fairly quickly. For example, they immediately covered the yellow hexagon with six of the green triangles and knew that the area of the hexagon was six area units. Two green triangles fit exactly over the blue parallelogram, yielding an area of two area units. Three green triangles fit on top of the red trapezoid, meaning it had an area of three area units.

Fig. 16.3. Students work in groups to find the perimeter of pattern block shapes.

Fig. 16.4. Students share their methods of determining perimeter.

Fig. 16.5. Students work in groups to determine the area of the [P]attern [B]lock shapes

Finding the area of the square and the small tan parallelogram proved to be challenging for the students. Although a couple of the groups made a visual conclusion that the areas of the tan parallelogram and the green triangle were equal, their conclusion is mathematically incorrect. Students could further test this conclusion with paper models of the tan parallelogram and the green triangle by cutting the parallelogram in half, rearranging the halves, and showing that the area of the parallelogram is just a little greater than that of the triangle.

Conclusion

The fifth-grade students in Miss Travis's class loved *Sir Cumference and the First Round Table*. The story provided the opportunity to review some of the attributes of rectangles, squares, parallelograms, octagons, ovals, and circles. The book also served as motivation for an area-and-perimeter activity using pattern blocks shapes. Teachers could extend the review of the attributes of shapes beyond what is discussed in this article and use additional activities on perimeter and area after reading the book.

Although *Sir Cumference* is a picture storybook, we found that the mathematics concepts reinforced in the book extend beyond the mathematical development of typical picture-book readers. In other words, the book could definitely be included with the many excellent picture storybooks recently published for older children. The fifth-grade students were interested in the story and the activities, and they related well to the mathematics contained in the story.

REFERENCES

National Council of Teachers of Mathematics (NCTM). *Principles and Standards for School Mathematics*. Reston, Va.: NCTM, 2000.

Neuschwander, Cindy. *Sir Cumference and the First Round Table: A Math Adventure*. Illustrated by Wayne Geehan. Watertown, Mass.: Charlesbridge Publishing Co., 1997.

"Adventures with Sir Cumference: Standard Shapes and Nonstandard Units"

by Betty B. Long and Deborah A. Crocker

Grade range:	4-6
Mathematical topics:	Shape recognition, spatial visualization, concepts of area and perimeter
Children's book:	*Sir Cumference and the First Round Table: A Math Adventure*, written by Cindy Neuschwander and illustrated by Wayne Geehan

Activity 1

Materials:	Paper rectangles, scissors, and transparent tape

Discussion of the mathematics: This task provides an opportunity to study different shapes, their attributes, and how they are related. Appropriate mathematics vocabulary will be naturally introduced and reinforced in the context of exploring the questions presented in the story. The questions also involve spatial visualization, because students need to consider how to transform one shape into another shape. Initially, some students may have difficulties with spatial visualization, but this skill is developed through experiences and over time.

Teaching notes and questions to ask students: This activity, which is done as the book is read, involves making the shapes encountered as Sir Cumference designs an appropriate table. Below are a suggested outline for the activity and possible questions. Additional examples of questions and sample discussions are included in the article.

Begin reading the book *Sir Cumference and the First Round Table: A Math Adventure*. Stop at the end of page 7. Distribute paper rectangles to each student.

- How could you make a square out of the rectangle? You can fold your rectangle and then cut along the fold. Do not throw away any part of the rectangle, because doing so would result in a smaller table for

Sir Cumference. Tape the pieces together to form your new shape.

Continue reading through the top of page 11.

- Fold one of the diagonals of your square, and then cut along the diagonal. What kind of shape can you make with these two pieces? Tape the pieces together to form your new shape.

Continue reading through page 16, and ask the students how the parallelogram can be transformed into an octagon. Give the students time to consider possible solutions. Guide the students on the cuts necessary to transform the parallelogram into an octagon; you might start by showing them how to cut off the corners as illustrated in the book on page 17. You will probably need to suggest that they cut and discard parts of the corners.

Continue reading through page 19.

- Can you visualize an oval or ellipse inside your octagon?

- Can you cut an oval or ellipse out of the center of your octagon? Try to cut as large an ellipse as possible.

Finish reading the book.

Activity 2 (Extension)

Materials: Pattern blocks, poster board or sheets of paper, and markers (red, green, blue, orange, yellow, and black)

Discussion of the mathematics: Exploring the concepts of perimeter and area at the same time provides an opportunity for students to compare the similarities and differences between the two measurement concepts. By using the green triangle as a nonstandard unit, students will need to focus on a length (the triangle's side) as one linear unit and the surface of the triangle as one unit of area. In this instance students will be counting how many "triangle" units of area will cover a surface instead of focusing on such standard units as square inches or square centimeters. Note: the length of the side of each pattern block is actually one inch, but the lengths are measured in terms of the green triangle's side in this activity.

Teaching notes and questions to ask students: The following activity is an extension that explores area and perimeter concepts and can be implemented after the book has been read.

Introduce the activity by using the quote "They want only to measure the area of their kingdom" from the book (p. 27) Elicit students' informal definitions of perimeter and area.

- What is perimeter?
- What is area?
- What types of units are used to measure each?

Put the students into groups of three or four. Hand out bags of pattern blocks to each student in each group. Give the students an opportunity to discuss the attributes of each of the shapes (i.e., number of sides, number and size of angles, and presence of parallel edges and planes).

- Can you name all the different shapes in your bag?
- What are some of the attributes of each shape?

Explain to students that they will first be collecting data on the perimeter and later the area of each shape. Give each group a recording sheet (a piece of poster board or at least two sheets of paper) and markers in the colors of the different pattern blocks

(red, green, blue, orange, yellow, and black [we outlined the white parallelogram in black and did not color it in]). On one sheet have the students write "PERIMETER"; on the other sheet have the students write "AREA."

- Let us use the green triangle to define our units of measure. What kind of triangle is it? We will use one side as one unit of length. Later we will use the green triangle's area as one unit of area.
- Use the triangle unit of length (length of one side of the triangle) to find the perimeter of each of the other shapes.
- Draw diagrams on your recording sheets to illustrate how you did so, and write your answers next to each shape on the poster board.

Have groups share results and some of their different strategies for finding the perimeters.

Next, have the students find areas using the green triangle. This pursuit will be a little harder and may take additional time. Finding the area of the square and the small parallelogram will be the most challenging tasks. After the students have finished this work, have each group share its methods and results for area.

- If the area of your triangle is one unit of area, what is the area of each of the other shapes?
- Draw diagrams on your poster board to illustrate how you found each area, and write your answers next to each shape.

REFERENCES

Long, Betty B., and Deborah A. Crocker. "Links to Literature: Adventures with Sir Cumference: Standard Shapes and Nonstandard Units" *Teaching Children Mathematics* 7 (December 2000): 242-45.

Neuschwander, Cindy. *Sir Cumference and the First Round Table: A Math Adventure*. Illustrated by Wayne Geehan. Watertown, Mass.: Charlesbridge Publishing, 1997.

17

Geometry Projects Linking Mathematics, Literacy, Art, and Technology

Catherine Little

How do you spark your students' interest in geometry? Which assignments connect geometry with other disciplines? Which assignments call on students' initiative and creativity?—Editorial Panel

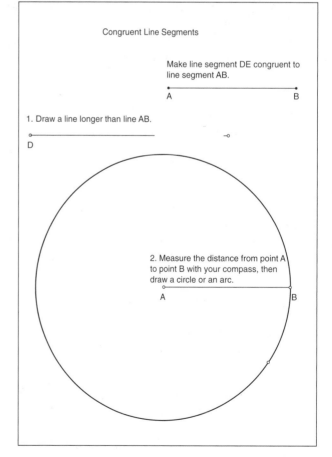

DURING the course of my eighth-grade geometry unit, I decided that the students were ready for a challenging project. I came up with the options for the assignments and their scoring rubrics in figure 17.1. The students were indeed up to the challenge! Four classes were assigned the project, including one class of gifted students and one class of learning-disabled students. Three of the classes were my own, and the fourth was that of one of my colleagues, who inspired the addition of the assignment using The Geometer's Sketchpad (Jackiw 1995).

The students had to choose one of three options and were given six weeks to complete the work; two of the weeks were holidays. The first choice was to create a Geometry Construction Manual using a computer program called The Geometer's Sketchpad (Sketchpad). The students had been shown the basics of construction work using conventional tools, but Sketchpad allowed them to use technology in a creative way. The students had also been exposed to Sketchpad through various class assignments. Combining the mathematics with the technology in a manual format meant that the students had to use technical writing to compose instructions. The students who chose this option had to do the whole assignment at school, since we were not licensed to duplicate the program for home use. See figure 17.2 for one student's instructions on geometric constructions.

The second option involved writing and illustrating a children's picture book. The only stipulation was that a character had to learn a geometry concept as part of the plot. Examples from previous students' projects were read in class, and we discussed various possible methods of illustration. The children's book option was chosen by the majority of the students. We read many of the

Congruent Line Segments

Make line segment DE congruent to line segment AB.

1. Draw a line longer than line AB.

2. Measure the distance from point A to point B with your compass, then draw a circle or an arc.

Fig. 17.2 Marion's instructions on geometric constructions

As part of your study of geometry, you will be required to complete *one* of the following assignments. This project will be due on _____. This time period allows you four weeks of school time as well as the two-week break in case you wish to work over the holidays. Please be advised that extensions will not be granted. Plan your time accordingly. START EARLY!

A) Constructions Manual

You may work by yourself or with one partner to write an instruction manual, which teaches students the method of construction for each of the basic constructions and an enrichment item. Each page must have a sequence of diagrams as well as written instructions. These must be presented in a logical manner using The Geometer's Sketchpad program. Please submit a disk as well as a printed copy of your manual.

Marking scheme

Clarity of diagrams	0 1 2 3 4 5 6 7 8 9 10
Clarity of written instructions	0 1 2 3 4 5 6 7 8 9 10
Overall organization and presentation	0 1 2 3 4 5 6 7 8 9 10

B) Children's Picture Book

You may work by yourself or with one partner to write and illustrate a children's book in which one of the main characters learns a geometry concept as part of the plot. This concept may or may not be one that has been or will be taught in our class. The book must be long enough to have an introduction, plot development, as well as conclusion.

Marking scheme

Quality of pictures	0 1 2 3 4 5 6 7 8 9 10
Quality of story (including grammar and spelling)	0 1 2 3 4 5 6 7 8 9 10
Overall organization and presentation	0 1 2 3 4 5 6 7 8 9 10

C) Escher Art

You may work by yourself to create a piece of art in the Escher style. You must research the life of M.C. Escher and write a one-page (three or four paragraphs) report on the relationship between Escher's art and mathematics. You must then learn to make a tessellation and use it to create your artwork.

Marking scheme

Written report	0 1 2 3 4 5 6 7 8 9 10
Complexity of tessellation	0 1 2 3 4 5 6 7 8 9 10
Overall appearance of artwork	0 1 2 3 4 5 6 7 8 9 10

This marking sheet must be attached to your project. A bibliography is required.

Fig. 17.1. Assignment options and rubrics

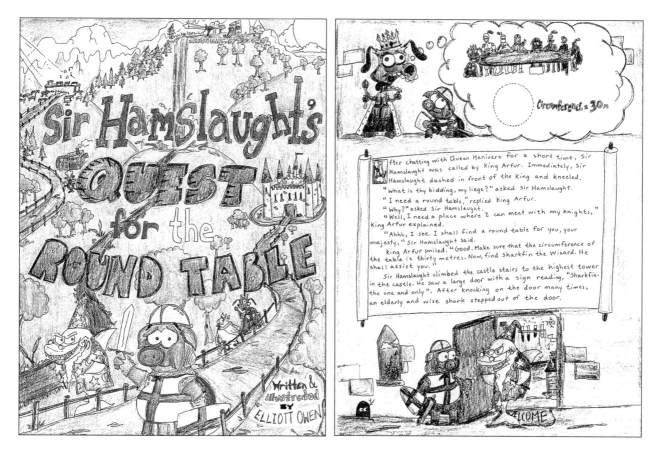

Fig. 17.3. Elliott's talent as mathematician and artist is obvious.

Fig. 17.4. Chris and Yalcin sleuth out a weapon whose "purpose was to suck up numbers."

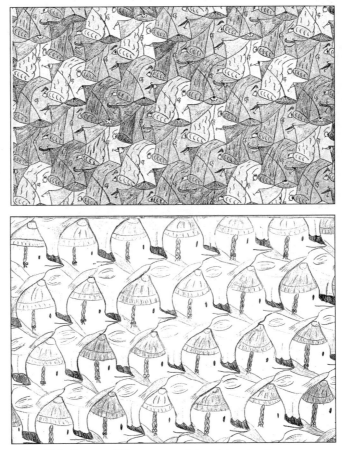

Fig. 17.5. Chuan and Fiana prepare Esher-style artwork.

books to our classes. Seventh-, eighth-, and ninth-grade students alike enjoyed the antics of Sir "Ham-slaught," a plump pig, in his quest for a round table with a circumference of 30 meters (see fig. 17.3). The students were delighted with the watercolors that illustrated the adventures of "Little Pi," agent 3.1415, and a former teacher who was depicted as the villain, FFOO Eisen. He had a powerful number-sucking machine that created chaos by eliminating numbers from the world. The secret agent had to solve riddles in the form of mathematics problems to solve the case (see fig. 17.4). A "Choose Your Own Adventure" book ended in several different ways depending on the path taken. The reader is called on to help when all the teachers at the school are mysteriously transformed into two-dimensional shapes.

The third choice involved Escher art (see fig. 17.5). The students were to study Escher's art and write a summary of its link to mathematics. They also had to create a piece of art in the Escher style,

meaning that each tessellation had to resemble an animate object. The results of this option have decorated the school hallway, a music-night program, and the director's office at the North York Board of Education. Students stopped to admire the work of their classmates and to discuss the techniques that they employed to achieve the desired effects.

The students had fun doing this project. Many favorable comments were made. One boy wrote that he thought the geometry unit was uninteresting until he had the opportunity to use the knowledge in creating his manual. He found this part of the course challenging. As teachers, we were very pleased with the process as well as the product. The students showed us that the potential of the learner is immense. A good project can help us to let that potential shine.

REFERENCE

Jackiw, Nicholas. The Geometer's Sketchpad, Ver. 3.0. Berkeley, Calif.: Key Curriculum Press, 1995. Software.

"Geometry Projects Linking Mathematics, Literacy, Arts and Technology"

by Catherine Little

Grade range:	6–8
Mathematical topic:	Connecting mathematics with other disciplines
Children's book:	A book such as *Math Curse*, written by Jon Scieszka and illustrated by Lane Smith, or *Socrates and the Three Little Pigs*, illustrated by Mitsumasa Anno and text by Tuyosi Mori
Materials:	"Geometry Project Guidelines" sheets, The Geometer's Sketchpad software

Discussion of the mathematics: The mathematics emphasized will vary. This investigation is an opportunity for students to learn more about a mathematics topic of their choice by researching that topic. The purpose of the projects is to help students build connections with other disciplines as well as learn to communicate what they have learned.

Teacher notes: Each of the three projects described in the article can be linked with an aspect of literacy. The challenge is to weave a seamless mix of mathematics and literacy skills in a manner that will do justice to both disciplines.

Children's picture book: Students may be enthusiastic about writing a children's storybook but be unsure about how to start one for mathematics class. Colleagues who teach language can be helpful in sharing the format used for story writing in their classes, so that students can use the same format for their mathematics stories. Some students will get carried away with the plot and dialogue in the story rather than focus on the mathematics. During brainstorming, emphasize that the mathematics must be the star in this story. Read such stories as *Math Curse* or *Socrates and the Three Little Pigs* to give the stu-

dents story ideas. Students who have difficulty with language might start their story-writing endeavors by modeling their story after an existing fairy tale but adding a mathematical twist. Younger students may be helped by the approach of starting the story as a class.

The main goal, however, is to encourage students to come up with an authentic challenge—a storyline that incorporates a real reason to need the included mathematics. Students often start with someone needing to learn a concept for a test and then progress to an adventure in which the hero solves mathematics problems as part of a quest or an adventure. The beauty of "Sir Hamslaught" is that the hero really needs to learn geometry to find that round table for the King!

Construction manual: Whereas writing the storybook is an example of a narrative project, writing the Sketchpad manual is an example of an explanatory or instructive project. Provide students with real life examples in which following step-by-step instructions is important to achieve the outcome. These examples will help students understand the need for clarity, precision, and accuracy. They should also appreciate the usefulness of a good diagram; for example, you might suggest that they imagine trying to put together a jigsaw puzzle without using the accompanying picture as compared with putting the puzzle together with the aid of a picture.

Prior to beginning this project, the class had worked with The Geometer's Sketchpad (Sketchpad) and had learned how to use rulers and compasses for such constructions as bisecting an angle and drawing an equilateral triangle. The new challenge for the students was to write instructions for using Sketchpad to make the constructions. To facilitate students' work, a computer lab was made available after school each day, and downloadable "test" copies of Sketchpad were available that students could use at home.

To evaluate their written instructions, students could ask a third party to try to follow the instructions; such feedback can help students write the final version of their instructions. Additionally, our students were given feedback from the computer teacher and the author.

Escher art: Although this project may be the most visual of the three, it is also a good opportunity to practice oral communication skills. Students could present their projects as if they were tour guides at an art gallery. Their talk could include information about the history of the genre, the personal interpretation of the artist, the use of color, and the like. If a large number of students pick this option, the class could organize an art show to present their work.

In preparing their projects, our students primarily found their own resources. The art teacher helped them get started researching Escher's art and related topics on the Internet. Their Internet searches garnered programs for making tessellations online. In earlier class work, all the students had been taught how to manually construct shapes that would tessellate.

REFERENCES

Friedman, Aileen. *A Cloak for the Dreamer*. Illustrated by Kim Howard. New York: Scholastic, 1994.

Little, Catherine. "Teacher to Teacher: Geometry Projects Linking Mathematics, Literacy, Arts, and Technology." *Mathematics Teaching in the Middle School* 4 (February 1999): 332–35.

Mori, Tuyosi. *Socrates and the Three Little Pigs*. Illustrated by Mitsumasa Anno. New York: Philomel Books, 1986.

Scieszka, Jon. *Math Curse*. Illustrated by Lane Smith. New York: Viking, 1995.

Geometry Project Guidelines

Name _____

Date _____

As part of your study of geometry, you will be required to complete *one* of the following assignments. This project will be due on _____. Please be advised that extensions will not be granted. Plan your time accordingly.

1. Constructions Manual

You may work by yourself or with one partner to write an instruction manual, which teaches students the method of construction for each of the basic constructions and an enrichment item. Each page should have a sequence of diagrams as well as written instructions. These components must be presented in a logical manner using The Geometer's Sketchpad program. Please submit a disk as well as a printed copy of your manual.

Marking scheme

Clarity of diagrams	0 1 2 3 4 5 6 7 8 9 10
Clarity of written instructions	0 1 2 3 4 5 6 7 8 9 10
Overall organization and presentation	0 1 2 3 4 5 6 7 8 9 10

2. Children's Picture Book

You may work by yourself or with one partner to write and illustrate a children's book in which one of the main characters learns a geometry concept as part of the plot. Your chosen concept may or may not be one that has been or will be taught in our class. The book must be long enough to have an introduction, development of the plot, and a conclusion.

Marking scheme

Quality of pictures	0 1 2 3 4 5 6 7 8 9 10
Quality of story (including grammar and spelling)	0 1 2 3 4 5 6 7 8 9 10
Overall organization and presentation	0 1 2 3 4 5 6 7 8 9 10

3. Escher Art

You may work by yourself to create a piece of art in the Escher style. You must research the life of M.C. Escher and write a one-page (three or four paragraphs) report on the relationship between Escher's art and mathematics. You must then learn to make a tessellation and use it to create your artwork.

Marking scheme

Written report	0 1 2 3 4 5 6 7 8 9 10
Complexity of tessellation	0 1 2 3 4 5 6 7 8 9 10
Overall appearance of artwork	0 1 2 3 4 5 6 7 8 9 10

This evaluation sheet must be attached to your project. A bibliography is required.

Content Strand:
Measurement

18

Exploring Measurement through Literature

Cheryl A. Lubinski and Diane Thiessen

THIS article focuses on how the children's book *How Big Is a Foot?* (Myller 1990) was used to prompt measurement experiences that reflect ideas embedded in the *Curriculum and Evaluation Standards for School Mathematics* (NCTM 1989). *How Big Is a Foot?* concerns a king's decision to surprise his wife, the queen, on her birthday by having a bed made for her. This gift would be a *big* surprise, since beds had not yet been invented.

This book was used to frame a discussion of children's reasoning about measurement. However, to understand how this experience occurred in one first-grade classroom, we must consider a synopsis of the story.

> To determine the size of the bed, the king asked the queen to lie on the floor while he measured her with his big feet (see fig. 18.1). He then told the Prime Minister who summoned the Chief Carpenter and commissioned a bed that was to measure three feet wide and six feet long, big enough to fit the queen "including the crown which she sometimes liked to wear to sleep" (Myller 1990, p. 10).
>
> In his shop, the carpenter's apprentice measured an area three feet by six feet with his little feet and made the bed accordingly.

When Ms. L. read this story to her first-grade class, even the six-year-olds realized the impending problem and were quick to smile at the mistake the apprentice was obviously going to make. They realized that the difference between the size of the king's foot and that of the apprentice's foot created

a problem. As the teacher continued reading the story, the children anticipated the outcome.

The bed was delivered to the king, who presented it to his wife. But alas, the bed was not suitable for the queen (see fig. 18.2). The apprentice was thrown in jail for displeasing the king and for failing to follow instructions. After much thought, since incarceration can be highly motivating, the apprentice resolved the problem and presented an explanation to the king. A new bed was made, and the apprentice was crowned a royal prince for his efforts.

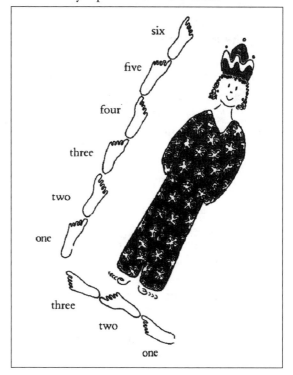

Fig. 18.1. The king measured around the queen with his big feet. From *How Big Is a Foot?* © 1990 by Rolf Myller. Reprinted with permission of Dell Publishing.

BUT

the bed was much too small for the Queen.

Fig. 18.2. The bed was not suitable for the queen. From *How Big Is a Foot?* © 1990 by Rolf Myller. Reprinted with permission of Dell Publishing.

This story line was the impetus for a discussion of measurement that continued for three weeks. During this time, the teacher was able to develop a learning environment that allowed her to create tasks based on students' thinking. Her intent was to develop children's thinking about linear measurement as being that form of measurement used to identify and count a defined unit in relation to an object's length. She believed that ongoing assessment was needed to ascertain how the children's thinking was developing in relation to her instructional goals.

Before rereading the book the following day, Ms. L. reflected on the following:

- *Children's thinking*: How will children communicate their understanding of the problems presented in the story?

- *Mathematical content*: What are the primary mathematical concepts that need to be addressed?

- *Additional resources*: What materials would help assess students' thinking?

To encourage discourse, she wanted the children to generate a list of questions related to the mathematical problems embedded in the story line.

She considered the following to be important:

1. What are the problems in this story? Who had them? What solutions were proposed for them?
2. Is the chief carpenter's role important? How could the chief carpenter have solved the problem?
3. What role did the apprentice play in the story? Could the apprentice have asked the king some questions to avoid the problem?

The children were able to pose similar questions during the subsequent rereading and discussion.

During the next several days, the children were involved in tasks that explored concepts related to linear measurement. The focus of these tasks and the time involved varied from day to day, but the common thread of the discourse among the tasks was *How Big Is a Foot?* Readers may want to consider how to extend or to modify the tasks that follow for students with regard to communication, reasoning, and connections to their experiences.

Tasks for the Learning Environment
Constructing a nonstandard unit

The children constructed paper footprints using one of their feet as a model. By using these models, they attempted to measure the length of various objects around the room, such as their desks, the reading table, and the door. However, this task was not easy. At times, even though the length of two children's paper footprints was the same, the answers they obtained were different. They debated on what factor accounted for these differences and discussed their conjectures about the discrepancies. They reasoned that using exactly one paper footprint was creating errors in measuring. It was not easy to determine the length of an object exactly by using one footprint, owing to its repeated use. At times overlapping occurred. It was suggested that perhaps it would be easier to measure longer lengths if several paper footprints were connected.

Iteration of nonstandard unit

For this task, an *Arithmetic Teacher* article (Bruni and Silverman 1974) was used as a resource, and sixth graders assisted the first graders. The older students were responsible for helping the first graders construct several footprints and link their footprints with brads and paper strips (see fig. 18.3) to make a longer measuring tool. This task allowed the teacher to discuss the ruler as being an object on which a unit of measurement is recorded, usually with subdivisions into smaller units. Then they measured and recorded the lengths of various objects in the room. At the same time, Ms. L. made a ruler using her foot as the unit model. After these initial measures, the question was then posed concerning whether the results would be the same if they had used the teacher's ruler to determine the length of an object. This discussion created an opportunity to consider estimation.

The next lesson focused on estimating students' heights in comparison with one student's footprint model. For example, after estimating Adelai's height using Maggie's footprint model, Maggie's paper footprint ruler was used to measure Adelai's height. After Maggie's height was measured, the children were asked what would happen if the teacher's footprint were used. Some children reasoned that if the length of the footprint was longer, the number of footprints needed to measure Maggie's height would be fewer. This conjecture was verified using the appropriate paper ruler. During the discourse that ensued, this situation was connected to the problem between the lengths of the king's foot and the apprentice's foot.

To reinforce the idea that unit measures have names, Ms. L. created a task that would explore a unit's name. During the second week of the discussion about measurement, she said, "I measured the length of the bulletin board this morning and I got 15." The children had reasoned that this number gave them some information about the unit used to measure the length of the bulletin board, but they did not know exactly what tool Ms. L. had used to measure it. Thus, they asked, "Fifteen what?" In a few days the class coined the phrase "How big was your foot?" that they understood to mean "What unit did you use when you measured?" On this

occasion, Ms. L. answered, "I used a pencil." This task was repeated not only by the teacher but by many students until Ms. L. was satisfied that the children connected the number representing length to the iteration of a specific unit. This activity took several days. However, the level of understanding developed by the students was well worth the time involved.

Extending to standard units of measurement

Once the children reasoned that the length of an object is determined by identifying a unit and iterating that unit over the length of the object, they began to use conventional units, such as centimeters, feet, and so on. The term *iterate* was used with the children because Ms. L. believes that it is important to use conventional mathematical terms even with young children. By this time, the unit was of little concern. Students knew that they could use the unit in the same manner that they had used their footprints to determine length. They easily connected the lesson to reality.

To extend their understanding of using a measuring tool, Ms. L. showed the class a centimeter ruler and pointed to two of its numerals. She asked, "How many centimeters long is it between these two lines?" Using different numbers, this task was repeated several times. The children focused on units, not numerals.

Discussion

In reflecting on the tasks that occurred in this first-grade classroom over three weeks, the teacher realized that several mathematical connections had been made. One of the most surprising outcomes was the skill that the children had developed using the ruler. In previous years, she had begun a discussion of linear measurement by introducing the ruler and measuring objects. Many of the children

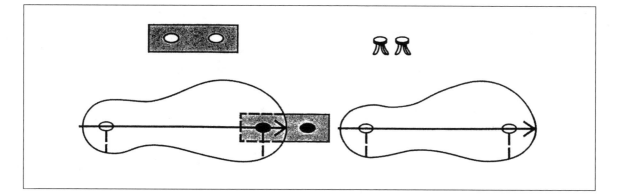

Fig. 18.3. First graders link their footprints (Bruni and Silverman 1974, p. 574).

had used the numeral 1 as the starting point and did not focus on unit length. Consequently, when they read their rulers, their measurements were always off by one unit.

This year, when measuring with a ruler, the children either lined up the edge of the ruler with the edge of the object *or* they started with any numeral on their ruler and counted units. Ms. L. had never had students make this connection as readily. She attributed their understanding to her decision to delay the discussion of using a ruler to an appropriate time.

Problem solving, communication, reasoning, and mathematical connections were evident in many of the measurement tasks. During the development of the linear-measurement concepts, it was important for the teacher to assess the students' understandings before proceeding to a more difficult task. The end of this story was a happy one because not only did the apprentice understand the problem, but the children did as well.

BIBLIOGRAPHY

Bruni, James V., and Helene Silverman. "Let's Do It! Developing the Concept of Linear Measurement." *Arithmetic Teacher* 21 (November 1974): 570-77.

Myller, Rolf. *How Big Is A Foot?* New York: Dell Publishing, 1990.

National Council of Teachers of Mathematics (NCTM). *Curriculum and Evaluation Standards for School Mathematics* Reston, Va.: NCTM, 1989.

———. *Professional Standards for Teaching Mathematics*. Reston, Va.: NCTM, 1991.

Thiessen, Diane, and Margaret Matthias, eds. *The Wonderful World of Mathematics: A Critically Annotated List of Children's Books in Mathematics*. Reston, Va.: National Council of Teachers of Mathematics, 1992.

"Exploring Measurement through Literature"

by Cheryl A. Lubinski and Diane Thiessen

Grade range:	Pre-K–2
Mathematical topics:	Attributes of measurement, standard and nonstandard units
Children's book:	*How Big Is a Foot?*, by Rolf Myller
Materials:	Squares of different sizes (paper or tiles), various-sized "cups" and containers, cubes, and "*How Big is a Foot?*" recording sheet

Discussion of the mathematics: Extensions to the task described in the article were developed by making connections with the NCTM's Measurement Standard for prekindergarten through grade 2, which states that students should "recognize the attributes of length, volume, weight, area, and time" (NCTM 2000, p. 102). "A measurable attribute is a characteristic of an object that can be quantified. Line segments have length, plane regions have area, and physical objects have mass"(NCTM 2000, p. 44). Young students need ample opportunities to explore various attributes.

"The types of units that students use for measuring and the ways they use them should expand and shift as students move through the prekindergarten through grade 2 curriculum" (NCTM 2000, p. 45). An important point for teachers to recognize is that "understanding that different units are needed to measure different attributes is sometimes difficult for young children" (NCTM 2000, p. 45). The purposes of the following tasks are to extend students' opportunities beyond understanding only the attribute of linear measures (as in the article) and to teach students to choose an appropriate unit of measurement.

Teacher notes: In the article "Exploring Measurement through Literature," the students progress through several tasks related to linear measurement. Initially they work with a nonstandard unit; then

they iterate that unit and begin to estimate and measure lengths; and finally, they discuss standard units of linear measurement. The tasks described below encourage students to explore other measurement attributes. These tasks should be related to the students' experiences with *How Big Is a Foot?* and connected with the idea that the size of the unit determines the number of units. A generalization for these tasks should be "the larger the unit, the fewer number of units needed to measure an object" or "the smaller the unit, the larger the number of units needed."

Attribute of area: To develop the concept that area is amount of surface covered, have students use a nonstandard square unit, such as small square tiles, to cover various small areas (the cover of a book, a sheet of paper, etc.) and discuss the number of square units that covered the object. Next have students estimate the number of square units for other objects (desktop, seat of their chair, etc.) and discuss *why* their estimates make sense. Have students measure these surfaces by covering them with tiles and then comparing their estimates with the actual measure. Note: Consider how to deal with partial square units that may be obtained or whether students should estimate to the nearest unit.

Finally, provide students with different-sized standard square units in the form of tiles or paper squares (square inch, square centimeter, square foot,

157

etc.). Have students determine the area measure of various surfaces, such as a desktop, a tabletop, or a carpet in the room, using the different-sized measures. As a summarizing activity, have the students discuss the different results they obtained for the same object. That is, the larger the unit, the smaller the number of units needed to cover the object.

Attribute of capacity/volume: Provide students with a paper cup that has a nonstandard volume. Have them estimate the number of paper cups of water (or sand) that will fill a larger container (bucket, juice container, etc.), and have them discuss *why* their estimate makes sense. Have students continue by measuring the volumes and then discussing how their estimates compare with their measures. Pose the following questions:

- If the bucket was half its size, how many paper cups of water would you need to fill it? Why?
- What if the bucket was twice its size; how many paper cups would you need? Why?

To help students develop referents for different-sized units and the relationships among them, provide measuring cups and containers of various capacities. Students can estimate and explore "how many" cups, half-cups, one-fourth cups, quarts, or gallons are needed to fill a specific container. They could also explore how many cups fill a quart, gallon, and the like. Metric units, such as liters, should also be considered.

Because we also measure volume in terms of cubic units, students can be given similar opportunities to measure containers by filling them with cubes. Such classroom materials as one-inch cubes or two-centimeter cubes are a more appropriate size than one-centimeter cubes for students beginning their explorations of volume.

Appropriate units of length, area, capacity, volume: As measurement situations are investigated during the school year, students should focus on what attribute is being measured and then what unit of measure makes sense to use, and why. For example, if students are investigating the area of a notepad (tabletop, wall, their bedroom floor), the teacher might ask, "What unit of measure makes sense to use, and why?"

To emphasize the importance of labeling measures, students may enjoy solving the following question:

Both the royal apprentice and the queen measured the height of the royal pooch's doghouse. The apprentice got 3 and the queen got 1. Can they both be correct? Explain.

Measurement in our lives: To help students acquire a broader perspective of measure and how it is used in daily life, students could interview family members on how they use measurement and why it is important. A class list could be constructed by summarizing their results. The chart could include a list of the objects measured; tell which units were most convenient to use, and why; and perhaps list the measuring tools that were used.

REFERENCES

Lubinski, Cheryl A., and Diane Thiessen. "Exploring Measurement through Literature." *Teaching Children Mathematics* 2 (January 1996): 260–63.

Myller, Rolf. *How Big Is a Foot?* New York: Dell Publishing, 1990.

National Council of Teachers of Mathematics (NCTM). *Principles and Standards for School Mathematics.* Reston, Va.: NCTM, 2000.

How Big Is a Foot?

Name_____

Date _____

Measure two different objects using the same unit.

Object to be measured _____

Unit of measure _____

Estimate _____

Measure _____

Object to be measured _____

Unit of measure _____

Estimate _____

Measure _____

(Continued on next page)

Remeasure each of the objects on the first sheet using a different-sized unit.

Object to be measured _____

Unit of measure _____

Estimate _____

Measure _____

Object to be measured _____

Unit of measure _____

Estimate _____

Measure _____

What did you learn by measuring the same object with two different-sized units?

Why is it important always to record the name of the unit as well as the number of units?

19

How Do You Measure a Dad?

Kathy Kubota-Zarivnij

BOYS and girls, you need to ask your mom for permission to borrow one of your dad's shoes for two weeks. It should be a shoe that he wouldn't use during this time because we don't want him to know that it is missing. You're going to use that shoe to prepare a special Father's Day gift," announced Mrs. Porter to her class of second-grade students. "What if I don't have a dad?" asked a few students. "Would you like to prepare a special gift for an uncle? Your grandfather? Your older brother? A special family friend?" asked Mrs. Vivona.

The children in these classrooms discussed the Father's Day activity and gift with excitement. This gift would include a series of pictorial and written descriptions about their dads' shoes, compiled in a booklet called "How Do You Measure a Dad?" On Friday, the teachers sent home an explanatory letter, outlining the request for a shoe and describing its use in the classroom. Throughout the next week, more than fifty shoes were collected, providing a concrete and relevant data set for students to analyze, classify, and describe mathematically.

Planning the Shoe Investigation

The shoe investigation was designed and implemented by a university mathematics course director and two second-grade teachers. The investigation uses the book *Shoes, Shoes, Shoes* (Morris 1995) and a series of mathematics activities (shown in fig. 19.1) based on the NCTM's Standards (1989) in data management, measurement, number sense and numeracy, and patterning. For example, students related "physical materials, pictures, and diagrams to mathematical ideas" (NCTM 1989, p. 26) using the book, shoe, measurement tools, and record sheets. When students interpreted their shoe graphs in mathematics journals, they communicated their interpretations and descriptions. Further, we assessed students' learning using observation, individual interviewing, and work-sample analysis, including mathematics journals and record sheets.

In addition, we arranged to have seventh- and eighth-grade students facilitate second-graders' small-group discussions. Before this activity began, these older students were given an overview of the shoe investigation and assigned responsibilities as facilitators, including recording students' ideas on chart paper, asking questions to promote discussion, gathering needed concrete materials, and interviewing students about their understanding of specific mathematical concepts. We discussed ways that the older students could help the second graders provide more detailed responses through probing questions and statements, such as, "Why did you say that?" "Explain your idea." "How do you know that your answer makes sense?" To encourage the younger students to listen actively to one another, we listed such questions as, "What else can you add to Vanessa's answer?" "What did Carlos say that makes sense to you?"

Qualitative Analysis: "What Makes Shoes the Same and Different?"

To introduce the shoe investigation, the teachers read aloud *Shoes, Shoes, Shoes*, which begins with the sentence, "Shoes, shoes, all kinds of shoes, wherever you find them shoes come in twos" (p. 7) The subsequent pages have photographs and rhyming descriptions of shoes in many real-life situations and cultural contexts. The book includes twenty-eight photographs from around the world and an index that describes each one. For example, in one photograph, Masai dancers leap in thick-soled sandals; in another, firefighters work in black rubber galoshes.

Activities for the Shoe Investigation

For the shoe investigation, the students—

- analyzed and described orally and on chart paper the characteristics of shoes depicted in the picture book *Shoes, Shoes, Shoes* (Morris 1995);
- classified the shoes in the book on a hula-hoop Venn diagram;
- classified the parents' shoes on a hula-hoop Venn diagram;
- analyzed the parents' shoes using nonstandard and standard measurement tools, such as cutout paper ants, string, measuring tape, rulers, centimeter-square grid paper, 8 cm × 8 cm cubes, and a triple-beam balance;
- recorded the measurements of the shoes on narrative sheets;
- collected and organized the shoe-measurement data (i.e., length, width, perimeter, area, volume, mass) into class graphs, including vertical and horizontal bar graphs, number-line plots, pie graphs, pictographs, and tree diagrams; and
- interpreted the class shoe graphs in a narrative journal.

Fig. 19.1. Activities for the shoe investigation

After the teachers finished reading the book to the class, they asked students, "What did you notice about the shoes in this story?" Some of the students said, "The shoes are from different cultures." Another student pointed out, "The shoes protect feet from water in that picture and from snow in that picture." Several students explained, "They're made of different stuff, you know … different material stuff, like leather."

To continue their analysis of the shoes for specific details, students worked in small groups, examining and brainstorming characteristics of different shoes from the picture book. The student facilitators listed the students' thoughts on chart paper and to help generate more ideas, posed probing questions, such as, "What else do you see?" "Why?" "What other ideas are related to this one?"

The students then shared their lists in the large group (see fig. 19.2). After recording some of their ideas on chart paper, the teachers asked the students, "What is special about these shoes?" After synthe-

sizing their ideas, the students identified the following categories using their own words:

- What it is used for (e.g., used for walking in the summer, helps you walk in the snow)
- How it looks (e.g., brown, open toes makes you look cool)
- Parts of a shoe (e.g., has straps, no zipper)
- What it is made of (e.g., leather, straw, rubber)
- Measurements (e.g., old, very heavy, tall)

Fig. 19.2. Charts showing characteristics of shoes

To further build on this experience, the students worked in groups to sort the pictures of shoes from the book according to the categories they had listed, then shared with, and explained their ideas to, the whole class (see fig. 19.3).

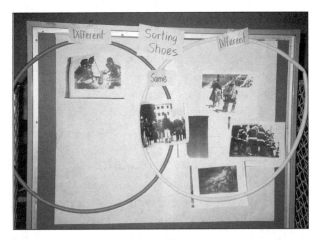

Fig. 19.3. Venn diagram showing shoes sorted into categories

Finally, the students examined and sorted their dads' shoes on the floor, using a Venn diagram made from hula hoops (see fig. 19.4). Students first sorted the shoes according to one attribute from their categories, then two attributes. The student facilitators recorded the sorting characteristics on strips of paper so that the groups had records of their sorting ideas. After about fifteen minutes, the students

EXPLORING MATHEMATICS THROUGH LITERATURE

chose one sorting rule and represented it on the hula-hoop Venn diagram. As the students walked around the classroom, examining and verifying one another's sorting rules, they offered comments, such as, "I agree with that rule." "I don't think that rule is correct; I'm going to check." "They're lucky that they had the shoes to do that rule; all the shoes in our group were almost the same."

Fig. 19.4. Venn diagram of two shoe attributes

Quantitative Analysis: "How Do You Measure a Dad's Shoe?"

The students continued analyzing their dads' shoes using a variety of nonstandard and standard measuring tools, such as uniform cutouts of ants (see fig. 19.5), string of varying lengths, measuring tapes, rulers, centimeter-square grid paper, and a triple-beam balance scale. As the students explored the relationship between the physical features of their dads' shoes and the measurements, they were "develop[ing] the process of measurement concepts related to units of measurement; making and using estimates of measurement; making and using measurements in problems and everyday situations" (NCTM 1989, p. 51) Most students used the ruler to measure the widest and longest parts of the shoe. The text of the record sheet prompted students to use the paper ants to estimate the perimeter of the shoe. I asked some students, "If you used pencils instead of paper ants, would the perimeter of the

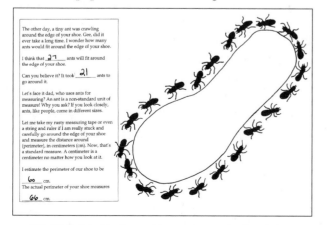

Fig. 19.5. Ant cutouts used to measure perimeter of shoe

shoe be bigger or smaller?" Several students said, "The perimeter would be smaller because it would have fewer pencils." Two students appeared to understand this concept. They said, "The perimeter of my dad's shoe would always be the same, but the nonstandard unit would change ... paper ants are shorter than pencils."

Many of the students remembered ways to estimate area using the centimeter grid paper to trace the soles of their dads' shoes, then count the number of squares. "This is what we always do for area," said one student, "we count squares." They counted squares, knowing that area is measured using square units. The students counted the whole squares, guessed the value of the total partial squares (e.g., "I think that those fourteen pieces make up five whole squares"), or meticulously counted half and quarter squares (see fig. 19.6).

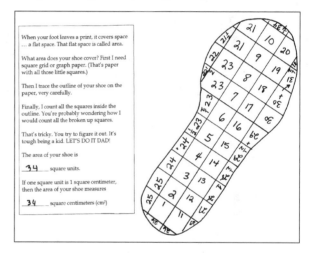

Fig. 19.6. Grid paper used to measure area of shoe

The second-grade students were eager to experiment with the triple-beam balance. As they inspected the machine, they discussed ways in which it was similar to their home bathroom scales. Their comments included, "If you push down on it, it moves"; "It has weight lines"; "You have to make sure that it starts at the center line, otherwise you might be cheating the weight." Most students thought that the triple-beam balance measured the "weight" of objects; however, through discussion, they became more familiar with the appropriate term, *mass*.

These investigations in measurement offered students opportunities to develop their understanding of measurement tools and concepts. Moreover, the students were asked to explain and justify their choices and uses of the different measurement tools. I asked some students, "Why are you using the measuring tape to measure length? Why don't you use the string?" Some students said, "Because that is what I always use," whereas others explained, "If I use the string, then I have to also use the ruler because the string doesn't have centimeters on it and the ruler is stiff." Another student said that he was "copying" his friend, yet realized, "The measuring tape has math on it … you know … a number line!"

Observing and interviewing students as they use mathematical ideas to solve problems helps them to "reflect on and clarify their thinking about mathematical ideas and situations" (NCTM 1989, p. 26). As I asked questions, the students often added explanatory details about their measurements or discussed other mathematical ideas. The seventh- and eighth-grade facilitators also noticed similar reactions from other students. One facilitator stated, "The kids seemed more into it when I showed I was interested in their measuring, especially when I asked them questions."

During questioning, I could also distinguish which students understood measurement as a procedure (e.g., "You put the ruler here and get the centimeters") and which students understood the measurement conceptually (e.g., "It doesn't matter if you use a tape measure, string, a ruler, or the ants—to get the real measurement you have to use a line and the centimeter ruler of some kind"). Thus, through interviewing, we gathered assessment data about students' knowledge of measurement concepts and their skills in applying measurement procedures. Although they demonstrated a range of mathematical knowledge and skill, their interactions with one another, their teachers, and the student facilitators enabled them to build on their measurement abilities by reflecting on, and clarifying their thinking about, mathematical ideas in the context of this shoe investigation.

"Dad, You Take Mighty Big Steps!": Using a Record Sheet

The teachers and I created a series of record sheets that included pictorial and written descriptions about the shoes. The written descriptions included first-person, teacher-generated narrative text and blank spaces for students to record and describe their estimated and precise measurements using words, numbers, and pictures (see figs. 19.5, 19.6, and 19.7). All the record sheets would be compiled into a booklet called "How Do You Measure a Dad?" and given as Father's Day gifts.

As we designed these record sheets, I wondered how the students would use them. I saw and heard students read the text of the record sheet aloud over

and over again, refining the quality of their oral reading skills, including intonation, pronunciation, and fluency; trying to make sense of the written words; and deciding which measurement tool to use in conjunction with the meaning of the text. One student explained, "I'm trying to read this so I can hear and know what to do." Another student said, "I'm pretending that I am talking to my dad as I am working." In fact, students explained that the story told them why they should be measuring the shoes using a certain type of measurement. "If my story part says [she reads from the text of the record sheet], 'How long is your step?' I don't put in my area measurement, right? I put my length measurement there. If I get them mixed up, then my dad will think that I don't know which is which. I know my math." (See fig. 19.7.)

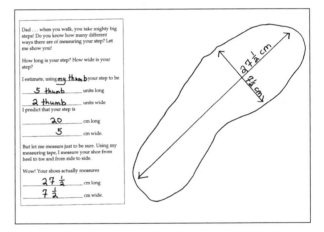

Fig. 19.7. Measuring the length and width of the shoe

How Does Your Dad Measure in the Class?

To make class shoe graphs, the students also recorded their measurements on data squares. These data squares were color coded (i.e., yellow for area, green for volume, blue for width, white for length, pink for perimeter, orange for mass) so that the measurement data could easily be distinguished and organized into different graphic representations, including vertical and horizontal bars, number-line plots, pie graphs, pictographs, and tree diagrams.

The students interpreted the shoe graphs orally. Both teachers noted that the students described a range of ideas that included naming the highest and lowest data values and explaining these values. For example, the students noted the large number of long shoes. Some students thought that if the dads' feet were long, then the dads would be tall, meaning that a lot of tall dads must be in the class.

Reflecting and Rethinking

The shoe investigation enabled us to think about how the design and implementation of this series of activities influenced the process and product of students' learning. This investigation also provided authentic learning contexts for students to "acquire confidence in using mathematics meaningfully" (NCTM 1989, p. 23). All the students were eager to share the details of their mathematics learning when they presented the gifts to their dads on Father's Day. As the students used the record sheet, they rethought their mathematical ideas and rehearsed explanations about the measurements out loud. One student said, "I can tell my dad how I counted the squares to find the area of his shoe. He needs to know that it [t]ook a lot of time to count the one-half and one-fourth squares. [She points at the text of the record sheet about area. See fig. 19.6.] I wanted to make sure it was right, just in case he checked."

This shoe investigation supported all the students in thinking both mathematically and narratively about their learning experiences (Bruner 1985; Gardner 1993; Robinson and Hawpe 1986). In the process of preparing and sharing the Father's Day gifts, the students used both mathematical and narrative thinking by listening to one another, discussing ideas, and raising questions about their analyses of the attributes of shoes (i.e., sorting and classifying the shoes; estimating and measuring the shoes using different materials; collecting, organizing, representing, and interpreting the shoe data).

Bruner (1985) and Robinson and Hawpe (1986) suggest that narrative thinking helps the learner organize and make sense of experience in ways that are different from logical-mathematical thinking. In fact, narrative thinking "involves the projection of story form onto some experience or event. This may occur as the experience is taking place, in reflecting upon the experience, or in recounting the experience at a later time" (Robinson and Hawpe 1986, p. 115). The process is much like answering a series of questions about a story, such as what happened, to whom, and why? Answering these questions enabled students to examine the shoes and identify relevant mathematical ideas as part of constructing their stories. In fact, students used the text in several ways. Many students read aloud from the record sheet to help them take measurements from their dads' shoes. Some students envisioned the text as a conversation with their dads, and others read the text to guide them through their investigations or to help them understand the mathematical ideas. I think that students who were using their mathematical and narrative modes of thinking were developing in-depth understanding about mathematical concepts, procedures, and terminology from the strands of data management, measurement, number sense and numeracy, and patterning.

Finally, the picture book furnished a setting and context for making real-life links to mathematical concepts. In fact, the book *Shoes, Shoes, Shoes* and the dads' shoes provided real-life data for the students to analyze, sort, and classify. The narrative aspects of the activity, including the story, class discussions, and the record sheet, furnished a context in which the students analyzed and described their dads' shoes using mathematical ideas. The discussions and questioning about the use of mathematical ideas enabled the students continuously to interpret phenomena, reflect on their learning experiences, and retell the experiences.

BIBLIOGRAPHY

Bruner, Jerome. "Narrative and Paradigmatic Modes of Thought." In *Learning and Teaching the Ways of Knowing*, edited by Elliot Eisner, pp. 97–115. Chicago, Ill.: University of Chicago Press, 1985.

Gardner, Howard. *Multiple Intelligences: The Theory in Practice*. New York: Basic Books, 1993.

Morris, Ann. *Shoes, Shoes, Shoes*. New York: Lothrop, Lee & Shepard Books, 1995.

National Council of Teachers of Mathematics (NCTM). *Curriculum and Evaluation Standards for School Mathematics*. Reston, Va.: NCTM, 1989.

Robinson, J., and L. Hawpe. "Narrative Thinking as a Heuristic Process." In *Narrative Psychology: The Storied Nature of Human Conduct*, edited by Theodore R. Sarbin, pp. 111–25. Westport, Conn.: Praeger Publishers, 1986.

Zanger, Virginia V. "Math Storybooks." *Teaching Children Mathematics* 5 (October 1998): 98–102.

"How Do You Measure a Dad?"

by Kathy Kubota-Zarivnij

Grade range:	2–3
Mathematical topics:	Measurement, data collection and analysis
Children's book:	*Shoes, Shoes, Shoes,* by Ann Morris
Materials:	Rulers, graph paper in different-sized units, *"Shoes, Shoes, Shoes"* recording sheets (photocopy recording sheets 1–3 in landscape orientation on 8.5-by-14-inch paper), data sheets in various colors

Discussion of the mathematics: Both qualitative and quantitative analyses of an object (shoes) are used to highlight different aspects of measurement. The emphasis is first placed on what attributes could be considered, then on estimating and measuring using both nonstandard and standard measures. After the measures are collected, the data are analyzed and interpreted using a variety of graphing techniques.

Teacher notes: A description of how to launch the task, including how to generate a list of attributes, is described in the article. Included below are additional comments to extend the description in the article and copies of recording sheets.

Creating a student narrative text for the recording sheets: In this investigation, the teachers created the narrative text for the recording sheets. The students often referred to the narrative text for a variety of purposes:

- to choose an appropriate measurement tool;
- to know the type of measurement to use;
- as a prompt for discussing the measurement concept with the teacher and other students; or
- to rehearse the presentation of the booklet to their dad or special person.

However, the students could have created their own narrative text for the booklet after they recorded their measurement data in the teacher-created recording sheets. Their own text could be their story about the measurement of their dad's shoe.

With the whole class, the teacher could lead a guided writing lesson that has students brainstorm and share ideas for a narrative text for each type of measurement data. As the students share ideas, the teacher could record the students' ideas on chart paper. Each piece of chart paper would focus on one type of measurement. In the end, the class would have a list of narrative text ideas for each type of measurement, from which students could choose text to include in their booklet for their dad or special person.

The students could write their choices for the narrative text in a booklet that was formatted with space for writing and a space for their pictorial representation of the measurement.

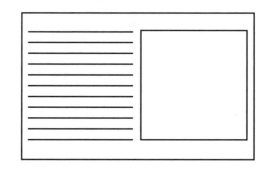

Booklet formatted with spaces for students' writing and their pictorial representation

Collecting the measurement data: Data squares were used to collect measurement data on such attributes as length, width, perimeter, area, volume, and mass about their dads' shoe data. Each student was assigned a number, so that identifying missing data was an easy task. The data squares included places for students to record their measurement data. Each type of data square was color coded to simplify sorting of the data into the different types of measurements.

Organization of the measurement data on different graphic organizers: Although the teachers and I expected that the students would collect the measurement data in the order of the booklet, it turned out that they first collected the data that made immediate sense to them. Most of the students started by collecting the linear data and later collected the other data in varying sequences. After the individual students filled in their data squares, they placed their color-coded squares into the appropriate piles.

When all the data for a particular measurement are collected, pairs or small groups of students should discuss and organize the data into a particular type of graphic organization (e.g., a horizontal or vertical bar graph, pictograph, a conceptual circle graph, a number plot, or a tree diagram.) With the teacher's guidance, small groups of students can organize the data on chart paper, identifying and drawing the necessary axes, title, labels, and scale intervals.

Interpreting the measurement data from the graphic organizers: Once the graphic organizers are completed, review different data measures with the whole class. In small groups, have students closely examine one graph at a time; discuss comparisons of their dad's shoe measurements with the other measurements; and review general trends in the graph, such as the range of measurements that includes most of the data and data outliers. Additionally, students should discuss reasons for the differences in measurement data, such as the dad's age and height.

As the small groups of students discuss and analyze the graphs, the teacher should facilitate intermittent whole-class discussions so that all students can share their interpretations of the graph. These observations could be recorded on chart paper.

Mathematics-journal prompts: Some mathematics-journal prompts to use throughout this shoe investigation follow:

- Why are length and width measurements important shoe measurements? How do you know that your length and width measurements best represent your dad's shoe?

- How did you use the ruler to find a linear measure? How do you know that your measurement is accurate?

- What other nonstandard units could you use to estimate the perimeter of your dad's shoe? How are the three different nonstandard units of measurement (e.g., ants, pencils, finger width) similar? How are they different? What did you learn?

- You used square units to estimate the area of your dad's shoe. Compare the area of your dad's shoe with the area of someone else's shoe. What did you find out? Note: some students may have used one-centimeter grid paper; others may have used a larger size, such as two-centimeter grid paper, or may have covered their diagram with square-inch tiles.

- Is it possible to use triangular or hexagonal units to measure the area of your dad's shoe? Explain.

REFERENCES

Kubota-Zarivnij, Kathy. "Links to Literature: How Do You Measure a Dad?" *Teaching Children Mathematics* 6 (December 1999): 260–64, 251.

Morris, Ann. *Shoes, Shoes, Shoes.* New York: Lothrop, Lee & Shepard Books, 1995.

Shoes, Shoes, Shoes

Recording Sheet 1

Name _____

Date _____

The other day, a tiny ant was crawling around the edge of your shoe. Gee, did it ever take a long time. I wonder how many ants would fit around the edge of your shoe?

I think that _____ ants would fit around the edge of your shoe.

Can you believe it? It took _____ ants to go around it.

Let's face it, dad, who uses ants for measuring? An ant is a nonstandard unit of measure! Why, you ask? If you look closely, ants, like people, come in different sizes.

Let me take my trusty measuring tape, or even a string and ruler if I am really stuck, and carefully measure the distance around (*perimeter*) in centimeters. A centimeter (cm) is a centimeter no matter how you look at it.

I estimate the perimeter of your shoe to

be _____ cm.

The actual perimeter of your shoe

measures _____cm.

Shoes, Shoes, Shoes

Recording Sheet 2

Name_____

Date_____

When your foot leaves a print, it covers a surface—a flat space. That surface is called *area*.

What area does your shoe cover? First I need a square grid or graph paper. (That's paper with all of those little squares.)

Then I trace the outline of your shoe inside the outline. You're probably wondering how I would count all the broken up squares.

That's tricky. You try to figure it out. It's tough being a kid. LET'S DO IT, DAD!

The area of your shoe is _____ square units.

If one square is 1 square centimeter, then the area of your shoe measures

_____ square centimeters (cm^2).

Shoes, Shoes, Shoes

Name _____

Date _____

Dad … when you walk, you take mighty big steps. Do you know how many different ways there are of measuring your step? Let me show you!

How long is your step? How wide is your step?

I estimate that using _____, your step is _____ units long and _____units wide.

I predict that your step is _____cm long and _____ cm wide.

But let me measure just to be sure. Using my measuring tape, I measure your shoe from heel to toe and from side to side.

Wow! Your shoe actually measures _____ cm long and _____ cm wide.

Student Name _____ Student Number_____

My Dad's Shoe Length

Length_____

Width_____

Picture of Shoe Measurement

Student Name _____ Student Number_____

My Dad's Shoe Perimeter

Nonstandard Unit_____

Estimation_____

Standard Unit_____

Measurement_____

Student Name _____ Student Number_____

My Dad's Shoe Area

Length_____

Width_____

Picture of Shoe Measurement

Student Name _____ Student Number_____

My Dad's Shoe Mass

Nonstandard Unit_____

Estimation_____

Standard Unit_____

Measurement_____

20

Students Use Their Bodies to Measure Animals

Eunice Hendrix-Martin

THE BIGGEST snake, the anaconda, can grow to be more than 25 feet long and to weigh 400 pounds. The smallest mammal, the Etruscan shrew, is little enough to sleep in a teaspoon. And the tiny flea can jump 130 times its own height. These are just a few of the interesting facts in Steve Jenkins's (1995) book *Biggest, Strongest, Fastest* (see figure 20.1). This book is an appealing introduction to the "world records" held by fourteen members of the animal kingdom.

I shared this book with my third- and fourth-grade students, hoping it would spark an interest in using these facts to investigate comparative lengths and heights. After we read the book, a lively discussion took place about which animals the students found most interesting. For many it was the sun jellyfish, which has tentacles that are 200 feet long.

Fig. 20.1. Cover illustration of book about animal-kingdom world records. Cover from *Biggest, Strongest, Fastest,* © 1995 by Steve Jenkins. Reprinted by permission of Houghton Mifflin Company. All rights reserved.

Others thought that the ant was amazing; the strongest animal for its size, the ant can lift five times its own weight. The students generated a list of almost every animal in the book, along with each animal's best-known characteristic. The discussion then focused on the biggest animal that has ever lived, the blue whale. Most students were shocked to learn that it is even longer and heavier than the largest known dinosaur.

I asked the students to close their eyes and picture in their minds what a 110-foot blue whale would look like. Cynthia said, "It doesn't fit in my head." "Bigger than a football field," Russell stated with confidence. Other descriptions included bigger than a three-story building, bigger than our playing field and blacktop put together, and bigger than the canal we had been learning about in social studies. All estimations described the whale as being bigger than something, rather than smaller, a fact that I found interesting.

Finding the Mean Height of the Class Using Unifix Cubes

To help students begin developing a better point of reference, we started with their own heights. I posed the question "Could you use your own height as a way to measure some of the animals in the book to understand how big they really are?" They were excited about this idea, and many began sharing how tall they were. Tammy said, "But we are all different heights, and I'm not sure how tall I am!" Nigel suggested that we find the average height of students in the class and use that value as our unit of measure. Students had had previous experience with range, the difference between the smallest and largest value in a set of data, and with mode, the value or values that appear most frequently in a set of data. Since most students had had no experience with the mean, we defined the mean to be the value that represents the amount each would have if all the data in a set, such as the set of all students' heights in the class, were evened out. This new understanding of average height helped students decide that it would be a good unit of measure to use. I now had a great opportunity to give my students a hands-on activity using manipulatives to investigate their mean height.

Together we developed a procedure for using Unifix cubes to find the average height of students in the class. Each student lay on the floor; a partner used tape to mark the spots that corresponded to the student's feet and head. Using these measures, each student made a train of Unifix cubes to represent his or her height. Once all the students had made their trains, we put the trains side by side to represent the heights of all the students in the class. "To find the mean height we need to make all the trains the same length," I explained to the class. Nikki said, "That will be easy because all we need to do is move cubes from the tallest trains to the smallest trains until they are all even."

After everyone took a turn moving a few of the Unifix cubes to make the trains the same length, students discovered twenty-one cubes remaining that could not be divided equally among the twenty-eight trains. We set these cubes to the side. The remainder helped the students recognize that we had found an approximation of the mean.

After the class agreed that the trains were all of the same length, we measured the length of one of the trains to determine the approximate mean height of the students in the class. "Why don't we just count the number of cubes in a train and that will tell us the number of inches?" suggested Sean. I asked the rest of the class if they agreed with Sean. Some agreed because they thought that each Unifix cube looked like it was about an inch long; therefore, counting the cubes would tell us the number of inches. Others disagreed, saying that until we measured a Unifix cube to see if it was an inch long, we could not be sure.

Brittany volunteered to measure a Unifix cube and discovered that it was three-fourths inch long. She then used a tape measure to measure the length of one of the trains, which was fifty-four inches.

Irwin responded by saying, "Four feet six inches." I wrote on the chalkboard "4' 6" or 54"" and explained how the notation "'" indicates feet and " " " indicates inches. Sean was still convinced that counting the cubes would give us the same information, so he proceeded to count them. He announced to the class that there were seventy-five cubes. He pulled out the tape measure again, and it showed fifty-four inches. He realized that the length in cubes and the length in inches were indeed different. Taking this time to help Sean construct his own understanding also helped others in the class to see why the relationship of cubes to inches was not numerically equal. Allowing this type of exploration of ideas also encourages students to take a risk and try their ideas.

Once we knew the mean height of a student, we were ready to begin our investigation. We recorded on chart paper animals from the book for which either the height or length was given. They listed the African elephant, 13 feet high; the giraffe, 19 feet high; the anaconda snake, 25 feet long; the blue whale, 110 feet long; and the tentacles of a sun jellyfish, 200 feet long. We developed the following problem: Given the mean student height of four feet six inches, how many students would it take to equal the height of the elephant? Of the giraffe? How many students would it take to equal the length of the snake? Of the blue whale? Of the tentacles of the jellyfish?

Problem-Solving Strategies

Everyone was excited. Most students chose to work with a partner so that they could discuss their thinking. I reminded them that they were responsible for recording their work individually using pictures, words, and numbers to help them communicate their thinking and understanding. We had done some measurement activities earlier in the year as part of a science unit on matter, and I was eager to see how they would apply that experience and their growing knowledge of multiplication and division to this activity.

Irwin began by multiplying 13 by 12. He was using the traditional algorithm to show his work. He explained, "The '13' is the height of the elephant in feet and the '12' is the inches in one foot. I need to multiply them together to find out how many inches tall the elephant is."

At another table Brian was also multiplying 13 by 12; however, he was not using the traditional algorithm to find the number of inches (see fig. 20.2).

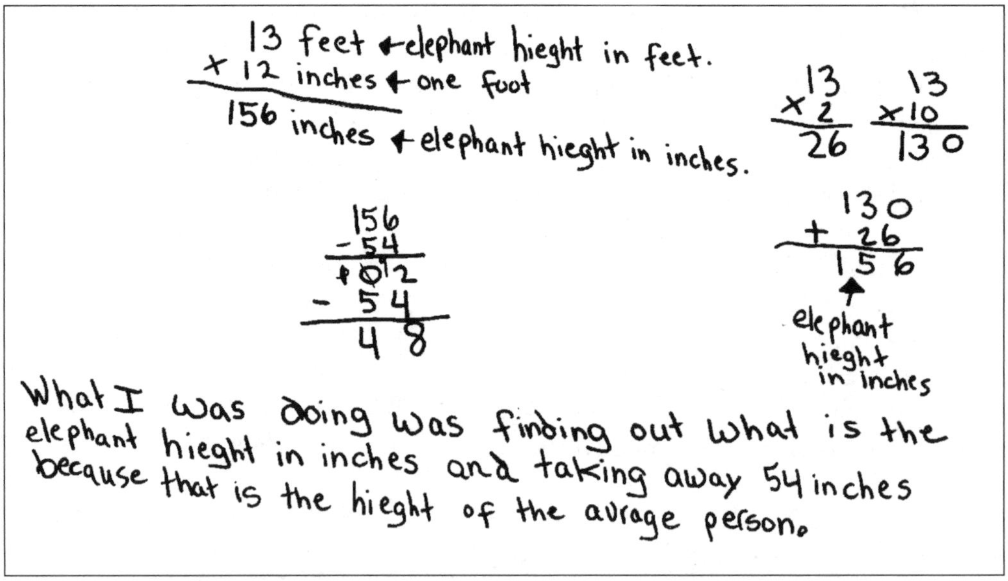

13 feet ← elephant hieght in feet.
+ 12 inches ← one foot
156 inches ← elephant hieght in inches.

13
× 2
26

13
× 10
130

156
− 54
102
− 54
48

130
+ 26
156
↑
elephant
hieght
in inches

What I was doing was finding out what is the elephant hieght in inches and taking away 54 inches because that is the hieght of the avrage person.

Fig. 20.2. Brian uses his knowledge of place value to complete the multiplication.

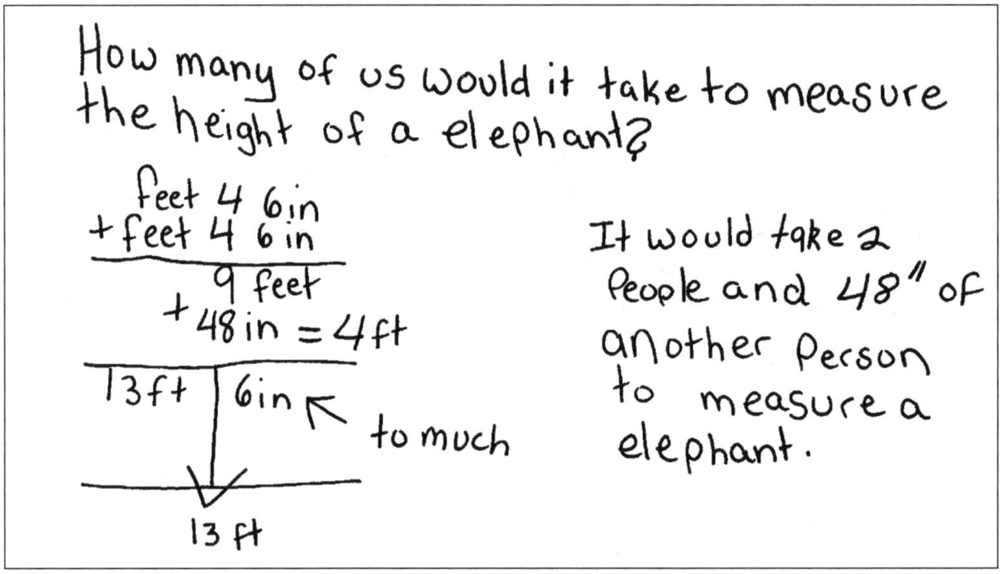

How many of us would it take to measure the height of a elephant?

feet 4 6 in
+ feet 4 6 in
9 feet
+ 48 in = 4 ft

13 ft   6 in ← to much

13 ft

It would take 2 People and 48″ of another Person to measure a elephant.

Fig. 20.3. Gladys uses addition and subtraction to determine the height of the elephant in "student" units.

Brian applied his understanding of place value to the multiplication problem by viewing the number 12 as 10 and two 1's and then multiplying. He explained confidently, "The number '156' is the number of inches tall of an African elephant. This is important to know because if I know how many inches tall the elephant is, then I can just subtract fifty-four inches, which is the mean height of our class, until I can't subtract anymore." To clarify his thinking further, he wrote down "156 – 54 = 102," under the "102," he wrote "54" and subtracted again. This time his answer was "48." Thus, not ready to divide by 54, Brian intuitively used repeated subtraction. "It will take two of us and forty-eight inches left over to measure the elephant," he explained. Not certain that Brian understood what the forty-eight inches represented, I asked him to explain. He said, "You can't use another person because that would be too much, so the forty-eight inches is what you would need to finish measuring the elephant."

While Brian calculated his answer using only inches, Gladys decided to use a combination of feet and inches (see fig. 20.3). I wanted to know how she came up with forty-eight inches. She explained that thirteen feet minus nine feet is four feet and that forty-eight inches is four feet. Although her written explanation was initially confusing, her oral explanation showed clear understanding. Gladys used addition and subtraction to solve the problem

EXPLORING MATHEMATICS THROUGH LITERATURE

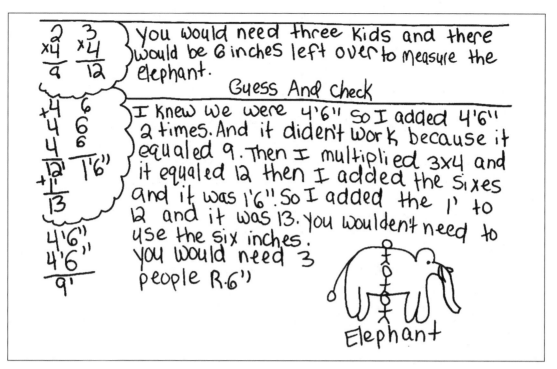

Fig. 20.4. Mia uses a guess-and-check approach.

on paper; however, her ability to convert inches to feet quickly in her head demonstrated skill in division.

Mia attacked the problem with a guess-and-check approach (see fig. 20.4) using multiplication and addition. Unlike Brian and Gladys, who saw the answer as two people plus forty-eight inches, Mia saw it as needing three people, with six inches left over. Mia's work clearly describes her mathematical thinking and understanding of the problem. These two different interpretations of the same quantity evoked a lively class discussion.

Class Discussion

Students were eager to share their answers and justify their thinking. Their responses were recorded on chart paper so that all students could visualize the strategies. Two answers quickly became apparent. Students were given a few minutes to discuss the answers with their groups. Ashley explained her group's thinking: "We think you would have to have at least three people or you wouldn't be measuring all of the elephant that you could using people, so two people plus the forty-eight inches is wrong." Another group defended two people plus forty-eight inches as correct because not all of the third person could be used; thus, in their view, the third person should not be included. Other groups justified their thinking in a similar way. Sean's group decided that the two answers were really very similar measure-

ments that were just written differently, because forty-eight inches was all but six inches of another person. It became clear during the discussion that many students were not yet ready to see the two answers as equivalent measurements.

Irwin, however, had an important discovery that he thought might help the others and that he wanted to share before we continued working. "Every time you add two people (4' 6" + 4' 6") together you get nine feet. The other animals will be simple because it's easier to add nine feet than four feet six inches. Isn't math lovely?"

As students began to work on the snake problem, an interesting connection to patterns was made. Mia shared that she had made a table (see fig. 20.5), which I then recorded on large paper. As students quietly studied the table, they began to see patterns.

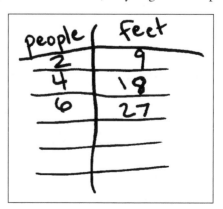

Fig. 20.5. Mia's table shows the relationship of students to feet.

"I see a pattern counting by twos under the people," said Gladys. "In the feet column, the ones are going down by one; and in the tens place, they're going up by one ten," announced Tammy. "If you add the digits together under the feet, they all equal nine, so the next number will be thirty-six. Hey, that's a pattern counting by nines!" exclaimed Shawn.

Almost everyone used a table to help measure the last two animals, the whale and the jellyfish. Most were able to quickly generate the list of people counting by twos and the number of feet counting by nines. For the whale, some students stopped at twenty-four people, or 108 feet, knowing they would need only 2 feet of another person. Other students said twenty-five people were required, with 2 feet 6 inches left over. Still others continued the table to twenty-six people, or 117 feet, not realizing that the twenty-sixth person was not needed. Students who finished the whale then used the table to compute the length of the jellyfish's tentacles.

Reflections

Biggest, Strongest, Fastest provided animal facts that were of interest to students and that could be used in a variety of ways. Although finding the mean turned out to be a pivotal point, other skills were involved, such as estimating; adding; subtracting; multiplying; dividing; measuring; and collecting, organizing, and using data. Measurement activities like the one my students did give students practical applications for the computational skills that they are learning.

Most students had access to the problem because they felt comfortable using a problem-solving strategy that made sense to them. This level of confidence comes when students are encouraged to solve problems in their own ways and justify their own thinking. Students' work is discussed and recorded for others to see. This process tells children that their thinking is valued and their work is important. When students are given opportunities to share their ideas, opinions, and questions, a classroom climate is created in which mathematical thinking is encouraged and valued.

One of the most valuable discussions in this lesson happened when Mia shared the table. Recognizing a pattern and applying a rule to the pattern proved to be a powerful problem-solving strategy for many students. Students who had difficulty working with feet and inches were able to use the table to see the relationship of people to feet. When students can look for patterns and express them mathematically in this way, they connect mathematics to their world.

By using themselves as a unit of measure, students had a real-world connection to the problem. Making comparisons between the length and height of the animals and themselves helped them see that measurement is never exact, that even careful measurements are approximations.

REFERENCE

Jenkins, Steve. *Biggest, Strongest, Fastest*. New York: Ticknor & Fields Books for Young Readers, 1995.

"Students Use Their Bodies to Measure Animals"

by Eunice Hendrix-Martin

Grade range:	3–5
Mathematical topics:	Computation and estimation strategies, averages, comparisons between different lengths
Children's book:	*Biggest, Strongest, Fastest*, by Steve Jenkins.
Materials:	Unifix cubes (about 1000), measuring tapes (1 per pair of students), "Biggest, Strongest, Fastest" recording sheets

Discussion of the mathematics: In this task, on the basis of the customary system of measurement, the mean height of the class is determined and used as a unit of measurement to make comparisons between the length and height of various animals. Two aspects of the NCTM Measurement Standards addressed in this task include the recommendations that students should "understand that measurements are approximations and understand how differences in units affect precision" and should be able to "select and use benchmarks to estimate measurements" (NCTM 2000, p. 170). Estimations as well as exact computations were used to determine the numerical (multiplicative) relationship between two quantities. This task provides opportunities for students to "develop fluency in adding, subtracting, multiplying, and dividing whole numbers" and "develop and use strategies to estimate the results of whole-number computations and to judge the reasonableness of such results" (NCTM 2000, p. 148). Additionally, students were involved in using representations to model and interpret the relationship between the sizes of different objects.

Teacher notes and questions for students: After reading the story, ask students which animals they found most interesting. As a class, generate a list of animals and each animal's best-known characteristic.

Ask students to try to picture in their minds what a 110-foot whale would look like. Explain that comparing the length with something known, such as the length of a football field, makes it easier to picture. These familiar referents are called *benchmarks*. Pose the question below, and encourage students to share their ideas about how they could use their own height.

> To help you understand how big some of these animals really are, how could you use your own height as a way to measure them?

Rather than use each individual's height, explain that the mean height of the class members will be used as a unit of measure. Ask the students what is meant by the mean and how it can be determined. Note: Define *mean* as an average: the value that represents the amount each would have if all the data in a set, such as the set of all students' heights in the class, were evenly distributed among all members of the set.

Explain that one way to find the mean height of the class is by using Unifix cubes. After each student has made a train of Unifix cubes to represent his or her height, all the trains are placed side-by-side to represent the heights of all the students in the class. To find the mean height, all the trains need to be made the same length. Ask the students to decide how to make all the trains the same length. As students redistribute some of the cubes to make the trains the same length, extra cubes will probably be left over. The extra cubes represent the remainder. This idea of remainder can help students build an understanding of the notion of approximating the mean.

After the students have equalized the lengths of the trains, have them use a measuring tape to measure the length of a train, which is the approximate mean height of the students in the class. (Note: a Unifix cube's dimension is not one inch. See the article for further discussion.)

Once students have determined the mean height as a point of reference, they can investigate the problem as posed on the recording sheet. Have students share and discuss their problem-solving strategies as they determine the measurements of each animal. Their responses can be shared through presentations, a class book, or a project bulletin board, so that all students have access to a written record of different approaches.

Editor's note: If a large number of cubes are not available, other uniform units, such as paper clips, could be used.

REFERENCES

Hendrix-Martin, Eunice. "Links to Literature: Students Use Their Bodies to Measure Animals." *Teaching Children Mathematics* 3 (April 1997): 426–30.

Jenkins, Steve. *Biggest, Strongest, Fastest*. New York: Ticknor & Fields Books for Young Readers, 1995.

National Council of Teachers of Mathematics (NCTM). *Principles and Standards for School Mathematics*. Reston, Va.: NCTM, 2000.

Biggest, Strongest, Fastest   Recording Sheet 1

Name_____

Date _____

How many students would it take to equal the height of an elephant? Of the giraffe? How many students would it take to equal the length of the snake? Of the blue whale? Of the tentacles of the jellyfish?

Choose an animal that you want to study, and compare it with our class's average height. In the space below, write about the comparison you found and show how you solved the problem.

21

Measuring Up with
The Principal's New Clothes

Maryann S. Wickett

The Principal's New Clothes by Stephanie Calmenson (1989) provides a delightful, whimsical context for investigations in measurement. This story is a modern-day adaptation of Hans Christian Andersen's *The Emperor's New Clothes.* Mr. Bundy, the principal of P.S. 88, is a very classy dresser. One day, Moe and Ivy come to town, offering to make Mr. Bundy a new suit from magic cloth. Children find the hilarious outcome very entertaining.

When I shared the book with my fourth-grade students, Suzanne suggested that we measure our principal and make a suit of clothes for him. Joey added that we should also measure the assistant principal and make some clothes for her.

"Pretend that you are Moe or Ivy. Suppose that you were going to make clothes for Mr. Wise, our principal, or Mrs. Singh, our assistant principal. What would you need to measure to ensure that their new clothes will fit?" I asked the class.

"How tall they are," shared Brenda. I wrote her suggestion on the chalkboard.

"How long their arms are. Otherwise, their clothes might come out with baby arms or gorilla arms," giggled Zach.

"You could just make tank tops, then it wouldn't be a problem," countered Sagan.

I continued to list the suggestions on the chalkboard. The children's ideas included measuring the length from the shoulders to the waist, the waist to the knees, and the waist to the ankles; the length of the arms; and the circumference of the shoulders and waist.

"Mr. Wise and Mrs. Singh are very busy. When are we going to do this measuring? How will we ever have time to check and see if things fit?" asked Casey.

"How about if we first made a life-sized model of Mr. Wise and Mrs. Singh? Then you could try the clothes on the model," I proposed.

"That would be way cool!" responded Sagan. "We'd have to measure a lot more than just length! We would also have to measure how big around stuff is, too!"

The students became very enthused about this idea. They brainstormed what they would need to measure while I listed their ideas on the chalkboard.

Mr. Bundy walked into the auditorium. As he walked down the aisle, he could hear whispers all around him. Mr. Bundy thought he must be the only stupid person in town.

Their suggestions included measuring the circumferences of the head, neck, arms, legs, waist, shoulders, and so on. I divided the students into eight groups of four and assigned them interesting school adults to measure, such as the principal, the assistant principal, the librarian, the student teacher, and me. From suggestions on the chalkboard, the groups made a list of the measurements that they thought they would need and set out to measure their school adult (fig. 21.1).

Fig. 21.1. The principal gets measured by a group of eager students.

Students Create Three-Dimensional Models

Students used their measurements, newspaper, and tape to create an internal frame for their models. Transforming their measurements into a three-dimensional model offered a true challenge for these fourth graders. Many hands, much patience, and much cooperation among the students were needed to measure and form the newspaper into a frame (fig. 21.2). Next they covered the newspaper model with butcher paper. Because the butcher paper was of poor quality and tore easily, students found it very difficult to cover the newspaper frame. Despite their problems, the students worked together cheerfully and completed their models (fig. 21.3). The students then decided not to make clothes for the models as originally planned because the slightest movement resulted in additional tears.

Fig. 21.2. Newspaper formed a "skeleton" for the student's models.

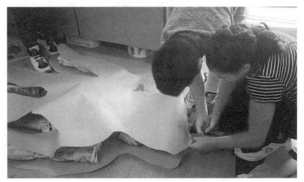

Fig. 21.3. A pair of students carefully applies the butcher-paper "skin."

Half-Size Me

"I think we should make clothes for ourselves," stated Johanna one afternoon as we were finishing our models.

"That's a cool idea! I could make sunglasses, too," added Isaiah.

"How about we make flat, two-dimensional, half-sized drawings of ourselves and make clothes for them?" I suggested, remembering an activity I had used in the past titled "A Half-Size Me" from *About Teaching Mathematics* (Burns 1992, p. 50).

During recess I gathered the needed materials, about three feet of white butcher paper and five feet of string for each child.

I began by having the children work in pairs to measure each other so that each child would have a piece of string equal to his or her height. Once every child had a piece of string of appropriate length, I instructed them to fold their string in half. "When you fold your string in half, what does it represent?" I asked.

"Half of how tall I am," replied Cameron.

"Lay your folded string on your paper with one end on the bottom of the paper and the rest of the string going up the middle of the paper. Mark with your pencil where your folded string ends. This represents half your height as Cameron said," I explained as I demonstrated to the students. Once students had marked half their height on the butcher paper, I asked them to cut or fold the paper to be the same length as half their height.

"Now use the string to measure your head's length. Fold your string in half, and measure down from the top of your paper. What does this represent?"

"Half of how long my head really is," ventured Lisa, a bit unsure of her explanation.

With my guidance, the students continued measuring in this way. They used the string to measure various parts of their body, such as the width of their head; the distance from the top of their head to their eyes, nose, mouth, and ears; and the length and width of their neck. They divided the string in half and marked the measurement on their paper to create "Half-Size Me" drawings. This part of the activity took about ninety minutes over two days.

Once students had completed their drawings, it was time to make the clothes. Students began by using measuring tapes to take needed measurements of their drawings. Using the measurements and plain newsprint, students created patterns, for example, a pattern of a shirt (fig. 21.4). Then students cut out their pattern and "tried it on" the drawing to make sure that it fit. I required the students to be very accurate at this point, which meant that a few students had to redo their measurements and patterns.

Fig. 21.4. A student focuses intently as she transfers a measurement.

By insisting on accuracy, I reinforced the idea that it is very helpful to put the leading end of the measuring tape at the beginning of what is being measured, a skill that children often do not take seriously. I gave students the choice of standard or metric measurement units, since my measuring tapes have both scales. Students favored metric units; they seemed to find it easier to deal with parts of centimeters than with parts of inches.

Once students created a pattern that fit their drawing, they used the pattern and colored construction paper to make clothing, which they then glued to their drawing (fig. 21.5). They cut out the completed projects, and I hung the "Half-Size Me's" around the room for all to admire.

Fig. 21. 5. A group of proud students with their half-size models

Student Reflections

"What did you learn from this activity?" I asked the children as we admired our efforts.

"Making three-dimensional stuff is really hard, and it takes a lot of hands and cooperation!" volunteered Jellian. Her classmates giggled and nodded in agreement. "But still it was fun to measure Mr. Wise and then to make him. I think his legs are too skinny, though!"

"I liked the part where we drew ourselves and did halves of everything. I knew I made a mistake one time because my arms went off my paper! I thought, 'Oh no! This can't be right!' Then I hit myself in the head and remembered I forgot to bend my string in half. Then when I did that, my arms looked right!" reflected Patrick.

"I think I learned you have to be really careful when you measure stuff. I wasn't careful at first, and then my pattern wouldn't fit, and then I had to do it again! I think I learned to be more careful and put the beginning of the tape at the beginning of what I am measuring. I get that part now!" shared Joey.

"Yep! Me too," added Lisa. "I kept on messing up and stuff didn't fit and then Sagan helped me. She showed me how to put the measuring tape, and then we worked together, and then finally my pattern fit my drawing. But it took two of us!"

"I figured out that my finger is about a centimeter. When I was measuring, my finger kept getting in the way and I couldn't see. Then I looked and thought, wow! My finger is about a centimeter, and if it is in the way, then I know it's about a centimeter and I can just go on and not get frustrated," explained Suzanne.

"I sure am short in half-size!" giggled Eric.

"I notice that the tall people in real life are mostly the tallest ones in half-size too," noticed Michael.

"Our pictures are half as tall as us, but they are also half as wide as we really are too, so is it really half?" wondered Alexandra.

"That's a very interesting point, Alexandra, and something we should investigate another day," I responded.

Alexandra makes a powerful point. Although the activity is called "Half-Size Me" and the *dimensions* are half-size, the picture created is really one-fourth of the actual *area* of the individual being drawn. To clarify this idea for yourself, fold a square piece of paper in half horizontally, creating a rectangle half the size of the original square. This result was achieved when the children divided their heights in half. The children also divided their widths in half, which can be represented by folding your rectangle in half vertically. By folding the square in half both horizontally and vertically, you end up with a square divided into fourths, or four squares, each one-fourth the size of the original square. This outcome is essentially what happened when the children drew themselves by dividing all their measurements, both height and width, in half.

Alexandra's point can be explored with students by having a child lie on a large sheet of grid paper. Trace around the child to create an outline of the child's body. Count the squares covered by the outline to find the area. Create a second outline drawing of the child with the same process as that used by the students for "Half-Size Me." That is, use a piece of string to find the height of the first outline then fold the string in half to determine the height of the second outline. Use the string to make all needed measurements of the first outline then fold the string in half to determine the measurements for the second outline. When the second outline is completed, count the squares that it covers on the grid to determine the area. The area will equal one-fourth the original area.

Teacher Reflections

Measurement is a basic skill that we frequently use in our adult lives. We are constantly in situations requiring the abilities to estimate various measurements and to use precise measurements. *The Principal's New Clothes* offers an enjoyable context in which to explore and apply measurement skills. Although my fourth-grade students enjoyed making the three-dimensional models of school adults, they found the task difficult. The activity required a great deal of patience and assistance from my student teacher and me. In the future, I would try this activity only with older students.

A more appropriate activity for fourth graders was "Half-Size Me." Using their own bodies gave students a real-life understanding of the meaning of half and furnished purpose and context for the necessity of using measurement tools accurately. When students were asked whether they would recommend this activity to others, they enthusiastically responded, "Yes!"

REFERENCES

Burns, Marilyn. *About Teaching Mathematics*. White Plains, N.Y.: Math Solutions Publications, 1992.

Calmenson, Stephanie. *The Principal's New Clothes*. New York: Scholastic, 1989.

"Measuring Up with *The Principal's New Clothes*"

by Maryann S. Wickett

Grade range:	4–6
Mathematical topic:	Measurement to build two- and three-dimensional models
Children's books:	*The Principal's New Clothes*, written by Stephanie Calmenson and illustrated by Denise Brunkus
Materials:	Newspaper, butcher paper, tape, measuring tapes, string, newsprint, construction paper, *"The Principal's New Clothes"* reflection sheets

Discussion of the mathematics: The two tasks described below provide an opportunity for students to consider different attributes of measure and to select the appropriate type of unit for measuring each attribute. Giving the students the choice of working with standard units in either the customary or the metric system caused them to consider the differences between the systems. Focusing on the relationship between area and linear dimensions was particularly striking in the "Half-Size Me" task because most individuals incorrectly assume that if the linear dimensions are halved, the area will also be halved.

Teacher notes: Both tasks described below began by sharing the book *The Principal's New Clothes* with the class.

Creating a three-dimensional model: Creating three-dimensional models as suggested in the article presents challenges for younger students. This task is best done with fourth graders or above.

After discussing the book, have students choose interesting school adults to measure. As a class, brainstorm what measurements are necessary to create a three-dimensional figure and list these measurements on the board. Each group of students should prepare a list of the needed measures and then collect the data of their chosen individual.

After collecting their data, each group of students uses newspaper and tape to create a model of the school adult on the basis of the measurements. Butcher paper, tape, and staples can be used to cover the newspaper "skeleton" (see fig. 21.2 from the article).

Creating a "half-size me": After discussing the book, pose the task of creating a "half-size me." Explain that the model will be flat, two-dimensional, and half-sized. As a class, make a list of what measures will need to be taken. Using string, students can work in pairs to measure each other's height. Students should fold their string in half to find the height of their "half-size me" and then mark this measurement on their piece of butcher paper as explained in the article. Each pair should repeat this process of measuring using string, halving the string, and then marking their butcher paper for the other measurements, such as the head, arms, shoulders, and legs.

When students have completed their drawings, they can make patterns for their clothes using tape measures and newsprint. After students have checked to verify that their patterns will fit their drawings, they can create their new clothes using construction paper.

To assess learning and promote retention, student reflection is highly important. See the section of the article titled "Student Reflections" for mathematical insights and points that came out in a discussion in one class.

REFERENCES

Calmenson, Stephanie. *The Principal's New Clothes*. Illustrated by Denise Brunkus. New York: Scholastic, 1989.

Wickett, Maryann S. "Links to Literature: Measuring Up with *The Principal's New Clothes*." *Teaching Children Mathematics* 5 (April 1999): 476–79.

The Principal's New Clothes   Reflection Sheet

Name_____

Date_____

Reflection: What did you learn from making your Half-Sized Me?

What did you notice about the area of your Half-Sized Me?

22

Incredible Comparisons:
Experiences with Data Collection

Vicki L. Oleson

THE MATHEMATICS curriculum for a typical sixth-grade classroom easily provides ample content for an entire school year. It can be difficult to take the time needed to develop a mathematics concept through the use of literature. However, I found that by focusing on content, I was able to incorporate literature into one sixth-grade mathematics classroom. This activity presented an interesting springboard to problem solving, an opportunity to research famous mathematicians, and an excellent vehicle to enhance the understanding of mathematics concepts.

Using "Easy Books" to Develop Difficult Concepts

After using the *Curriculum and Evaluation Standards for School Mathematics* (NCTM 1989) and multiple textbook resources to plan a general curriculum that included each Standard, I began searching for resources to assist me in integrating literature into that curriculum. Two helpful resources for locating literature that would relate to the concepts being taught were *Math and Literature: Grades 4–6* (Bresser 1995) and *The Wonderful World of Mathematics* (Thiessen and Matthias 1992). Both were valuable in finding the right piece of literature to illustrate or extend sixth-grade concepts.

Using literature, especially picture books, to stimulate learning in a mathematics classroom is typically associated with younger students. Initially, reading books like *A Million Fish … More or Less* (McKissack 1992) that develop number sense sometimes leaves a middle-grades teacher open to groans and complaints from students. I have found that per-sistence and a light-hearted attitude on my part are well rewarded when I ask my students to think through the mathematics of the story. For some of my students, the images created in books like *Is a Blue Whale the Biggest Thing There Is?* (Wells 1993), which incorporates measurement, makes comparisons, and illustrates large-number concepts, provided a valuable tool for constructing conceptual understanding. They also came to genuinely enjoy and appreciate the author's thinking and the content of such quality children's literature as *The King's Giraffe* (Collier and Collier 1996), which incorporates the mathematics strand of estimation and the skill of finding averages.

The Math Curse (Scieszka 1995) is a hilarious piece of literature rich in mathematical ideas. When encountered and then revisited by students at various points during the year, the concepts illustrated in the book allowed students to experience a completely different level of understanding. For instance, after we studied the Mayan base-twenty numeration system, the book's wonderfully illustrated pages on various ways of counting took on a whole new meaning.

Literature also introduced the sixth graders to famous mathematicians. The students were delightfully open to developing role models. By reading aloud throughout the year, we explored fascinating lives through *Celebrating Women in Mathematics and Science* (NCTM 1992) and *Mathematicians Are People, Too* (Reimer and Reimer 1990). Stories of real-life struggles and accomplishments build confidence in adolescents who are developing their own mathematical power.

"E" Means "Everybody," Not "Easy": *Incredible Comparisons*

The final step in overcoming the problem of making picture books appeal to these upper elementary school students occurred through a delightful journey. Throughout the year, using pieces of literature to illustrate and develop mathematical concepts became an interesting part of the curriculum. As a year-end culminating activity for this group of sixth graders, we built a unit around Russell Ash's *Incredible Comparisons* (1996). The end of the year was an excellent time to introduce this book. In their science units, the students had already studied such topics as space, the solar system, the universe, oceans, and the human body. The information that they encountered in *Incredible Comparisons* supplied wonderful connections because this beautifully illustrated book contains a wealth of information. Each page—some of which fold out to display four pages of information—is fascinating enough for students to spend a great deal of time simply considering its statistics.

Incredible Comparisions by Russell Ash, © 1996 by Dorling Kindersley Ltd., London; used with permission; all rights reserved

The students had just completed two units that were beneficial in preparing them for real-life statistical analysis, and they were eager to make the connections illustrated in the book. For example, proportional relationships were integrated into our study of fractions and percents and developed through the use of diagrams and models. Our study of statistics emphasized basic statistical concepts, such as mean, median, and mode. Data analysis of statistical information was taught by using various graphing techniques, such as stem-and-leaf plots and number-line plots, and by using line and bar graphs to create a story about data.

Following these directly taught units, we gave the students their first activity related to *Incredible Comparisons*—simply to enjoy the book. Using six copies of the book, students worked in groups or independently to read and react to the literature. Then the whole class read and discussed the first section, titled "How to Use This Book." The introduction of the book recommended that those pages be read as a guide to using *Incredible Comparisons* effectively in creating the upcoming projects. The first section explained the proportional representations found in the book. For instance, the surface area of each planet was transformed into a flat surface to make comparisons. Scales and mathematical expressions were also described. After their immersion in this book, students broke into groups to create their own page for a class book of comparisons (fig. 22.1). This task required four separate and sequential mind-stretching steps.

Fig. 22.1. Lizzie's group analyzes its problem as members create a page titled "Food Comparisons with Animals."

First, students were required to use logical reasoning to develop analogies that could be used as comparisons for the subject matter for their page. This step involved brainstorming various possibilities as a group and then discussing the feasibility of the ideas. The concept of an analogy is cross-curricular and involves language arts skills as well

EXPLORING MATHEMATICS THROUGH LITERATURE

as mathematical reasoning. Students were asked to find a correspondence in some aspects between two otherwise unrelated things. They then used mathematics to make and describe meaningful comparisons. For example, while measuring "tall things," a group of students compared the length of a pencil with the height of the Sears Tower and the height of a computer with that of a television signal tower seen in North Dakota. This step proved to be rich in connections for all students and was a great help in launching the next part of the project.

Second, in their small groups, students were required to use various resources to access the data necessary to make accurate mathematical comparisons. For one group, this step simply involved using data in *Incredible Comparisons* and measuring items in the classroom. Other groups used the Internet and collected data. Although accessing information was a challenge for some groups, others viewed the task as a direct and simple part of the research process (fig. 22.2).

Fig. 22.2. Elizabeth uses data collected from the Internet to make dinosaur comparisions.

Third, the students used estimation and an understanding of measurement to illustrate their comparisons. The task was designed to employ the NCTM's measurement standard to "estimate, make, and use measurements to describe and compare phenomena" (NCTM 1989, p. 116). Jake's group estimated the speed of an average sixth-grade runner for its page, "From Zero to Supersonic Speed" (fig. 22.3).

Finally, using proportional thinking, students verified their comparisons and then communicated their findings. Formulas for solving proportions had been discussed earlier in class, but this task actual-

ly helped students develop that formula independently out of the necessity to think proportionally. The illustrations and descriptions on the pages that students created reflected their degree of understanding.

Fig. 22.3. Jake concentrates on a joke to add humor to "From Zero to Supersonic Speed."

Student Work

Developing the initial idea was the most difficult step in the process of creating a page for the data-collection book. We spent a great deal of time discussing the concept of comparison. One group of students wanted to compare Olympic sports, which raised the question of what to compare. Comparing the speed of one runner with that of another runner was one suggestion. At that point, an in-depth discussion was held concerning what made the comparisons in Ash's book powerful and understandable to the reader. The apparent power of the comparisons in the book seemed to lie in making comparisons between unlike subjects versus making comparisons between like subjects or in comparing various like objects from a different perspective. For example, the surface areas of various planets are transformed from a three-dimensional area as a sphere into a two-dimensional area as a flat surface. The flat-surface areas of each planet are then compared.

At that point, it was back to the drawing board for the groups. The work was painstaking, but the end result was a dramatic paradigm shift for the sixth graders in terms of their understanding of comparisons. This shift can be traced through the progression of Jillian's group. The group's concept of comparisons developed from making simple speed comparisons between two runners, even if one was male and one was female, to making far more impressive comparisons of speed. These students compared the speed of a sixth-grade runner with the speed of a rocket-powered car traveling from Des Moines to Seattle (fig. 22.4). Interestingly, each group had to go through the same process of shifting its ideas about comparisons. For some, the shift was easier and more complete than for others.

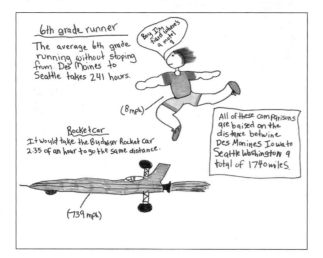

Fig. 22.4. "From Zero to Supersonic Speed" is illustrated by artistically inclined students.

Entwined in the process of developing a comparison was the availability of data to *prove* that comparison. Lizzie's group observed others struggling to find data to substantiate their comparisons and chose another way to address the data problem. This group chose to develop an idea *after* its data had been found. They discovered a book on nutrition that showed the weight of various servings of fast food. They then used the fast-food information as the basis for showing the amount of fast food that would be consumed by different animals if they consumed this food at the same rate as they ate their usual diet. See figure 22.5.

Ben's group measured various items found around the classroom and then used a ratio to compare the height of each object with the height of something very different. For example, they compared the height of a fifteen-ounce bottle of hand lotion with the height of the Eiffel Tower. They determined that "it takes 1485 fifteen-ounce bottles of hand lotion to equal the height of the Eiffel Tower, which is 1052 feet."

The final step of verifying and communicating the comparisons mathematically proved to be one of the least difficult steps. This ability emphasizes the

Fig. 22.5. "Food Comparisons with Animals" uses intriguing fast-food data.

importance of the NCTM's *Standards* document's (1989) recommendation to take more time to develop an understanding of ratio, proportion, and percent and to give less emphasis to memorizing procedures without understanding. We observed in the classroom that the procedure for making a mathematical comparison arose naturally from the task of proving the comparison and that the idea was easily grasped by students. It was also easily confirmed as students examined the reasonableness of the comparison through estimation.

For instance, the statement made by Jon's group that "it takes 2904 Comet cans to equal the height of the CN Tower, which is 1815 feet tall" could be easily estimated as accurate by knowing that if a Comet can were one foot tall, it would take 1815 cans to equal the height of the CN Tower. If it were six inches tall, it would take 3630 cans of Comet to reach that height. Comet cans are less than one foot tall but more than six inches tall, so the group's solution is reasonably accurate. This thinking demonstrated the NCTM *Standards'* goal to "verify and interpret results with respect to the original problem situation" (NCTM 1989, p. 75).

Kate's group made the observation that "when we polled 15 sixth graders, the average amount of TV watched each week was 18 hours. That is 72 hours a month and 936 hours a year. That would be like staying up and watching TV for 39 days straight with no sleeping" (fig. 22.6). The accuracy of the statements depends on a month's being four weeks long and on a year's being fifty-two weeks long.

EXPLORING MATHEMATICS THROUGH LITERATURE

Fig. 22.6. Television-viewing habits are considered in this group's comparison.

The humor found in the voice balloons of the book added to its student appeal. Therefore, the students decided that their pages should also contain these items, and their sense of humor was delightfully reflected in the pages they created. Lizzie's group recognized a common problem that occurs when large quantities of liquid are consumed (fig. 22.5).

Conclusion

In planning the sixth-grade mathematics curriculum, my goals were driven by the NCTM's *Standards* document (1989). I placed a strong emphasis on Mathematics as Problem Solving (Standard 1), Mathematics as Communication (Standard 2), and Mathematics as Reasoning (Standard 3). My use of children's literature throughout the year, and especially my focus on *Incredible Comparisons*, provided a natural springboard for implementing Standard 4, Mathematical Connections. The literature formed the basis for asking sixth graders to "formulate problems from situations within and outside mathematics" and to "verify and interpret results with respect to the original problem situation" (NCTM 1989, p. 75). The task of creating their own pages required students to "model situations using oral, written, concrete, pictorial, graphical, and algebraic methods," and the discourse arising from the group work promoted "discussion of mathematical ideas [leading to] making conjectures and convincing arguments" (NCTM 1989, p. 75).

Finally, this project was an opportunity to promote mathematical connections through the wonderful conceptual ideas that Russell Ash's book depicts. Connections were emphasized not only to science and social studies but also between mathematical ideas. The use of literature in my sixth-grade classroom enhanced our mathematical power and opened another avenue for understanding. This well-constructed piece of literature proved invaluable as a catalyst for complex problem solving.

REFERENCES

Ash, Russell. *Incredible Comparisons*. New York: Dorling Kindersley Publishing, 1996.

Bresser, Rusty. *Math and Literature: Grades 4–6*. Sausalito, Calif.: Math Solutions Publications, 1995.

Collier, Mary Jo, and Peter Collier. *The King's Giraffe*. New York: Simon & Schuster Books for Young Readers, 1996.

McKissack, Patricia. *A Million Fish … More or Less*. New York: Alfred A. Knopf, 1992.

National Council of Teachers of Mathematics (NCTM). *Curriculum and Evaluation Standards for School Mathematics*. Reston, Va.: NCTM, 1989.

———. *Celebrating Women in Mathematics and Science*. Reston, Va.: NCTM, 1996.

Reimer, Luetta, and Wilbert Reimer. *Mathematicians Are People, Too*. Palo Alto, Calif.: Dale Seymour Publications, 1990.

Scieszka, John. *The Math Curse*. New York: Viking, 1995.

Thiessen, Diane, and Margaret Matthias. *The Wonderful World of Mathematics*. Reston, Va.: National Council of Teachers of Mathematics, 1992.

Wells, Robert E. *Is a Blue Whale the Biggest Thing There Is?* Morton Grove, Ill.: Whitman & Co., 1993.

"*Incredible Comparisons:* Experiences with Data Collection"

by Vicki L. Oleson

Grade range:	5–8
Mathematical topics:	Measurement relationships, ratio and proportion
Children's book:	Multiple copies of *Incredible Comparisons*, by Russell Ash (recommend at least one book per four students)
Materials:	"*Incredible Comparisons*" recording sheets

Discussion of the mathematics: Helping students make sense of number and measures is an essential component of understanding these concepts. In the tasks described below, students make comparisons between two numbers or two measures to better understand the magnitude of their multiplicative relationship. Additionally, the examples from *Incredible Comparisons* will help students better understand our world as they analyze the numerical relationships and representations involving population, speed, continents, growth and age, big buildings, and so on. Creating and studying these multiplicative relationships should enhance students' proportional reasoning skills.

Teacher notes: *Incredible Comparisons* is an incredibly rich book. You will find that if you set the book out on a table, students will naturally gravitate toward the wonderful illustrations and mind-stretching comparisons found in it.

We have used this book in the classroom during our study of measurement and of ratio and proportion. Following some general discussion about ratios and how to solve proportions, I bring my set of *Incredible Comparison* books (I have seven available) and place them on a table at the front of the room for a few days. Invariably a few students will page through one of the books, get interested in the content, and subsequently pique the interest of others in the class. This book is not a read-aloud story, nor a book that can easily be absorbed in one sitting. It calls to be picked up and perused over and over. Students find new information each time they look. The best way to introduce this book is simply to make it available to students for a period of time.

We use *Incredible Comparisons* to create our own class book of comparisons, but it could also be used to create comparisons to be displayed in the classroom or hallways. When we get ready to actually create our own pages for a class book of incredible comparisons, we start by getting serious about how to use the book. Two excellent pages at the beginning of the book are worth taking time to study directly. I designed the "*Incredible Comparisons*" recording sheet to help students discover ways to enjoy and understand this book to the fullest. I have used *Incredible Comparisons* both with and without using this introductory guide; however, using the guide is a timesaving device, in that it helps students attain the proper mindset to understand the comparisons and then create their own comparisons. The guide also directs students to details and captions in the book that they may otherwise overlook.

After we spend some time getting to know how to use the book, I place students in pairs or groups of three to explore the book. As they explore, I ask them to think about what comparisons they might want to make. During this time, group interactions and a free-flowing movement between small-group work and whole-class discussion provide direction. For instance, an early suggestion for a comparison might be that one student wants to compare a golf ball with a basketball. Probing questions from either the other students or me usually lead the students to understand that we need to decide what attribute we are going to compare—circumference, weight, bouncing ability, or the like. Next we discuss the richness of the comparison: Would it be more effective to compare things that are not alike or things that are alike? Would it be more interesting to compare things that are used in different ways or those that we think of in different circumstances? Would it be fun to determine how long it would take the average spider to crawl around the circumference of earth—even though it could never happen? Can we find some humor in our comparisons?

During this stage, students start to bounce ideas among themselves and also start to look to the information in the *Incredible Comparisons* book and in other sources to make measurements. For instance, one group had a Barbie doll in the classroom for a project in another class; the group decided to measure the height of the Barbie and then compare it with that of the Empire State building. Another group measured all the students in the class and then found the average height of the class members to make a comparison.

In this phase of the activity, rich opportunities for mathematics instruction really begin. We have to make comparisons that are accurate and then must prove mathematically the accuracy of the comparison. The task set before the students is to find an interesting comparison; accurately state the comparison in words; illustrate the comparison; and then, to demonstrate the comparison, write a ratio that shows the mathematics. In my classroom, I have given sixth graders a blank sheet of paper and verbally stated the task. I have found that imposing any more structure limits students' creativity. Sometimes their comparison is stated in the form of a caption that accompanies an illustration. Sometimes the mathematics or ratio is embedded in the stated comparison.

Each time *Incredible Comparisons* is used as a springboard for the task of creating comparisons, different mathematical problems and solutions arise. The problems arise from the students themselves, and the solutions can also come from the students through the structure of the task and the questions posed by the teacher.

REFERENCES

Ash, Russell. *Incredible Comparisons*. New York: Dorling Kindersley Publishing, 1996.

Oleson, Vicki. "Links to Literature: *Incredible Comparisons*: Experiences with Data Collection." *Teaching Children Mathematics* 5 (September 1998): 12–16.

Incredible Comparisons

Name _____

Date _____

1. On page 8 of *Incredible Comparisons*, read the first section, titled "How to Use This Book." How is this book going to answer such questions as "How big is it?" or "How fast is it?" How will using this book answer those questions?

2. Next read the rest of page 8. What can you find out from captions?

3. What kinds of things can scales tell us?

4. Fill in the following equivalent measures:

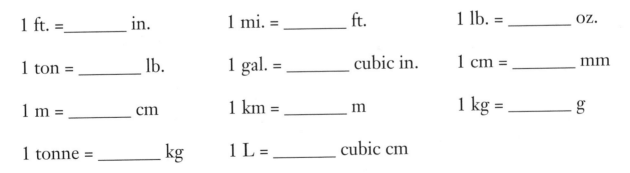

1 ft. = _____ in.   1 mi. = _____ ft.   1 lb. = _____ oz.

1 ton = _____ lb.   1 gal. = _____ cubic in.   1 cm = _____ mm

1 m = _____ cm   1 km = _____ m   1 kg = _____ g

1 tonne = _____ kg   1 L = _____ cubic cm

5. If the line segment below represents one foot, draw a second line segment that would represent one inch.

_____

6. Name something that you think is about one mile from our school.

7. Name something that weighs about one-half pound. Name something that weighs about 5 pounds.

_____ one-half pound _____ 5 pounds

8. Can you name something that comes in two-liter bottles?

9. About what part of a ton do you weight?

10. How many gallons of water do you think it might take to fill the wading pool, or baby pool, at the nearby public swimming pool?

(Continued on next page)

11. About how many meters tall are you?

12. Next read page 9. Below write at least five facts from that page that you found interesting:

_____

_____

_____

_____

_____

_____

Enjoy a look through the rest of this book!

Content Strand:
Data Analysis and Probability

23

Scrumptious Activities in the *Stew*

Sally Schneider

THE WEEK-LONG venture began with reading *The Wolf's Chicken Stew* (Kasza 1987). The children engaged in predicting outcomes and quickly recognized that the wolf's favorite number seemed to be 100. "First he made a hundred scrumptious pancakes . . . The next night he brought a hundred scrumptious doughnuts . . . And on the next night he brought a scrumptious cake weighing 100 pounds."

Keiko Kasza's *The Wolf's Chicken Stew* presented a way to involve forty children enrolled in two multi-age primary classes in activities focusing on thinking, one of the main goals of mathematics education. Five open-ended tasks were designed that involved children in problem solving; estimating; conducting probability experiments; and collecting, sorting, classifying, displaying, and interpreting data. The students expressed themselves orally and in writing during the investigation as they worked in both large and small groups.

Creating *100 Favorite Scrumptious Foods*

Once the story was read, the class decided to make a book of their favorite 100 scrumptious foods. This activity produced a lively discussion on how to ensure that exactly 100 pages were in the book. Students grappled with this idea by suggesting that everyone make 2 or 3 pages for the book, that the students make 2 pages and the teachers make 3 pages, and that other classes or the entire school participate in the book's production.

During the discussion, students analyzed their classmates' thinking and either offered support or disagreed. Sean reasoned that 3 pages per person were too many because 3 times 40 is 120. Joy agreed, stating that 40 + 40 equals 80 and 40 more makes 120. She justified her answer by explaining, "If you take off the 0's, it's 4 plus 8 equals 12. Put the 0's back on and it's 40 plus 80 equals 120."

After determining that 2 pages per student were not enough and that 3 were too many, the class decided to keep a running tally on the chalkboard. Each time someone picked up a new page for the book, a tally would be made until 100 marks were drawn. The class counted how many pages had been made and how many more were needed. This constant monitoring enabled students to begin forming part-whole relationships for 100. On reaching 100 tally marks, they observed that 20 groups of 5 equaled 100 as well as did 10 groups of 10.

Kara, whose favorite scrumptious food is cookies, was trying to represent the total number of chips in the cookies (see fig. 23.1). Originally she wrote 5 + 9 = 14. When asked to explain her work, she noted that she had made three rows of cookies with five cookies in each row and nine chips on each cookie. When asked if fourteen total chips were in the cookies, Kara looked at the teacher askance and patiently explained that the first cookie had 9 chips and so did the second cookie. When she was given a calculator, she used repeated addition to determine that 9 + 9 + 9 + 9 + 9 = 45. Without further prompting, she added 45 + 45 + 45 = 135, which was the total number of chips in her cookies. Although

Kara has difficulty expressing mathematics symbolically, she understands the concepts. When given the opportunity to explain her reasoning, Kara demonstrated her mathematical power.

Fig. 23.1. Kara's favorite scrumptious food

Collecting data

The class-authored book, *100 Favorite Scrumptious Foods*, led the students to wonder about other people's favorite foods. For homework, each child interviewed two people and recorded each person's favorite scrumptious foods on a separate index card. Students were encouraged to sort and classify their cards in as many different ways as possible while working in small groups. Each group reported to the class how it had sorted the cards. Some groupings suggested by the students included spicy/not spicy, red/not red, hot/cold, desserts/not desserts, pizza/not pizza, and meat/vegetables/pasta.

The class decided to sort all the cards into the categories of vegetables, meat, pasta, fruit, and desserts. Before counting and sorting all the cards, students were asked to predict which category would contain the most favorite scrumptious foods and to explain why. Predictions ranged from such responses as "Meat, because that's what we have the most of in our group" to "Desserts, because that's my favorite." Their sharing and predictions were interesting examples that displayed their mathematical thinking.

After approximately one-third of the students had placed their cards on the data display, students were allowed to adjust their predictions. Everyone chose meat as the category most likely to have the most favorite scrumptious foods by citing that "It already has the most cards." When the data display had been completed, students were asked to share their observations about the graph. Students noted that they had created a bar graph, meat was chosen the most often with forty-two cards, fruit had the fewest votes with two cards, and the meat category had forty more cards than fruit.... Once again, number relationships were being explored, this time through analyzing the data display.

Predicting the height of 100 pancakes

While paging through the book, several students speculated on the height of 100 pancakes. Their inquiries prompted a new investigation in which the children worked in groups to estimate the height of 100 pennies. Ten pennies were stacked on top of each other. Students used this benchmark of ten to mark their estimates of the height of 100 pennies on the butcher paper taped to the wall. One group decided to organize the various piles of pennies into groups of 10, reasoning that they needed nine more groups of 10 to make 100, since they already had one stack of 10. The students connected this new task to their previous discussions when they tallied the pages in their class-authored book. Midway through the stacking and again when all 100 pennies were stacked, students shared their thinking about which predictions were good and why they thought they were reasonable.

When determining the height of a stack of 100 pancakes, Brennan predicted that the pancakes would be higher than the pennies because pancakes are bigger. When asked to explain, he used his hands to show that not only were pancakes bigger around than pennies but, more important, they were thicker too.

Ten frozen waffles stacked on a plate became the center of the class's attention. Using this stack as a reference, the children marked their predictions for the height of 100 pancakes (waffles) on butcher paper taped to the wall. However, the class had a problem in that the four boxes of waffles in the classroom did not contain 100 waffles. The students thought about and discussed ways to determine the height of 100 pancakes if fewer pancakes were available. Students decided that the height of 10 pancakes could be measured, the spot marked on a ruler, and this marking used nine more times. The students connected this measuring task with the strategies they used to solve the tally for 100 pages by using ten groups of 10.

After marking the point for 50 pancakes, the children began speculating about which predictions would be closest to 100. Sarah suggested that instead of marking off five more groups of 10, they measure the group of 50 and mark that interval. She justified her idea by stating that 50 is one-half of 100 because 50 + 50 = 100. Students remarked that 100 pancakes would be hard to carry because a stack of 100 pancakes was taller than many children in the class. Naturally, the next step was to toast the contents of the four boxes of waffles, which the class enjoyed.

Counting Cookies

At the end of *The Wolf's Chicken Stew*, the wolf contemplates, "Maybe tomorrow I'll bake the little critters a hundred scrumptious cookies." With this thought, the class was shown a big bowl of animal-cracker cookies and a scoop. This question was posed, "How can we help the wolf scoop out enough cookies for all the chicks without touching each one?" Again a lively discussion ensued in which the children suggested various methods for helping the wolf scoop out enough cookies.

One idea was to see how many cookies were in one scoop. The teacher modeled this idea by taking a scoop from the bowl and determining that 16 cookies were in the scoop. She asked how this information could help the wolf obtain 100 cookies. One child suggested continually adding 16 + 16 + 16 . . . until 100 is reached; another child proposed using multiplication in a guess-and-check manner; and a third child recommended using a calculator to divide 100 by 16. This brainstorming and discussion time allowed the children to extend their thinking and prepared them to work in small groups to complete the activity. Each group was given a scoop, a bowl or bag of animal crackers, and a calculator.

Selena, a first-year student, used her knowledge of mathematical representations to record the results for her group (see fig. 23.2). First, she recorded that 17 cookies were in one scoop. To determine how many scoops would be needed to obtain 100 cookies, the group used a calculator to determine $100 \div 17 = 5.8$. (In fig. 23.2, 5.8 appears as 2.8 owing to a reversal.) Selena used a tally to record the number of scoops removed from the bowl and the total number of cookies. She and Ronnie, another first-year student, were concerned with sharing the cook-

ies fairly among the members of their group, thus setting up another problem-solving situation in which the students could stretch their thinking.

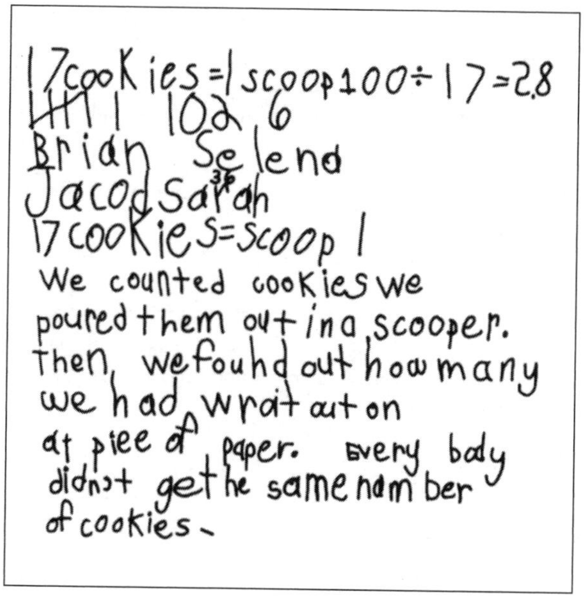

Fig. 23.2. Selena's record of her group's problem-solving approach

Fixing Chicken Stew

The final activity was a probability experiment in which the students made "pretend" chicken stew. Working in groups of three with a cook, taster, and recorder, students were given a brown-paper bag (the stew pot), two green linking cubes (celery), two orange cubes (carrots), four yellow cubes (onions), six brown cubes (chicken) and a recording booklet. The cook was instructed to "cut" the celery in half and add it to the stew pot. The children were asked, "If we put our tasting spoon into the pot, what would we be most likely to taste?" Naturally all groups predicted celery, since that was the only ingredient in the pot. Next, students "cut" their carrots in half but only added half the carrot pieces to the pot. Again, students were asked, "If we put our tasking spoon into the pot what would we be most likely to taste?" Students discussed the question within their groups, and the recorder wrote down the group's prediction (see fig. 23.3).

To validate their predictions, each taster pulled a cube out of the pot and then returned it to the pot while the recorder tallied the result, which was repeated ten times in each group. Class results were tallied on an overhead recording sheet, and a discussion ensued. Did each group get the same results? Did the students have more celery in the tasting? Why? What will happen if another piece of carrot is added? Why?

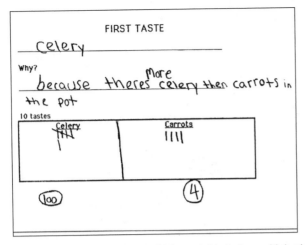

FIRST TASTE

Celery _____

Why? because theres ^{more} celery then carrots in the pot

10 tastes

Celery	Carrots
ⅢⅢ	‖‖‖

⑩⓪   ④

Fig. 23.3. Students predicted which vegetable taste would dominate the soup, then tested their predictions and recorded the data. The circled numbers record the class's data.

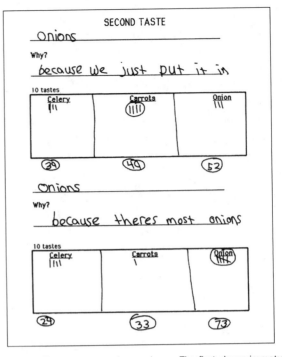

SECOND TASTE

Onions _____

Why? because we just put it in

10 tastes

Celery	Carrots	Onion
‖‖‖	⑪‖‖	‖‖‖

㉚   ㊵   ㊾

Onions _____

Why? because theres most onions

10 tastes

Celery	Carrots	Onion
‖‖‖	‖	㊄ⅢⅢ

㉔   ㉝   ㊃

Fig. 23.4. Two group records are shown. The first shows immature thinking; the second shows intuitive thinking about probability. The circled numbers below the chart record the class's data.

The other piece of carrot was added, group predictions were recorded, and ten tastings were made. Again, class results were compiled and discussed. This process was repeated for the other ingredients. The students' predictions and reasoning varied from taste to taste. Sometimes students thought that whatever had been added to the pot most recently would be tasted; at other times, they believed that the ingredient with the largest amount inside the pot would be tasted. (See fig. 23.4.)

Several mathematical processes and concepts were involved in this last task: fractional parts and equivalent fractions were discussed when students "cut" the different ingredients into halves, fourths, and sixths; probability, data gathering, recording, and analysis occurred; predictions were made and verified; reasoning was explained in their recordings and discussions; and addition of whole numbers was needed to total the class's results.

The Wolf's Chicken Stew became an excellent vehicle for fostering children's reasoning and building their mathematical power. Children's literature can be used to create activities that foster children's thinking. Additionally the author has found that children's literature helps establish a nonthreatening classroom environment wherein ideas are shared and thinking is encouraged. After all, the essence of good teaching is getting children to think.

REFERENCE

Kasza, Keiko. *The Wolf's Chicken Stew*. New York: G. P. Putnam's Sons, 1987.

Teaching Notes for

"Scrumptious Activities in the *Stew*"

by Sally Schneider

Grade range:	1–4
Mathematical topics:	Estimation, measurement, probability and data collection, sorting and classifying
Children's book:	*The Wolf's Chicken Stew*, written by Keiko Kasza

Discussion of the mathematics: Each task focuses on different topics in mathematics, but they all center on the benchmark of 100, involve problem solving, and focus on sense making both through estimation and predictions and through verification.

Teacher notes and questions to ask students: A number of investigations based on *The Wolf's Chicken Stew* are described in the article. Students' questions and observations prompted many of these tasks after we read the book. Sample questions and additional comments are given below.

Materials: Blank paper (at least 100 sheets), crayons or markers

Creating 100 favorite scrumptious foods: Have students estimate how many pages each student would be allotted, and have them share their reasoning. Have them explore an initial estimate to determine whether this number would be too much or too little. Have them use the information about that estimate to determine a closer one.

- How will we know when we have 100 pages in our book?
- How many pages should each student make so that we have exactly 100 pages in our book?
- If each student in our class made (3) pages, would we have more or fewer than 100 pages?

How many more pages would we need? This amount would be how many pages too many? How can we use this information to come up with a better estimate?

Be sure to have students justify their answers by explaining their reasoning.

- Tell the class how you came up with that estimate.
- How do you know that 3 times 40 is 120?

Most likely the number of students will not evenly divide 100. Have students determine the maximum number of pages each student can make, then decide how to handle the remaining pages fairly. If the class makes its own 100-page book, a helpful tactic is to have students mark a tally each time a page is added to the book. Have the tallies grouped in tens, as working with groups of ten is the foundation for place-value work.

Materials: Two index cards per child

Collecting data: Making a book of the 100 favorite scrumptious foods of our class members prompted us to wonder about the favorite foods of others. As we discussed who to ask and how to survey them, issues about sampling came up. The students discussed surveying school friends but decided that they would have no way to tell

203

whether a person had already been interviewed and observed, "It wouldn't be fair for someone to get asked twice." Consequently, the students decided to collect data from two people outside of school and record each person's favorite food on a separate index card. Later, in small groups, the students sorted and classified the foods named in as many ways as possible. The questions they posed included these:

- Can you think of another way to put these foods into two groups?
- Why does this (food) belong in this (group)?

After compiling all the sorting categories from each group, we determined which classification groups the entire class would use. We displayed our data on the wall by creating a bar graph with our index cards. The students were asked to make predictions and to read the completed graph.

- Which group do you think will have the most cards? Why? The fewest cards? Why?

- What can you tell me about favorite foods from looking at our graph?

- What comparison questions could you ask using data from our graph?

We recorded students' observations about the data on strips of paper and posted them around the graph, thus providing models for reading and interpreting data.

Materials: Objects that can be stacked, rulers, frozen waffles

Predicting the height of 100 pancakes: The picture of the wolf scurrying with a stack of 100 pancakes begs the question "How high is a stack of 100 pancakes?" Since a stack of 100 items is unwieldy if not inconvenient, a sample of ten items can serve as a benchmark. Engage the students in estimating how high the final stack will be when they know the height of ten of the items. Ask such questions as this:

- Will 100 pennies be as high as the table, or taller than you?

After the students have discussed their estimates, have them measure the height of their benchmark and then determine the height of 100 items. Some students may find it helpful to consider the height

of two sets or five sets before estimating the height of ten sets. My students investigated the height of a stack of ten pennies to use as their benchmark; other items, such as ten mathematics books or ten plates, could also be used. Having students determine the height of 100 frozen waffles is a motivating culminating activity.

Materials: Animal-shaped crackers, a scoop, and a bowl for each group

Counting cookies: At the end of the story, the wolf contemplates, "Maybe tomorrow I'll bake the little critters a hundred scrumptious cookies." This closing line often generates a question about what 100 cookies would look like. Pose the question to the class, and show them a large bowl of animal-shaped crackers and a scoop that will be used to collect a sample. Ask them such questions as these:

- What would 100 cookies look like? How many cookies would you estimate are in this container? Why?

- How can we help the wolf scoop out enough cookies for all 100 chicks without touching each cookie?

After students have discussed different strategies for solving the problem, have them work in small groups and provide each group a bowl or bag of animal-shaped crackers and a scoop. In my classroom students used calculators to help them solve the problem, because we had previously discussed how to interpret the display when decimals are involved.

Materials: A set of *"The Wolf's Chicken Stew"* recording sheets, connecting cubes, and a paper sack for each group

Fixing chicken stew: As this activity was one of the children's early experiences with probability, the investigation alternated between class discussion and directions and small-group investigations through role-playing. To help structure the investigation, each member of a group of three students had a specific role (i.e., a cook, a taster, and a recorder) to play. Each group was given a paper sack (stew pot), two green linking cubes (celery), two orange cubes (carrots), four yellow cubes (onions), six brown cubes (chicken), and a recording booklet. The number of cubes for the different ingredients varied so that halves, fourths, and sixths could be considered. Since the size of the wholes varied, students would be considering different representations of halves when they placed half the celery or onions or chicken in the pot. As described in the article, we started with just one cube in the pot. Each time the cook added another ingredient, we discussed our predictions, the taster sampled the soup ten times, and the recorder tallied the data.

- If we put our tasting spoon into the pot, what would we most likely taste? Why?

- Let's check our prediction by having the taster pick one cube out of the pot. The recorder will mark the result on your group's recording sheet. Place the cube back in the pot, and sample and record nine more times.

After we compiled the class's results, I posed such questions as the following:

- Did each group get the same results?

- Did the students have more celery or more carrots in the tasting? Why?

- What will happen if another piece of carrot is added? Why?

REFERENCES

Kasza, Keiko. *The Wolf's Chicken Stew*. New York: G. P. Putman's Sons, 1987.

Schneider, Sally. "Links to Literature: Scrumptious Activities in the *Stew*." *Teaching Children Mathematics* 1 (May 1995): 548–52.

Scrumptious Activities

Name _____

Date _____

First Taste

Which vegetable taste will dominate the soup? _____

Why? _____

_____

10 tastes

Celery   Carrots

Second Taste

Which vegetable taste will dominate the soup? _____

Why? _____

_____

10 tastes

Celery   Carrots   Onions

Scrumptious Activities Recording Sheet—*Continued*

Name _____

Date _____

<u>Third Taste</u>

Which vegetable taste will dominate the soup? _____

Why? _____

_____

<u>10 tastes</u>

Celery   Carrots   Onions   Chicken

24

Investigating Probability and Patterns with
The Thirteen Days of Halloween

Maryann Wickett

IT WAS week 2 of a probability unit in my 3–4 multigrade class. My students had experienced several activities that involved making predictions based on sampling with replacement, but for most students, their understanding was fragile. *The Thirteen Days of Halloween* by Carol Greene (1983) (fig. 24.1) provided an appropriate context to explore and reinforce

On the first day of Halloween, my good friend gave to me a vulture in a dead tree.

3

this notion further. The book was also the basis for experience in number and patterns. This four-day, high-interest investigation gave students a variety of access points, encouraging their persistence and enabling them to solve complex problems and think more deeply about probability.

"On the first day of Halloween, my good friend gave to me a vulture in a dead tree." Delighted by the words and illustrations, the students giggled as I continued, "On the second day of Halloween, my good friend gave to me two hissing cats and a vulture in a dead tree."

"This is like 'The Twelve Days of Christmas,'" observed Tiffany.

I paused after reading the fourth day. "Does anyone notice a pattern that would allow them to predict what might come next?" I asked.

"A new thing gets added each day, and the new group has one more in it than the new group had from the day before," explained Yessica.

"Each day all the stuff from the days before is added, and the list of things always ends with a vulture in a dead tree," John observed.

After reading day 5 to verify what the students had noticed about the pattern, I posed the following question: "How many things did the witch receive on the fifth day of Halloween?"

The students talked about this situation among themselves for a few moments; then several eager hands went up. "You add 5 + 4 + 3 + 2 + 1, so she got 15 things," Breanna shared. "We added 5 for the worms, 4 for the ghosts, 3 for toads, 2 for cats, and 1 vulture."

"We agree with Breanna, and we think she will get 21 things for day 6 and 28 things for day 7, because you would add 15 for what she has on day 5 to 6 for the number of things for day 6, which is 21, and then add 7 more for the 7 things on day 7, and that would make 28. It's a pattern and you could keep on going," shared Christina. As the students listened to Christina's explanation, several nodded their agreement.

On the thirteenth day of Halloween, the witch gives her friend a gift in return. The illustration shows a huge box with the witches standing beside it. A pair of scary eyes peer out one of the dark holes, and a tail hangs out of another. A long green trunk is reaching around the corner of the box (fig. 24. 2).

Fig. 24 2. The mysterious gift on day 13. Illustration for *The Thirteen Days of Halloween* by Carol Greene, © 2000 by Troll Bridgewater Books. All rights reserved.

The children loved the picture and broke into an animated discussion of the contents of the box. They were disappointed to find out that the book does not tell what was in the box. Somewhat incensed, Christina declared, "I'm going to write to the author and demand to know what was in the box!"

Patterns and Probability

On the second day, Emily began by rereading the story as I recorded each day's gift on the chalkboard. "How many gifts did the witch receive on day 12?" I asked the class. "How could we figure out this answer?"

"We could add … , like, 12 cauldrons plus 11 bats, and so on, down to 1 vulture in a dead tree," Fercie said.

"We could use a chart. One column would be the item, the next would be the number of items, and the third would be all the different items together," offered Anton.

"I think I could draw a picture and count," volunteered Tiara.

"Tally marks would be like Tiara's idea, only it would be faster than drawing pictures," Manuel suggested.

"You may work with your group to solve this question, but I would like for each of you to make your own recording sheet and justify your answer," I explained.

I was interested in the approaches that the students took. A few grabbed calculators, some used counters or beans, and several used tally marks. Tiara used a combination of pictures, tally marks, counting, and addition to get her answer. In my multilingual, multigrade classroom, all students had access to this problem because of its visual nature, our cooperative-group structure, and the high interest of the problem.

After a class discussion focusing on students' strategies for finding that 78 gifts were given on day 12, I held up a clear, empty jar. "What if I put 1 pink cube into the jar. What is the probability that I will draw a pink?"

"One!" quickly responded the class.

"What if I added a yellow cube to the jar. Now what is the probability I will draw a pink?" I continued.

"Fifty percent," responded Maritza.

"Another way of saying that would be 1 out of 2. There are 2 cubes, and 1 is pink, so that is 1 out of 2 chances, which is half, which is 50 percent," added Anton.

"What if I put in 1 pink cube for the vulture in a dead tree, 2 light blue for the hissing cats, and so on, and then 12 purples for the cauldrons? Which would I be most likely to draw?" I asked. (I added different-colored Unifix cubes to represent the different gifts.)

"Purple because there are the most. You would have 12 chances out of 78. There are 12 purple cubes out of 78," shared Todd.

"Which would be least likely?" I asked.

"The pink because there is only 1 out of 78 chances of getting it," explained Hannah.

"Does 'most likely' guarantee that something will happen?" I asked the class. "Talk with your neighbor about your ideas. Then I would like to hear what you are thinking about this."

"Well, I think that 'most likely' doesn't mean it will happen, it just means it's the best guess," explained Hannah.

"If something is guaranteed, then I think that it is the only thing that can happen. Like, to be guaranteed of a purple, then you would only have purple as your choice. And for something to be impossible, then it would not be there, like, there is no polka-dotted cube, so it is impossible to get one. So if it's in the jar, then it is possible," explained Christina.

"How many times do you think we would have to draw cubes from the jar to predict what is in it?" I probed, wanting to give students an opportunity to think about predicting based on sampling.

"Thirty-six," replied John quickly. "That seems to be how many times we have been doing it in other activities." John's memory was correct.

"Let's try two draws per student," I suggested. "How many samples will that be?"

"That's 31 times 2, which is 30 two times, which equals 60, and then two more for the 31st, so that's 60 plus 2, so that would be 62!" shared Tiara.

Each student drew a cube twice. We decided to go beyond 62 to a "nice" sample size of 70. Each time a student drew a cube, I noted the color then the student returned the cube to the jar (see fig. 24.3). As the sample size grew, we discussed how it compared with what we actually knew about the contents of the jar. After 60 draws the students agreed that the sample looked similar to the contents of the jar; that is, the greatest number of cubes were purple, the least number were pink, and the others fell somewhat accordingly.

More Patterns and Sampling

"We needed 78 cubes to represent the gifts for just the 12th day. How many cubes do you think we would need to represent *all* the gifts given on *all twelve* days?" I asked on the third day of our investigation. "How could you solve this question?"

"We could use the same ways we talked about before with day 12, things like calculators, pictures, charts, addition, and stuff like that," Yessica reminded us.

"Using any of these ideas or any idea that makes sense to you, work with your groups to figure how many gifts were given for all twelve days. Be sure to make your own recording sheet and explain your thinking."

As I observed the students, they were using a variety of approaches. All students were involved and had some way of approaching the problem. Manuel was using a chart that he and his tablemates had developed. Hannah and her partner, Monica, were using a combination of a chart, symbols, counting, and addition. Adrian was using a color code and drawing cubes to represent each of the gifts given for each day. A variety of charts were developed and used meaningfully by the students; figure 24.4 shows one student's method.

When most students were about halfway through the solution, I asked for their attention to

	Number of Draws for Each Color						
Colors of Cubes	10 Draws	20 Draws	30 Draws	40 Draws	50 Draws	60 Draws	70 Draws
Pink	0	0	0	0	0	0	0
Light blue	1	2	2	3	3	3	3
Tan	1	3	5	5	5	5	7
Light green	1	2	3	3	3	6	6
Yellow	0	0	0	1	2	2	2
White	2	3	3	4	6	6	6
Dark blue	0	1	5	5	5	9	9
Red	0	0	0	2	4	4	5
Brown	0	0	0	2	3	3	4
Orange	0	0	0	2	4	4	5
Black	2	3	6	6	6	7	10
Purple	3	6	6	7	8	10	12

Fig. 24.3. Sampling cubes

EXPLORING MATHEMATICS THROUGH LITERATURE

consider for a few moments what a reasonable answer would be. This problem was complex for third and fourth graders. Talking about reasonable answers at this point was an effective way to help them stay focused and on track. As part of the discussion, I made a chart on the chalkboard. On the left I listed the day number, and on the right I listed the total number of cubes, or gifts, given up to that point. Day 1, 1 gift; day 2, 4 gifts; day 3, 10 gifts; and so on up to day 5. After some discussion, most students seemed to think that the total number of gifts should be somewhere between 190 and 500. (The actual number is 364.) The students went back to work enthusiastically.

When most of the students had finished, I asked them to sit on the floor. We continued to fill in the chart we had started before. As we moved from day to day, we built a Unifix train to represent the gifts given for the day. When we got to day 9, I asked the students to predict which color cube I would be most likely to draw when I had finished putting in cubes for all twelve days.

"I think it would be purple, because purple is the cauldrons and there will be twelve of them, and so that will be the most," suggested Tiffany.

"I don't think it would be purple because there is only one day you would get them, you would get 12, which is the most, but you only get it once, on the twelfth day," explained Theresa.

"It won't be pink. You get one every day, but you only get one, so you only get 12 altogether. You see, it's sort of a pattern, you get twelve purples once to equal 12 and one pink twelve times, which is also 12," shared Christina.

"Oh, I see a pattern! So for light blue, that's two cubes for eleven days, which is 22, and the black is eleven cubes for two days, which is also 22, so I think the color with the most will be somewhere in the middle if the pattern keeps getting bigger. The tan is three cubes for ten days, and that's 30, which is

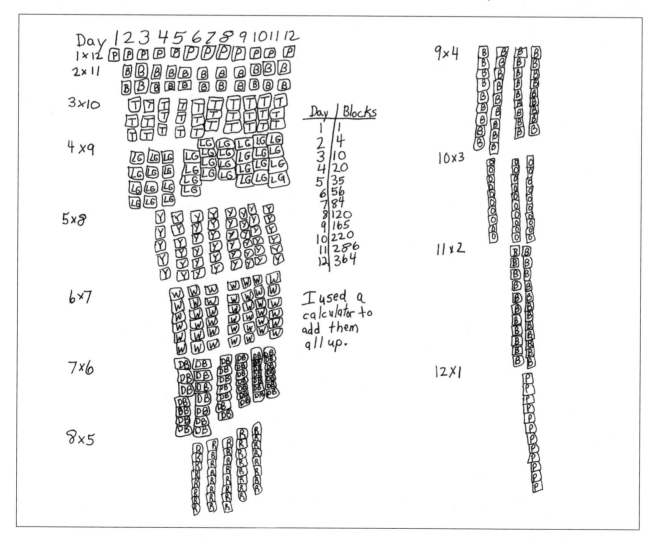

Fig. 24. 4 Theresa's method for finding the total number of gifts

bigger than 22, so I think I might be right!" exclaimed Hannah.

We continued to explore and did discover that the total gifts for all twelve days was 364. The colors that appeared most often were those for gifts introduced in the middle, on days 6 and 7.

Many students had predicted that purple cubes, representing the cauldrons given on day 12, would appear the most, because that was the case when we looked only at day 12. Several thought it might be one of the colors in the middle because a medium number of gifts was given a medium number of days. Students continued to sample and recorded their results to investigate whether the results of their sampling would resemble the distribution of blocks representing the gifts given for all twelve days. The students predicted that as the sample size grew, it would more closely represent the distribution of blocks, which proved to be true as they did the activity (fig. 24.5).

Pink	/
Light blue	//
Tan	//
Light green	//
Yellow	//LH
White	//LHT
Dark blue	//LHTT
Red	///
Brown	/
Orange	
Black	/
Purple	/

Fig. 24.5. Data after thirty samples

Reflections and Assessment

"I would like for you to reflect on what we have been investigating for the past three days," I began. "I am curious to know about the following," I continued as I wrote two sentence starters on the chalkboard: "These are some things I learned" and "These are some things I am still wondering about."

The students wrote quietly. In the text that follows, you will note that we have retained students' spelling. Christina wrote, "… it was a long problem and I learned that it had a lot to do with probability. You had to add a lot too. I had to count and add, count and add, count and add untile I got the answer. I learned that there were patterns that I had to salove and there were some gusstamating too. We had to sample size too. There were 78 cubes for 12 days. All the days blocks came up to 364." Maritza was still wondering about "… what was in the box it seems mystyrias."

I wanted the students to evaluate their own work. Together we generated a list of activities and attributes related to this investigation, including their reflections and the clarity of their explanations. I asked each student to use a +, √ +, √, or √ – symbol to assign himself or herself a grade for each item, as well as an overall grade. They were also asked to give at least one reason for each grade they gave themselves. For example, Tiara gave herself a + on the activity to figure out the total gifts, or blocks, for all twelve days because "It was done diffiret for eney other and it had the righ anser." She gave herself a √ + for the number of gifts on day 12 because "I got the rong anser but did the rest good."

The students' work showed persistence and many creative solutions. Considering their ages, their explanations made sense. Although students were aware of the correctness of their answers, they also showed an appreciation of their thinking and problem-solving skills (fig. 24.6).

OTHER RESOURCES

The following books could be used for similar investigations:

Chwast, Seymour. *The 12 Circus Rings*. San Diego: Harcourt Brace Jovanovich, 1993.

Trivas, Irene. *Emma's Christmas*. New York: Franklin Watts, 1988.

The Twelve Days of Christmas. Many versions and authors of this book exist.

REFERENCE

Greene, Carol. *The Thirteen Days of Halloween*. Chicago: Children's Press, 1983.

EXPLORING MATHEMATICS THROUGH LITERATURE

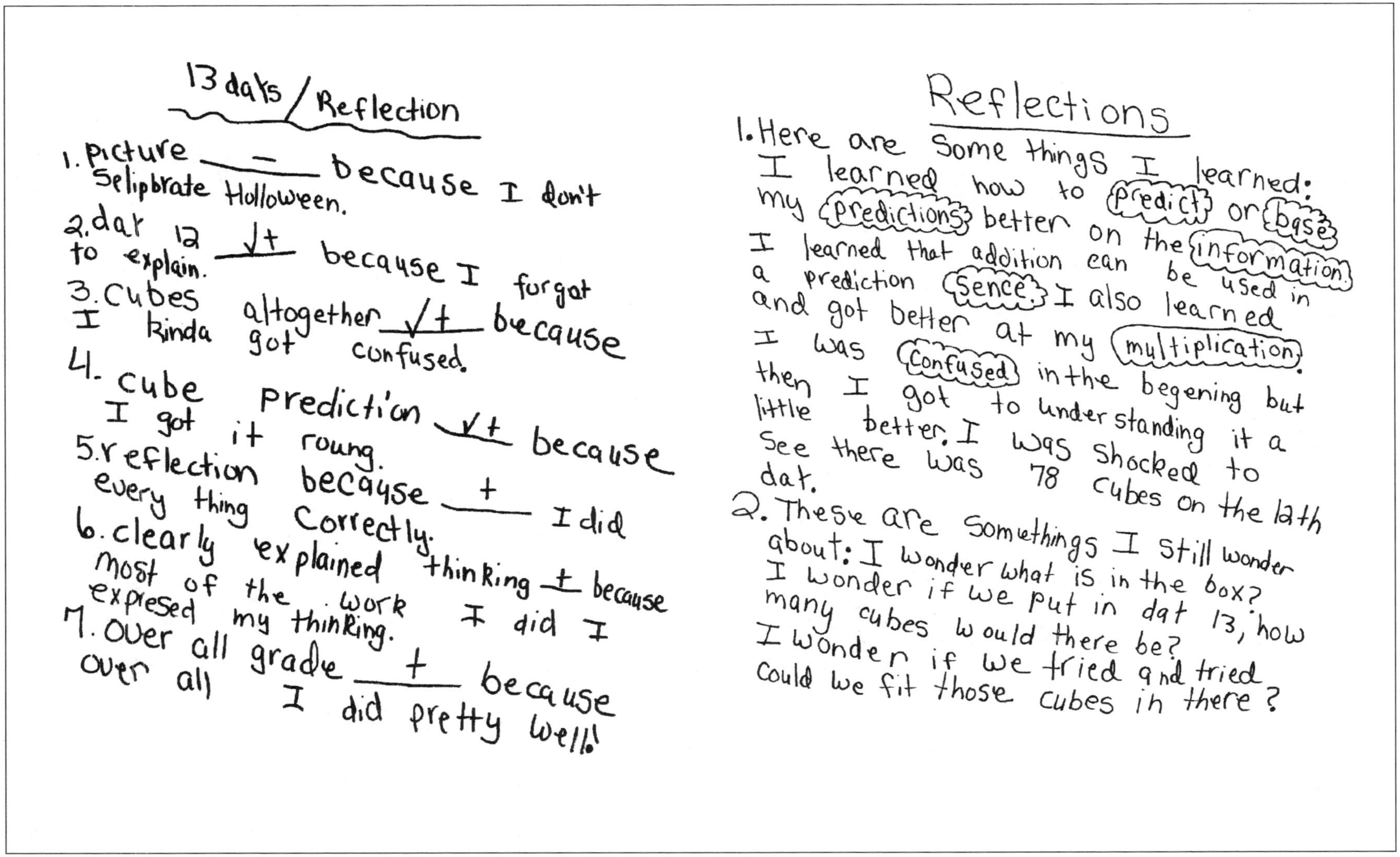

Reflections

1. Here are some things I learned:
I learned how to Predict or base
my predictions better on the information.
I learned that addition can be used in
a prediction. Sence. I also learned in
and got better at my multiplication.
I was confused in the begening but
then I got to understanding it a
little better. I was shocked to
See there was 78 cubes on the 10th
dat.

2. These are somethings I still wonder
about: I wonder what is in the box?
I wonder if we put in dat 13, how
many cubes would there be?
I wonder if we tried and tried
could we fit those cubes in there?

13 dat/s Reflection

1. Picture — because I don't
Selipbrate Holloween.

2. dat 13 -/+ because I forgot
to explain.

3. Cubes altogether -/+ because
I kinda got confused.

4. cube Prediction -/+ because
I got it roung.

5. reflection because + I did
every thing correctly.

6. clearly explained thinking + because
most of the work I did I
expresed my thinking.

7. Over all grade + because
over all I did pretty well!

Fig. 24.6. Hannah's reflection

"Investigating Probability and Patterns with *The Thirteen Days of Halloween*"

by Maryann Wickett

Grade range:	3–5
Mathematical topics:	Probability, number operations and patterns
Children's books:	*The Thirteen Days of Halloween*, by Carol Greene (Alternatives: *The Twelve Circus Rings*, by Seymour Chwast; *Emma's Christmas*, by Irene Trivas; or one of the many versions of *The Twelve Days of Christmas*)
Materials:	Snap, multilink, or Unifix cubes in twelve colors; large plastic jar or other clear plastic container; "*The Thirteen Days of Halloween*" recording sheet

Discussion of the mathematics: *The Thirteen Days of Halloween* provides a context to explore ideas in data collection and probability. This task includes describing events as likely or unlikely, predicting the probability of outcomes of simple experiments, and testing the predictions. The problems also involve finding sums of sequences and multiplication situations.

Teacher notes and questions to ask students: After reading a few pages of the book, pose and discuss the following questions and then read the rest of the story.

- What pattern do you notice that you could use to predict what might come next?
- How many things did the witch receive on the fifth day of Halloween?
- How many on the sixth day? How many on the seventh day? What pattern do you notice?

Have a student reread the story while you list each day's gifts on the board, and then pose the questions that follow. As a class, brainstorm and record ideas about how the problem could be solved. Ask students to solve the problem, showing how they arrived at their solution.

- How could we figure out the number of gifts the witch received on the twelfth day of Halloween?

Begin the probability discussion by representing the gifts with cubes and posing questions about the first gift-giving days, then discussing students' understandings about "most likely" and "least likely." Use a clear plastic jar and different-colored cubes to represent the gifts.

- If I place one cube in the jar, what is the probability that I will draw a red cube?
- What if I added a yellow cube? What is the probability that I will draw a red cube now?
- What would I be most likely to draw if I put one red cube in the jar to represent the vulture, two yellow cubes for the hissing cats, and so on, until I put in twelve black cubes for the cauldrons?
- Which would be the *least likely*? How do you know? Does *most likely* guarantee that something will happen?

To help students understand that they can use sampling to predict the distribution of colors in the jar, pose the following question:

- How many times do you think you will have to draw cubes from the jar to predict its contents?

Conduct the foregoing experiment by having each student draw a cube from the container and then replace it before a second draw. You may need to transfer the cubes to a paper sack so that the students cannot see the colored cubes. Record their results on the board; ten draws for each accumulating sample worked well (see fig. 24.3 in article).

- What did you already know about the contents of the jar?
- What do you notice about the results of our sampling? How does this outcome compare with what you know about the contents of the jar? Why do you think this relationship is so?

To begin the next part of the investigation, pose the following questions and have students brainstorm ways they could solve the problem.

- How many cubes do you think we would need to represent *all* the gifts given on *all twelve days?*
- How could you solve this question?

Have the students work on their solutions using paper and pencil. When they appear to be about halfway through the process of solving the problem, ask for their attention to discuss what would be a reasonable answer.

- What do you think a reasonable answer will be?

Record the students' responses, and ask them to justify their thinking. Note: This problem is complex for many children. Stopping to consider what a reasonable answer might be helps to keep students focused and on track and will help some students clarify their thinking. As part of the discussion, create a chart listing the days on the left, and across from each day, list the number of gifts received through day 4 or 5. This format creates a self-check for students.

When students have completed their solution, gather for a class discussion. Finish the chart started previously. As you move from day to day, have a few students represent the gifts given by building cube trains. When you get to day 9, ask the following:

- When we finish adding cubes for all the gifts, which color (gift) will most likely be drawn?
- What patterns have you noticed so far?
- How can the patterns you have noticed help you predict what will happen when all twelve days are completed?

To investigate the number of draws (experimental probability) needed to represent the distribution of colored cubes, have students sample by drawing out a cube and recording the results of their draw. The number of draws could be quite large before the results start to resemble the actual probability, thus providing an opportunity to discuss sample sizes and how close is close enough.

Student reflection and assessment: To help students build generalizations and reflect on their learning, have them reflect on all the work that they have pursued in this investigation. Have them respond to the following prompts:

- These are some things I learned....
- These are some things I am still wondering about....

REFERENCES

Chwast, Seymour. *The Twelve Circus Rings.* San Diego: Harcourt Brace Jovanovich, 1993.

Greene, Carol. *The Thirteen Days of Halloween.* Chicago: Children's Press, 1983.

The Twelve Days of Christmas. Many versions and authors of this book exist.

Trivas, Irene. *Emma's Christmas.* New York: Franklin Watts, 1988.

Wickett, Maryann. "Links to Literature: Investigating Probability and Patterns with *The Thirteen Days of Halloween.*" *Teaching Children Mathematics* 4 (October 1997): 90–94.

The Thirteen Days of Halloween   Recording Sheet

Name_____

Date _____

Clearly show how to solve the problem below:

How many cubes do you think we would need to represent ALL the gifts given on ALL twelve days?

Wait for guidelines from your teacher.

> On the back of this sheet, write a reflection:
> These are some things I learned....
> These are some things I am still wondering about....

25

Socrates and the Three Little Pigs: Connecting Patterns, Counting Trees, and Probability

Denisse R. Thompson and Richard A. Austin

EXPLORATIONS of concepts of chance should be a part of the middle school curriculum, as indicated in the mathematics curriculum frameworks developed by several states (Florida 1996; South Carolina 1993; New Jersey 1996). The challenge for teachers is to find contexts that interest middle school students and motivate them to explore these ideas.

The use of literature to engage students in exploring mathematics topics has been well documented at the elementary level (Burns 1992; Whitin and Wilde 1992, 1995; Welchman-Tischler 1992). Many middle-grades teachers have also begun to investigate the use of literature to motivate students at this level (Austin and Thompson 1997). Our experience has been that middle-grades students enjoy stories. When concepts are introduced through literature, students can often productively investigate concepts beyond those in their current curriculum.

This article features the use of the children's book *Socrates and the Three Little Pigs* (Anno 1986) to engage middle-grades students in exploring patterns related to counting. All the activities described here have been used with regular seventh-grade students during one blocked period of roughly ninety minutes; parts of these activities have also been used with seventh graders during a typical forty-five- to fifty-minute class period.

Summary of *Socrates and the Three Little Pigs*

Socrates, the philosopher wolf, needs to catch a little pig for his wife, Xantippe, who is rather hungry. Three pigs, dressed in blue, red, or yellow pants, live in any of five houses in the meadow. Socrates wants to determine in which house to look to have the best chance of catching a pig. His mathematician friend, Pythagoras the Frog, helps Socrates look at the problem in an orderly fashion. The remainder of the book contains illustrations and discussions about all the different ways in which the three pigs can be in the five houses. Through the story and illustrations, the reader is introduced to counting trees, permutations, and combinations.

Setting the Stage

To set the stage for the activities, students were asked to brainstorm the meaning of *probability*, even though this topic had not yet been studied during the school year. Students commented that probability means "how likely" something is to occur. They connected this term to the lottery and the chances of winning and to tossing a coin and obtaining either heads or tails. They understood that probability deals with matters of chance. One student had just completed a report on Pascal and mentioned Pascal's triangle; however, the student was unable to explain how Pascal's triangle connects to probability.

To further set the stage for using the book, students were shown the three problems in figure 25.1 and asked to comment on how the problems are similar. Students noted that all the problems have

---

The Mom and Pop Ice Cream Shop is rather small and has a limited supply of ice cream for sundaes. They carry only vanilla, chocolate, strawberry, and butter-pecan ice cream. On sundaes you get a choice of either hot fudge or caramel sauce. The only toppings available are sprinkles, chopped nuts, or chocolate chips. Every sundae has a bit of whipped cream and a sauce and only one topping. Ann wants to get a different kind of sundae every day. How many days can Ann get a sundae from Mom and Pop's shop before she must get a duplicate kind of sundae? Can you list the possible types of sundaes?

Uncle Vito's Pizza Palace is having a special on one-topping pizzas. You can choose betwen thick crust, regular crust, or very thin crust. You must then choose between traditional tomato sauce or gourmet white sauce. Finally, you must choose from one of the following toppings: pepperoni, sausage, olives, green peppers, onions, ham, or ground beef. The cheese is included, and you will love the results. How many different one-topping pizzas are possible from Uncle Vito's?

Peter bought a new CD player that holds three CDs at a time and plays one after the other. He has three types of CDs that he likes. Peter decided to put one CD from each category into the CD player. If he has ten rock CDs, eight jazz CDs, and eleven rap CDs, how many different arrangements can he have on his CD player?

Fig. 25.1. Real-world counting problems used to set up the lesson

---

groups in which one item is taken from each category and that all three problems involve different arrangements. Students also commented that "all are about stuff we like," an interesting comment for teachers to consider as we incorporate more real-world applications into the curriculum.

Students were encouraged to conjecture about how to obtain an answer to the pizza problem. Some thought that they should add the number of options in each category and multiply by 3; others wanted to add the number of options and divide by 3. Still others thought that the number of options in each category could be multiplied.

The students' comments indicated that solving these problems was not trivial, even though such problems are often found in textbooks. Having students consider the problems and make conjectures about the solutions provided the springboard and motivation for reading the beginning of the book. Students were told that the story would help develop mathematical strategies useful for solving these problems. The goal of the activities was to develop the use of counting trees as a tool to generate patterns leading to the multiplication counting principle, the mathematical strategy used to solve these three problems and other similar problems.

Activity 1: Counting Trees and Patterns

One of the instructors read the first fourth of the book, including the portion in which a counting tree is used to illustrate the number of ways that three pigs can be in five houses if more than one pig can be in a house. Although the story describes the arrangements for three pigs and five houses, we were interested in having students consider patterns, generalize those patterns, and develop algebraic representations for those patterns. Hence, students considered the number of arrangements possible for numbers of pigs and houses other than those in the story. To help students record their ideas in an organized fashion, they were given a blank copy of the table that is shown in a completed form in figure 25.5.

To help students understand the structure of the counting trees and to lay the foundation for the entries in the remainder of the table, the instructor sketched out the tree diagram for two pigs in three houses, as illustrated in figure 25.2. The thick lines represent the three possible houses in which the first pig can be found; for each of these situations, the three thin lines represent the three houses

EXPLORING MATHEMATICS THROUGH LITERATURE

in which the second pig can be found. The number on the branch of the tree corresponds to the house in which the given pig is found. With the students' help, the instructor then listed the nine possible arrangements for two pigs in three houses. Notice that "11" means that the first pig is in house 1 and the second pig is also in house 1; similarly, "31" means that the first pig is in house 3 and the second pig is in house 1.

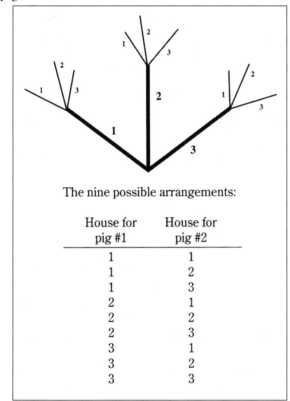

The nine possible arrangements:

House for pig #1	House for pig #2
1	1
1	2
1	3
2	1
2	2
2	3
3	1
3	2
3	3

Fig. 25.2. Counting tree and arrangements for two pigs in three houses, where more than one pig can be in a house

With the different arrangements listed, students answered probability questions directly related to this situation. For instance, the probability that both pigs are in the same house is 3/9; the probability that at least one pig is in house 1 is 5/9. Students determined the probability by counting how many of the nine arrangements satisfy the stated conditions. When asked to determine the probability that no pig is in house 3, one student responded with 2/3 because "if [a pig] is not in house 3, then it must be in house 1 or 2, so the answer is 2 out of 3." Others disagreed, noting that only four of the nine arrangements had no pig in house 3. Listing the arrangements presented an opportunity for self-correcting by the students.

After this introduction, students were asked to construct a tree diagram that would show all the ways that two pigs could be in four houses and then

to list the different possible arrangements. Figure 25.3 contains one sample tree diagram, together with a student's response to probability questions about the likelihood of finding both pigs in the same house or finding no pig in house 4.

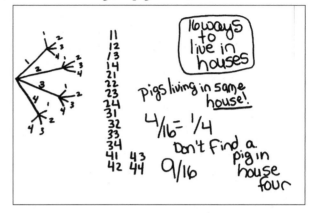

Fig. 25.3. Student tree diagram and arrangements for two pigs in four houses, where more than one pig can be in a house

Before constructing a tree diagram for two pigs in five houses, students were asked to conjecture the number of possible arrangements that they thought would occur. The purpose was to have students recognize that making conjectures is a viable mathematical activity; conjectures may be true or false. Evidence must be produced to support a conjecture or to prove it false; in this example, a completed counting tree was used to test the validity of the conjectured value.

At this point, students had constructed two counting trees and had completed the first three rows of the second column of the table. Many students were beginning to recognize a pattern in the table. Students had a chance to test their pattern when the number of pigs increased to three. They were expected to conjecture the number of ways in which three pigs could be in four houses and then to construct a counting tree displaying all the arrangements.

The change in the number of pigs from two to three created a dilemma for students trying to construct the tree diagram. Initially, several students struggled with the idea of creating another level of branches to describe the location of the third pig given the location of the first two pigs. Students constructed two levels of branches as in the situations with only two pigs and needed a small hint to think about constructing branches for the third pig. This tree diagram and the number of arrangements approach the limit of what can reasonably be expected for students to complete with a sketch.

Although not discussed within the context of this activity, clearly a side benefit is the use of the tree to make an orderly list of the arrangements. Many times when students of all ages try to make an exhaustive list, they are not organized in the process. Hence, when the list is large, it becomes difficult to locate omissions in arrangements.

At this point, students worked individually or with a partner to complete the second column of the table. Having constructed several counting trees, students had little difficulty recognizing the pattern. Students described the pattern by noting that "the main number is the number of houses, and the exponent is the number of pigs." After stating this rule, students were able to represent the number of arrangements for p pigs in h houses as h^p.

To help students consider the case in which only one pig can be in a house, the instructor read another fourth of the book, specifically the portion of the book describing this new condition. Students revisited the original counting tree for two pigs in three houses and considered which branches would no longer be acceptable. The resulting tree diagram and possible arrangements are shown in figure 25.4.

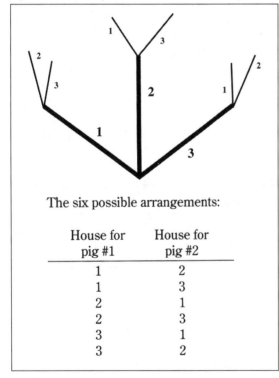

The six possible arrangements:

House for pig #1	House for pig #2
1	2
1	3
2	1
2	3
3	1
3	2

Fig. 25.4. Counting tree and arrangements for two pigs in three houses, where only one pig can be in a house

With this information, students again worked individually or with partners to complete the last column of the table. For the most part, students were able to complete the rows of the table. The only rows creating difficulty were those with a given number of pigs in h houses. Although students recognized the pattern, many struggled with denoting one less than h. Initially, some students tried to express the arrangements for three pigs in h houses as $h \bullet -1 \bullet -2$; others tried $h \bullet g \bullet f$. A few were able to express the number of arrangements correctly as $h \bullet (h-1) \bullet (h-2)$. Figure 25.5 contains one student's completed table. Observe that the last row of the third column is not completed. Although the instructor worked with students to discuss the appropriate result, $h \bullet (h-1) \bullet (h-2) \bullet ... \bullet (h-(p-1))$, most students did not seem to understand this expression. These students had had only minimal work with variables, so dealing with an unknown number of pigs was too abstract for them.

Activity 2: Revisiting the Three Real-World Problems

To bring the lesson in this double period to a close, students revisited the three problems from figure 25.1. Figure 25.6 contains sample responses from three students to the ice-cream-parlor problem. The transfer from pigs in houses to real-world problems was not trivial for students. Many students struggled with creating a tree diagram to describe the situation. Some students constructed the diagram and used numbers just as in the situations with the pigs. Whether these students understood that the numbers in this example referred to flavors of ice cream, types of sauces, and types of toppings is not clear. Response (a) shows a diagram in which the ice-cream choices are reflected on the diagram. Response (b) illustrates a situation in which the student tried to list the possible sundaes using a strategy similar to that with the pigs; the student would likely have benefited from using different letters for the sauces and the toppings to avoid confusion. Although the student listed only twenty-one possibilities, it is clear that those combinations could be translated into sundaes if the student interpreted the first letter to be the flavor, the second letter to be the topping, and the third letter to be the sauce. Response (c) illustrates a solution in which the student used the results from the pigs to generalize the multiplication counting principle to other situations.

The difficulties experienced in transferring from pigs in houses to ice-cream flavors and toppings constitute an interesting reminder to educators that students do not automatically transfer concepts learned in one context to another context. In this situation, students would likely have benefited from

Number of pigs in houses	Number of possible arrangements if more than 1 pig can be in a house and the order of the pigs in the house is not important	Number of possible arrangements if only 1 pig can be in a house and the color of the pig is important
2 pigs in 3 houses	$3 \cdot 3 = 3^2$ 9	$3 \cdot 2$ 6
2 pigs in 4 houses	$4 \cdot 4 = 4^2$ 16	$4 \cdot 3$ 12
2 pigs in 5 houses	$5 \cdot 5 = 5^2$ 25	$5 \cdot 4$ 20
3 pigs in 4 houses	$4 \cdot 4 \cdot 4 = 4^3$	$4 \cdot 3 \cdot 2$ 24
3 pigs in 5 houses	$5 \cdot 5 \cdot 5 = 5^3$	$5 \cdot 4 \cdot 3$
3 pigs in 6 houses	$6 \cdot 6 \cdot 6 = 6^3$	$6 \cdot 5 \cdot 4$
3 pigs in h houses	$h \cdot h \cdot h = h^3$	$(h)(h - 1)(h - 2)$
4 pigs in 5 houses	$5 \cdot 5 \cdot 5 \cdot 5 = 5^4$	$5 \cdot 4 \cdot 3 \cdot 2$
4 pigs in 6 houses	$6 \cdot 6 \cdot 6 \cdot 6 = 6^4$	$6 \cdot 5 \cdot 4 \cdot 3$
4 pigs in 7 houses	$7 \cdot 7 \cdot 7 \cdot 7 = 7^4$	$7 \cdot 6 \cdot 5 \cdot 4$
4 pigs in 10 houses	$10 \cdot 10 \cdot 10 \cdot 10 = 10^4$	$10 \cdot 9 \cdot 8 \cdot 7$
4 pigs in h houses	$h \cdot h \cdot h \cdot h = h^4$	$(h)(h - 1)(h - 2)(h - 3)$
5 pigs in 6 houses	$6 \cdot 6 \cdot 6 \cdot 6 \cdot 6 = 6^5$	$6 \cdot 5 \cdot 4 \cdot 3 \cdot 2$
p pigs in h houses ($p \leq h$)	h^p	

Fig. 25.5. Sample completed table

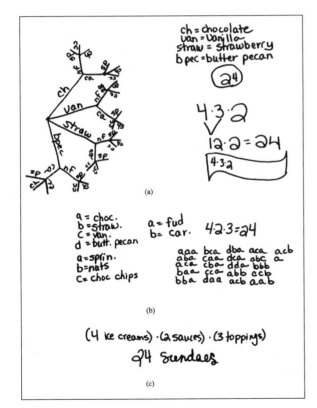

Fig. 25.6. Solutions to the ice-cream-parlor problem from figure 25.1

discussing, as a class or in small groups, the similarities of these problems to the pigs-in-houses problems. Explicitly drawing attention to the connections would probably have facilitated the transfer of the mathematical strategy of counting trees from one context to another. This explicit discussion is an important part of completing a lesson.

Reactions to the Lesson

After conducting this lesson, the regular classroom teacher shared her insights on the effectiveness of the lesson and also surveyed students about their reactions to the lesson. Although students were able to construct counting trees, the teacher thought that a broad-based introduction to counting trees might have made it easier for students to generalize to different situations. In addition, the teacher suggested the use of a concrete model to illustrate the placement of pigs in houses. Both suggestions are ones that other teachers using this lesson might want to consider on the basis of the needs and abilities of the students in the class.

As might be expected, students' reactions to the book and the activities varied. When asked to describe the purpose of a counting tree, ten of the twenty-four students indicated that it is used to show possible arrangements, five indicated that it is used to figure out a problem, and six specifically indicated that it is used to solve probability problems. Students were also asked, "How did the tree help you determine a mathematical method for solving the same problem?" Fourteen indicated that it simplified the problem, helped organize the counting arrangements, or helped to figure out the problem.

The teacher surveyed the students about what they liked about the lesson. Seven commented on the new and enjoyable material, two indicated that working with the professors was interesting, five indicated that the material was easy with no home-work, and three indicated "the story." When asked what they disliked about the lesson, eight said, "Nothing." A few commented that it was too long or too short or too hard. When asked what they thought about the story, seven thought that it was a good or "cool" story, five thought that it was educational and interesting, and six thought that it was too childish or dumb.

Even though some students considered the story to be a bit childish, none of the students indicated that the mathematical tasks or the introductory problems were too easy for them. For many, the story was a positive motivator to engage in the tasks and problems presented. In fact, several students stayed after class to find out the ending of the story.

Conclusion

This article has presented ideas for introducing counting trees to students and connecting those counting trees to patterns and probability. The children's story *Socrates and the Three Little Pigs* (Anno 1986) was the basis around which this lesson was built. The activities can serve as an introduction to probability and combinatoric problems that are accessible to middle-grades students. The activities are also feasible for students in the upper elementary grades as they extend their conceptual understanding of multiplication to include contexts solved by the multiplication counting principle. We encourage you to consider using this book to have your students explore some rich mathematics.

REFERENCES

Anno, Mitsumasa. *Socrates and the Three Little Pigs.* New York: Philomel Books, 1986.

Austin, Richard A., and Denisse R. Thompson. "Exploring Algebraic Patterns through Literature." *Mathematics Teaching in the Middle School* 2 (February 1997): 274–81.

Burns, Marilyn. *Math and Literature (K–3): Book One.* Sausalito, Calif.: Math Solutions Publications, 1992.

Florida Department of Education. *PreK–12 Sunshine State Standards and Instructional Practices: Mathematics.* Tallahassee, Fla.: Florida Department of Education, 1996.

New Jersey State Board of Education. *State Mathematics Framework.* Trenton, N.J.: New Jersey State Board of Education, 1996.

South Carolina State Board of Education. *South Carolina Mathematics Framework.* Columbia, S.C.: South Carolina State Board of Education, 1993.

Welchman-Tischler, Rosamond. *How to Use Children's Literature to Teach Mathematics.* Reston, Va.: National Council of Teachers of Mathematics, 1992.

Whitin, David J., and Sandra Wilde. *It's the Story That Counts: More Children's Books for Mathematical Learning, K–6.* Portsmouth, N.H.: Heinemann, 1995.

———. *Read Any Good Math Lately? Children's Books for Mathematical Learning, K–6.* Portsmouth, N.H.: Heinemann, 1992.

Teaching Notes for

"*Socrates and the Three Little Pigs*: Connecting Patterns, Counting Trees, and Probability"

by Denisse R. Thompson and Richard A. Austin

Grade range:	7–8
Mathematical topics:	Permutations, probability, and generalizing patterns
Children's book:	*Socrates and the Three Little Pigs*, written by Tuyosi Mori and illustrated by Mitsumasa Anno
Materials:	"*Socrates and the Three Little Pigs*" recording sheets, dots or counters in three colors

Discussion of the mathematics: Such representations as a model of the problem, tables, and tree diagrams are effective ways to help students understand the interrelated concepts of permutations, combinations, and probability. These concepts and strategies are effectively presented in the story line in *Socrates and the Three Little Pigs*. Because this topic is at a sophisticated level, you will need to guide the class to closely analyze the problems and the different representations to help students build and connect these concepts and strategies.

Teacher notes and questions to ask students: In the story, the three pigs can be identified because each wears an outfit of a different color (red, yellow, or blue). The author shows all the various arrangements of pigs in houses, but the diagrams are small. As noted in the article, we read only a fourth of the book because we needed time to discuss the problems posed and analyze the representations used to solve them. Additionally, students need opportunities to solve similar problems in terms of the number of pigs and the number of houses. These problems can then be related to the book's representations. In the article, we noted the problems used for whole-class and individual or

small-group work, including samples of students' thinking. Also, we simplified matters for the tree diagrams by numbering the houses.

In investigating a simpler situation with students, the teacher could have students represent different pigs visually. One scenario might be to develop the case for two pigs and four houses when a house can have more than one pig. The teacher could have students represent the pigs with color dots, chips, or similar materials. An additional task would be to place two pigs in four houses where no house has more than one pig.

"*Socrates and the Three Little Pigs*" recording sheet 1 helps students draw out and organize the arrangements for the simpler problem of two pigs and four houses and then answer probability questions using the data collected. For students who need a physical representation of the arrangements, "*Socrates and the Three Little Pigs*" recording sheet 2 provides sets of houses in which students can show with dots (or draw) the actual arrangements.

"*Socrates and the Three Little Pigs*" recording sheet 3 extends the work of the other two recording sheets to look for patterns describing the number of arrangements for various numbers of pigs and houses. By investigating the pattern in the table, students

223

are led to a generalization of the problem of p pigs in h houses ($p \leq h$).

The story moves very quickly through the possibilities and mixes the permutations and combinations. Our article focuses only on permutations because of the limited amount of time available with the students. A teacher could use the story and expand on the simpler case of permutations to develop the notion of combinations—arrangements in which the color of the pig's outfit does not matter and no more than one pig can be in a house. "Socrates and the Three Little Pigs" recording sheet 3 (fig. 25.5 in the article) could be expanded to include an additional column on the right that asks students to find the number of possible arrangements if only one pig can be in a house and the color of the pig's outfit is NOT important.

Connections with history: In the story, the wolf is named Socrates, his wife is named Xanthippe, and the mathematician frog is named Pythagoras. Have students investigate historical figures who had those names and find their contributions, particularly to mathematics. Students might need a hint that they consider ancient Greeks.

REFERENCES

Anno, Mitsumasa, illustrator. Socrates and the Three Little Pigs. Text by Tuyosi Mori. New York: Philomel Books, 1986.

Thompson, Denisse R., and Richard A. Austin. "Socrates and the Three Little Pigs: Connecting Patterns, Counting Trees, and Probability." Mathematics Teaching in the Middle School 5 (November 1999): 156–61.

Author's note: First, we have received several e-mail messages from teachers who wanted to try some of the things that we did with this book but who were unable to purchase a copy of the book. We have been able to find the book Socrates and the Three Little Pigs in several public libraries and a few school libraries.

Second, as noted previously, we read only about a fourth of the book to use it as a springboard for the lesson. However, the class needs to finish reading the story at some point. When we have failed to do so, several students have asked us about the ending.

Third, some teachers have commented on the anatomical drawing of the female wolf, Xanthippe. In particular, the female wolf is drawn with two large teats, and teachers have expressed concern about potential issues that might arise when using this book in the classroom. We did not have any problems when we used the book in two different mathematics classrooms in public schools. We should note that we read the book to the class and did not pass the book around.

Socrates and the Three Little Pigs

Name _____

Date _____

In the space below, construct a tree diagram that shows all the ways that two pigs could be in four houses, where more than one pig can be in a house.

Use your tree diagram to list all possible arrangements in the table on the next page, and then answer the questions below.

a) What is the probability of finding both pigs in the same house? _____

b) What is the probability of finding no pigs in house 4? _____

Socrates and the Three Little Pigs

House for Pig No. 1   House for Pig No. 2

Consider the situation for two pigs and five houses. Make a conjecture about the total number of arrangements of the pigs in the houses. Discuss your conjecture with classmates. On the back of this sheet, use a tree diagram or a table to find all the arrangements of two pigs and five houses. Compare the number of arrangements with your conjecture. Additionally, answer the following questions for this new situation:

a) What is the probability of finding both pigs in the same house? _____

b) What is the probability of finding no pigs in house 5? _____

Name _____

Date _____

Place a red dot for one pig and a blue dot for the other pig. Find all of the possible arrangements for two pigs in four houses if a house may have more than one pig.

(Continued on next page)

Socrates and the Three Little Pigs

Revisit the problem above, and find all the possible arrangements for two pigs in four houses if no house may have more than one pig.

Socrates and the Three Little Pigs Recording Sheet 3

Name _____

Date _____

Number of pigs in houses	Number of possible arrangements if more than 1 pig can be in a house and the order of pigs in the house is not important	Number of possible arrangements if only 1 pig can be in a house and the color of the pig is important
2 pigs in 3 houses		
2 pigs in 4 houses		
2 pigs in 5 houses		
3 pigs in 4 houses		
3 pigs in 5 houses		
3 pigs in 6 houses		
3 pigs in h houses		
4 pigs in 5 houses		
4 pigs in 6 houses		
4 pigs in 7 houses		
4 pigs in 10 houses		
4 pigs in h houses		
5 pigs in 6 houses		
p pigs in h houses ($p \leq h$)		

26

From *The Giver* to *The Twenty-One Balloons*: Explorations with Probability

Ann Lawrence

BASING an activity in the mathematics classroom on an event or a story from children's literature offers a vivid, engaging context for mathematical investigation. The following problem (see fig. 26.1) stems directly from *The Giver*, by Lois Lowry (1993):

> Each class of 50 children in the Community has 25 girls and 25 boys. Assuming that the probability of a woman giving birth to a boy or a girl is the same, how often do you think exactly 25 out of 50 babies will be girls?

Students were asked to predict the result, design a model, and carry out fifty trials to determine the experimental probability. Finally, they were to explain any differences between their predictions and the experimental results.

When the teacher presented this problem, pairs of seventh graders immediately began to chatter eagerly, making their predictions. They made comments like "Well, we know it will be way less than half the time" and "I wish I had a Pascal's triangle that showed fifty rows." Because these students had had a number of related experiences involving probability, they were confident in their educated guesses. Similarly, the students had little trouble determining an appropriate method for modeling the problem. A few pairs used dice; a few, coins or two-color chips. But most used their calculators to generate random numbers. The class compiled its results to establish the experimental probability,

which was about 12 percent, and the students worked together to support their findings by working out the theoretical probability

$$\frac{_{50}C_{25}}{2^{50}},$$

since $_{50}C_{25}$ represents the number of ways that twenty-five girls can be chosen from a group of fifty children and that must be compared with 2^{50}, which is the total number of possibilities for a group of fifty children. To compute the theoretical probability, students needed to rewrite $_{50}C_{25}$ as

$$\frac{50!}{(50-25)!\,(25)!}.$$

Finally, the teacher asked each student to design a problem with a solution similar to this one. Most of their results reflected a clear understanding of probability.

If the teacher had made this assignment without previously having given the students related experiences, the positive results would have been unlikely. Indeed, students need many experiences with probability if they are to develop the skills and confidence that they need for independent explorations involving chance.

Therefore, we take an important look back. The activities that students carried out before the one with *The Giver* were designed to focus on the following concepts:

- An informal definition of probability

Will Girls and Boys Be Equal?
For use with *The Giver*, by Lois Lowry (1993)

Each class of 50 children in the Community has 25 girls and 25 boys. Assuming that the probability of a woman giving birth to a boy or a girl is the same, how often do you think exactly 25 out of 50 babies will be girls?

I. Model this problem. Do 50 trials. Record your results below.

II. Combine your data with those of your classmates to simulate a large number of years.

III. Now how would you answer the original question, "How often do you think exactly 25 out of 50 babies will be girls?" Explain your answer, using the data your class gathered.

Extension: Suppose the Committee of Elders decided that the Community should expand so that each family has five children. If the babies are randomly assigned to each family, how often will a family have no boys, one boy, etc.?

> Related Writing Activity: In the Community, there was Sameness. For example, there was Climate Control—no snow, no sunshine, always the same weather conditions. Write a paragraph describing the one characteristic of Sameness, and create a related problem and solve it.

Fig. 26.1. Probablility problem based on *The Giver*

- The difference between experimental and theoretical probability
- The importance of order in listing possible outcomes
- The importance of determining an accurate outcome set

The students completed each of the carefully ordered activities described subsequently, and, as often happens in middle school classes, some unexpected extensions resulted.

The Initial Probability Experience

As an initial warm-up, the teacher led the class in a brief exploration of basic probability. For most of the students, the discussion was review, but for a few, it was their first exposure to the topic. Students were prompted with the following probes:

- Tell me what you remember about probability.
- What is the range of values for probabilities?
- What is an outcome set?
- In what forms are probabilities expressed?

To make a connection with children's literature, the teacher asked, "Who has read the book *The Twenty-One Balloons*, by William Pène Dubois?" and "Who can summarize the story for us?" In the book, a man discovers a remote, uninhabited island that has numerous diamonds. He selects twenty-five families to join his own and live there permanently; moreover, when he chooses families to go to Krakatoa, he picks only those with exactly one girl and one boy (Dubois 1986).

Once the setting was established, the teacher posed this problem:

> In a family with two children, how often do you think that the family has exactly one girl and one boy?

Next, the teacher distributed the activity sheet (see fig. 26.2) and directed the students to "use a fraction to predict the probability of one girl and one boy in a family of two children."

Students shared their estimates and explained their reasoning. The most common estimate was 1/3. As Alison explained, "There were three ways the family could happen: two boys, two girls, or one

Will Girls and Boys Be Equal?

For use with *Twenty-One Balloons* by William Pène Dubois (1986)

When Mr. M chose families to go to Krakatoa, he picked only those with exactly one girl and one boy. How often do you think this happens in a family with two children?

Use a fraction to predict the probability of one girl and one boy in a family of two children. _____

Design a model you can use to find the experimental probability of one girl and one boy in a family of two children. Describe it below.

Do twenty trials, using your model. Record your results below.

Compare your results with those of your classmates. Combine the data from your entire class, and record the experimental probability (results) below.

How did the results of the experiment compare with your prediction? Why do you think this happened?

Show all the possibilities for a family with two children. Then give the theoretical probability of one girl and one boy in a family of two children.

Write two paragraphs below about this activity.

What we found ….

What I learned …

> Extension: List all possibilities for a family of four children to determine the theoretical probablility of exactly two girls and two boys. Then answer this question: As the number of children in a family increases, what happens to the probablity of having the same number of girls and boys? Explain why this happens.

Fig. 26.2. Probability problem based on *The Twenty-One Balloons*

boy and one girl. So the probability was one good thing out of three things, or one-third." Other estimates varied widely and were explained with "I thought of families I knew" and "I just took a wild guess." Among the small number who estimated one-half, many said the equivalent of "It felt right." Very few students, one or two in each class, explained their estimates of one-half as Fuller did: "There are four ways to have a family with two children: first, a boy, then another boy; second, a girl, then another girl; third, a girl, then a boy; and fourth, a boy, then a girl. So the probability of one girl and one boy is two-fourths, or one-half." At this point, a lively debate broke out in every class. The teacher did not comment either way. Clearly, most students did not demonstrate intuitive understanding of this situation.

Next, the teacher led a brief discussion about experimental probability and asked each pair of students to develop a model to simulate this problem. Most had no difficulty determining an appropriate model. In each class, all the following models were suggested:

- Flip a coin or a two-color chip.
- Roll a number cube.
- Use a calculator to generate random numbers.

The most unusual model was designed by Garrett and his partner, who counted to three then showed one or two fingers. When the numbers matched, they designated a girl; with no match, they designated a boy. Obviously, this pair had intuition about the underlying mathematics of the problem.

EXPLORING MATHEMATICS THROUGH LITERATURE

Students described their model in writing, and a volunteer read a description of each suggested method to the class. For example, Yaicha shared, "We will use a two-color chip. We will flip it two times for each family. If it lands on yellow, it will stand for a girl. If it lands on red, it will be a boy. We will do this twenty times." In each class, someone requested a demonstration of how to generate random numbers with a calculator. Seeing a reason to learn this skill, students quickly mastered both the needed keystrokes and the application of random numbers in the context of this problem. Allowing students to choose their own model accommodated a wide range of interest and skill levels easily and subtly.

As each pair worked to complete, record, and total the results for twenty trials, the teacher circulated among them. A few pairs needed help because they thought that it was appropriate simply to generate data to represent forty births: they did not grasp that two events were needed to complete each trial. As Charles later wrote, "We did not understand at first that we were sort of acting out the problem. We found out we needed to roll the cube twice for each family, since there were two kids. Then we started over for the next family." The opportunity to redirect student thinking *on the spot* was an important ingredient in the success of this activity.

After each pair of students totaled its results, the class built on the wall a histogram of the results, compiled the results for the entire class, expressed the results as a fraction, and recorded them on the activity sheet. After the students discussed the combined results, they agreed that the fractional value—and thus the probability of exactly one girl and one boy in a two-child family—was close to 1/2. The teacher then asked students to compare in writing their original predictions with the experimental results. Some students then understood why their prediction was incorrect. As Katherine wrote, "My prediction was totally wrong. This is why. I did not think about a boy and a girl being different from a girl and a boy." Because others were stymied and needed class discussion to clarify their understanding, the teacher asked volunteers to read their explanations and led a brief discussion of theoretical probability.

The class next listed the outcome set for this problem: GG, BB, BG, and GB. As Mignon pointed out in her class, "We have one boy and one girl in my family, and I am the oldest. That is certainly different than if my brother was the older child!" Such examples from people they knew quickly convinced reluctant students that BG and GB were two different outcomes. Students then listed the outcome set and found the theoretical probability.

After a discussion about such topics as the reason that the experimental results did not exactly match the theoretical ones and the effects of sample size, each student wrote two summary paragraphs about the activity, titled "What We Found" and "What I Learned." Sample student responses to these prompts are in figures 26.3 and 26.4. As the students' writings suggest, almost all the students could verbalize the results of the activity and believed that they had gained a better understanding of some aspects of probability.

> Write two paragraphs below about this activity.
>
> What We Found . . . .
>
> We found that a little bit more than half the time from our experiment that a family with two children would have 1 boy and 1 girl.
>
> I found out that a family would have a half of a chance to get a boy and a girl. I found out the information by getting a die and making the even numbers girls and the odd boys. My results were $\frac{12}{20}$ families would be one boy and one girl. As a class the results equalled $\frac{85}{180}$.
>
> This was a fun activity in that you can get an estimate of what people are trying to find out in the real world. The class found that $\frac{62}{133}$ are Boys and girls in the world.
>
> What We Found . . . . out was that there are more ways than 1 to solve this problem. Also, people could say a boy and a Girl then a Girl and a boy can be 4ths or altogether a half which then makes it a 50%, 25%, and 25% of chances.

Fig. 26.3. Student responses to the "What we found" prompt

> What I Learned . . . .
>
> I learned that there are two parts of probability; experimental and theoretical.
>
> I learned that if you look at a simple problem there might be a little bit more than you think. I also learned how to use the calculator in a different way. I got to freshen up in my probability and fractions.
>
> What I Learned . . . . about probability is that you can put probability in 3 ways fraction, percentage, or decimal. I also learned that a G+B + a B+G can be counted as a 1/4 each or a 1/2 together.
>
> You need a large sample to get a good idea what might really happen.

Fig. 26.4. Student responses to the "What I learned" prompt

More Probability Activities

The next activities were slightly different in each class, depending on the written responses and the questions raised by the students during the first activity. The students in every class were asked to find the sample space for a family of four children to determine the theoretical probability of exactly two boys and two girls, or 3/8. They were then asked the following question:

> As the number of children in a family increases, what happens to the probability of having the same number of girls and boys, and why does this happen?

Students had little difficulty transferring their learning from the first problem and using mathematical reasoning to explain the different results. David gave a typical explanation: "The reason the two-children families were different from the four-children families is because when you add more children, you add more possibilities for each family, therefore decreasing your chance to get the same number of boys and girls. For the two-children family, the expected probability is 4/8. For the four-children family, it is 3/8."

Students next predicted the probability of three boys and three girls in a family with six children. This task initially gave some students trouble, as evidenced by comments like those of Sarah, who wrote, "When you have two children, you have one girl and one boy only half the time. When you have four children, you have six out of sixteen chances of having half girls, half boys. I think that if you have six children, you will have half girls, half boys only one-fourth of the time." Since listing the outcome set became unwieldy at this point, the teacher introduced Pascal's triangle. If the rows are numbered starting with row 0 for the apex, the numbers in each row represent the frequency of occurrence of a given outcome. Students used the triangle to find the probabilities for equal numbers of boys and girls in families of various sizes. Their writing reflected an understanding of why the probabilities diminished as the number of children increased.

At this point, students were again asked to write what they had learned. Typical comments follow:

- I learned [that] my prediction [should] always have a meaning. I know predictions don't have to be exactly right, but you need to think hard about all the possibilities.

- I learned that if you switch the order of happenings, it counts as a different way. I also learned that probability can be fun.

- I learned that questions you have can often be answered by doing a simple experiment.

- We found out that a larger sample usually gives you results in the experiment that are nearer the theoretical ones.

Finally, the foregoing problem related to *The Giver* was presented as a culminating assessment activity. Students were successful and justifiably proud of their growth. They discussed the real-world chances of a girl or boy being born, but all classes were satisfied that the 50-50 model was sufficient. One class insisted on designing a spreadsheet to produce row 50 of Pascal's triangle and cheered when it validated the results of their experiments. But the clearest evidence of student understanding was the content of the original problems that the students designed. Students presented them for their classmates to solve. A few samples are shown in figure 26.5.

In the Community, you get two pets. The Elders pick the pets for each family. There were six choices of pets to have: dog, cat, fish, snake, bird, and hamster. What was the probability of getting a dog and a cat?

Mark

The elders decided [that] all families can have five children. How often will there be no boys?

Charlie

The Elders wanted hair color to come out even. So out of 40 people they wanted 10 to have blond hair, 10 red, 10 black, and 10 brown. Obviously, the Elders cannot just make someone have a certain color hair. What are the chances it would come out "just right"?

Elizabeth

Fig. 26.5. Student-generated problems

And, finally, we present Graeme. In his seventh-grade class, Graeme was a basketball star who was reluctant to admit that he liked mathematics and even more reluctant to take risks in mathematics class. Not this time. Graeme devised the following problem:

EXPLORING MATHEMATICS THROUGH LITERATURE

In the Community, people were randomly assigned a truck, jeep, or a car. There are plenty of each kind of vehicle. The people have no control over which kind they get. Each person gets one vehicle. If there are 50 people, how many will get a car?

(See fig. 26.6). He not only insisted on presenting his problem in class but also took time at lunch to make a transparency for his presentation. As Graeme proudly showed his creation to the class, I simply thought, "Slam dunk!"

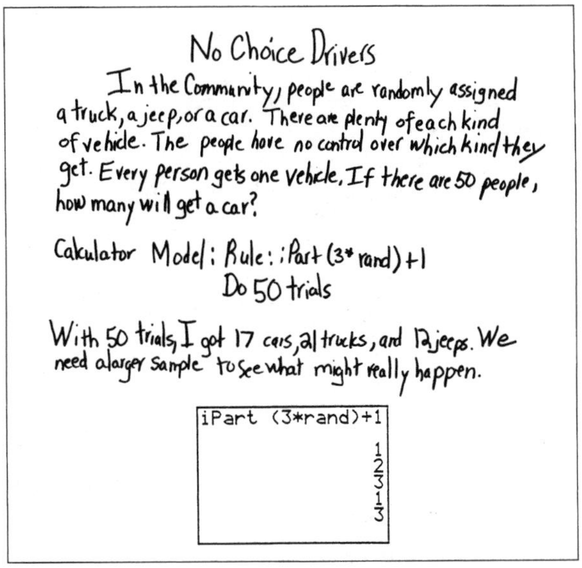

Clearly, blending connections to literature with intriguing yet accessible problems and opportunities for cooperative learning and writing can increase both the interest and confidence of middle school students in dealing with probability.

REFERENCES

Dubois, William Pène. *The Twenty-One Balloons*. New York: Puffin Books, 1986.

Lowry, Lois. *The Giver*. New York: Bantam Doubleday Dell, 1993.

No Choice Drivers

In the Community, people are randomly assigned a truck, a jeep, or a car. There are plenty of each kind of vehicle. The people have no control over which kind they get. Every person gets one vehicle. If there are 50 people, how many will get a car?

Calculator Model: Rule: :Part (3* rand) +1
Do 50 trials

With 50 trials, I got 17 cars, 21 trucks, and 12 jeeps. We need a larger sample to see what might really happen.

```
iPart (3*rand)+1
                1
                2
                3
                1
                3
```

Fig. 26.6. Graeme's problem

"From *The Giver* to *The Twenty-One Balloons*: Explorations with Probability"

by Ann Lawrence

Grade range:	6–8
Mathematical topics:	Experimental and theoretical probability
Children's books:	*The Giver*, by Lois Lowry; *The Twenty-One Balloons* by William Pène Du Bois
Materials:	*"The Twenty-One Balloons"* recording sheets; *"The Giver"* recording sheets; problem-solving materials, such as coins, two-color counters, number cubes, and graphing calculators

Discussion of the mathematics: Explorations in experimental probability are the foundation for understanding theoretical probability. Experimental probability provides an opportunity to explore different possibilities, observe the effects as the sample size increases, and experience the range of likely and unlikely results. It also leads to an estimate of what is a reasonable result.

Teacher notes and questions to ask students

Task 1—*The Twenty-One Balloons*: To launch the task, I use such prompts as the following to create an opportunity for students to review what they know and to start to build a common class background.

- What do you remember about probability?
- What is the range of values for probabilities?
- What is an outcome set?
- In what form are probabilities expressed?

If students are unfamiliar with the plot of *The Twenty-One Balloons*, have one of the students summarize the story. In the book a man discovers a remote, uninhabited island that has numerous diamonds. He selects twenty families to live there permanently. Unfortunately, the island has an active volcano that could erupt at any time, so the families must have an escape plan.

After discussing the plot of *The Twenty-One Balloons*, pose the question below. As a class, have the students discuss their predictions and explain their reasoning. A surprising number of middle school students estimate the probability of one girl and one boy in a family of two children to be one-third. They do not think of BG as different from GB in the outcome set. Thus, this activity helps establish the importance of order is listing outcomes.

- In a family with two children, how often do you think that the family has exactly one girl and one boy?

Discuss experimental probability with the class, and have each pair of students develop a model to represent the situation from the book and determine the results for twenty trials. For modeling, students may suggest flipping a coin, rolling a die, and so on. (A graphing calculator can be used to generate random numbers for modeling this problem situation; see the description in the next task, but change the last step to indicate twenty families.) Often students are surprised to find that their experimental results indicate that families with one boy and one girl seem to occur about half the time. They may decide to do more trials.

The class results should be compiled, and after the students have an opportunity to reflect on their data, a discussion should center on their understandings and original misconceptions. This class discussion should lead naturally into theoretical probability and examples of sample spaces. Have students list the possible outcomes for two children to see that actually four outcomes are possible, two of which include one boy and one girl. Thus, the theoretical probability for a family with two children having one boy and one girl is 1/2.

The discussion should include a comparison of the results for the theoretical and experimental probabilities, the reasons they are not exactly alike, and the effects of sample size. As a reflection on this initial lesson, each individual should write about what was found and what he or she learned.

Task 2—*The Giver*: Briefly discuss *The Giver*, by Lois Lowry. In this futuristic book, much conformity was observed because most aspects of people's lives were planned by the Committee of Elders. Jonas, the twelve-year-old main character of the book, begins to question the way things work in the Community. Focus on the situation from the book described at the top of the recording sheet for *The Giver*. Have students estimate an answer to the question posed on their papers, then share their estimates and reasoning.

Ask students how they might model this situation or carry out an experiment to get an estimate of the probability of exactly twenty-five girls if fifty children were born. Some students may point out that slightly more boys than girls are actually born, but considering the chances for a girl or a boy to be equal is close enough to get a good estimate. For modeling, students may suggest flipping a coin, rolling a die, and the like. If no one suggests using random numbers, briefly explain this technique and how to program a calculator to randomly generate 1s and 2s to represent girls and boys. Use the steps below for a TI-73.

- Clear the screen by pressing CLEAR.
- Press MATH.
- Arrow over to PRB.
- Choose # 2: RandInt(.
- Press 1 and ,.
- Press 2 and ,.
- Press 1.
- You should see RandInt (1,2,1 on your screen.
- Press ENTER 50 times.

Have students work in pairs to simulate the births of fifty babies. After each pair has recorded its findings on a large class chart, have several students comment on the findings. Next the class can combine all the data to find the experimental probability from the enlarged sample; they will probably be surprised at the results.

For many seventh- or eighth-grade classes, conducting at least two other experiments will be appropriate before students are prepared to explain their results. Students benefit from reconsidering the probability of one girl and one boy when there are two children (1/2) and following that with an experiment to find the probability of having two girls and two boys when there are four children (6/16 or 3/8). Often they need to list all the possibilities to understand these probabilities. By examining these situations, students usually conclude that the probability for the same number of girls as boys becomes smaller as the total number of children increases, because more outcomes are possible. They should realize that with a group as large as fifty children, so many ways would exist to combine girls and boys that the probability for one particular way, twenty-five girls and twenty-five boys, would be rather small.

If your class expresses interest in the theoretical probability of exactly twenty-five girls and twenty-five boys, introduce them to Pascal's triangle. Such an exploration would conclude with the observation that the theoretical probability for this situation can be found by locating the middle item on the fiftieth row of Pascal's triangle or by computing $_{50}C_{25}/2^{50}$ (.11227…).

Two appropriate ways to display the results of this activity are in a histogram or in a box-and-whisker plot. If your students are not familiar with this type of graph, you will need to guide them step-by-step through the process.

After each student has done a set of fifty random numbers, you may want to use program 26.1 to produce many sets of fifty trials quickly.

Assessment: Students should write paragraphs about what the class found and what they learned. Allow students to share their responses.

- What were the results of the experiment? How do they relate to your estimate? Were you surprised? Why or why not?
- As the number of possible outcomes for an event increases, what happens to the probability of a particular outcome?

PROGRAM 26.1

Computer Program to Simulate the Births of Fifty Babies

```
CHILDREN     E Program
:ClrHome
:Ø →C: Ø → D: Ø → E: Ø →F
:Disp "HOW MANY BIRTHS?"
:Input F
:Lbl A
:C+1→ C
:iPart (2*rand)+1ˣB
:If B=1
:Then
:Disp "BOY"
:D+1 →D

:If B=2
:Then
:Disp "GIRL"
:E+1 →E
:End
:If C ≠F
:Goto A
:Disp "NUMBER OF BOYS"
:Disp D
:Disp "NUMBER OF GIRLS"
:Disp E
```

• How did this activity add to your understanding of probability?

Extension: For the extension activity, through class discussion establish that each trial will need five random numbers, one for each child in the family. The activity can be modeled in a variety of ways, including the use of a program similar to the one shown in program 26.1 but that produces results in sets of five, for instance, 11121, for each family. At some point, this problem should be related to row 5 of Pascal's triangle to determine the theoretical probability. Have the students extend their solutions by considering families of increasing sizes and using Pascal's triangle to generate the appropriate sample space. After analyzing their results, each individual should write about what they found and what they learned.

• As the number of children in a family increases, what happens to the probability of having the same number of girls and boys, and why does this outcome occur?

REFERENCES

Lawrence, Ann. "From *The Giver* to *The Twenty-One Balloons*: Explorations with Probability." *Mathematics Teaching in the Middle School* 4 (May 1999): 504–9.

Lowry, Lois. *The Giver*. Boston: Bantam Doubleday Dell, 1993.

Pène Du Bois, William. *The Twenty-One Balloons*. New York: Puffin Books, 1986.

Group Name_____

Date _____

<u>Will Numbers of Girls and Boys Be Equal?</u>

Problem: When Mr. M chose families to go to Krakatoa, he picked only those with exactly one girl and one boy. How often do you think this arrangement happens in a family with two children?

• Use a fraction to predict the probability of one girl and one boy in a family of two children.

• Design a model that you can use to find the experimental probability of one girl and one boy in a family of two children. Describe it below.

• Do twenty trials, using your model. Record your results below.

(Continued on next page)

- Compare your results with those of your classmates. Combine the data from your entire class, and record the experimental probability (results) below.

- How did the results of the experiment compare with your prediction? Why do you think this outcome happened?

- Show all possibilities for a family with two children, then give the theoretical probability of one girl and one boy in a family of two children.

- Write two paragraphs about this activity on the back of this sheet.

  What we found:

  What I learned:

Extension: List all possibilities of four children to determine the theoretical probability of exactly two girls and two boys. Then answer the question "As the number of children in a family increases, what happens to the probability of having the same number of girls and boys?" Explain why this outcome happens.

Group Name_____

Date _____

Will Numbers of Girls and Boys Be Equal?

Problem: Each class of 50 children in the community has 25 girls and 25 boys. Assuming that the probability of a woman giving birth to a boy and that of giving birth to a girl are the same, how often do you think exactly 25 out of 50 babies will be girls?

• Model this problem. Do 50 trials. Record your results below.

• Combine your data with those of your classmates to simulate a large number of years.

(Continued on next page)

- Now how would you answer the original question, "How often do you think exactly 25 out of 50 babies will be girls?" Explain your answer, using the data your classmates gathered.

Extension: Suppose the Committee of Elders decided that the Community should expand so that each family has five children. If the babies are randomly assigned to each family, how often will a family have no boys? One boy? Two boys? Three boys? Four boys? Five boys?

Related writing activity: In the Community, there was Sameness. For example, there was Climate Control—no snow, no sunshine, always the same weather conditions. On a separate sheet of paper, write a paragraph describing the characteristic of Sameness, create a related problem, and show its solution.

Theme-Related Articles

27

Dumpling Soup: Exploring Kitchens, Cultures, and Mathematics

Nancy L. Smith, Carolyn Babione, and Beverly Johns Vick

MANY TEACHERS understand the importance of discussing diversity and celebrating cultural heritage. One way that these two goals can be accomplished is by looking at the lives of others through multicultural literature. Teachers often use such literature in language arts and social studies but may be unsure how to use it in mathematics.

The NCTM's *Curriculum and Evaluation Standards for School Mathematics* states, "Children also need to understand that mathematics is an integral part of real-world situations and activities in other curricular areas. ... Many children's books present interesting problems and illustrate how other children solve them" (NCTM 1989, pp. 18, 28). Exposure to literature helps children gain insights into mathematical ideas and cultures.

The first step in selecting appropriate multicultural literature for use in any curriculum area is to be sure that the literature does not contain biases. Teachers selecting multicultural literature should consider the following criteria:

1. The illustrations are not stereotypes or over-simplifications.
2. The story lines include minorities and females solving problems.
3. The text fosters genuine insight into lifestyles.
4. The relationships depict minorities and females sharing equal status.
5. The heroes serve the interests of minority groups.
6. The positive role models can be identified.
7. The authors and illustrators are qualified to deal with the subject matter.
8. The author's perspective presents other world views.
9. The text is free from loaded words with offensive overtones.
10. The copyright date indicates relevance to the rapid changes in society. (Derman-Sparks and the Anti-Bias Curriculum Task Force 1989, pp. 143–45)

These criteria were used to select the multicultural children's literature for these lessons. The inspiration for *Dumpling Soup* (1993) grew out of author Jama Kim Rattigan's childhood memories of celebrating the New Year with her Korean-American extended family in Hawaii, where nearly fifty different cultures are represented. The story is written in the voice of a young female who presents a child's perspective on preparing and eating the traditional dumpling soup. The story contains examples of equal-status relationships, as everyone—young and old, male and female—has a role to play to prepare for the New Year celebration. The illustrations by Chinese-American Lillian Hsu-Flanders are full of detail and rendered without oversimplification or stereotypes.

The following description illustrates how Beverly Vick, a second-grade teacher in a culturally diverse school outside of Washington, D.C., started with this multicultural story and launched numerous investigations of mathematical concepts, including patterns, measurement, estimation, area, fractions, graphing, and probability. This particular class comprised children from over eight countries in various parts of the world. Although no Asian children were present in this particular classroom, Asian children did attend the school, and the Chinese New Year was part of the winter celebration in the school. Within the context of learning mathematics, the children in this classroom learned about Asian traditions, as well as the cultures in their own classroom.

Patterns

As the story opens, the women of the family gather in the grandmother's kitchen to prepare dumplings. Seven-year-old Marisa describes the family gathering and her first attempt at making dumplings for her grandmother's soup (fig. 27.1).

Fig. 27.1. Marisa in her grandmother's kitchen. From *Dumpling Soup* by Jama Kim Rattigan. Copyright © 1993 by Jama Kim Rattigan (text); Copyright © 1993 by Lillian Hsu-Flanders (illustrations). By permission of Little, Brown and Company, Inc.

First, the children identified the patterns in the cooking sounds described in the story, "chop-chop pounding, chop-scrape-scrape" (Rattigan 1993, p. 4). Next, students numbered off, each child saying the number and identifying it as odd or even: "one–odd, two–even, three–odd …." The odds and evens created patterns using clapping, desk tapping, and foot stomping (fig. 27.2). The next day, the children brought in safe kitchen utensils from home to create sound patterns (fig. 27.3). Doing so presented an opportunity to discuss the function of the utensils and the various ethnic foods with which they are used.

Measurement and Estimation

After reading the story, the class discussed cultural differences in food preparation. Many cul-

tural groups prepare delicious foods without using such standardized utensils as measuring cups or spoons. Pinches, bunches, and handfuls of ingredients are used instead.

Fig. 27.2. Students snap and clap. Photograph by Beverly Vick; all rights reserved

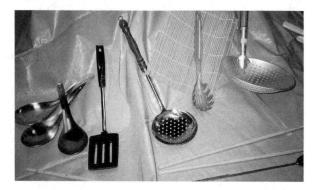

Fig. 27.3. Kitchen utensils from home. Photograph by Nancy Smith; all rights reserved

In the story, the dumplings were placed in wrappers. Minicupcake wrappers were used to represent the dumpling wrappers (fig. 27.4). Students brought small food items from home to use for estimating. For example, Douglas brought black beans, Michael brought rice, Vanessa brought corn meal, and Shellante brought macaroni. The task was to choose a food item and estimate the quantity needed to fill the minicupcake wrapper. Cupcake tins helped to hold the wrappers in place. Each child shared how the food item was used in the home.

Fig. 27.4. Cooking with estimates and measurements. Photograph by Nancy Smith; all rights reserved

EXPLORING MATHEMATICS THROUGH LITERATURE

The children learned to connect a term common to their vocabulary, *guess*, with the term *estimate*. They discussed how an estimate involves more thinking than a guess. They selected a food item then recorded their estimates of the amount needed to fill the minicupcake wrapper. Next, they actually filled the wrapper, counting how much was required, and recorded the actual amount. Besides experiencing estimation, children practice counting quantities less than 100. Students' estimates were often lower than the actual amount needed. After the first estimate and count were completed, students repeated the activity with a different item that was larger or smaller than the first. Again, the students estimated, filled, and counted. Students not only develop number sense by such counting but also discover an important number-sense idea related to measurement: the larger the unit, the fewer the units used.

The cooking context also presented natural opportunities to estimate and compare quantities using the customary measures of teaspoon, tablespoon, cup, pint, quart, and gallon. For example, the class made two recipes, one with estimated quantities and the second using exact measurements (fig. 27.5). The class agreed that the recipe made with estimates tasted awful. Although the standardized utensils provided accurate measurements, students' estimates were inaccurate. The students discovered that one person's handful might be equivalent to a cup, whereas another's is equivalent to only a half-cup. Measuring without utensils takes a lot of practice. Family traditions of preparing recipes and measuring food were shared by the children.

Fig. 27.5. Measuring ingredients. Photograph by Beverly Vick; all rights reserved

Fractions

The students explored the fractional concept of parts of a set with halves, thirds, and fourths by shar-

ing the candy in their cupcake wrappers among imaginary friends. The students were first asked to share candy in their wrapper with a friend, making sure that each child had the same amount. Any extras would be set aside for "Marisa's grandma." They followed the same idea for thirds and fourths, and with each fractional sharing, they compared their results with those of their classmates.

In a follow-up lesson, the students continued to investigate fractional parts of a set. They shared color-tile "dumplings." Everyone had twelve tiles. They were challenged to show two different ways to share their dumplings equally. For example, Ashley gave three friends four dumplings each. Each friends' dumplings were a different color. Jose chose to give himself and one friend six dumplings each. He kept all the blue tiles and gave his friend all the red tiles. Shazad shared his dumplings among four people, giving everyone two reds and one of another color. The students discussed the color patterns that had emerged and compared them with those from other activities that they had completed. They talked about how the color pattern might be represented as a rhythm and how sharing the tiles was similar to what they did when they divided up the candies from the cupcake wrappers.

To further develop the notions of fractions, fair shares, and parts of a whole, groups of four children could be given paper "dumplings" to share among group members. For example, to share five dumplings among their group members, the students could be led to find that each person received one whole dumpling and one-fourth of another.

Area

To introduce the concept of area, each child was given a sheet of one-inch graph paper to use as a "tray" and five to seven color tiles to represent dumplings. Students investigated different ways to arrange the dumplings on their trays (fig. 27.6). Even though the shape of the figure changed, the students found that the area or number of tiles remained the same. The concept of perimeter could also be introduced, and children could investigate the relationship between area and perimeter.

In a follow-up activity, the children used one to nine tiles to build rectangles with a base of two. The students noticed that the even numbers formed rectangles with a base of two and that those formed by the odd numbers had an extra tile on top. This visual representation further reinforced the concept of odd and even numbers (fig. 27.7).

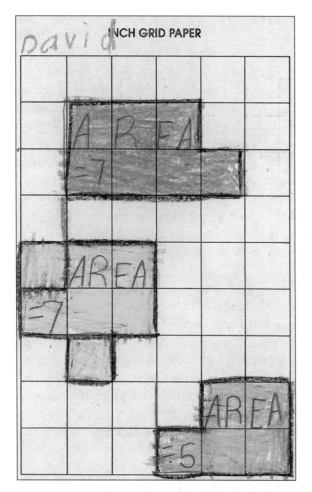

Fig. 27.6. Color-tile dumplings

The children also enjoyed playing a game involving estimation of area. Small groups of students estimated the number of dumplings, or individual color tiles, that would fit on a dumpling tray. The dumpling trays were in irregular shapes, like those shown in figure 27.6, cut from one-inch graph paper and laminated. Once the estimate was made, the students covered the shape with color tiles and counted them to find the actual area of the figure. For larger shapes with an area of more than twenty, the students covered their trays with ten tiles of one color, then used a different color for the next ten tiles, and so on. When the figure was covered, the students counted by tens and ones. For example, one figure was covered by 3 groups of ten and 4 ones, revealing that the total number of tiles was thirty-four. As the children practiced this activity, their estimation skills improved.

Graphing

As the story continues, on New Year's Eve Day the rest of the family arrives and the children play various games as they wait for the new year to begin. It is the custom in Marisa's family to leave one's shoes outside the front door. "By six o'clock Grandma's front steps are covered with big, medium, and little slippers, sandals, and shoes" (Rattigan 1993, p. 14).

To focus attention on graphing and probability, the children examined the illustration of the family's shoes outside the front door. First, the children used their own shoes to classify, sort, and make shoe graphs answering questions that they generated, such as, "How many tennis shoes? How many black shoes? How many shoes with ties? How many shoes all together?" (fig. 27.8). They discussed how a graph helps to organize information.

Next, the children used color tiles to represent the shoes on a plastic floor graph. For example, everyone with white tennis shoes placed a green color tile on the graph; those with black tennis shoes, a red tile; those with dress shoes, a yellow tile; and those with any other shoes, a blue tile. The class

EXPLORING MATHEMATICS THROUGH LITERATURE

transferred the information to the chalkboard. For each graph, the children counted the shoes in each column and added them. When another graph was created comparing boys' and girls' shoes, the children concluded that the total number of shoes would be the same for both graphs, even though they had used four categories on the first graph and two on the second. Finally, The Graph Club graphing software (1996) was used on the classroom computer to create the graphs, which allowed the children to see their data organized as pie, picture, and bar graphs (fig. 27.9).

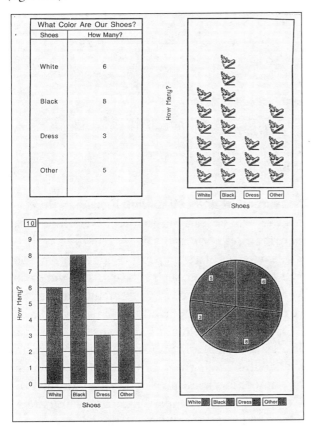

Fig. 27.9. Computer graphs

Probability

The children in the story play with the family's shoes until they get mixed up on Grandma's yard. This vignette led to activities involving the concept of probability and to introduce terms, such as *equally likely events*. The students investigated the chances of drawing a matching pair of shoes from a bag. Once the procedure was demonstrated with students' shoes, color tiles were substituted for small-group use. The children found that a better chance of getting a match occurred when fewer different kinds of shoes, or tiles, were in the bag.

In a follow-up activity, four paper bags were filled with ten tiles each. The contents were as follows:

> Bag 1: 5 red and 5 yellow tiles
> Bag 2: 6 red and 4 yellow tiles
> Bag 3: 2 red and 8 yellow tiles
> Bag 4: 8 red and 2 yellow tiles

The combinations for each bag were written on the chalkboard using abbreviations, for example, 2r (two red) + 8y (eight yellow) = 10 tiles. The students enjoyed the color codes and continued to use them frequently. The class selected a bag, and students took turns drawing a tile while a recorder noted the results on the chalkboard with tally marks. After several draws, they tried to guess which bag they had chosen. This guessing game became quite popular, but the students found it was particularly difficult to distinguish between bags 1 and 2, regardless of the number of draws.

Conclusion

The students enjoyed learning and applying mathematical skills and concepts as they were involved in the situations depicted by the story. As illustrated here, multicultural children's literature can furnish a rich context for students to explore a variety of mathematical content in a real-life setting. We encourage teachers to view the literature they share with their students through a multicultural lens and to take advantage of opportunities to teach mathematics through multicultural children's literature.

REFERENCES

Derman-Sparks, Louise, and the Anti-Bias Curriculum (A.B.C.) Task Force. *Anti-Bias Curriculum: Tools for Empowering Young Children*. Washington, D.C.: National Association for the Education of Young Children, 1989.

National Council of Teachers of Mathematics (NCTM). *Curriculum and Evaluation Standards for School Mathematics*. Reston, Va.: NCTM, 1989.

Rattigan, Jama Kim. *Dumpling Soup*. Boston, Mass.: Little, Brown & Co., 1993.

Stearns, Peggy Healy. The Graph Club. Watertown, Mass.: Tom Snyder Productions, 1996. Software.

"*Dumpling Soup:* Exploring Kitchens, Cultures, and Mathematics"

by Nancy L. Smith, Carolyn Babione, and Beverly Johns Vick

Grade range:	1–3
Mathematical topics:	Measurement, estimation and area
Children's book:	*Dumpling Soup*, written by Jama Kim Rattigan and illustrated by Lillian Hsu-Flanders

Discussion of the mathematics: Estimation that is based on strategies and number ideas will help students develop better number sense. Asking students to give a rationale for their estimates instead of accepting wild guesses will help facilitate learning. Helping students process overestimates and underestimates will also help. In estimating the number of units in an item, students should generalize that the larger the item, the fewer you need of them, and that the smaller the item, the more you need of them. The second task introduces area as counting tiles to cover a shape and recognizing that different shapes can have the same area.

Teacher notes and questions to ask students: Read through the entire book for an opportunity for the class to enjoy and discuss the many dimensions of the story. Reread the appropriate sections of the book as different aspects of the story line are explored. A number of activities involving various topics are described in the article; two of these tasks are expanded below.

Materials: *"Dumpling Soup"* recording sheets; mini-cupcake wrappers; a variety of uncooked foods, such as dried beans, macaroni, chickpeas, and the like.

Measurement and estimation: Explain to the class that they will be learning about different foods that their families cook and eat. Ask them to bring a small container of a small, uncooked food item from their family's kitchen, such as beans, rice, and so on. Some nonstandardized measurement units, such as pinches, bunches, and handfuls, may be discussed. Choose an item such as pinto beans, and have the class explore the variations in the number of beans in a handful. Each group could estimate and count the number in a handful. Note: Having the class fix a recipe using nonstandard measuring units reinforces the importance of standardized measures.

- Tell the class about the food you brought from home. How does your family prepare this food? How does your family measure food when cooking?
- How many beans are in your handful? What is the smallest number obtained? The largest number? If the teacher (principal) scooped a handful of beans, how do you think that amount would compare with your handful?

Another estimation activity involved filling the same-sized container with different-sized objects. Have each group of four students select four different-sized foods brought from home. For one of the items, have the students estimate how many pieces would fit inside the mini-cupcake wrapper before filling and then counting the number it holds. Repeat this process for the other items. After each estimate and measure, the groups should discuss their results; additionally they should give a reason for their choice of an estimate. One of the generalizations the students should make is that the larger the item, the fewer you need of them.

- Estimate how many beans (rice kernels, dried peas, etc.,) will fill a mini-cupcake wrapper, and record your estimate. Why did you estimate that number? Fill the cupcake wrapper, count the number of beans, and record the actual number on the recording sheet. Compare your estimate with the actual number. How can you use your results from this item to help you estimate the number of the next item?

Materials: *"Dumpling Soup"* recording sheets 2–4, sheets of one-inch grid paper, one-inch color tiles (fifty per student or group of students), a sheet of centimeter grid paper, and paper for recording results

Area: For this activity, the dumpling tray is represented by a sheet of one-inch graph paper, and a dumpling, by a set of contiguous tiles (each tile exactly covers one square on the tray, and each tile must touch at least one other tile with a side, not just a corner). A good teaching strategy is using the overhead to show examples of appropriate and illegal tile placement to define "These are Dumplings" and "These are Not Dumplings." Have each student or small group use five tiles to find different shapes. Twelve distinct, "legal" shapes, commonly called *pentominoes*, are possible. As the students finish this task, have them focus on the fact that each dumpling, no matter what its shape, covers five squares, so all of them have an area of five squares.

- How can you arrange the tiles so that each dumpling is a different shape? See how many different shapes you can make with your tiles. When you find a new shape, color it on your centimeter grid paper. The number of squares the dumpling covers is called the *area*.

Estimation and Area: Use *"Dumpling Soup"* recording sheet 2—"Which Shape Is Largest?" Before measuring the areas of the shapes with tiles, have students estimate which shapes are the largest and then estimate the area for each shape.

- Here are some dumplings already formed on the tray. Estimate the area of each dumpling (the number of squares it covers). Write your estimate on the shape. Then cover it with color tiles to find the actual area.

For *"Dumpling Soup"* recording sheet 3 and 4—"How Big Is This Shape?" have students work in pairs to estimate and then determine which of the two shapes is larger. To extend the activity, students can make a new shape on graph paper and have another student solve it. Because these shapes are larger and more tiles are needed to cover them, this task presents an opportunity to reinforce the representation of two-digit numbers with tiles in groups of ten and numerals in a place-value chart.

- Compare shapes 1 and 2. Without counting, which one do you think is larger? Again, without counting, estimate the area of each shape. Next cover each shape with color tiles. When covering each shape, use ten tiles of one color, then ten of another, until the shape is covered. Count the number of groups of tens and the number of ones, and then record the result in the place-value chart.

- Make your own dumpling shape. Cut it out, and trade with a friend. Cover the dumplings with color tiles to find the area of each.

REFERENCES

Rattigan, Jama Kim. *Dumpling Soup.* Illustrated by Lillian Hsu-Flanders. Boston: Little, Brown & Co., 1993.

Smith, Nancy L., Carolyn Babione, and Beverly Johns Vick. *"Dumpling Soup:* Exploring Kitchens, Cultures, and Mathematics." *Teaching Children Mathematics* 6 (November 1999): 148–52.

Dumpling Soup

Group Members _____

Date _____

Estimate and then measure one food item. Discuss your estimates and results.

Cupcake Wrapper Estimates

Food Item	Estimate	Actual
1. _____	_____	_____
2. _____	_____	_____
3. _____	_____	_____
4. _____	_____	_____

What did you learn?

Group Members _____

Date_____

Which Shape Is Largest?

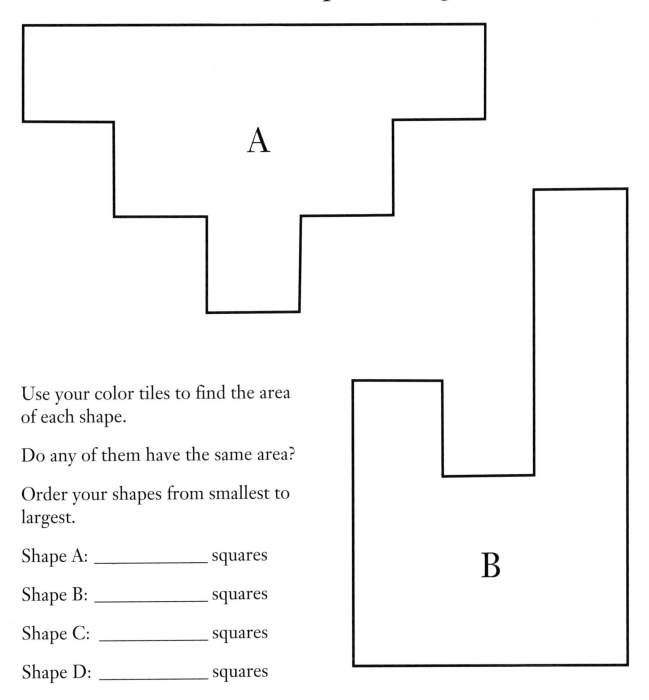

Use your color tiles to find the area of each shape.

Do any of them have the same area?

Order your shapes from smallest to largest.

Shape A: _____ squares

Shape B: _____ squares

Shape C: _____ squares

Shape D: _____ squares

(Shapes C and D on next recording sheet)

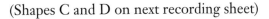

Group Members _____

Date_____

Which Shape Is Largest?

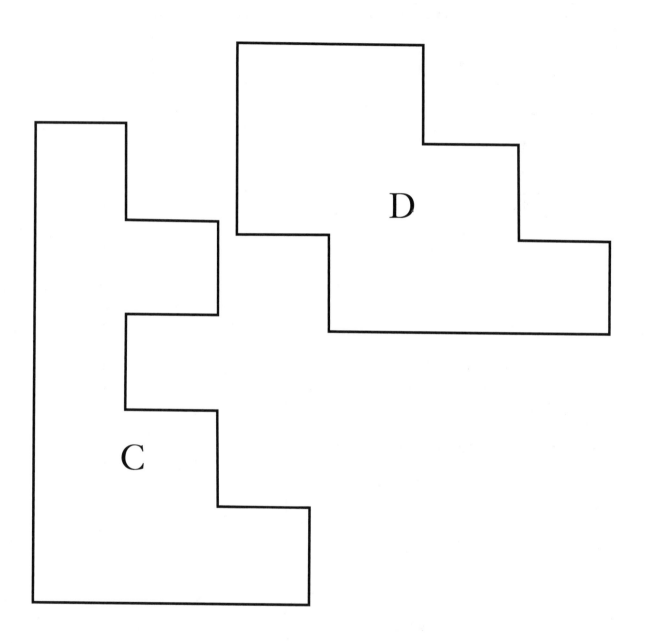

(Shapes A and B on previous recording sheet)

Group Members _____

Date_____

How Big Is This Shape?

Estimate _____

Actual _____

Shape 1

Tens | Ones

Dumpling Soup

Group Members _____

Date_____

How Big Is This Shape?

Estimate _____

Actual _____

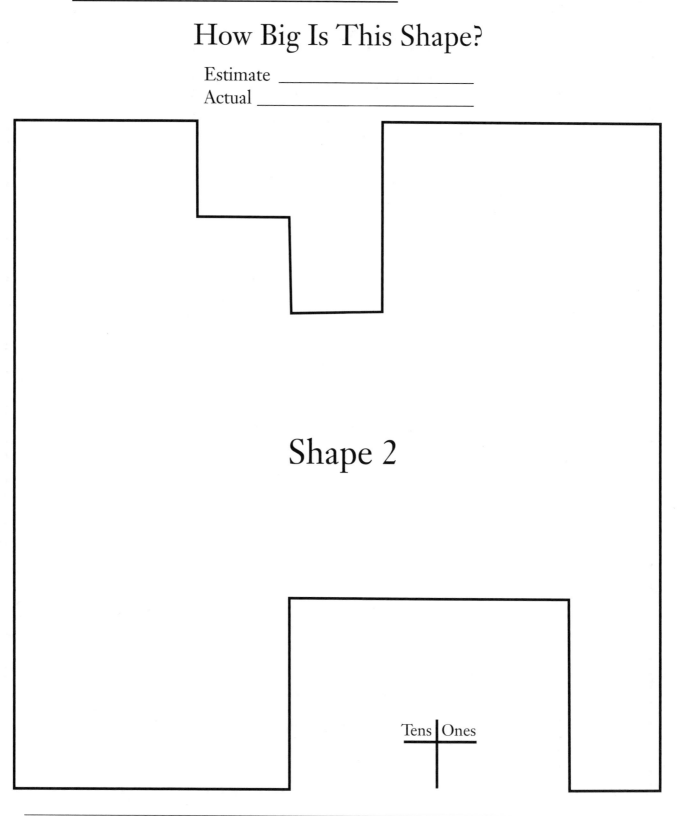

Shape 2

Tens | Ones

28

Telling Tales: Creating Graphs Using Multicultural Literature

Karen S. Karp

THE FOCUS in primary classrooms on children's literature through the whole-language approach to reading encourages the elimination of artificial divisions among subjects through such natural and desirable mixtures as mathematics and storybooks. Egan (1989) states that the use of stories is an excellent foundation for teaching all subjects. A setting or scenario in children's literature can be used as a direct lead-in to a mathematics exercise or can act as a catalyst to motivate students to pursue a related mathematical activity that includes the development of such mathematics process skills as problem solving and making inferences. When children are engaged in reading a book or story, they can become familiar with the characters and plot in sufficient depth that these literary elements can function as the nucleus for more authentic mathematics activities.

Mathematical problem solving based on familiar settings and contexts has been shown to increase the skills children need to make sense of their world. Research evidence consistently points out that students achieve higher levels of performance when confronted with problem-solving situations to which they can relate (Bradbard 1990; Davis-Dorsey 1991). Teachers must build bridges between settings with which their students are comfortable and the realm of mathematical ideas.

The Critical Link

In particular, mathematics skills involving examining problems, collecting and recording data, representing data, describing and interpreting data, and developing hypotheses and theories based on data are significant components of explorations in which elementary students will be engaged as envisioned in the National Council of Teachers of Mathematics's *Curriculum and Evaluation Standards for School Mathematics* (1989) and in the quantitative-literacy movement (TERC 1990). Linking these vital forms of representing mathematical concepts with literature gives students opportunities to communicate in mathematics on two levels. First, when students transform and analyze the information gleaned from the stories they are interpreting and enjoying in class, they develop skills in both critical thinking and mathematical reasoning. Second, such data collection based on stories enables students to increase their fluency in connecting written or oral language to mathematical language. Cultivating facility in communicating through multiple means equips students with the ability to "tell tales" through both traditional stories and graphic representations.

The Need for Multicultural Literature

Although numerous books can be used for these purposes, multicultural literature is a rich source for encouraging students of all backgrounds to experience a variety of perspectives. Students need to have the "opportunity to benefit from the knowledge, perspectives, and frames of reference that can be gained from studying and experiencing other cultures and groups" (Banks 1989, p. 189). In light of the growing population of second-language learners, investigations of actual situations taken from their own real-world experience or an event described through the eyes of children from similar cultural backgrounds are critical for meaningful mathematics learning. In addition, a curriculum that neglects multicultural materials is moving away from achieving equity in learning mathematics, a goal that has been highly desirable yet equally evasive. Therefore, the following links between stories and data-collecting activities have the potential of meeting several points that represent the vision of the *Curriculum and Evaluation Standards for School Mathematics* (NCTM 1989).

Collecting peanut butter preferences

In a thematic, integrated unit on inventions, Eva Moore's book *The Story of George Washington Carver* (1990) generates fascinating information about Carver's discoveries involving peanut plants. In celebrating the accomplishments of this scientist, children recognize evidence of his original thinking that relates directly to their everyday eating experiences. This accounting of Carver's life was an ideal inspiration for a graph on peanut butter preferences. This activity included an actual taste test in which children decided whether they liked creamy peanut butter or crunchy peanut butter or that they didn't care for peanut butter at all. After the taste test, each student glued a peanut shell on a five-centimeter-square portion of an appropriate bar on poster paper to create a graph incorporating real materials. When all responses were recorded through this process, children totaled the frequency for each category by counting the peanuts (see fig. 28.1).

Next another poster-board graph organized in the same fashion as the first graph was incorporated to demonstrate how the data could be transformed into a more abstract representation. Instead of gluing peanuts on the graph, students colored in squares similar to those that held the peanuts to form single colored bars (see fig. 28.2). At this point, word problems based on the data were introduced. Then pairs of children were given an opportunity to create their own problems, which included such questions as "How many more children like peanut butter than those who do not?"

To extend the sample and create more possibilities for analysis, children in groups of three were assigned to poll other classrooms in the school to collect additional data on peanut butter preferences. The children passed out one peanut to each child in the classroom. Then the students were able to vote for their choice by placing their peanuts in an appropriately marked container (each group member was responsible for one of the labeled containers). When the data-collection team members returned to their own classroom, they continued to work in the small groups, tallying the peanuts by categories and illustrating the data on a graph. When all graphs were completed, they were posted in an area where they were interpreted by the class. A question such as "If a new child came into the school from a similar community, what would we expect that his or her choice would be?" was used to encourage predictions. Additional conclusions were drawn, and word problems comparing classes or grades were written by the students. Students

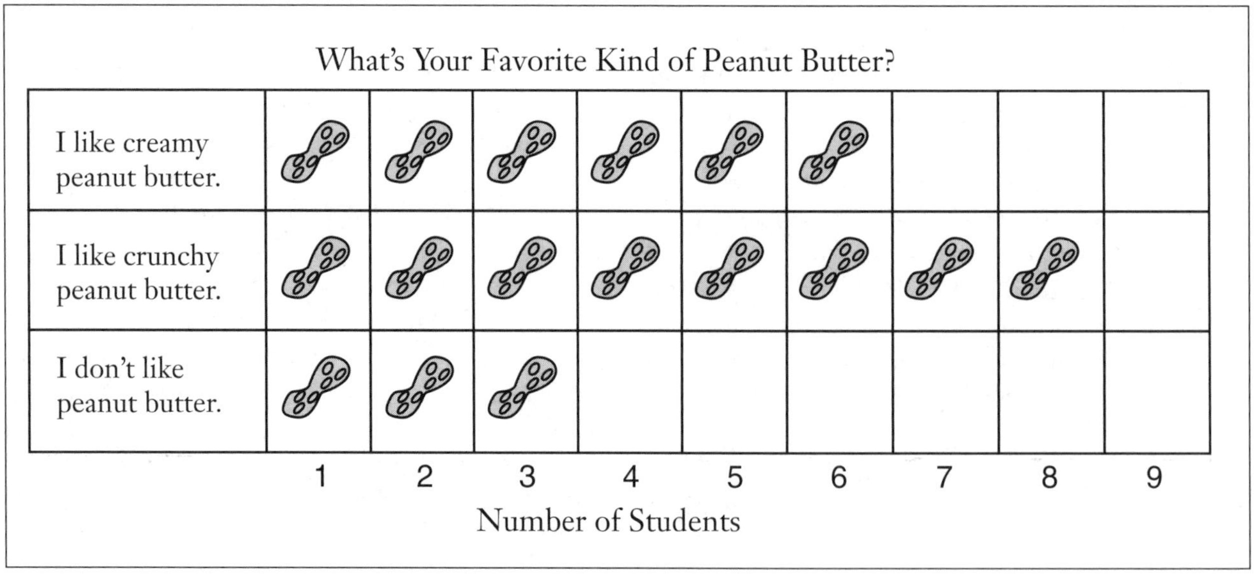

Fig. 28.1. Object graph of peanut butter preferences

EXPLORING MATHEMATICS THROUGH LITERATURE

were curious to examine the data for evidence that children's taste preferences change as they grow older. For example, are they more likely to have tried and enjoyed crunchy peanut butter by sixth grade as compared with the figure for kindergarten? The children were given a choice of writing a story about the project findings or creating a commercial appealing to their age group as suggested by the actual results.

Students can be further challenged by totaling the data from all the classroom graphs and compiling the information on another graph, using one-to-many correspondence through incorporating a one-to-five or one-to-ten icon. Taking advantage of the circumstance of dealing with such large numbers helps to demonstrate realistically the need for a representation other than one-to-one.

Reading knots

The intergenerational tale *Knots on a Counting Rope* by Bill Martin Jr. and John Archambault is a moving story of a Native American boy and his grandfather. The boy implores the old man to relate the story of the boy's birth and early years, as is evident the grandfather has done many times before. The grandfather repeats these past events, including the challenges and trials the boy had already successfully faced in what appears to be an effort to nurture courage and confidence in the child. As this dramatic tale unfolds, the reader learns that the young boy is blind. Thus, this tale is both a story of determination and a celebration of an individual's ability to overcome physical challenges. Consequently, the reader discovers that the title of the story represents the tactile way the boy is able to record the number of times his grandfather tells this story. Each knot make by the grandfather remains a permanent record of the storytelling experience.

A natural way that the author incorporated this concrete image into the classroom was to have children keep individual counting ropes to record the number of books that they had read. To represent the data accurately, the students' ropes were marked at ten-centimeter intervals so that the knots formed parallel number lines when they were hung vertically as a group graph from a bulletin-board strip (see fig. 28.3).

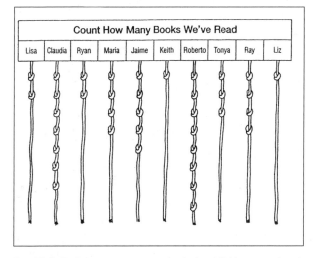

Fig. 28.3. Each knot represents a book the child has completed.

Cultivating cherries

The perfect opportunity to initiate both a science and mathematics activity through literature

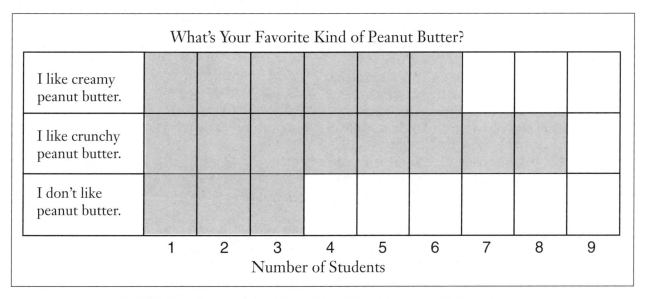

Fig. 28.2. More abstract representation of figure 28.1's data on peanut butter preference

and multicultural characters is with the actual planting of cherry pits as suggested in the story *Cherries and Cherry Pits* by Vera B. Williams. Students measured the growth of their burgeoning seeds by using the edge of computer paper that is interspersed with holes at equal intervals and matching it to the length of their plant's stem. At the point where they reached the top of the stem, they tore off the strip and used it as a record of the height of their plant. Recording measurements in three-day intervals, the resulting strips were placed on a continuum and thereby created a visual representation of the plant's growth. To connect to the theme of the story and make an appealing presentation, the strips were arranged on red paper so that the red color peeked through the holes and reminded the students of the small cherries in the story. The most critical component of this recording process was the analysis of the data. The students made comparisons of the graphs to generalize about successful plant care and environmental conditions best for growth.

Measuring baby

In another book, *She Come Bringing Me That Little Baby Girl*, Eloise Greenfield relates the gentle story of an African American boy's emotional dealings with the arrival of a new baby sister. Initially, the diminishing attention from all the adults turns the boy's world around for the worse. Eventually, his new role as big brother seems to garner appeal. With many students in the primary grades facing similar situations at home, this book is a welcome validation of their feelings as well as a foundation for a long-term graph.

To encourage positive feelings about a new sibling and to examine human growth over time, a graph of a new baby's length is an interesting class project. When a new baby was born to a family in the class, records of the baby's length were collected each month and recorded with a strip of paper cut to the same size as the baby's most recent measurement. As the newborn made monthly visits to the doctor, the sibling reported the actual growth to the class, and a corresponding strip of paper was added to the graph. The children enjoyed making regular predictions estimating the baby's length. Not surprisingly, this baby became a class favorite and received both invitations to visit—where comparisons to the graph were made—and an especially warm welcome.

Other books that invite follow-up experiences in the form of graphs were found in the annotated bibliography at the conclusion of this article. Surveys based on children's literature can also generate interesting graphing activities (see the appendix).

In the school day, fragmented with curricula ranging from the "three Rs" to moral development, the necessity for the intentional and rational integration of subjects is acute. The link between literature and mathematics can and should be encouraged and strengthened, capitalizing on the abilities, interests, and heritage of children who inspire connections between these subjects.

APPENDIX

Additional topics for graphing exercises might include literature-related surveys, such as the following:

- Which author do you like best—Donald Crews, Eloise Greenfield, or John Steptoe?

- Which Caldecot Medal winner did you enjoy most—*Arrow to the Sun: A Pueblo Indian Tale* by Gerald McDermott; *Why Mosquitoes Buzz in People's Ears: A West African Tale* by Verna Aardema; or *Lon Po Po: A Red Riding Hood Story from China* by Ed Young?

- Who is your favorite character in *"More, More, More," Said the Baby: Three Love Stories* by Vera B. Williams?

- Which version of the Cinderella story is your favorite? Select any three of the following: *Cinderella* (Italian) by David Delamare; *Yeh-Shen* (Chinese) by Ali-Ling Louie: *Rough Face Girl* (Native American) by Rafe Martin; *The Brocaded Slipper and Other Tales from Vietnam* by Lynette Vuong; *The Egyptian Cinderella* by Shirley Climo; or *Moss Gown* (Southern United States) by William H. Hooks?

BIBLIOGRAPHY

Aardema, Verna. *Why Mosquitoes Buzz in People's Ears: A West African Tale*. New York: Dial Books, 1978.

Banks, James A. "Integrating the Curriculum with Ethnic Content: Approaches and Guidelines." In *Multicultural Education: Issues and Perspectives*, edited by J. Banks and C. M. Banks, pp. 189–206. Boston: Allyn & Bacon, 1989.

Bradbard, Paula. "Improving Problem Solving through Writing Based on Children's Literature." Ph.D diss. University of Lowell (Mass.), 1990.

Climo, Shirley. *The Egyptian Cinderella*. New York: HarperCollins Publishers, 1989.

Crews, Donald. *Bigmama's*. New York: Greenwillow Books, 1991.

Davis-Dorsey, Judy. "The Role of Rewording and Content Personalization in the Solving of Mathematics Word Problems." *Journal of Educational Psychology* 83 (March 1991): 61–68.

Delamare, David. *Cinderella*. New York: Simon & Schuster, 1993.

Egan, Kiernan. *Teaching as Story Telling*. Chicago: University of Chicago Press. 1989.

Greenfield, Eloise. *She Come Bringing Me That Little Baby Girl*. New York: HarperCollins Children's Books, 1990.

Hooks, William H. *Moss Gown*. New York: Clarion Books, 1987.

Louie, Ai-Ling. *Yeh-Shen*. New York: Clarion Books, 1982.

McDermott, Gerald. *Arrow to the Sun: A Pueblo Indian Tale*. New York: Puffin Books. 1977.

McKissack, Patricia, and Frederick McKissack. *George Washington Carver: The Peanut Scientist*. Hillside, N.J.: Enslow Publishers, 1991.

Martin, Bill, Jr., and John Archambault. *Knots on a Counting Rope*. New York: Henry Holt & Co., 1987.

Martin, Rafe. *Rough Face Girl*. New York: Putnam Publishing Group, 1992.

Moore, Eva. *The Story of George Washington Carver*. New York: Scholastic, 1990.

National Council of Teachers of Mathematics (NCTM). *Curriculum and Evaluation Standards for School Mathematics*. Reston, Va.: NCTM, 1989.

Steptoe, John. *Mufaro's Beautiful Daughters: An African Tale*. New York: Lothrop, Lee & Shepard, 1987.

TERC (Technical Education Research Centers) and Lesley College. *Used Numbers*. Palo Alto, Calif.: Dale Seymour Publications, 1990.

Vuong, Lynette. *The Brocaded Slipper and Other Tales from Vietnam*. New York: HarperCollins Publishers, 1992.

Williams, Vera B. *Cherries and Cherry Pits*. New York: Greenwillow Books, 1986.

———. *"More, More, More," Said the Baby: Three Love Stories*. New York: Greenwillow Books, 1990.

Young, Ed. *Lon Po Po: A Red Riding Hood Story from China*. New York: Putnam Publishing Group, 1989.

Annotated Bibliography

Mosel, Arlene. *Tikki Tikki Tembo*. New York: Holt, Rinehart & Winston, 1989.

This Asian Folktale about a boy with a dangerously long name lends itself to a graph of the lengths of children's names.

Yashima, Taro. *Crow Boy*. New York: Viking Books, 1976.

Children can use this story of a little Japanese child who has a significant distance to walk to school as a stimulus for a graph that communicates the length of their walk to school.

Baer, Edith. *This Is the Way We Go to School: A Book about Children around the World*. New York: Scholastic, 1990.

In a book that examines not only various regions of the United States but countries all over the world, we find descriptions of many different ways that children travel to school. A graph depicting students' mode of transportation to school would be a natural reply.

Cameron, Ann. *The Stories Julian Tells*. New York: Alfred A. Knopf, 1989.

This book contains a delightful chapter called "Because of Figs." On his fourth birthday the little African American boy in the story is given a fig tree that is to grow as fast as he grows. A graph representing children's heights might be a motivating response.

Brown, Marcia. *Stone Soup*. New York: Macmillan Child Group, 1986.

McGovern, Ann. *Stone Soup*. New York: Scholastic, 1986.

In a classic take of trickery, soldiers turn a soup made from a stone into a vegetable soup fit for a feast. A graph representing students' favorite vegetables would be an appropriate link between this old French folktale and data collections and interpretation.

"Telling Tales: Creating Graphs Using Multicultural Literature"

by Karen S. Karp

Grade range:	2–5
Mathematical topics:	Independent and dependent variables, averages, sampling and probability
Children's books:	*She Come Bringing Me That Little Baby Girl*, written by Eloise Greenfield and illustrated by John Steptoe; *Knots on a Counting Rope*, written by Bill Martin Jr. and John Archambault and illustrated by Ted Rand; *Stone Soup* by Marcia Brown; *Stone Soup* written by Ann McGovern and illustrated by Winslow Pinney Pels

Materials: *"Knots on a Counting Rope"* recording sheets, rope (cotton clothesline works best), rulers or tape measures, graph paper

Discussion of the mathematics: In the task called Knots on a Counting Rope, the length of the rope (dependent variable) is dependent on the number of knots (independent variable). Graphing provides an opportunity to discuss the relationship between variables and to predict the results for larger numbers.

Teacher notes and questions to ask students: *Knots on a Counting Rope:* One task described in the article was to use individual counting ropes to create a class graph that was a record of the number of books each student had read. As more books are read, the counting rope becomes longer. An extension is to explore the relationship between the number of knots and the length of the rope: the students will generalize that as knots are accumulated, the length of the rope becomes shorter and shorter. Have the students work in groups of three. Have each group take a piece of rope about one yard long, measure the length of the rope, and record the result on the chart on their recording sheet. Have each group make one knot in the rope and measure again. Each group should collect five more pieces of data

by knotting and measuring five more times and recording its data on the chart.

Have students use coordinate graphs to predict the length of the rope for a large number of knots. They could use centimeter graph paper or large chart-sized graph paper to mark their results. Have them label the horizontal axes of the graph with the number of knots (0–6), because the number of knots is the independent variable. After labeling the vertical axis as the length of the rope, have the students decide on reasonable interval lengths for the axis. After graphing their results, ask the class such questions as these:

- What do you notice?

- Without making any additional knots, can you predict how long the rope will be when it has 10 knots? Twenty knots? How do you know?

Materials: Bags of rice, baby blanket

Discussion of the mathematics: The task called Measuring Baby gives students an opportunity to start forming referents for different weights and to compare weights. When asked about the average weight for a baby, students may focus on different averages, such as mean, median (middle number in ordered data), or mode (number occurring the most frequently). Depending on the background of the students and the purpose of the lesson, one or more of these averages may be pursued.

Teacher notes and questions to ask students:
Measuring Baby: In the article, the book *She Come Bringing Me That Little Baby Girl* was the basis of a task for recording the changing length of a baby month by month. Another task is to collect data on the birth weight of the individual class members. Have each student check with their parent or guardian for his or her original birth weight, record this information in pounds and ounces, and bring the results to class. Set up a class chart for each student to record his or her birth weight. Have students figure out a way to find the average birth weight. After finding the average weight, use one- or two-pound bags of rice to create the same weight. Wrap the "baby" in a baby blanket, and give students an opportunity to hold it. Was the "baby's" weight what they expected? Make a "rice" model of the smallest baby and the largest baby. How do they compare?

- What does an "average" baby weigh? How would you find that weight? After holding the average baby, what do you notice?

- "How does the "rice" model of the smallest baby compare with that of the largest baby?

Have students write statements that compare their birth weight with the average, the smallest, or the largest birth weight in the class.

Materials: Paper bags, colored cubes, recipes, and *"Stone Soup"* recording sheets

---

Discussion of the mathematics: The task based on the book *Stone Soup* gives students an opportunity to explore sampling through data collection. Students are asked to explain their choices on the basis of the collected data.

Teacher notes: *Stone Soup*: In the article's annotated bibliography, the book *Stone Soup* is the basis of a task that involves data collection, sampling, and probability. After reading the book to the class, discuss the likelihood that they would get a stone in their cup of stone soup. To investigate this question, each group has a paper lunch bag that serves as the soup pot and inside it, colored cubes to represent a particular recipe.

Different soup combinations can be created using colored cubes. For example, use yellow cubes for chicken, orange for carrots, green for celery, white for onions, and blue for stones. Some soups should have just carrots, celery, and one stone. Other soups could have one cube of each. Depending on the background of the students, you may choose to have them analyze a few or several recipes. Additionally, the difficulty level will vary depending on how similar or different the recipes are. Use your own preferences, and on separate cards list the ingredients of each of the different soups you create.

Explain to the class that the different recipes posted on the cards were used to make different soups. They are to sample their own soup and then discuss which recipe matches their soup. Next, each group conducts another taste test of twelve draws from the same paper bag and reflects on all its results.

REFERENCES

Brown, Marcia. *Stone Soup*. New York: Macmillan Child Group, 1986.

Greenfield, Eloise. *She Come Bringing Me That Little Baby Girl*. Illustrated by John Steptoe. New York: Harper Collins Children's Books, 1990.

Karp, Karen S. "Telling Tales: Creating Graphs Using Multicultural Literature." *Teaching Children Mathematics* 1 (October 1994): 87–91.

Martin, Bill, Jr., and John Archambault. *Knots on a Counting Rope*. Illustrated by Ted Rand. New York: Henry Holt & Co., 1987.

McGovern, Ann. *Stone Soup*. Illustrated by Winslow Pinney Pels. New York: Scholastic, 1986.

Knots on a Counting Rope
Recording Sheet

Group members _____

Date _____

1. Take a piece of rope about one yard long, measure the length of the rope, and record the result on the chart below. Make one knot in the rope, and measure again. Knot and measure five more times using the chart below to fill in the measurements.

Number of Knots	Length in Inches
0	
1	
2	
3	
4	
5	
6	
10	
20	

2. Take a piece of graph paper, and mark your results, labeling the axes of the graph with the number of knots along the bottom (0–6) and the length along the side (in intervals of 2–5 inches depending on the paper).

What do you notice? Without making any additional knots, can you predict how long the rope will be when it has 10 knots? Twenty knots? How do you know?

Stone Soup

Group members _____

Date _____

"Taste" your soup by pulling one cube out of your bag without looking. Record the result on your chart. Put the cube back, and stir the soup by shaking your bag. Do this eleven more times, recording the results from each draw on the chart. Think about which recipe matches your soup. Then do another taste test of twelve draws from the paper bag.

Taste Test 1 _____

Total _____

Carrots
□ □ □ □ □ □ □ □ □ □ □ □ _____
1 2 3 4 5 6 7 8 9 10 11 12

Celery
□ □ □ □ □ □ □ □ □ □ □ □ _____
1 2 3 4 5 6 7 8 9 10 11 12

Onions
□ □ □ □ □ □ □ □ □ □ □ □ _____
1 2 3 4 5 6 7 8 9 10 11 12

Chicken
□ □ □ □ □ □ □ □ □ □ □ □ _____
1 2 3 4 5 6 7 8 9 10 11 12

Stones
□ □ □ □ □ □ □ □ □ □ □ □ _____
1 2 3 4 5 6 7 8 9 10 11 12

(Continued)

Stone Soup

Group members _____

Date _____

Taste Test 2
_____

Total _____

Carrots □ □ □ □ □ □ □ □ □ □ □ □   _____
       1 2 3 4 5 6 7 8 9 10 11 12

Celery □ □ □ □ □ □ □ □ □ □ □ □   _____
       1 2 3 4 5 6 7 8 9 10 11 12

Onions □ □ □ □ □ □ □ □ □ □ □ □   _____
       1 2 3 4 5 6 7 8 9 10 11 12

Chicken □ □ □ □ □ □ □ □ □ □ □ □   _____
       1 2 3 4 5 6 7 8 9 10 11 12

Stones □ □ □ □ □ □ □ □ □ □ □ □   _____
       1 2 3 4 5 6 7 8 9 10 11 12

After the first taste test, what do you think is the recipe that matches your soup? Did you change your mind after the second taste test? Give a reason for picking your recipe. Why is that one the best match for your data?

29

Feisty Females: Using Children's Literature with Strong Female Characters

Karen Karp, Candy Allen, Linda G. Allen, and Elizabeth Todd Brown

GIRLS ENTER school more mathematics ready than boys. By the time they graduate from high school, however, females have been outdistanced by males in the number of higher-level mathematics courses taken and in the results of crucial tests, such as the mathematics portion of the Scholastic Achievement Test (American Association of University Women 1991). They are also much less likely to pursue majors and careers that relate to mathematics. Why? What happens to girls as they age from eight to sixteen that puts them at a disadvantage in mathematics?

The change in girls' interest and confidence in mathematics during this developmental period is part of a larger phenomenon. As girls progress through the late elementary school years and enter middle school, they are frequently seen as losing their daring nature (Brown and Gilligan 1992). They change from outspoken ten-year-olds into young adolescents who respond, "I don't know," to most questions. Specifically, researchers Ouellette and Pacelli (1983) report that adolescent females often lack a "hardy personality," which they define as the propensity to look forward to changes and challenges, feel in control of one's life, be responsible for one's own actions, and survive unfavorable conditions.

Interestingly, Ouellette and Pacelli also connect the characteristics of a hardy personality to successful problem-solving skills. Although the problem-solving skills that they discuss are not exclusively mathematical, their findings could connect with young females' loss of interest in mathematics at this same age. When female students lack confidence in their ability to prevail in novel or challenging situations, then approaching mathematics problems with risk-taking behaviors seems unlikely. Mathematics educators suggest that the kinds of mathematical problem-solving strategies that we teach should directly relate to solving the problems that students face in the real world. The reverse seems true, as well. Girls who do not develop hardy inner personalities, or what we describe as the characteristics of a "feisty female," may not be prepared to tackle problem-solving situations. How can we build this strength and nurture these students to mature mathematically?

One strategy is to present girls with models of hardy female personalities through examples of young problem solvers found in children's literature. These characters can act as springboards to mathematics lessons as teachers link these "feisty females" to mathematical activities. Children's literature is a way to supply a powerful context in which to build mathematical tasks and is a strong influence in the development of children's perceptions about their world. Through books we can find young and feisty females who face adventure bravely; make hard decisions; solve problems of their own and of others; and use their connections to, and relationships with, other people as ways to both develop a sense of spirit and face new challenges. Walkerdine states that stories are "one of the powerful ways in which constructions of gender are authorized and regulated" (1994, p. 128). Gilbert notes that "through constant repetitions and layering, story patterns and logic become almost 'naturalized' as truths and common sense" (1994, p. 128). Therefore, the stories that we read to children often become the essence of their reality.

When adult females are asked to recall books that they were required to read during their school years, many are able to remember only books with male protagonists (Fields and Karp 1995). Other current research shows that the read-aloud preferences of elementary school teachers show a strong bias toward books with male characters (Smith, Greenlaw, and Scott 1987). As we approach the turn of the century, students in our classes need a more diverse pool of models.

In addition, individuals with hardy personalities often come from families that encourage their members to go out and tackle stressful situations. In these changing times, we often see the role of the family being taken on by schools, with teachers often acting to mentor girls and foster autonomous learning behaviors. "If she learns to tolerate anxiety and act anyway, she will be more likely to persist when she gets her first really tough assignment or fails her first test" (Bingham and Stryker 1995, p. 80).

We have generated several mathematics lessons that incorporate books with feisty female characters and have tested them in elementary, multiaged classroom settings. We worked with upper elementary students ranging in age from eight to eleven in classes with an age spread of at least two years. In contrast with some initial concerns, we found that boys in the class are just as interested in these stories as girls are.

In each situation, the book is read in its entirety with no interruptions. After the children experience the story, the teacher customarily begins a "grand conversation" about such literary elements as plot, theme, and message. The children discuss characters for their qualities and personalities as they make connections between the characters' lives and their own. The children are asked, "What mathematics do you find in the story?" Then the mathematical wisdom of the story is shared. We do not introduce books with an overt discussion of the story's being about a strong female. Instead, we allow the discourse to take its own path. The following example represents some of the children's literature that can engage all children with hardy characters in an effort to generate exciting and motivating mathematical activities.

Swamp Angel, a Caldecott honor book by Anne Isaacs (1994), spins a Tennessee folk tale about Angelica Longrider. Angelica was "scarcely taller than her mother at birth, and although she was given an ax in the cradle she was already two before she built her first log cabin." Angelica was a very special young woman. Her nickname, Swamp Angel, was bestowed after she rescued a wagon train from a marsh at the age of twelve.

When a call goes out across the land for someone to rid the territory of a huge bear known as Thundering Tarnation, who was stealing the townspeople's food, Angelica is ready to try. After unsuccessful attempts by male competitors, Angelica rises to the challenge. The battle of strength and will lasts for days and nights, but Angelica persists and succeeds then treats all of Tennessee and Kentucky to a bear feast.

The tall tale of Angelica led to interesting student discussions of fantasy, reality, and fictional writing. Students even touched on issues of animal rights when Angelica battled the bear, pointing out that "the bear was just doing what was natural. If we saw some food just sitting there, we would want to take it, too." The outrageous situations created in this tale, however, helped them see the exaggerations as being part of the humor.

The students found that thinking about what Angelica was able to do at a given age stirred their imagination. Thinking about what could be done by a person 200 feet tall encouraged everyone to fantasize. One child observed, "She would be the first one to know if it was going to rain, because she would feel it first." Another child saw a relationship between a recent investigation of the Olympic torch relay and Swamp Angel's size when she suggested, "If she were running in the relay, she would need to take only one step to go one kilometer."

Connecting Literature and Mathematics

Mathematical connections came about from the fact that Angelica was not like everyone else in size, strength, and skill. Discussions about the story led to the mathematical opportunity to think about measures of central tendency as students gathered data about themselves and made comparisons. The mathematics-portfolio prompt (see fig. 29.1) was introduced, and it encouraged an exploration of what students would like to know about children their age. They first agreed that they wanted to collect numerical data.

Next, students brainstormed questions, discussed possibilities, and came to consensus on what information they would like to discover. They decided to survey students in their age range, nine to

What Is Average?

After reading the tall tale *Swamp Angel* by Anne Issacs, we can imagine what being above average in size, strength, and skill can do for you. What is average in your life? Conduct a mathematical investigation to find out about your averageness.

Fig. 29.1. *Swamp Angel* mathematics-portfolio prompt

eleven years old, and gather information on height, weight, shoe size, and hours of television watching a day. They were also persistent about knowing whether most children were left- or right-handed. These data did not fit the criterion of numerical responses and later presented a challenge when students began using spreadsheets. Each student was responsible for collecting data on the five questions from twenty individuals within the designated age range. The students worked independently to gather their data and to compile and average the information.

Measures of central tendency was not a new concept for this group. Students had already discovered the formula for finding the mean by redistributing cubes in different-sized towers until the towers all had the same height. In identifying the median and mode, they were able to generalize when one method of finding an "average" might be more appropriate than another. Although they knew the mechanics of the calculations, the *Swamp Angel* survey gave them a "real life" application for their knowledge.

Students in the class had been previously introduced to spreadsheets. They decided that they wanted to put their information from their survey in this format. With help from our technological support team, they designed a spreadsheet for organizing and analyzing the data (see fig. 29.2). An examination of the spreadsheet in figure 29.2 will reveal in the "height" column a misunderstanding that turned into a teachable moment. When the children returned to class with their initial data on the twenty respondents, some had recorded a height as

	A	B	C	D	E	F
			Swamp Angel Random Survey			
	NAME	HEIGHT	WEIGHT	SHOE SIZE	HRS. TV	R/L
1	NAME	HEIGHT	WEIGHT	SHOE SIZE	HRS. TV	R/L
2	Brad J.	62	110	10.5	2	1
3	Danny	48	55	2.5	2.5	1
4	Leah	56	65	4	5	1
5	Brandy	60	82	7.5	8	1
6	Christy	58	49	6.2	4	1
7	Kenya	53	84	6.2	4	1
8	Tye	56	84	6.2	4	1
9	Jessica	66	63	5.2	4	1
10	Irania	73	100	6	1	1
11	Tyler	57	95	8	6	1
12	Brandon	4.8	65	5.2	1	1
13	Jenny	56	70	4	2.2	1
14	Victor	56	54	3	2.2	1
15	Ben B.	59	80	7	2	0
16	Jonathen	5	80	7	3	1
17	Ariel F.	4	70	5.2	2.2	1
18	Heather	5.3	95	4	2	1
19	Mike B.	5.8	64	7	5	1
20	Nicole I.	4.8	65	3	5	1
21	Travis	4.8	74	7	3	0
22	AVERAGE	39.725	75.2	5.735	3.405	
23					right	18
24					left	2

Fig. 29.2. *Swamp Angel* spreadsheet

4 feet 8 inches and others had recorded the same height as 56 inches. In some instances, however, children recorded a mix of units on the same spreadsheet (see fig. 29.2), recording 4 feet 8 inches as 4.8. When the computer calculated the average height of the twenty students as 39.7 inches, the children knew that the answer did not make sense, so they started to compare their data and look for patterns and discrepancies. They decided that they needed to be consistent. The teacher posed a question: "Which unit should we use in our average formula on the computer, feet and inches or just inches?" They discussed the advantages and disadvantages of both and consulted the technology support person, as well. They even drew some conclusions about what data are more logical to report in feet, in inches, or in combinations of feet and inches. What initially seemed to be a problem for some students actually became a relevant learning opportunity.

Another dilemma emerged from the students' desire to use the nonnumerical data generated by the survey question "Are you right- or left-handed?" To use this information, the children decided to code the data for right and left hands into ones and zeros. Instead of finding the mean, they discussed which measure of central tendency would be best. Therefore, they set the spreadsheet to do a count, to help identify the mode.

The students had also made their own calculations with a calculator and had checked their work against the averages computed on the spreadsheets. The students spent time reviewing their work when averages were significantly different. Going back and validating their work is something that nine- and ten-year-old mathematicians do not always like to do. But they discovered that the use of spreadsheets made errors easy to fix, especially when the numbers had been misplaced or deleted. The spreadsheet activity helped students rethink their data and gave them more practice in developing appropriate formulas to calculate totals and the mean. One student explained in her reflections (see fig. 29.3), "We had to put formulas in the computer to get the average, the formula for weight, for example, =avg(C2..C21)." She also added that the computer calculated the average faster and more accurately than she could with by-hand computations. This reorganization of information also reinforced the NCTM curriculum standard relating to students' constructing, reading, and interpreting displays of data (NCTM 1989).

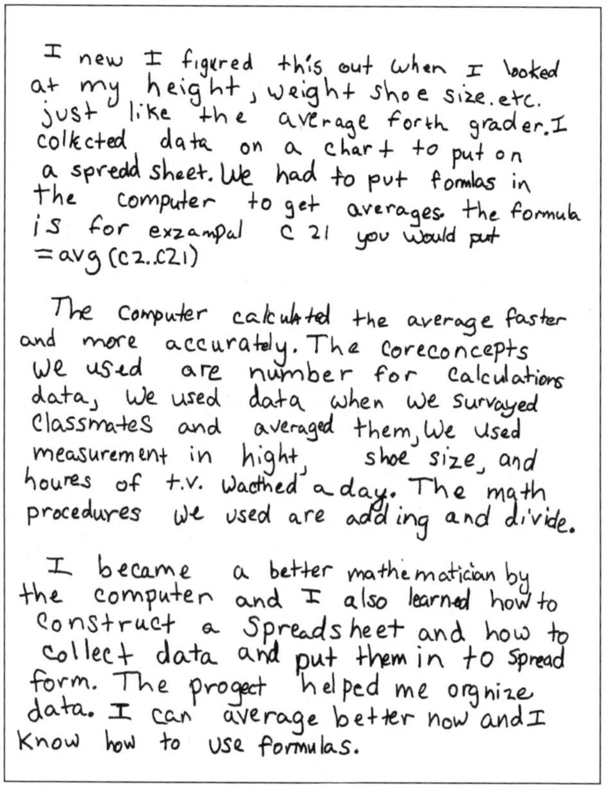

I new I figured this out when I looked at my height, weight shoe size, etc. just like the average forth grader. I colected data on a chart to put on a spredd sheet. We had to put fomlas in the computer to get averages. the formula is for exzampal C 21 you would put =avg (c2..c21)

The computer calculated the average faster and more accurately. The coreconcepts we used are number for calculations data, we used data when we survayed classmates and averaged them, we used measurement in hight, shoe size, and houres of t.v. wached a day. The math procedures we used are adding and divide.

I became a better mathematican by the computer and I also learned how to construct a spreadsheet and how to collect data and put them in to spread form. The proget helped me orghize data. I can average better now and I know how to use formulas.

Fig. 29.3. Students' reflections

Some students then raised a question: How might students in other parts of the country respond? With the help of friends at the university and neighboring school districts, the students sent the questions by e-mail to other parts of the United States and Canada. When the data were received from various locations, the students had an opportunity to revisit the data-analysis concepts and the use of spreadsheets. Since some time had passed, the teacher used the opportunity to assess who still understood the mathematics. Most students quickly transferred the data to spreadsheets, and they compared and contrasted the averages in height, weight, shoe size, hours of television watching, and the totals of right- or left-handedness. Their experience with putting data on the first spreadsheet streamlined the process of creating a second spreadsheet.

Several mathematical activities emerged as a result of the e-mail information. The children had an opportunity to place their class's numerical data side by side with the data from a class in another city and to write mathematical conjectures about the comparisons. A child wrote, "The tallest and shortest came from the other class [New York] data." In looking at other comparisons, a student wrote, "For example, our average height was 56.35 (inches) and theirs was 59, so that proves that they were taller than us. The average shoe size was 5.8 but the other class average was 6.1, so that meant they also had bigger feet than us." Another child summarized her data in the following way: "We found out the average fourth grader is right-handed, watches 1 hour of TV a day, has a shoe size of about 5, weighs 76.75 pounds, and their height is 56 inches."

After interpreting their survey data, students wrote reflectively about what they had found, with references to students in their corner of the world. This written component linked well with the NCTM's communication standard, which suggests that students should realize that representing, discussing, reading, writing, and listening to mathematics are vital parts of their lives (NCTM 1989).

Since the children are enrolled in the multiage classes for more than one year, this activity began at the end of one school year and awaited them at the beginning of the next year. Throughout the investigation and data collection, the teacher kept questioning the students about who would be interested in shoe sizes, height, weight, television watching, and the handedness of children in different parts of the continent. How could they share their findings with the real world? Students considered whether this information might be valuable in marketing products to the people their age. The consensus came down to several groups that might be able to use the findings: shoe companies, clothing companies, and manufacturers of scissors. The students wrote letters to these groups regarding the possible implications of the survey results; at the time of this writing, the class was still waiting for a response.

Conclusion

Angelica Longrider was a risk taker. Her example led the class on a continent-wide search for data on how the students compared with other nine-, ten-, and eleven-year-olds. Her "hardy personality" gave us an avenue along which to grow more knowledgeable about our world and ourselves.

Swamp Angel has been only one of many mathematics-literature connections that we have made. At this time, more than sixty stories about strong female characters have been linked to powerful mathematics lessons with exciting results. Three other book suggestions and the corresponding mathematics are briefly described here:

- *Cinder Edna*, by Ellen Jackson (1994), is a humorous rendering of the tales of both Cinderella and her next-door neighbor, Cinder Edna. In a style that moves back and forth from one character to the other, the author involves the reader in how these two women faced similar problems but solved them in very different ways. This piece of literature enabled us to reinforce the possibilities of multiple problem-solving strategies through nonroutine problems and to develop the concepts of combinations and probable outcomes. In an effort to compare and contrast these stories as well as other multicultural Cinderella tales, such as *Rough Faced Girl* (Martin 1992) and *Yeh Shen* (Young 1982), we incorporated Venn diagrams to help students visualize relationships among the differing versions of the classic fairy tale.

- *City Green*, by DyAnne DiSalvo-Ryan (1994), shares a real-world experience about living in a large city and working cooperatively. Marcy, the young girl in the story, decides to make a difference in her neighborhood by transforming a cluttered vacant lot into a community garden for everyone to enjoy. By depicting the actual activity of the characters, this story line generated mathematical investigations with fractional parts, growth over time, estimated plant size, area, spatial sense, and perimeter.

- *The Rag Coat*, by Lauren Mills (1993), is the touching story of a mountain girl named Minna. She loves a new coat that has been quilted for her by neighbors, but the children in school make fun of her "rag coat." Minna uses problem-solving skills and develops a strategy to deal with this situation. This story was used as a springboard to develop a quilting unit that included an exploration of the geometrical shapes, reflective symmetry, and rotational symmetry found in a nine-patch square.

Through all these activities, we have found that the hands-on, cooperative tasks that connect mathematics to both girls and stories create exciting opportunities to engage students actively in important concepts. In addition, our heightened awareness about including a variety of role models in the lessons made us more effective with all children in the class. Every child became an enthusiastic participant.

Researchers in psychology consistently find that males can look at the pursuits of either other males or females and feel fully able to attack similar situations. Females, in contrast, often perceive only the activities they see other females doing as being possible for them. If we wish to develop the underlying traits that strengthen the problem-solving abilities of females, we need to consider using female models with hardy personalities. Clearly, it is essential to include female role models in classrooms where we want to meet the needs of all children. Repeatedly, research shows that as we seek ways to help create more equitable classrooms, we find the means to help all students become more mathematically literate.

The Goals 2000 report (National Educational Goals Panel 1994) calls for the United States to be first in the world in mathematics by the year 2000 and to promote a significant increase in the numbers of females and minorities entering mathematics, science, and engineering careers. If these goals are to be reached, we must face a crucial need to create learning situations that encourage all children to be a part of the equation. Perhaps through establishing links between "feisty females" and mathematics, an important portion of the puzzle can be completed.

REFERENCES

American Association of University Women. *Shortchanging Girls, Shortchanging America: A Call to Action.* Washington, D.C.: American Association of University Women, 1991.

Bingham, Mindy, and Sandy Stryker. *Things Will Be Different for My Daughter: A Practical Guide to Building Her Self-Esteem and Self-Reliance.* New York: Penguin Books, 1995.

Brown, Lyn Mickel, and Carol Gilligan. *Meeting at the Crossroads.* Cambridge: Harvard University Press, 1992.

Fields, Teesue, and Karen Karp. "Positive Role Models in Children's Literature." Paper presented at the annual conference for the Association of Women in Psychology, Indianapolis, Indiana, 1995.

Gilbert, Pam. " 'And they lived happily ever after': Cultural Storylines and the Construction of Gender." In *The Need for Story*, edited by Anne H. Dyson and Celia Genishi. Urbana, Ill.: National Council of Teachers of English, 1994.

National Council of Teachers of Mathematics (NCTM). *Curriculum and Evaluation Standards for School Mathematics.* Reston, Va.: NCTM, 1989.

National Educational Goals Panel. *The National Education Goals Report.* Washington, D.C.: National Educational Goals Panel, 1994.

Ouellette, Suzanne Kobasa, and Mark C. Pacelli. "Personality and Social Resources in Stress Resistance." *Journal of Personality and Social Psychology* 45 (1983): 839–50.

Smith, Nancy J., M. Jean Greenlaw, and Carolyn J. Scott. "Making the Literate Environment Equitable." *Reading Teacher* 40 (1987): 399-407.

Walkerdine, Valerie. *Schoolgirl Fictions.* London: Verso, 1990.

BIBLIOGRAPHY

DiSalvo-Ryan, DyAnne. *City Green.* New York: Morrow Junior Books, 1994.

Isaacs, Anne. *Swamp Angel.* New York: Dutton Children's Books, 1994.

Jackson, Ellen B. *Cinder Edna.* New York: Lothrop, Lee & Shepard Books, 1994.

Karp, Karen, Todd Brown, Linda Allen, and Candy Allen. *Feisty Females: Inspiring Girls to Think Mathematically.* Portsmouth, N.H.: Heinemann, 1998.

Martin, Rafe. *Rough Faced Girl.* New York: Scholastic, 1992.

Mills, Lauren A. *The Rag Coat.* Boston: Little, Brown & Co., 1991.

Young, Ed. *Yeh Shen.* New York: Philomel Books, 1982.

Teaching Notes for

"Feisty Females: Using Children's Literature with Strong Female Characters"

by Karen Karp and Elizabeth Todd Brown

Grade range:	4–6
Mathematical topics:	Collecting data, finding averages
Children's book:	*Swamp Angel*, written by Anne Isaacs and illustrated by Paul O. Zelinsky
Materials:	*"Swamp Angel"* recording sheet; measuring instruments, such as tape measures, scales, stopwatches, or watches with second hands

Discussion of the mathematics: The process of data collecting is important, but data should be collected with a purpose rather than simply for the sake of collecting data. Posing such questions as "Who would want to know about head circumference? Or about the number of hours of TV watched?" will produce lively conversations. The differences between numerical and categorical data need to be discussed before survey questions are finalized. As discussed in the article, data on left- and right-handed individuals presented a challenge when the data were to be analyzed, but the dilemma was resolved using coding. Finally, such tools as e-mail to collect data and spreadsheets to analyze data are used in solving problems.

Teacher notes and questions to ask students: Discussions about the heroine of *Swamp Angel* led naturally to speculations about what a person who is 200 feet tall can do, as well as discussions about what is average. A class discussion should center on what information is to be collected and who is to be surveyed. Students are particularly motivated to collect data about their age group. Additionally, the class conversation should focus on who would be interested in knowing or using this information. Students can work in small groups, write their own survey questions for the information they are interested in pursuing, and then collect and analyze the data.

The "What's an Average Kid? Recording Sheet" can be used for the students to collect numerical information about themselves in the areas of interest generated by their survey questions. They may include such items as these:

Height
Weight
Head circumference
Number of hours of TV watched each day
Number of books read in a month
Number of teeth lost
Shoe size
Backpack weight
Heartbeats per minute

The data could then be entered on a spreadsheet to calculate attributes and characteristics of an "average kid." Students were also highly motivated to collect data about other students who lived in different areas; as described in the article, e-mail linkages provided an excellent way to work with other students. Students can draw comparisons or make conjectures about data from different groups.

REFERENCE

Isaacs, Anne. *Swamp Angel*. Illustrated by Paul O. Zelinsky. New York: Dutton Children's Books, 1994.

Karp, Karen, Candy Allen, Linda G. Allen, and Elizabeth Todd Brown. "Feisty Females: Using Children's Leterature with Strong Female Characters." *Teaching Children Mathematics* 5 (October 1998): 88–94.

Swamp Angel

Group Members _____

Date _____

With three other students, conduct a mathematical investigation to gather numerical data.

In the spaces below, write the questions that your group would like to use in your survey:

1. _____

2. _____

3. _____

Collect and record responses from at least six individuals:

Group Members _____

Combine your group's data, making sure you do not repeat answers from the same people. Find the average answer for each question.

What mathematical conclusions can you draw?

Who would be interested in this information?

Swamp Angel

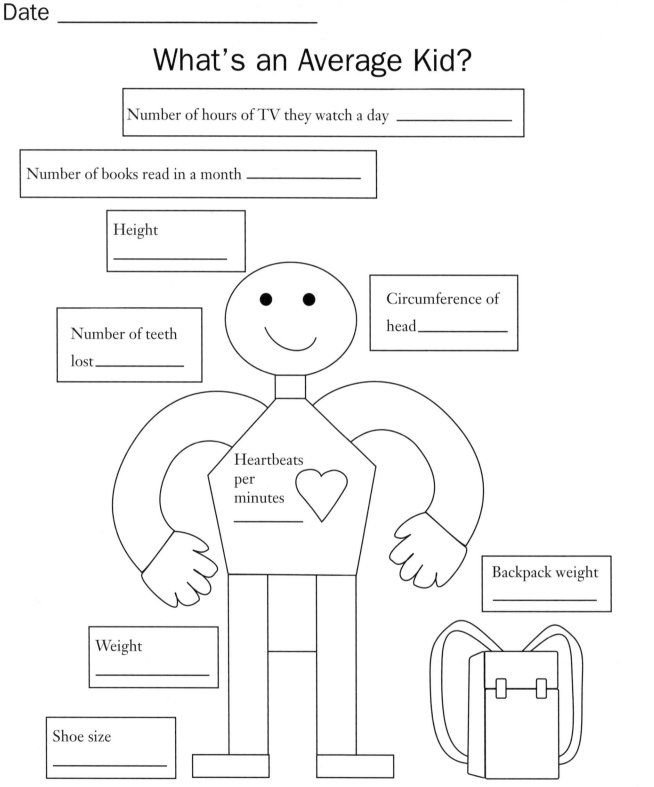

Recording Sheet

Group Members _____

Date _____

What's an Average Kid?

Number of hours of TV they watch a day _____

Number of books read in a month _____

Height
_____

Circumference of head_____

Number of teeth lost_____

Heartbeats per minutes
_____

Backpack weight
_____

Weight
_____

Shoe size
_____

30

On the Road with Cholo, Vato, and Pano

Frederick L. Silverman, Abbilynn B. Strawser, Donna L. Strohauer, and Noel Nevada Manzano

TYPICALLY, elementary school mathematics experiences for children in the United States have stood almost completely apart from their lives outside school. Children's voices simply do not come through in the common arithmetic-driven curriculum. Although the NCTM's Standards movement, which began in the 1980s and continues to this day with the recent publication of *Principles and Standards for School Mathematics* (NCTM 2000), had had an impact in the professional, political, and public realms, much teaching and learning of mathematics is still detached from children's personal experiences.

Children's literature offers a context for teaching and learning mathematics, especially in the elementary grades. Such books as Pat Hutchins's *The Doorbell Rang* (1986) and Rod Clement's *Counting on Frank* (1991) certainly come to mind when we recall books that youngsters enjoy and that have evident mathematics content in a social context. Other books have the effect of heightening youngsters' awareness of, and appreciation for, the abundance of mathematics in the daily lives of us all. Such books include Marilyn Kaye's *A Day with No Math* (1992) and Jon Scieska's *Math Curse* (1995). Poetry has also been a venue for mathematics, as in Carl Sandburg's "Arithmetic" (1970) and Shel Silverstein's "Reflection," "Shapes," and "Smart" (1981, 1974). Controversy sometimes arises, as it did over Virginia Grossman's and Sylvia Long's *Ten Little Rabbits* (1991), which inspired healthy discussions in the cultural sphere. Other examples of multicultural children's literature include Ann Tompert's *Grandfather Tang's Story* (1990) and Claudia Zaslavsky's *Count on Your Fingers African Style* (1999). All these selections enable youngsters to experience mathematics in a context that adds meaning to their mathematical thinking as they read about characters who encounter problematic situations.

This article describes a lesson that the authors prepared for a fifth-grade class in Greeley, Colorado, using the book *A Migrant Child's Dream: Farm Worker Adventures of Cholo, Vato, and Pano*, written by George Rivera and illustrated by Tony Ortega (1994). Many children at the school are Hispanic, and some have had migrant experiences similar to those in the book. Our students knew that migrant workers must travel from one place to another, depending on where the crops need to be planted, cultivated, or harvested.

Combining Spanish and English

The book tells a story of a Hispanic family and other workers who are traveling through the Rocky Mountain region and the north central United States, working the crops from state to state. Cholo, Vato, and Pano are two dogs and a young boy, respectively. Pano and his family, along with their beloved dogs and other migrant workers, are on the road in a moderately sized panel truck. Their travels and experiences are described in Spanish and English with Ortega's colorful and lively illustrations. This story enables students to glimpse the culture of Hispanic families who are doing important, hard agricultural work. It challenges stereotypes by portraying dedication, warm family ties, and a vision of a future that includes school and education. The book offers creative teachers a number of natural opportunities for integrating mathematics with other elementary school curriculum areas. Students and teachers together can study mathematics in a real context, one in which children and teachers use the book to answer questions that arise out of natural curiosity.

The book is written in English and Spanish. Abbilynn Strawser asked one of her students, a Spanish-speaking youngster who had limited proficiency in English, to read the Spanish text. The versions closely approximate each other in meaning, but they are not identical. Rivera indicates that he left the translations loose so that Spanish and English speakers would have unexpected details to share. Strawser engaged her students by describing how the author wrote of his mother's and aunt's experiences years ago on the "migrant stream." The children were enthralled, quietly anticipating the story about to unfold. They were sitting below a map of Colorado, and Strawser showed her students the cities where author Rivera and illustrator Ortega live and where Rivera teaches.

"Pretty close to us," she and the children agreed as they estimated the distance. The mathematics was already subtly present in the lesson as the children located these cities around the state. "Locating" is one of six categories of human behavior in which Alan J. Bishop (1988) has found that mathematics occurs naturally. The others are counting, measuring, designing, explaining, and playing. These six behaviors can be found in virtually every culture, a fact that highlights the similarities of people around the world. (See Alan J. Bishop's article, "Research into Practice: What Values Do You Teach When You Teach Mathematics?" in this issue, as well as the poster titled "Mathematics Makes a World of Difference in Our Lives!" that illustrates and describes the six mathematical activities identified by Bishop as universal human behaviors.) Our differences lie in how our cultures influence the ways in which we name, describe, and use mathematics. Strawser was aware of these behaviors and knew that she could use them to have her students propose and solve a number of mathematical questions resulting from experiences described in the story. She began reading out loud in English; the first page

is decorated with an illustration of Pano and his two dogs in front of a colorful map of the United States. Strawser and her Spanish-speaking partner then read from the book alternately in English and Spanish.

> Where there are many vegetables and fruit,
> A farm worker's family is enroute.
> *Donde hay muchas verduras y fruta*
> *La familia de un campesino está.*

> Familias from all over get ready:
> Mama, Cholo, Vato, Pano, Daddy.
> *Familias de todas partes están aquí:*
> *Mamá, Cholo, Vato, Pano y Papi.*

Integrating Mathematics

The characters pile into their truck in May and head off, first to Montana for sugar beets, then east to Ohio for tomatoes, then back west to Idaho for potatoes. The families crisscross the country, visiting seven states and tending eight different crops. Strawser read the book aloud twice; the first time allowed students to understand and enjoy the story, and the second time enabled them to gather data to create their problems.

The students worked in small groups to compose problems and explain how they would solve them. Each group shared a map that showed such details as state names and boundaries, cities, and topographical features. These maps helped students recreate the route traveled. The fifth graders' natural curiosity led them to connect Bishop's suggested mathematical behaviors with Pano's exploits. In this article, we share several of the many mathematical problems that the students suggested, described, and solved. The questions included, How many and what states did the characters visit (counting)? How long were Pano and the others on the road (measuring)? How far did they travel (measuring)? Where did they start (locating)? and What route did they take (locating and explaining)?

As Strawser read, one group traced a route that Pano might have followed. The students wanted to see where Pano went and how far he traveled. They sketched a possible route from one state to the next, usually using straight lines to the capitals of the states. The students began their calculations by estimating the trip's distance on the large classroom map. They decided to measure the route with twelve-inch pipe cleaners that were available in the classroom, knowing that they could use the pipe

EXPLORING MATHEMATICS THROUGH LITERATURE

cleaners to easily calculate the number of inches covered on the scaled map. The map's legend indicated the number of miles per inch. The students multiplied the number of inches by the number of miles per inch to find an answer to their question. They naturally turned to calculators as they busily computed the mileage estimates between capital cities. The students estimated Pano's journey to be about 6700 miles!

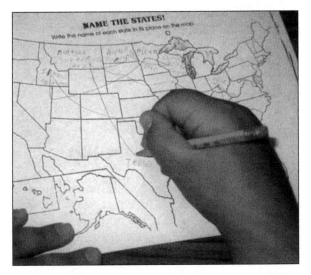

As Strawser read, one group traced a route that Pano might have followed. Photograph by Noel Manzano: all rights reserved.

Strawser also led the whole class in a problem-solving inquiry to calculate the durations of Pano's journey. From the story, the students knew that the trip began sometime in May and ended at Christmastime in Eagle Pass. Strawser helped the students apply their calendar knowledge to estimate the number of days that the travelers might have been on the road. With her guidance, the youngsters recalled the refrain "Thirty days has September, April, June, and November. All the rest have thirty-one, except February, which has twenty-eight, except for leap year when it has twenty-nine." The class consolidated this information with a month-by-month chart that showed the approximate number of days that the family in the story was away from Eagle Pass: May—31, June—30, July—31, August—31, September—30, October—31, November—30, December—25. The students concluded that Pano and the others would have been away from Eagle Pass for about 239 days. Of course, this total is an estimate because the story is fuzzy on beginning and ending dates. The fifth graders gained perspective on mathematics as a discipline in which problem solvers must often make assumptions to arrive at approximate solutions. For this inquiry, an estimate

was quite satisfactory, but the youngsters still had some unanswered questions: About how long might the characters have stayed in each locale? About how long might they have been on the highway between locales? Those questions were saved for another day.

At the end of this inquiry, Strawser said, "Your lives are filled with school. Pano's travels didn't allow much time for school. Pano's life was filled with tomatoes, sugar beets, potatoes, cherries, and other crops." She reminded them of Pano's dream, shared at the end of the story:

At home far away from the migrant stream,
A school forever is in Pano's dream.

En casa, lejos de un campo migrante,
Una escuela para siempre es el sueño gigante.

Conclusion

Strawser learned a great deal about her students by allowing them to share personal stories of road trips as they continued to pose and answer their own questions and share the solutions with others. She also witnessed their growing realization that much of what Pano did was mathematical and observed that their use of mathematics allowed them to better understand Pano's experiences. Strawser concluded the lesson by having the students write about their insights and reactions to the story. One student, writing in emergent English, stated, "What I remember is how Mrs. Abbi read the book to us and we used pipe cleaners to see how many miles Cholo, Vato [the dogs], and Pano [the little boy] went as they digged suger beets, corn, cotton, potatoes, and tomatoes. How I reacted to this lesson is I didn't know what to say because it was so fun. . . ."

We hope that our lesson encourages other teachers who are interested in using Bishop's six categories to frame the mathematics in stories that they and their students may enjoy. For our students, the unifying opportunities and the touching and lively story of *A Migrant Child's Dream: Farm Worker Adventures of Cholo, Vato, and Pano* would be tough to beat. For information on how to obtain a copy of this book, please contact the Emma Eccles Jones Center for Early Childhood Education, Utah State University, 2885 Old Main Hill, Education Building, Room 340, Logan, UT 84322-2885; telephone: (435) 797-8629; fax: (435) 797-0372; e-mail eejcenter@coe.usu.edu; Web site: www.coe.usu.edu/ ecc/.

REFERENCES

Bishop, Alan J. *Mathematical Enculturation*. Norwell, Mass.: Kluwer Academic Publishers, 1988.

Clement, Rod. *Counting on Frank*. Milwaukee, Wis.: Gareth Stevens Children's Books, 1991.

Grossman, Virginia, and Sylvia Long. *Ten Little Rabbits*. San Francisco: Chronicle Books, 1991.

Hutchins, Pat. *The Doorbell Rang*. New York: Greenwillow Books, 1986.

Kaye, Marilyn. *A Day with No Math*. Orlando, Fla.: Harcourt Brace Javanovich, 1992.

National Council of Teachers of Mathematics (NCTM). *Principles and Standards for School Mathematics*. Reston, Va.: NCTM, 2000.

Rivera, George. *A Migrant Child's Dream: Farm Worker Adventures of Cholo, Vato, and Pano*. Illus. by Tony Ortega. Boulder, Colo.: University of Colorado Art Galleries, 1994.

Sandburg, Carl. "Arithmetic." In *The Complete Poems of Carl Sandburg*, rev. ed. New York: Harcourt Brace, 1970.

Scieska, Jon. *Math Curse*. New York: Penguin Books USA, 1995.

Silverstein, Shel. "Reflection" and "Shapes." In *A Light in the Attic*. New York: Harper & Row, Publishers, 1981.

———. "Smart." In *Where the Sidewalk Ends*. New York: Harper & Row, Publishers, 1974.

Tompert, Ann. *Grandfather Tang's Story*. New York: Crown Publishers, 1990.

Zaslavsky, Claudia. *Count on Your Fingers African Style*. New York: Black Butterfly Children's Books, 1999.

"On the Road with Cholo, Vato, and Pano"

by Frederick L. Silverman, Abbilynn B. Strawser, Donna L. Strohauer, and Noel Nevada Manzano

Grade range:	4–7
Mathematical topics:	Estimation and reading map scales
Children's book:	*A Migrant Child's Dream—Farm Worker Adventures of Cholo, Vata, and Pano,* written by George Rivera and illustrated by Tony Ortega
Materials:	"A Migrant Child's Dream" recording sheets, maps, pipe cleaners or string

Discussion of the mathematics: The mathematics integrated in this lesson includes such skills as computation, estimation, and using map scales. The story line provides a context for solving mathematics problems, and the calculation and estimation of the time spent and the distances traveled will help students better understand the story line.

Teacher notes: Introduce this task to the students by reading the book twice. The first reading gives students an opportunity to understand and enjoy the story. The second reading enables them to gather data to create their own problems and to answer questions. To help structure the data collection, a map and recording sheets are helpful. The recording sheets that follow were created from the questions posed by one fifth-grade class.

Younger children will also enjoy *A Migrant Child's Dream*. They can keep track of the states that Pano visits, the number of states he visits more than once, the crops and the states in which they grow, and the number of months Pano is on the road. A large map could be available for students to locate the states as the story is read.

Map—using a diagram to represent the situation: Initially students used a map of the United States to locate the various states that Pano and his family worked. Later, the map was used to sketch a route that Pano and his family might have followed

from state to state as they worked the crops. Some students used the map to get a general idea of Pano's travels by drawing straight lines between the capital cities of the states he visited. Other students will have additional ideas on how to represent Pano's road trip. Useful maps are available at the World Wide Web site worldatlas.com.

Collecting information on states and crops: This table was used to keep track of the states that Pano and his family visited and the crops they tended in each state.

STATES	CROPS

Fig. 30.1. States that Pano and his family visited and the crops they tended in each state

Timeline to record Pano's location and estimated travel time: Some students think that Pano's story began in early May or late April in Texas. Have your students discern where they think Pano was during each month the story takes place, then draw a timeline that indicates these locations. To determine the length of the total time, have students use the table to list the months that Pano's story takes place. Next estimate the number of days, from the time he left until the time he returned, that Pano might have been away. Note: When the story is ambiguous with respect to either location or time, students should explain their choices of time estimates and Pano's location.

Estimating the distances traveled: Have students list the states in the order that Pano visited them and use this information to sketch his travels on a map. To estimate the distance that Pano traveled on each leg of his trip, students can use pipe cleaners or strings to mark the various estimated distances on a large classroom map. By measuring these lengths and consulting the map's legend to determine the scale, students can calculate the estimated distances.

REFERENCES

Rivera, George. *A Migrant Child's Dream—Farm Worker Adventures of Cholo, Vata, and Pano.* Illustrated by Tony Ortega. Boulder, Colo.: University of Colorado Art Galleries, 1994.

Silverman, Frederick L., Abbilynn B. Strawser, Donna L. Strohauer, and Noel Nevada Manzano. "Links to Literature: On the Road with Cholo, Vato, and Pano." *Teaching Children Mathematics* 7 (February 2001): 330–33.

Name _____

Date _____

Mark the locations where Pano and his family worked. Sketch a route that Pano and his family might have followed from state to state as they worked the crops.

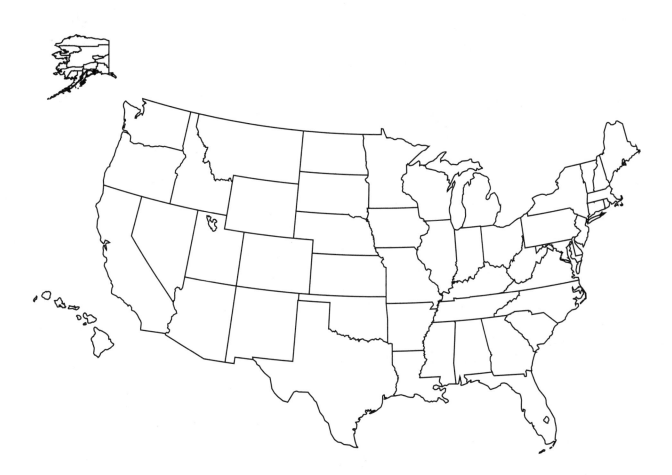

Name_____

Date_____

STATES AND CROPS

List the states that Pano and his family visited and the crops they tended in each state.

STATES	CROPS

A Migrant Child's Dream

Name_____

Date_____

STATES AND DISTANCE PANO TRAVELED

List the states in the order that Pano and his family visited them. Use this information to sketch their travels on the United States map. Estimate the distance Pano traveled on each leg of his trip, and enter that estimate in this table.

STATES	ESTIMATE OF DISTANCE TRAVELED

A Migrant Child's Dream

Recording Sheet 4

Name_____

Date_____

TIMELINE TO ESTIMATE PANO'S LOCATION DURING THE STORY

Draw a timeline that indicates where you think Pano was each month from the start to the end of this story.

Jan	Feb	Mar	Apr	May	June	Jul	Aug	Sept	Oct	Nov	Dec

⟵──────────────────────────────────────⟶

TX

Use this table to list the months that Pano's story takes place. Then estimate the number of days that Pano might have been away from the time he left until the time he returned.

MONTHS	DAYS IN EACH MONTH	ESTIMATED NUMBER OF PANO'S DAYS AWAY
TOTALS		

A Migrant Child's Dream

Name_____

Date_____

SUMMARY TABLE FOR DATA ABOUT PANO'S TRAVEL
Here you can summarize the information you gathered or figured out about Pano's story.

STATES	CROPS	ESTIMATE OF DISTANCE OF SEGMENTS	MONTHS	ESTIMATE OF NUMBER OF DAYS
TOTALS				

Readers of *Exploring Mathematics through Literature: Articles and Lessons for Prekindergarten through Grade 8* might be interested in the following resources from the National Council of Teachers of Mathematics (NCTM) on teaching mathematics with literature as the springboard:

◆ ***Connecting Mathematics across the Curriculum: 1995 Yearbook,*** edited by Peggy A. House. Reston, Va.: NCTM, 1995. This rich resource illuminates ways that mathematics can be connected with other topics in the curriculum, including literature along with many other subject areas. It helps classroom teachers and other educators broaden their views of mathematics and suggests practical strategies for making mathematics come alive in the classroom.

◆ ***How to Use Children's Literature to Teach Mathematics,*** by Rosamond Welcman-Tischler. Reston, Va.: NCTM, 1992. This wonderfully illustrated book shows teachers how to use popular children's tales, such as "Caps for Sale" and "Stone Soup," to teach mathematics concepts, including classification, graphing, measurement, monetary concepts, patterning, and symmetry.

◆ ***Integrated Mathematics,*** edited by Sue Ann McGraw. Reston, Va.: NCTM, 2003. With a focus on using various tools and approaches to teach meaningful, significant, and useful mathematics using an integrated approach, this resource includes two chapters that specifically deal with using literature to teach mathematics concepts. This book helps educators at all levels understand how to teach mathematics through an integrated approach and how to plan, implement, and assess an integrated curriculum.

◆ ***The Wonderful World of Mathematics: A Critically Annotated List of Children's Books in Mathematics, 2nd ed.,*** by Diane Thiessen, Margaret Matthias, and Jacquelin Smith. Reston, Va.: NCTM, 1998. This excellent resource reviews more than 550 books to help teachers select high-quality children's literature as a basis for teaching mathematics concepts. It analyzes each book for appropriate content and accuracy and discusses the writing style, illustrations, and included activities. The second edition contains a new section on series and a new subsection on quilting.

Please consult www.nctm.org/catalog for order and price information.

For the most up-to-date listing of NCTM resources on topics of interest to mathematics educators, as well as information on membership benefits, conferences, and workshops, visit the NCTM Web site at www.nctm.org.